FEMALE OFFENDERS

Recent Titles in
Research and Bibliographical Guides in Criminal Justice

Criminal Activity in the Deep South, 1700–1930: An Annotated Bibliography
A.J. Wright, compiler

Criminal Justice Ethics: Research and Bibliographical Guide
Frank Schmalleger, compiler, with the assistance of Robert McKenrick

Comparative Criminology: An Annotated Bibliography
Piers Beirne and Joan Hill, compilers

Criminal Justice in Israel: An Annotated Bibliography of English Language Publications, 1948–1993
Robert J. Friedmann

FEMALE OFFENDERS

An Annotated Bibliography

Compiled by
KATHLEEN A. O'SHEA
and
BEVERLY R. FLETCHER

Foreword by
Sister Mary Vincentia Joseph, DSW

Research and Bibliographical Guides in Criminal Justice,
Number 5

GREENWOOD PRESS
Westport, Connecticut • London

Library of Congress Cataloging-in-Publication Data

O'Shea, Kathleen A.
Female offenders : an annotated bibliography / compiled by Kathleen A. O'Shea and Beverly R. Fletcher ; foreword by Mary Vincentia Joseph.
p. cm.—(Research and bibliographical guides in criminal justice, ISSN 1042-4636 ; no. 5)
Includes index.
ISBN 0-313-29228-0 (alk. paper)
1. Female offenders—Bibliography. 2. Women prisoners—Bibliography. I. Fletcher, Beverly R. II. Title. III. Series.
Z5703.4.P75075 1997
[HV6046]
016.3643'74—dc20 96-42163

British Library Cataloguing in Publication Data is available.

Library of Congress Catalog Card Number: 96-42163
ISBN: 0-313-29228-0
ISSN: 1042-4636

First published in 1997

Greenwood Press, 88 Post Road West, Westport, CT 06881
An imprint of Greenwood Publishing Group, Inc.

Printed in the United States of America

The paper used in this book complies with the Permanent Paper Standard issued by the National Information Standards Organization (Z39.48-1984).

10 9 8 7 6 5 4 3 2

Para Los Desaparecidos

CONTENTS

FOREWORD

Although the female offender population is comparatively small in relation to the male, it is growing at an increasingly higher rate than the population of men in the correctional system. Despite this fact and the increasing literature in this area, there is still a paucity of scholarly research on women in prisons and in other correctional facilities. This suggests a lack of serious study of women and crime as well as a lack of interest in their rehabilitation. Critiques of the literature to date cite not only the striking exclusion of research on the experience of women offenders but a distortion of the reality of their experiences. Some commentators contend that this is related to negative and obsolete models of the nature of women and a displacement of hostility toward the feminist movement onto women in marginal segments of society. Moreover, the causes of criminal activity generally have been attributed to the individual person without an adequate examination of the social and economic forces in society that contribute to dysfunctional behavior. Too often women in the criminal justice system as well as those who are victims of spousal abuse are viewed in this context, as both the cause and effect of the problem. They have been considered to be of little worth, a disposable population.

This book, an annotated bibliography, provides an overview of the literature that has emerged in this neglected field. It shows the scope of the problem which is only beginning to attract the attention of the scholarly community. It covers a range of topics. These include the criminal justice system and women, women in prison and on death row, race and gender issues, probation and parole, female juvenile delinquents, prostitution, health and mental health issues of women in prison, social justice concerns as well as programmatic issues and curricula in criminal justice education. The references included here not only identify available resources in these areas but also highlight the interdisciplinary nature of the issues involved and how they cross fields such as law, criminal justice, criminology, social work, and psychology.

Importantly, this work provides a small window through which we can see the intensity of racism and sexism in our society as well as their effects in terms of undervalued and wasted human resources. The social justice issues break through forcibly and are vividly dramatized in this vulnerable population. This review reflects in a profound way that despite the advances of women in society, or maybe as a result of them, discrimination against women is still with us. Perhaps no other area captures the power of racism and sexism in our society more than the experience of women in the nontherapeutic environments of our correctional systems and of the models used to deal with social dysfunction. The continued use of unenlightened approaches that emphasize maintenance and custodial care rather than education and treatment demonstrates in an impressive way society's ethical insensitivity to these invisible members of our community.

Annotated bibliographies have long been recognized as serving a highly useful purpose in presenting the scope of material available in a given field. Although computer indexes are highly valuable in locating relevant material and saving time they still do not provide the scope of review presented here, which spans disciplines. These references serve as an indispensable guide, not only for students and researchers, but for practitioners who are working with this increasingly important population. Certainly, they will provide a significant and useful resource for social workers who serve women in spousal abuse programs, substance abuse programs, and in the criminal justice system. Traditionally, social workers have been concerned with the person in the environment, that is both the micro environment, such as the family, and the macro environment which embraces larger societal systems. The social work focus is not only on the individual person, but also on the contextual forces that contribute to problems in living and social dysfunction. Annotated bibliographies help to identify gaps in a scholarly literature as well as dominant themes that thread its major works. The literature here clearly shows the need to address the environmental forces that negatively impact this population at the direct practice level, in the social policy arena, and through serious empirical research. In this respect, it should be of enormous help to the social work community and to other professional groups that have targeted women's issues as a priority in the formulation of their research and action agendas.

Much of the theoretical and research literature in the helping professions fails to build on the works of others and often literature reviews in the preparation of even rigorous research fail to cross disciplines. This guide helps to avoid this pitfall. It provides an important resource for theoreticians and researchers in indexing the relevant literature in this area in their own professions and across disciplines.

The range of material in this work raises important questions that need to be confronted. One needs to ask: What is the view of the nature of woman reflected in this body of literature? What is the nature of crimes committed by women and how is the causation of these crimes viewed? What are the dominant models of intervention used in providing services to women in the areas covered by this bibliography? What theories underlay these service provisions and what does research have to say about their effectiveness? An important and significant question which will influence not only the selection of the models utilized in practice but will affect research efforts is: What are the values that *inform the selection of* contemporary models and, of more importance, what values *should be inherent* in these models? What do the gaps in the literature suggest, not only in terms of research but also in terms of interventive approaches and social policy change? As the literature presented here shows, female offenders, and particularly women of color, have fewer opportunities for educational, vocational, and health programs than their male counterparts. Reasons most often cited for this situation include the fact that women comprise a smaller percentage of this population, are less demanding, and less likely to riot. Systems developed to deal with these problems were designed largely for men and the needs of women, without regard for any cultural dimensions, have been forced to fit into them. Such a structure speaks to the value or lack thereof placed on women in this and in other segments of society. The increasing interest in forgotten groups of women represented in these pages is certainly a sign of hope but also presents an immense challenge, especially in the social and political climate of today.

The authors, Kathleen A. O'Shea and Beverly R. Fletcher, have made a major contribution in keying important works on female offenders and organizing them in a logical fashion. Thus, these works are more accessible to educators, researchers, and students as well as to practitioners who daily face the profound human service needs of these women at all ages and in a variety of settings. In an environment of cost constraints and sexist attitudes, they find themselves faced with innumerable practice concerns and ethical dilemmas. The authors are well qualified for the task that they undertook as they have both direct practice and research experiences in working with these underserved female groups. They have contributed to creative and ethically sensitive approaches to working with these women and know, first-hand, the shortcomings of our social structures which are purported to help these women. They are keenly aware of the institutional oppression these women face.

In conclusion, Kathleen O'Shea and Beverly Fletcher deserve our gratitude as it was not an easy task to produce a work of this nature and magnitude. It not only gives us access to a wide range of information, but it pulls together a substantive literature that should contribute to both the development and organization of theory on female offenders. Moreover, it should influence more humane and effective services--services which are consistent with the value orientations of the professions represented in this field of practice and the value commitments of the professionals involved.

Sr. Mary Vincentia Joseph, DSW
Associate Dean and Chair of Doctoral Program
National Catholic School of Social Service
The Catholic University of America, Washington, DC

ACKNOWLEDGMENTS

Although every book owes its existence to many people, a bibliography is unique in that it is the end result of research by hundreds and hundreds of individuals. With this in mind, we acknowledge everyone who is engaged in doing research on female offenders and, in particular, the contributors to *Women Prisoners: A Forgotten Population*, whose enthusiasm and thirst for knowledge inspired us first to look beyond the information we had at hand.

A special thanks to Dr. Rita Simon at The American University for inviting us to discuss the project with her and for her feedback and expertise. At the Catholic University of America, Mullen Memorial Library, we acknowledge and extend our thanks to Harrriet Nelson, Reference Librarian, who could always be counted on to cheerfully steer us in the right direction. At The American University, Bender Memorial Library, we were fortunate to know and benefit from the efforts of Mary Alice Baish, and at the University of Maryland, College Park, McKeldin Library, we appreciate and acknowledge the assistance of Deborah Stefany. For all of these we are most grateful.

Finally, we extend our gratitude to Sr. Mary Vincentia Joseph, DSW, Associate Dean and Chair of the Doctoral Program at the National Catholic School of Social Service, The Catholic University of America, Washington, DC, for supporting our efforts and joining us in our desire to make this information available to all those engaged in research.

INTRODUCTION

This bibliography, like many, we suspect, was born out of necessity. In doing research on female offenders for the book, *Women Prisoners: A Forgotten Population* (Praeger, 1993), we became keenly aware of two things. First, contrary to what many people seem to think, a great deal has been written about female offenders and second, the information that exists has not, until now, been collected categorically in one place.

Nevertheless, when we first proposed the project to an editor, we were faced with the task of convincing her, that in an age of daily computer miracles, there is really a need for this kind of work. Based on our experiences, the references found here, both in quantity and quality, cannot be retrieved in one sitting and would, in fact, take many hours to accumulate from various sources and disciplines that include social work, psychology, sociology, law, education, history, criminology, health, literature, medicine, and many other areas. We were, in fact, amazed, that the female offender has been looked at, speculated on, talked about, and planned for from such a variety of disciplines, and for so long. References span from a decree in 1820 to "repeal an Act to abolish the public whipping of female offenders" (C.0424) to Coramae Richey Mann's *When Women Kill*, in 1996 (B.0420).

The entries found in this book have taken over two years to compile and, in the end, there is much that page constraints forced us to leave out. We found, for example, a wealth of information in *Book Reviews* and collected several hundred which are not included. Regretfully, we have not included any of the many foreign language articles we found, unless they were translated and published in an English journal. Although we included some reports and some dissertations, as well as some conference papers, there were hundreds we left out. There is also a profusion of information and debates about women offenders in the popular media, i.e., newspapers and magazines. Beyond this we found radio shows, TV talk shows, videos, documentaries, and even plays on women offenders, though none are included. One record from the Library of Congress of women's prison songs is included because we liked it and it is, after all, our book.

The categories, or chapters, formed themselves. We sorted the information we had on hand, and certain themes emerged. We would have liked to have done more in certain areas. You may have done differently, but we hope you will find our arrangement useful. Each chapter has a smaller heading which emphasizes topics to look for. The commentaries after each citation are meant to give an overview and in no way are meant to reflect an opinion. We limited ourselves to no more than two lines per entry. This was out of a desire to include more material. If a study was done, that is what the citation says. We did not attempt to list results or outcomes. We would hope that users will find the source and do that themselves. Do not be slighted if we have reduced several years of your life to one line. It was not out of disrespect and it was not easy. We have sat at your table and savored your wine and we are in awe.

The chapter on *Criminology* has references pertaining to studying, teaching, and understanding emerging criminological theories about women as well as articles on research and the practitioners of Criminology, Criminal Justice, and Corrections. The *Crimes* chapter looks at the crimes women commit. You will find information on newer topics, such as fetal abuse and battered women who kill, as well as substance abuse and white collar crime. In *Arrest, Prosecution, and Sentencing* we included issues of race and gender because of the obvious intersection of race, gender, and the courts. In this section, you will also find information on alternative sentencing and the death penalty. The Battered Woman's Syndrome is in this chapter because of its use as a defense. Chapter 4 focuses on *Female Juveniles* in the criminal justice system, specifically in the areas of delinquency, gangs, and prostitution. Chapter 5, *Corrections,* includes citations on jails, prisons, and other issues such as mothers in prison, prison programs, and health issues of incarcerated women. *Probation and Parole* is the focus of Chapter 6. Chapter 7 lists references about female *Political Prisoners*, and the final chapter contains *Bibliographies* on female offenders or related topics.

This bibliography is a work-in-progress. We have made every effort to track citations and list them correctly. However, we are human, not to mention the unfathomable cliches of our computers, which are not. If we have left you out or listed you incorrectly, if you know of someone who should be listed but isn't, or if you simply want to tell us something, please write us at *P.O. Box 29026, Washington, DC 20017-0026.* The bottom line is we put this bibliography together because it is the kind of reference tool we needed and one we would like to have for the future, and it gives us great pleasure to share it with you. We plan to update to assure it continues to be a useful tool.

1

CRIMINOLOGY

Theories; Education; Practitioners

A.0001 Abell, Jennie, & Geller, Gloria (1985). Women and crime: Recent developments in research and theory. *Resources for Feminist Research, 14,* 25-37. Discusses new research and theory on women and crime.

A.0002 Adelberg, Ellen, & Currie, Concetta (1993). In conflict with the law: *Women and the Canadian justice system.* Vancouver, BC: Press Gang Publishers. Anthology of ten papers on women and the Canadian criminal justice system.

A.0003 Adelberg, Ellen (1986, January). Not enough: A review of research for women in conflict with the law. *Resources for Feminist Research, 14,* 56-57. Reviews available research on women and crime and suggests more needs to be done.

A.0004 Adler, Freda (1980). The interaction between women's emancipation and female criminality: A cross-cultural perspective. In S. Datesman & F. Scarpitti (Eds.), *Women, crime and justice.* New York, NY: Oxford University Press. Discusses the impact of the women's movement on the criminality of women.

A.0005 Adler, Freda (1977). The interaction between women's emancipation and female criminality: A cross-cultural perspective. *International Journal of Criminology and Penology, 5*(2), 101-112. Discusses the impact of the women's movement on the criminality of women.

A.0006 Adler, Freda (1976, May). Crime: The feminine challenge. *Criminal Defense, 3*(3), 17-19. Focuses on role of women in the criminal justice system as practitioners and offenders.

A.0007 Adler, Freda, & Simon, Rita (1979). *The criminology of deviant women.* Boston, MA. Houghton Mifflin. Collection of essays on women in crime. Emphasis on theoretical selections.

A.0008 Ageton, Suzanne (1983, November). The dynamics of female delinquency, 1976-1980. *Criminology, 21*(4), 555-584. Considers developments in thinking on the criminality of women during 1976-1980.

A.0009 Ahuja, R. (1981-82). Women and crime: A new theoretical perspective. *The International Journal of Critical Sociology, 5,* 1-13. Theoretical discussion of new (1981) ideas on the criminality of women.

A.0010 Akins, Jerry (1994, Fall). An investigation of the correlation between high school dropouts and subsequent criminal activity: A look at causality. *Masters Abstracts International, 32*(3), 773. Analysis of data on educational, sociological and criminal histories of prisoners to explore causality. 100 female felons incarcerated in Missouri included.

A.0011 Alarid, Leanne, et al. (1994, March). *Understanding the nature of adult female criminality.* Paper presented at the 1994 ACJS Annual Meeting, Chicago,IL. Discusses factors that lead women to nontraditional street crimes. 104 female felons involved in the study.

A.0012 Alpert, Geoffrey (1984, August). The needs of the judiciary and misapplication of social research: The case of female guards in men's prisons. *Criminology An Interdisciplinary Journal, 22*(3), 441-456. Legal cases pertaining to women serving as guards in male institututions.

A.0013 Atway, R. (1984). Physiognomy, photography, and prostitution: Cesare Lombroso and the female offender. *Research Communications in Psychology, Psychiatry and Behavior, 9*(4), 353-364. Critiques ideas and methodologies of Lombroso.

A.0014 Austin, Roy (1982, November). Women's liberation and increases in minor, major, and occupational offenses. *British Journal of Criminology, 20*(3-4), 407-430. Discusses the impact of the women's movement on trends in crimes committed by women.

A.0015 Austin, Roy (1981, October). Liberation and female criminality in England and Wales. *British Journal of Criminology, 21*(4), 371-374). Discusses the impact of the women's movement on female criminality in England and Wales.

A.0016 Babcock, Barbara (1973, Winter). Introduction: Women and the criminal law. *The American Criminal Law Review, 11*, 291-294. Examines women in criminal law.

A.0017 Barack, Leonard, & Widom, Cathy (1978, November). Eysenck's theory of criminality applied to women awaiting trial. *British Journal of Psychiatry, 133*, 452-456. Discusses Eysenck's theory of criminality.

A.0018 Bardsley, Barney (1987). *Flowers in hell: An investigation into women and crime.* London: Pandora Press, Routledge & Kegan Paul Ltd. Discusses stereotypes of women criminals, treatment of women by the courts, and political crime.

A.0019 Bartel, Anne (1979, January). Women and crime: An economic analysis. *Economic Inquiry, 17*(1), 29-51. Looks at the economics of women's crimes.

A.0020 Baskin, Deborah, et al. (1993, Spring). The political economy of female violent street crime. *Fordham Urban Law Journal, 20*, 401-417.

A.0021 Baunach, Phyllis, & Hahn-Rafter, Nicole (1982). Sex-role operations: Strategies for women in the criminal justice system. In N. Rafter-Hahn & E. Stanko (Eds.), *Judge, lawyer, victim, thief: Women, gender roles, and criminal justice* (pp. 341-358). Boston, MA: Northeastern University Press. Focuses on the problems of women employed in the criminal justice system and strategies women use to overcome difficulties.

A.0022 Belknap, Joanne (1996). *The invisible woman: Gender, crime, and justice.* Belmont, MA: Wadsworth Publishing. Discusses the lack of research on women in criminology.

A.0023 Belknap, Joanne (1991). Women in conflict: An analysis of women correctional officers. *Women and Criminal Justice, 2*(2), 89-115. Discusses the employment of women as correctional officers.

A.0024 Benedek, Elissa (1990). Female offenders. In J. Spurlock & C. Robinowitz (Ed.), *Women's progress: Promises and problems: Women in context: Development and stresses* (pp. 159-171). New York, NY: Plenum Press. Considers existing theoretical perspectives on female criminality.

A.0025 Bentzon, A. W. (1986, August-November). Comments on women's law in Scandinavia. *International Journal of the Sociology of Law, 14*(3-4), 249-254. Discussion of women as they are regarded by the law in Scandinavia.

A.0026 Berger, L. (1977, Fall). Profile of the woman criminal. *Quarterly Journal of Corrections*, 43-45. Ties women's crimes to economic forces, inflation, and unemployment.

A.0027 Berger, Ronald (1989, September). Female delinquency in the emancipation era: A review of the literature. *Sex Roles: A Journal of Research, 21*(5-6), 375-400. Discusses changes in female delinquency. Emphasizes research on women's race, class, and ethnic groups.

A.0028 Best, Joel, & Luckenbill, David (1990, Winter). Male dominance and female criminality: A test of Harris's theory of deviant typescripts. *Sociological Inquiry, 60*(1), 71-86. Tests Harris's theory of deviant typescripts which predicts higher female participation in deviance when male dominance is low.

A.0029 Bishop, C. (1931). *Women and crime.* London: Chatto & Windus. Early discussion of criminal women.

A.0030 Boles, Jacqueline, & Tatro, Charlotte (1979). The female offender: The 1980's and beyond. In J. O'Brien & M. Marcus (Eds.), *Crime and justice in America: Critical issues for the future* (pp. 255-282). New York, NY: Pergamon Press. Examines the participation of women in crime identifying trends for the future.

A.0031 Boles, Jacqueline (1975, April). *Women in crime: Changing patterns.* Paper presented at the 38th Annual Meeting of the Southern Sociological Society, Washington, DC. Discusses trends in female crime using data from police records over a period of twelve years.

A.0032 Bowersox, Michael (1981). Women in corrections: Competence, competition, and the social responsibility norm. *Criminal Justice and Behavior, 8*(4), 491-499. Reviewed 263 male and 70 female officers' attitudes toward females employed as correctional officers in a men's prison.

A.0033 Box, Steven, & Hale, Chris (1984, November) Liberation, emancipation, economic marginalization, or less chivalry: The relevance of three theoretical arguments to female crime patterns in England and Wales, 1951-1980. *British Journal of Criminology, 22*(4), 473-497.

A.0034 Box, Steven, & Hale, Chris. (1983, January). Liberation and female criminality in England and Wales. *British Journal of Criminology, 23*(1), 35-49. Explores statistical relationship between 4 measures of female liberation and female crime rates in England and Wales between 1951-1979.

A.0035 Boyd, S., & Sheehy, Elizabeth (1986). Feminist perspectives on law: Canadian theory and practice. *Canadian Journal of Women and the Law, 2*(1), 1-52. Discusses feminism and the theory and practice of Canadian law.

A.0036 Boyle, Christine, et al. (1985). *A feminist review of criminal law.* Ottawa: Status of Women in Canada & Ministry of Supply and Services. Discusses the practice of criminal law from the feminist point of view.

A.0037 Brewer, Stephanie (1994, March). *General theories of delinquency: A feminist analysis.* Paper presented at the 1994 ACJS Annual Meeting, Chicago, IL. Reviews content of existing theories for references to women. Suggests developing a more inclusive theoretical base.

A.0038 Brodsky, Annette (1974). *Sexual justice: Research on female offenders.* Tuscaloosa, AL: University of Alabama Press. Course conducted at the University of Alabama addressed socialization of women, patterns of deviant behavior, and frequently committed crimes.

A.0039 Broskowski, Anthony, et al. (1971, August-November). Actuarial assessment of criminality in women. *Criminology, 9*(2-3), 166-184. Attempted to determine if data from the Psychological Screen Inventory differentiates between women criminals and women non-criminals.

A.0040 Brown, Beverly (1986). Women and crime: The dark figures of criminology. *Economy and Society, 25*(3), 355-402. Discusses attacks by feminist criminologists since the 1970's on male dominated theories of criminology.

A.0041 Bynum, Victoria (1992). *Unruly women: The politics of social and sexual control in the old South.* Chapel Hill: University of North Carolina Press. Discusses the constraints of social expectations and the idea of a "good woman" in the early South.

A.0042 Cain, Maureen (1990, February). Towards transgression: New directions in feminist criminology. *International Journal of the Sociology of Law, 18*(1), 1-18. Addresses feminist criminology and unequal treatment as well as the nature of female criminality.

A.0043 Cain, Maureen (1986). Realism, feminism, methodology and law. *International Journal of the Sociology of Law, 14,* 255-267. Discusses feminist methodology in the practice of law.

A.0044 Carlen, Pat (1994). Why study women's imprisonment? Or anyone else's? An indefinite article. *British Journal of Criminology, 34*(1), 131-140. Discusses problems of studying women's imprisonment separately from men's. Offers suggestions for further prison research.

A.0045 Carlen, Pat (1992a). Women, crime, and realism. In John Lowman & B. D. Maclean (Eds.), *Realist criminology: Crime control and policing in the 1990's* (pp. 203-220). Toronto: University of Toronto Press. Discusses the need for theories of women's lawbreaking, the potential for feminist criminology, and limitations of realist criminology in relation to women.

A.0046 Carlen, Pat (1992b). Criminal women and criminal justice: The limits to, and potential of, feminist and left realist perspectives. In R. Matthews & J. Young (Eds.), *Issues in realist criminology* (pp. 51-69). London: Sage. Looks at the feminist perspective and its limitations.

A.0047 Carlen, Pat (1990, Winter). Women, crime, feminism, and realism. *Social Justice, 17*(4), 106-123. Discusses women and crime from a feminist perspective.

A.0048 Carlen, Pat, & Collison, M. (1980). *Radical issues in criminology.* Oxford: Martin Robertson. Discusses new issues in researching the criminality of women.

A.0049 Carrington, Kerry (1994). Postmodernism and feminist criminologies: Disconnecting discourses? *International Journal of Sociology of the Law, 22*(3), 261-277. Considers the implications of postmodernism for feminist criminological research.

A.0050 Caufield, Susan, & Wonders, Nancy (1994). Gender and justice: Feminist contributions to criminology. In G. Barak (Ed.), *Varieties of criminology: Readings from a dynamic discipline* (pp. 213-229). Westport, CT: Praeger. Outlines key contributions to criminology by feminist theorists in context, process and theories of social change.

A.0051 Chapman, Jane (1984). *Economic realities and the female offender.* New York, NY: Macmillan. Discusses economic nature of crimes committed by women and lack of coordination among criminal justice agencies in providing rehabilitative programs geared toward economic stability.

A.0052 Chapman, Jane, et al. (1985). *Women employed in corrections.* Washington, DC: Center for Women's Policy Studies. Profile of women employed in corrections identifies correctional occupations for women and factors affecting recruitment, placement, and advancement.

A.0053 Chesney Lind, Meda (1989, January). Girls' crime and women's place: Toward a feminist model of female delinquency. *Crime and Delinquency, 35*(1), 5-29. Argues that existing theories are fundamentally inadequate for explaining female delinquency.

A.0054 Chesney-Lind, Meda (1986, Autumn). Women and crime: The female offender. *Signs: Journal of Women in Culture and Society, 12*(1), 78-96. Discusses female criminality.

A.0055 Chesney-Lind, Meda (1980). Re-discovering Lilith: Misogyny and the new female criminal. In C. T. Griffiths & M. Nance (Eds.), *The female offender: Selected papers from an international symposium* (pp 1-35). Burnaby, BC: Criminology Research Center, Simon Fraser University.

A.0056 Chester, B. (1976). *Personality and life history of female offenders and their sibs: A taxonomic and genetic analysis.* Dissertation, University of Minnesota. Clinical psychometric approach to the concept of criminality in female offenders.

A.0057 Chiqwada, Ruth, et al. (1989). Toward a women-wise penology. *Probation Journal, 36*(3), 100-114. Discusses how penology might equalize treatment of female inmates. Reports on interviews with 10 black female ex-prisoners in the UK.

A.0058 Clark, Roger (1989, September-December). Cross-national perspectives on female crime: An empirical investigation. *International Journal of Comparative Sociology, 30*(3-4), 195-215. Three theoretical approaches explaining cross-national variations in female crime, Durkheimian modernization, Marxian world systems, and ecological opportunity.

A.0059 Clonginger, C., & Guze, S. (1970, December). Psychiatric illness and female criminality: The role of sociopathy and hysteria in the anti-social woman. *American Journal of Psychiatry, 127*(3), 303-311. Study of 66 convicted female felons on parole.

A.0060 Cloward, Richard, & Piven, Frances (1979, Summer). The channeling of female innovation and resistance. *Signs: Journal of Women in Culture and Society, 4*(4), 651-669. Examines the social context of female deviant behavior.

A.0061 Cohen, Sherrill (1992). *The evolution of women's asylums since 1500: From refuges for ex-prostitutes to shelters for battered women.* New York, NY: Oxford University Press. Views early gender-specific institutions as training grounds for current practices in the field of corrections.

A.0062 Crites, Laura, & Pearson, Rose (1977, Winter). The female offender. *British Journal of Law and Society, 4*(2), 297-299. Discusses the image of the female offender in criminology.

A.0063 Crouch, Ben (1985). Pandora's box: Women guards in men's prisons. *Journal of Criminal Justice, 13*(6), 535-548. Discusses problems of women guards in men's prisons, meeting security demands, relating to male co-workers, and occupational socialization and advancement.

A.0064 Crump, Anna (1987). Women and crime: A contemporary controversy. *International Journal of Offender Therapy and Comparative Criminology, 31*(1), 31-40. Discusses controversy in criminological theories of women.

A.0065 Culliver, Concetta (1993). *Female criminality: The state of the art.* New York, NY: Garland, Library of Sociology. Focuses on three aspects of criminal justice: Law enforcement, courts, and corrections.

A.0066 Curran, D. J. (1984, July). The myth of the "new" female delinquent. *Crime and Delinquency, 30*(3), 386-399. Examines the idea that the women's movement resulted in change in quantity and quality of offenses committed by women.

A.0067 Dahl, T. S. (1986, August-November). Taking women as a starting point: Building women's law. *International Journal of the Sociology of Law, 14*(3-4), 239-247. Discusses women as they are viewed by the law.

A.0068 Dallam, Audre (1987, June). The "New female criminal": A test of Adler's hypothesis. *Dissertation Abstracts International, 49*(12), 3877. Partial replication of a 1968 study. Data collected from female inmates to produce a profile of female offenders in the 1980's.

A.0069 Daly, Kathleen (1989). Criminal justice ideologies and practices in different voices: Some feminist questions about justice. *International Journal of the Sociology of Law, 17,* 1-18. Discusses the feminist practice of criminal justice.

A.0070 Daly, Kathleen, & Chesney-Lind, Meda (1988). Feminism and criminology. *Justice Quarterly, 5*(4), 497-538. Describes core elements of feminist thought and their relevance to criminology. Discusses issues in building theories of gender & crime and gender equality.

A.0071 Datesman, Susan, & Scarpitti, Frank (1980). *Women, crime and justice.* New York, NY: Oxford University Press. Essays on the treatment of women in the criminal justice system.

A.0072 Datesman, Susan, et al. (1975). Female delinquency: An application of self and opportunity theories. *Journal of Research in Crime and Delinquency, 12*(2), 107-123. Discusses the criminality of women from a theoretical perspective.

A.0073 Daunton-Fear, M. W. (1975). *Women as participants in the criminal justice system.* Woden, Australia: Australian Institute of Criminology. Discusses the treatment of women in the criminal justice system.

A.0074 Del Olmo, Rosa (1986, September). Female criminality and drug trafficking in Latin America: Preliminary findings. *Studies in Third World Societies, 37,* 163-178. Discusses female criminality, behavior theory, economic necessity theory, and the new female criminal theory.

A.0075 Deming, Richard (1977). *Women: The new criminals.* New York, NY: Thomas Nelson. Discusses new (1977) theories of female criminality.

A.0076 Denmark, Florence, & Rutschmann-Jaffee, Ruth (1979). The emerging female criminal. *International Journal of Group Tensions, 9*(1-4), 50-58. Discusses female offenders statistically, sociologically, psychologically and some etiological factors that influence women criminals.

A.0077 Devasia, L., & Devasia, V. V. (1989). *Female criminals and female victims: An Indian perspective.* Nagpur: Dattsons. Discusses the view of female criminality in India.

A.0078 Diaz-Cotto, Juanita (1991). Women and crime in the United States. In C. Mohanty et al. (Eds.), *Third world women and the politics of feminism* (pp. 197-211). Bloomington, IN: Indiana University Press. Discusses the criminality of women in the United States.

A.0079 Doerkson, Lorna (1985-1986, December-January). Women and crime: Recent developments in research and theory. *Resources for Feminist Research, 14*(4), 3-4. Theoretical discusssion of the criminality of women.

A.0080 Donaldson, G. (1976). *Women in crime.* London: Phoebus. Discusses the criminality of women.

A.0081 D'Orban, P. T. (1971). Social and psychiatric aspects of female crime. *Medicine, Science, and Law, 11*(3), 104-116. Discusses the "treatment" of female deviance as a socio-medico problem.

A.0082 D'Orban, P. T., & Dalton, J. (1980, May). Violent crime and the menstrual cycle. *Psychological Medicine, 10*(2), 353-359. Study of 50 women (15-38 yrs), 44% committed offenses during the paramenstruum.

A.0083 Dorworth, Vicky, & Henry, Marie (1992, Fall). Optical illusions: The visual representation of blacks and women in introductory criminal justice textbooks. *Journal of Criminal Justice Education, 3*(2), 251-260. Discusses traditional portrayals of blacks and women in textbooks.

A.0084 Ebbe, Oloi (1985). Correlates of female criminality in Nigeria. *International Journal of Comparative and Applied Criminal Justice, 9*(1-2), 83-95. Examines the relationship between socioeconomic and family bond measures and female criminality in Nigeria.

A.0085 Edwards H. (1982). Women crime and criminal justice: The state of current theory and research in Australia and New Zealand. *Australian and New Zealand Journal of Criminology, 15*(2), 69-89. Discusses current (1982) research in female criminality in Australia and New Zealand.

A.0086 Edwards, Susan (1986). Neither bad nor mad: The female violent offender reassessed. *Women's Studies International Forum, 9*(1), 79-87. Looks at traditional representation of violent female offenders as mentally ill or socially deviant.

A.0087 Ehrlich Martin, Susan, & Jurik, Nancy (1996). *Doing justice, doing gender: Women in law and criminal justice occupations.* Thousand Oaks, CA: Sage Publication. Looks at occupations for women in law and in the criminal justice system.

A.0088 Eigenberg, Helen, & Baro, Agnes (1992, Fall). Women and the publication process: A content analysis of criminal justice journals. *Journal of Criminal Justice Education, 3*(2), 293-314. Examines publication patterns in five criminal justice journals .

A.0089 Erez, Edna (1988). Myth of the new female offender: Some evidence from attitudes toward law and justice. *Journal of Criminal Justice, 16*(6), 499-509. Examines attitudes of female/male inmates in three federal prisons.

A.0090 Erickson, Nancy (1990). Final report: Sex bias in the teaching of criminal law. *Rutgers Law Review, 42*(2), 309-630. Examines sex bias in the teaching of criminal law.

A.0091 Erskine, C. (1984). Female delinquency, feminism, and psychoanalysis: An overview. In C. R. Keith (Ed.), *The aggressive adolescent: Clinical perspectives* (pp. 403-431). New York, NY: The Free Press. Examines the current status of literature on female delinquency.

A.0092 Esser, Mary, & Mueller, Charles (1983). *The relationship of sex-role orientation, self-concept and self-control to female criminality.* Paper presented at the Annual Meeting of the Midwestern Psychological Association, 1983, Chicago, IL. Investigates the female offender as a masculinated, and anguished woman possessing low self-esteem and low self-control.

A.0093 Estep, Rhoda (1982). Women's roles in crime as depicted by television and newspapers. *Journal of Popular Culture, 16*(3), 151-156. Looks at stereotypical representations of women as suspects, victims, and law enforcers.

A.0094 Evans, Mary, & Morgan, D. (1979). Crime and deviance. In. M. Evans & D. Morgan (Eds.), *Work on women: A guide to the literature* (pp. 39-44). New York, NY: Tavistock Publications. Discusses female criminality and contemporary (1979) theories.

A.0095 Fagan, J. A., et al. (1993). The political economy of female violence: Social and economic influences in the onset of assault by women. *Fordham Urban Law Review, 20*(3), 401-417. Discusses the criminality of women from a causal perspective.

A.0096 Faith, Karlene (1993a). *Historical perspectives on female crime and punishment: From witch hunts to PMS.* Barnaby, BC: Simon Fraser University. Historical look at criminal behavior in women from witch hunts in the 15th century to premenstrual syndrome in the 19th.

A.0097 Faith, Karlene (1993b). An interview with Freda Adler. *Criminologist, 5*(1), 3-10.

A.0098 Faith, Karlene (1993c). *Unruly women: The politics of confinement and resistance.* Vancouver, BC: Press Gang Publishers. Challenges stereotypes of "unruly" and "deviant" women in North America.

A.0099 Feeley, M., & Little, Deborah (1991). The vanishing female: The decline of women in the criminal process, 1687-1912. *Law and Society Review, 25*(4), 719-757. Historical perspective indicates that 45% of the criminals indicted for property crimes in the 18th century were women.

A.0100 Feinman, Clarice (1986). *Women in the criminal justice system* (2nd ed.). New York, NY: Praeger. Historical and theoretical perspective regarding the treatment of female offenders and female criminal justice practitioners from the 19th century to the present.

A.0101 Felthous, A., & Yudowitz, B. (1977, August). Approaching a comparative typology of assaultive female offenders. *Psychiatry, 40*(3), 270-276. Two-part study exploring assaultive behavior in women.

A.0102 Ferdinand, T. N. (1978). Female delinquency and Warren's typology of personality patterns: An evaluation. *Social Work Research and Abstracts, 14*(4), 32-41. Discusses female delinquency from a review of Warren's typology of personality patterns.

A.0103 Fielding, J. (1977). Female delinquency. In P. Wilson (Ed.), *Delinquency in Australia: A critical appraisal.* Queensland, Australia: University of Queensland Press. Discusses disinterest in female delinquency in Australia and factors that influence female delinquency.

A.0104 Figueira-McDonough, Josefina (1992, September). Community structure and female delinquency rates: A heuristic discussion. *Youth and Society, 24*(1), 3-30. Establishes the relevance of community structural dimensions for two distinct theories of women's criminal behavior.

A.0105 Figueira-McDonough, Josefina (1984, October). Feminism and delinquency: In search of an elusive link. *British Journal of Criminology, 24*(4), 325-342. Discusses the connection between feminism and female delinquency.

A.0106 Figueira-McDonough, Josefina, & Selo, Elaine (1980, July). A reformulation of the "equal opportunity" explanation of female delinquency. *Crime and Delinquency, 26*(3), 333-343. Expands the equal opportunity hypothesis into a comprehensive predictive model.

A.0107 Finley, Nancy (1982). *Gender and the inhibitors of crime: An issue of traditionalism and social control.* Dissertation, University of Oklahoma. Focuses on two explanations for the narrowing gap between male and female criminality.

A.0108 Fishbein, D. H. (1992). The psychobiology of female aggression. *Criminal Justice and Behavior, 19*(2), 99-126. Discusses female aggression .

A.0109 Fishman, Gideon, & Weimann, Gabriel (1985). Presenting the victim: Sex-based bias in press reports on crime. *Justice Quarterly, 2*(4), 491-503. Examines media images of female criminality. Survey of all reports of offenses in Israel's leading newspapers during 1981-1982.

A.0110 Flowers, Ronald (1995). *Female crime, criminals and cellmates: An exploration of female criminality and delinquency.* Raleigh, NC: McFarland & Company. Touches on various aspects of female crime. Includes statistics and charts.

A.0111 Flowers, Ronald (1987). *Women and criminality: The woman as victim, offender, and practitioner.* Westport, CT: Greenwood Press. Analysis of the role of women in criminology and criminal justice. Theoretical and statistical approaches.

A.0112 Flynn, Edith (1982). Women as criminal justice professionals: A challenge to change tradition. In N. Rafter-Hahn & E. Stanko (Eds.), *Judge, lawyer, victim, thief: Women, gender roles and criminal justice* (pp. 305-340). Boston, MA: Northeastern University Press. Considers women in law enforcement, and as judges, lawyers, court employees, and correctional officers.

A.0113 Fox, J., & Hartnagle, T. F. (1979). Changing social roles and female crime in Canada: A time series analysis. *Canadian Review of Sociology and Anthropology, 16*(1), 96-104. Examines female crime rates in Canada. Hypothesized that the female crime rate varies inversely with the rate of female involvement in the family.

A.0114 Frank, Susan, & Quinlan, D. (1976, October). Ego development and female delinquency: A cognitive-developmental approach. *Journal of Abnormal Psychology, 85*(5), 505-510. Discusses female delinquency and ego development.

A.0115 Freedman, Estelle (1995). *Maternal Justice: Miriam Van Waters and the female reform tradition.* Chicago, IL: University of Chicago Press. The life of social activist and reformer Miriam Van Waters, 1887-1974.

A.0116 Friend, Roxanne, & Leibowitz F. (1992, May-June). Sexual harassment: An issue for women in corrections. *American Jails,* 11-14. Discusses the issue of sexual harassment for women working in the correctional system.

A.0117 Frigon, S. (1994) Women, heresies and social control: From witches to midwives and beyond. *Canadian Journal of Women and the Law, 7*(1), 133-155. Highlights the social construction of woman as witch. Examines witch as mental patient, healer, scapegoat, and sexual deviant.

A.0118 Garrison, Carole, et al. (1992, Fall). Gender balancing the criminal justice curriculum and classroom. *Journal of Criminal Justice Education, 3*(2), 203-222. Discusses the need to balance the gender perspective in criminal justice curriculums.

A.0119 Gavigan, Shelley (1988). Law, gender and ideology. In A. Bayefsky (Ed.), *Legal theory meets legal practice* (pp. 283-295). Edmonton, Alberta: Academic Press. Discusses legal perspectives and gender in Canadian law.

A.0120 Gavigan, Shelley (1987). Women's crime: New perspectives and old theories. In E. Adelberg & C. Currie (Eds.), *Too few to count: Canadian women in conflict with the law* (pp. 112-126). Vancouver: Press Gang Publishers. Discusses the need for new theories of female criminality in Canadian law.

A.0121 Gavigan, Shelley (1982, Fall). Women's crime and feminist critiques: A review of the literature. *Canadian Criminology Forum, 5*(1), 40-53. Reviews selected documents related to women and criminality. Emphasis on relevance to understanding the oppression of women.

A.0122 Geller, Gloria (1987). Feminism and criminal "justice": An uneasy partnership. *Resources for Feminist Research, 17*(3), 100-102. Focuses on the relationship between feminism and the Canadian criminal justice system. Examines perspectives on women's equality and the law.

A.0123 Gelsthorpe, Loraine (1990). Feminist methodologies in criminology: A new approach or old wine in new bottles? In L. Gelsthorpe & A. Morris (Eds.), *Feminist perspectives in criminology* (pp. 89-106). Philadelphia, PA: Open University Press. Discusses the feminist perspective in criminology.

A.0124 Gelsthorpe, Loraine, & Morris, Allison (1990). *Feminist perspectives in criminology.* Philadelphia, PA: Open University Press. Explores approaches to feminist criminology.

A.0125 Gelsthorpe, Loraine (1989). *Sexism and the female offender: An organizational analysis.* Brookfield, VT: Gower Publishing Company. Discusses viewing female criminality in terms of social forces and influences rather than in terms of individual characteristics.

A.0126 Gelsthorpe, Loraine, & Morris, Allison (1988a). Feminism and criminology in Britain. In P. Rock (Ed.), *History of British Ciminology.* Oxford: Clarendon Press. Discusses the place of feminism in British criminology.

A.0127 Gelsthorpe, Loraine, & Morris, Allison (1988b). Feminism and criminology in Britain. *British Journal of Criminology, 28*(2), 93-110. Argues that criminology has not yet accepted and integrated the importance of gender with factors such as race and class.

A.0128 Ghosh, Srikanta (1993). *Women and crime.* New Delhi: Ashish Publishing. Looks at the criminality of women in India.

A.0129 Gibson, Mary (1982, September). The female offender and the Italian school of criminal anthropology. *Journal of European Studies, 12*, 155-165. Discusses tradtional theories of female criminality .

A.0130 Gido, R. (1990). Teaching "women and criminal justice." *Journal of Criminal Justice Education, 1*, 263-266. Discusses the need to incorporate theories of women in criminal justice education.

A.0131 Gilfus, Mary (1988). *Seasoned by violence, tempered by love: A qualitative study of women and crime.* Dissertation, Brandeis University. Theoretical model for understanding women's crime patterns.

A.0132 Giordano, Peggy, et al. (1981). The economics of female criminality: An analysis of police blotters, 1890-1976. In L. Bowker (Ed.), *Women and crime in America* (pp. 65-81). New York, NY: Macmillan. Considers why women commit crime.

A.0133 Goldman, Mimi (1971). Women's crime in a male society. *Juvenile Court Journal, 22*(2), 33-35. Discusses society's ideas about women criminals.

A.0134 Goodstein, L. (1992). Feminist perspectives and the criminal justice curriculum. *Journal of Criminal Justice Education, 3*(2), 165-181. Discusses the place of feminism in the criminal justice classroom.

A.0135 Gora, Joanne (1982). *The new female criminal: Empirical reality or social myth?* New York, NY: Praeger. Discusses the concept of a "new" female criminal.

A.0136 Gora, Joanne (1979). A longitudinal analysis of sex role changes in crime rates: 1939-1976. *Dissertation Abstracts International, 40*(7), 4246-A. Examines female criminality from 1939-1979. Contrasts biological and psychological theories with sex-role socialization theory.

A.0137 Gora Joanne (1976, August). *The changing nature of female criminality: A methodological dilemma.* Paper presented at the 26th Annual Meeting of the Society for the Study of Social Problems. Explores differences in theories that explain female and male crime.

A.0138 Greenwood, V. (1981). The myth of female crime. In A. Morris & L. Gelsthorpe (Eds.), *Women and crime*. Cambridge, MA: Institute of Criminology. Discusses the criminality of women and women's crimes.

A.0139 Gregory, Jeanne (1986). Sex, class and crime: Towards a non-sexist criminology. In R. Matthews & J. Young (Eds.), *Confronting crime*. London: Sage Publications. Discusses sexism in the criminal justice curriculum.

A.0140 Guibord, A. S. B. (1917). Physical state of criminal women. *Journal of the American Institute of Criminal Law and Criminology, 8*, 82-95. Early ideas about the criminality of women.

A.0141 Gwynn, Carolene (1993). Women and crime: The failure of traditional theories and the rise of feminist criminology. *Monash University Law Review, 19*, 92-103. Discusses why traditional theories do not adequately explain female criminality.

A.0142 Hagan, J. (1985). Toward a structural theory of crime, race, and gender: The Canadian case. *Crime and Delinquency, 31*(1), 129-146. Tests a theory of race, gender, and crime with data from offenders admitted to the Ontario Correctional Institutions during 1974 and 1980.

A.0143 Hagan, J., et al. (1979, March). The sexual stratification of social control: A gender-based perspective on crime and delinquency. *British Journal of Sociology, 30*(1), 25-38. Discusses the place of gender in criminological theory.

A.0144 Haggart, Joy (1973, Fall). Women and crime. *Humboldt Journal of Social Relations, 1*(1), 42-47. Discusses social-psychological analysis of female criminology based on socialization.

A.0145 Hahn-Rafter, Nicole, & Heidensohn, Frances (1995). *International feminist persepctives in criminology: Engendering a discipline.* Buckingham, UK: Open University Press. Analyzes the impact of feminism on international criminological thought.

A.0146 Hahn-Rafter, Nicole (1980). Too dumb to know better: Cacogenic family studies and the criminology of women. *Criminology. 19*(1). 3-25. Discusses how family studies (1874-1926) remodeled the traditional image of the "bad woman."

A.0147 Harris, Anthony (1977). Sex and theories of deviance: Toward a functional theory of deviant type-scripts. *American Sociological Review, 42*(1), 3-16. Examines major criminal paradigms of deviance for the inclusion of women.

A.0148 Harris, Kay (1987, Fall). Exploring the connections between feminism and justice. *National Prison Project Journal, 13.* Discusses the concept of feminist justice.

A.0149 Harry, Bruce, & Blacer, Charlotte (1987, Summer). Menstruation and crime: A critical review of the literature from the clinical criminology perspective. *Behavior Sciences and the Law, 5*(3), 307-322. Considers the relationship between menstruation and crime and the limitations of such studies.

A.0150 Hartnagel Timothy, & Mizanuddin, Muhammad (1986, January-April). Modernization, gender role convergence and female crime: A further test. *International Journal of Comparative Sociology*(Leiden, Netherlands), *27*(1-2), 1-14. Looks at gender roles and female crime.

A.0151 Hartnagle, Timothy (1982, Autumn). Modernization, female social roles, and female crime: A cross-national investigation. *Sociological Quarterly, 23*(4), 477-490. Examines the relationship between modernization and female crime rates. Data from 40 countries.

A.0152 Hartnagle, Timothy (1974, August). *Female crime in Canada.* Paper presented at the Annual Meeting of the Sociology and Anthropology Association, 1974, University of Toronto. Reviews historical variations in female crime rates in Canada.

A.0153 Heide, Wilma (1974, December). Feminism and the "fallen woman." *Criminal Justice and Behavior, 1*(4), 369-373. Discusses the concept of the female offender as "fallen woman" as being indicative of the male-dominated social system.

A.0154 Heidensohn, Frances (1994). From being to knowing: Some issues in the study of gender in contemporary society. *Women and Criminal Justice, 6*(1), 13-37. Demonstrates the development (1960-1991) of feminist critiques of, and contributions to, criminology.

A.0155 Heidensohn, Frances (1987). Women and crime: Questions for criminology. In P. Carlen & A. Worrall (Eds.), *Gender, crime and justice* (pp. 16-27). Philadelphia, PA: Open University Press. Critiques theories of female criminality and makes suggestions for further research.

A.0156 Heidensohn, Frances (1986, August-November). Models of justice: Portia or Persephone? Some thoughts on equality, fairness and gender in the field of criminal justice. *International Journal of the Sociology of Law, 14*(3-4), 287-298. Looks at models of justice.

A.0157 Heidensohn, Frances (1985). *Women and crime: The life of the female offender:* New York, NY: New York University Press. Advocates a shift from criminological and deviance perspectives to a perspective that considers family life, male dominance and feminist theory.

A.0158 Heidensohn, Frances (1968, June). The deviance of women: A critique and an inquiry. *British Journal of Sociology, 19*(2), 160-175. Comments on the absence of studies on the deviant behavior of women. Discusses positivism, neo-functionalism, and the interactional perspective.

A.0159 Henson, S. D. (1980). Female as totem, female as taboo: An inquiry into the freedom to make connections. In E. Sagarin (Ed.), *Taboos in criminology* (pp. 67-80). Newbury Park, CA: Sage Publications. Discusses how the feminist movement may have affected female criminality.

A.0160 Hill, Gary, & Harris, Anthony (1981). Changes in the gender patterning of crime, 1953-1977: Opportunity vs. identity. *Social Science Quarterly, 62*(4), 658-671. Explores the theory that women's participation in crime increases as women's participation in the labor force grows and traditional stereotyping erodes. Reviewed data for 1953-1977.

A.0161 Hing, B. (1993, July). Raising personal identification issues of class, race, ethnicity, gender, sexual orientation, physical disability, and age in lawyering courses. *Stanford Law Review, 45,* 1807-1833. Discusses the place of personal identity issues in law courses.

A.0162 Hoffman-Bustamante, Dale (1973, Fall). The nature of female criminality. *Issues in Criminology, 8*(2), 117-136. Explores whether or not female criminality is uniquely different from male criminality. Looks at five factors that lead women to crime.

A.0163 Holtman, R. (1989, November). The power of legal concepts: The development of a feminist theory of law. *International Journal of the Sociology of Law 17*(4), 481-502. Discusses the place of feminism in law theory.

A.0164 Horne, Peter (1985, September). Female correction officers: A status report. *Federal Probation, 49*(3), 46-54. Discusses problems and issues that restrict women in certain aspects of corrections.

A.0165 Howe, Adrian (1994). *Punish and critique: Towards a feminist analysis of penalty.* London: Routledge. Discusses the need for a feminist analysis of punitive theory.

A.0166 Howe, Adrian (1990, Summer). Prologue to a history of women's imprisonment: In search of a feminist perspective. *Social Justice, 17*(2), 5-22. History of women's imprisonment in Australia in the context of neo-Marxist theories of crime, social control, and feminist criminology.

A.0167 Hutter, Bridget, & Williams, G. (1981). *Controlling women: The normal and the deviant.* London: Croom Helm in association with the Oxford University Women's Studies Committee. Discusses traditional ideas of what is normal and what is deviant.

A.0168 Ireland, Robert (1992, Winter). Frenzied and fallen females: Women and sexual dishonor in the nineteenth-century United States. *Journal of Women's History, 3*(3), 95-117. Discusses the double-standard of sexual conduct and the male domination of the legal sytem.

A.0169 James, Jennifer (1980, July). Women's liberation and the female delinquent. *Journal of Research in Crime and Delinquency, 17*(2), 230-244. Discusses the impact of the women's movement on ideas of female delinquency.

A.0170 Johnson, Holly (1986). *Women and crime in Canada.* Ottawa: Office of the Solicitor General of Canada. Traces women in the Canadian Criminal Justice System from 1975 1984.

A.0171 Johnson, Rubye (1984, May). *Socialization impact on women and economically motivated crimes.* Dissertation, Howard University. Examines the impact of socialization on incarcerated women and explores the social roles society ascribes to them.

A.0172 Jurik, Nancy (1985, April). An officer and a lady: Organizational barriers to women working as correctional officers in men's prisons. *Social Problems, 32*(4), 375-388. Considers barriers to women employed as correctional officers in men's prisons.

A.0173 Jurik, Nancy, & Halemba, G. (1984). Gender, working conditions and the job satisfaction of women in a non-traditional occupation: Female correctional officers in men's prisons. *Sociological Quarterly, 25*(4), 551-566. Compares work-related attitudes of male and female correctional officers at the same prison.

A.0174 Kendall, Kathleen (1991, Fall). Masking violence against women: The case of premenstrual syndrome. *Canadian Women's Studies, 12,* 17-20. Discusses the idea that the reality of women's experiences is being masked through scientific, legal and popular discourse on PMS.

A.0175 Kennedy, Helena (1992). *Eve was framed: Women and British justice.* London: Chatto & Windus. A crtique of the British legal systems discrimination against female crime victims, offenders, and attorneys.

A.0176 Klein, Dorie, & Kress, June (1979). Any woman's blues. In F. Adler & R. Simon (Eds.), *The criminology of deviant women.* Boston, MA: Houghton Mifflin. Discusses the place of feminist consciousness in the analysis of female criminality.

A.0177 Klein, Dorie (1977). The etiology of female crime: A review of the literature. In L. Crites (Ed.), *The female offender* (pp. 5-31). Lexington, MA: Lexington Books, DC Heath. Reviews literature on the etiology of female crime from Lombroso to the 70's.

A.0178 Klein, Dorie, & Kress, June (1976, Spring-Summer). Any woman's blues: A critical overview of women, crime, and the criminal justice system. *Crime and Social Justice, 5,* 34-49. Discusses experiences of women contrasting traditional literature with radical criminology.

A.0179 Koser Wilson, Nanci (1991). Feminist pedagogy in criminology. *Journal of Criminal Justice Education, 2*(1), 81-94. Discusses the development of a new feminist methodology in criminology.

A.0180 Koser Wilson, Nanci, & Rigsby, Constance (1975). Is crime a man's world: Issues in the exploration of criminality. *Journal of Criminal Justice, 3,* 131-140. Discusses the absence of feminist theories of criminality.

A.0181 Kruttschnitt, Candace (1982). Women, crime, and dependency: An application of the theory of law. *Criminology, 19*(4), 495-513. Discusses the image of women in law.

A.0182 Kunzel, Regina (1993). *Fallen women, problem girls: Unmarried mothers and the professionalization of social work, 1890-1945.* New Haven, CT: Yale University Press. Discusses the influence of social workers on early rehabilitation practices for "deviant" women.

A.0183 Laberge, Danielle (1991). Women's criminality, criminal women, criminalized women? Questions in and for a feminist perspective. *The Journal of Human Justice, 2*(2), 37-56. Discusses the feminist perspective in criminology.

A.0184 Lake, M. B. (1913). Relation between occupation and criminality of women. *Journal of Home Economics, 5,* 224-230. Early ideas about the causes of criminality in women.

A.0185 La Prairie, Carol (1989). Some issues in aboriginal justice research: The case of aboriginal women in Canada. *Women and Criminal Justice, 1*(1), 81-91. Reviews research documenting the over-representation of aboriginal women in the Canadian Criminal Justice System.

A.0186 La Prairie, Carol (1987). Native women and crime: A theoretical model. *Canadian Journal of Native Studies, 7*(1), 121-137. Discusses the disproportionate incarceration of native women in anadian correctional institutions.

A.0187 Lasley, J., et al. (1985, February). Relationship of non-traditional sex role attitudes to severity of women's criminal behavior. *Psychological Reports, 56*(1), 155-188. Examined the hypothesis that a rise in women's criminality is a response to nontraditional self-perceptions.

A.0188 Laster, Kathy (1989). Infanticide: A litmus test for feminist criminological theory. *Australian and New Zealand Journal of Criminology, 22*(3), 151-166. Discusses the challenge to account for infanticide without "essentializing" the offense and its perpetrators.

A.0189 Leonard, Eileen (1982). *Women, crime and society: A critique of criminology theory.* New York, NY: Longmans. Critiques five influential theories of criminology and their adequacy in explaining female patterns of crime.

A.0190 Leonard, V. A. (1953, January-February). The American woman as a criminal. *Journal of Criminal Law, Criminology, and Police Science, 43*(5), 643. Early ideas about the criminality of women.

A.0191 Levanthal, Gloria (1977, December). Female criminality: Is women's lib to blame? *Psychological Reports (Part 2), 41*(3), 1179-1182. Discusses the idea that the rise in female criminality in America may be due to changes in women's roles influenced by the Women's Movement.

A.0192 Lombroso, Cesare, & Ferrero, G. (1958). *The female offender.* New York, NY: Philosophical Library. (first printed in London, 1895). Classic work by Lombroso on female criminality.

A.0193 Lory, Marie (1985, July). Women and the criminal justice system: A study of women offenders in the criminal justice system. *Dissertation Abstracts International, 46*(1), 347-358. Uses historical research and clinical process notes to examine the relationship between societal attitudes, social structures, and women offenders.

A.0194 Los, Mario (1986). Social change and female crime under Communism: A study of the USSR and Poland. *International Annals of Criminology*(Paris), *24*(1-2), 111-135. Examines Polish and Soviet women's participation in crime.

A.0195 Lynch, M., et al. (1992). Cutural literacy, criminology, and female gender issues: The power to exclude. *Journal of Criminal Justice Education, 3,* 183-202. Discusses the relevance of traditional theories of female criminality.

A.0196 Macey, Nora, et al. (1977). The prison project: A proposed model for a clinical course. *Journal of Legal Education, 28*(4), 573-591. Review of a project that took place at the Indiana Women's Prison where ten law students taught a course in criminal law and prisoners rights,

A.0197 MacKinnon, Catherine (1987). Feminism, Marxism, method and the state: Toward feminist jurisprudence. In S. Harding (Ed.), *Feminism and methodology* (pp. 125-156). London: Open University Press. Discusses the importance of feminist theories of law.

A.0198 MacKinnon, Catherine (1983, Summer). Feminism, Marxism, method, and the state. Toward a feminist jurisprudence. *Signs, 8*(4), 635-658. Discusses feminist jurisprudence.

A.0199 Maguire, M., & Shapland, Joanna (1980, December). Is he the villian, she the victim? *New Society, 54*(944-945). Discusses patterns of criminality among women and concerns about the negative effects of the women's movement on women's behavior.

A.0200 Mahan, Sue, & Anthony, Aimee (1992, Fall). Including women in corrections texts. *Journal of Criminal Justice Education, 3*(2), 261-275. Discusses the need to be more inclusive in criminology texts.

A.0201 Mandle, J. D. (1981). Women, crime and social change. In Lagoy (Ed.), *New perspectives on urban crime* (pp. 5-15). Jonesboro, TN: Pilgrimage Press. Discusses the effects of social change on the criminality of women.

A.0202 Mann, Cora Mae (1984). *Female crime and delinquency.* Tusculoosa, AL: University of Alabama Press. Explores theory and concepts of female criminality, female offenders and the law, females and the courts, and females and the correctional system.

A.0203 Mannheim, Hermann (1965). The sex factor: Female delinquency. In H. Mannheim *Comparative criminology* (pp. 690-707). London: Routledge & Kegan Paul. Discusses historical differences in male and female crime rates.

A.0204 Marshall, Ineke (1982, Spring-Winter). Women, work, and crime: An international test of the emancipation hypothesis. *International Journal of Comparative and Applied Criminal Justice, 6*(1), 25-37. Uses Interpol statistics to test the emancipation hypothesis of female criminality, and Adler's aggressive hypothesis.

A.0205 Martin, Ronald, et al. (1978, February). Female criminality and the prediction of recidivism: A prospective six-year follow-up. *Archives of General Psychiatry, 35*(2), 207-214. Discusses the possibility of predicting recidivism in female offenders.

A.0206 Mathew, A. (1992). *Fair sex in unfair society: Women and crime.* New Dehli: Ashish. Discusses female criminality in India.

A.0207 McCabe, Sarah (1968, April). Studies of female offenders. *Criminal Law Review* (London), 207-209. Reviews available literature (1968) on female offenders.

A.0208 McDermott, Joan (1994a, March). *American pragmatism and feminist criminology.* Paper presented at the 1994 ACJS Annual Meeting, Chicago, IL. Discusses links between American pragmatism and feminist philosophy and the implications for the development of feminist criminology.

A.0209 McDermott, Joan (1994b). Criminology as peacemaking: Feminist ethics and the victimization of women. *Women and Criminal Justice, 5*(2), 1-20. Identifies similarities between ethical concerns and criminological priorities.

A.0210 McDermott, Joan (1992, Fall). The personal is empirical: Feminism, research methods, and criminal justice education. *Journal of Criminal Justice Education, 3*(2), 237-249. Discusses feminist research in criminal justice education.

A.0211 McGinnis, J. E. (1953, April). Delinquency in women. *California Medicine, 33,* 56-62. Early discusssion of the causes of female criminality.

A.0212 McLachlin, B. M. (1991). Crime and women--feminine equality and the criminal law. *University of British Columbia Law Review, 25*(1), 1-22. Discusses equality and criminal law.

A.0213 McLeod, Eileen (1985, December; 1986, January). Feminist action research and the criminal justice system: Lessons from the PROS campaign on prostitution. *Resources for Feminist Research, 14,* 40-41. Discusses the viability of feminist action research.

A.0214 McNeill, Pat (1990, January). Female trouble: Why do women commit fewer crimes than men? *New Statesman & Society, 3*(85), 28. Discusses why women commit crimes.

A.0215 McSherry, Bernadette (1993, September). The return of the raging hormones theory: Premenstrual syndrome, Postpartum disorders and criminal responsibility. *The Sydney Law Review, 5,* 292-316. Discusses theories that advocate diminished responsibility for crime.

A.0216 Menzies, Robert, & Chunn, Dorothy (1991). Kicking against the pricks: The dilemmas of feminist teaching in criminology. In B. McLean & D. Milovanovic (Ed.), *New directions in critical criminology* (pp. 63-70). Vancouver, BC: Collective Press. Discusses some of the difficulties in presenting a feminist perspective in criminology classes.

A.0217 Messerschmidt, J. (1988, Fall). From Marx to Bonger: Socialist writings on women, gender, and crime. *Sociological Inquiry, 58*(4), 378-392. Discusses contemporary socialist criminology and the role gender plays in crime.

A.0218 Messerschmidt, J. (1987). Feminism, criminology, and the rise of the female sex "delinquent" 1880-1930. *Criminal Law and Social Change, 11*(13), 243-264. Discusses early theories of female criminality that focused on sexual misconduct.

A.0219 Messerschmidt, J. (1986). *Capitalism, patriarchy, and crime: Towards a socialist feminist criminology.* Totowa, NJ: Rowan and Littlefield. Asserts that an adequate theory of crime requires both a socialist and a feminist perspective.

A.0220 Miller, Eleanor (1983). International trends in the study of female criminality: An essay review. *Contemporary Crises, 7*(1), 59-70. Reviews three books on female criminality exploring women's liberation, shifts in sex-roles, and increased female participation in the labor force.

A.0221 Millman, Marcia (1975). She did it all for love: A feminist view of the sociology of deviance. In M. Millman & R. Kanter (Eds.), *Another voice: Feminist perspectives on social life and social science* (pp. 251-279). Garden City, NY: Anchor Books. Discusses causality in female crime.

A.0222 Mills, Crystal (1984, August). *Sex-role adaptation and female criminal behavior.* Dissertation, University of Michigan. Tested hypothesis that female criminals are more masculine than females who do not demonstrate criminal behavior.

A.0223 Mitchell, Edwina (1994, March-April). The woman offender of today: All women offenders are not criminals. *Prison Journal, 6*(2), 10. Discusses the female offender today.

A.0224 Monahan, Florence (1941). *Women in crime.* New York, NY: Ives Washburn. Early theories about female criminality.

A.0225 Morash, Merry (1988). *Teaching about women in criminal justice and criminology courses: A resource guide.* Columbus, OH: American Society of Criminologists. Guide to available resources for teaching about women in criminology courses.

A.0226 Morris, Allison, & Gelsthorpe, Loraine (1991). Feminists perspectives on criminology: Transforming and transgressing. *Women and Criminal Justice, 2*(2), 3-26. Describes achievements of feminism in criminology and explores potential for transforming criminology.

A.0227 Morris, Allison (1987). *Women, crime and criminal justice.* New York, NY: Basil Blackwell. Reappraises women's criminality and criminological theories as applied to women.

A.0228 Morris, Ruth (1964, October). Female delinquency and relational problems. *Social Forces, 43*(1), 82-89. An early discussion of possible causes for female delinquency.

A.0229 Morton, Joann (1994). Martha Wheeler: Redifining women in corrections. *Women & Criminal Justice, 5*(2), 3-20. Discusses the leadership of Martha E. Wheeler in redefining the standards of correctional practice for the treatment of female offenders.

A.0230 Morton, Joann (1976, November-December). Women offenders: Fiction and facts. *American Journal of Corrections, 38*(6), 32-34. Examines assumptions about the nature of female criminality.

A.0231 Moyer, Imogene (1992) *The changing roles of women in the criminal justice system: Offenders, victims, and professionals.* Prospect Heights, IL: Waveland Press. Indicates that conflict theory is an appropriate perspective to explain traditional research and theories by male criminologists.

A.0232 Moyer, Imogene (1984, Fall). The life and works of Ruth Shonle Cavan: Pioneer women in criminology. *Journal of Crime and Justice, 12*(2), 171-201. Presents the life of a woman pioneer in criminology.

A.0233 Mukherjee, S., & Scutt, Jocelynne (1981). *Women and crime.* Winchester, MA: Australian Institute of Technology in association with Allen & Unwin. Essays on women and crime.

A.0234 Mullings, Janet, & Scarsborough, Kathryn (1994). *A comparison of empirical research on women in policing and women in corrections.* Paper presented at the ACJS Annual Meeting, 1994, Chicago, IL. Analyzes issues in the literature on women in policing and literature on women in corrections. Suggests direction for further research.

A.0235 Muraskin, Rosyln, & Alleman, Ted (1993). *It's a crime: Women and justice.* Englewood Cliffs, NJ: Regents/Prentice Hall. Essays defining the criminal woman.

A.0236 Murphy, K. M., & D'Angelo, R. Y. (1963). The intelligence factor in the criminality of women. *American Catholic Social Review, 24,* 340-347. Early discussion of intelligence and the female offender.

A.0237 Naffine, Ngaire (1987). *Female crime: The construction of women in criminology.* Winchester, MA: Allen & Unwin. Reviews major schools of criminology for the image of the female offender from the late 1960's to mid 1980's.

A.0238 Naffine, Ngaire (1985, October). The masculinity, femininity hypothesis: A consideration of gender-based personality theories of female crime. *British Journal of Criminology, 25*(4), 365-381. Discusses gender-based theories of female criminality.

A.0239 Naffine, Ngaire (1981). Theorizing about female crime. In S. Mukherjee and J. Scutt (Eds.), *Women and crime* (pp. 70-91). Sydney, Australia: Allen & Unwin. Reviews theories of female crime and the symbolic interaction perspective.

A.0240 Nagla, B. K. (1991). *Women, crime and law.* New Delhi: Jaipur Rawat Publications. Discussion of women, crime, and criminal law in India.

A.0241 Nagla, B. K. (1982, October). The criminality of women in India. *Indian Journal of Social Work, 43*(3), 273-282. Reviews research and theories of female criminality from a perspective of social conditioning and the changing aspects of social roles in India.

A.0242 Newberg, Paula (1967, Spring). The female of the species: A systematic review of theories, evaluations and studies of the female criminal. *Interdiscipline, 4*(1), 29-42. Concept of criminal behavior is discussed as well as some theories of female criminality.

A.0243 Norland, Stephen, & Shover, Neal (1977, May). Gender roles and female criminality: Some critical comments. *Criminology: An interdisciplinary Journal, 15*(1), 87-104. Discusses theoretical problems between gender roles and criminality.

A.0244 O'Donavan, Katherine (1989, Spring). Engendering justice: Women's perspectives and the rule of law. *University of Toronto Law Journal, 39*(2), 127-148. Examines contributions of feminist theory to jurisprudence, with particular emphasis on the promise of equality.

A.0245 Offen, L. (1986). Female offender and psychiatric referral: The Medicalisation of female deviance. *Medicine and Law, 5*(4), 339-348. Looks at female deviance from the context of psychiatric court referrals.

A.0246 Omodei, Roslyn (1981). The mythinterpretation of female crime. In Mukherjee & Scutt (Eds.), *Women and crime* (pp. 51-69). Sydney, Australia: Allen & Unwin. Examines the myth that female delinquency is predominantly sexual delinquency.

A.0247 Ostrander, M. R. (1964). Meeting the challenge of our problem girls. *Law and Order, 12*(2), 22. Discusses sociological and pyschological factors that motivate female offenders.

A.0248 Ostrander, M. R (1963). The female offender. *Law and Order, 11*(11), 40-41; *11*(12), 70-73. Early studies on the female offender.

A.0249 Pace, Helen (1992). All the nice girls: A case study in the social control of women, Melbourne, 1942. *Hecate: A Women's Interdisciplinary Journal, 18*(1), 38-59. Discusses the social construction of the term "nice girls" examining 3 murders involving women during WW II.

A.0250 Parisi, Nicolette (1984). The female correctional officer: Her progress toward and prospects for equality. *Prison Journal, 64*(1), 92-109. Explores the evolution of the role of matron to correctional officer.

A.0251 Parisi, Nicolette (1982). Exploring female crime patterns. In N. Rafter-Hahn & E. Stanko (Eds.), *Judge, lawyer, victim, thief: Women, gender role and criminal justice* (pp. 111-129). Boston, MA: Northeastern University Press. Investigates data on the level of female crime including type, extent of participation, and relationship of sex-roles to criminal behavior.

A.0252 Payak, Bertha (1963, December). Understanding the female offender. *Federal Probation, 27*(4), 7-12. Early discussion on the female offender.

A.0253 Payne, S. (1992). Aboriginal women and the law. In *Aboriginal perspectives on criminal justice: Institute of Criminology Monograph Series #1.* Sydney, AU: The Australian Institute of Criminology. Discusses aboriginal women and the law in Australia.

A.0254 Pierce, C. R., et al. (1978). Patterns of female delinquency: Toward differential treatment of female offenders. *South African Journal of Criminal Law and Criminology, 2*(1), 278-287. Discusses the discriminatory treatment of female offenders.

A.0255 Pogrebin, Mark, & Poole, Eric (1994). *Women as jail correctional officers: Their problems and prospects.* Paper presented at the ACJS Annual Meeting, 1994, Chicago, IL. Explores the occupational problems faced by female jail officers in five jails in Colorado.

A.0256 Pollak, O. (1950). *The criminality of women.* Philadelphia, PA: University of Pennsylvania Press. Early study on the criminality of women.

A.0257 Pollock, Joy (1978). Early theories of female criminality. In L. Bowker (Ed.), *Women, crime and the criminal justice system* (pp. 25-55). Lexington, MA: Lexington Books. Discusses Lombroso, Kellor, Lekkerkerker, Thomas, Pollak and others.

A.0258 Pradesk, K. N. (1986, December). Female criminality: Patterns and consequences. *Indian Journal of Social Research, 27*(4), 362-370. Discussion of female criminality in India.

A.0259 Prewitt, A., & Schram, Pamela (1994, March). *Women in criminological theories: Social realities and multiple hierarchies.* Paper presented at the Annual Meeting of the ACJS, Chicago, IL. Explores the place of women in crime causation theories.

A.0260 Price, Barbara, & Sokoloff, Natalie (1982). *The criminal justice system and women: Offenders, victims, and workers.* New York, NY: Clark Boardman. Essays on women in all aspects of the criminal justice system.

A.0261 Price, Ray (1977, April). The forgotten female offender. *Crime and Delinquency, 23*(2), 101-108. Discussion on the lack of studies and information on female offenders.

A.0262 Quade, Vicki, & Dadisman, Mary Ann (1993, Fall). Redefining notions: Feminist legal theory pushes into the mainstream. *Human Rights, 20*(4), 8-11. Discusses feminist legal theory.

A.0263 Quarles, M. S. (1964). How one woman's reformatory interests students in the correctional field. *American Journal of Corrections, 26*(3), 32-35. Discusses the need for correctional workers and what attracts individuals to the field.

A.0264 Radosh, Polly (1990). Women and crime in the United States: A Marxian explanation. *Sociological Spectrum, 10*(1), 105-131. Reviews predominant theories of the causes of female crime in the U.S. and proposes a theory based on a Marxist approach.

A.0265 Radzinowicz, L., & King, Joan (1977). The rise of crime amongst women. In L. Radzinowicz & J. King (Eds.), *The growth of crime: The international experience* (pp. 13-17). New York, NY: Basic Books. Discusses reasons for the increase in the number of crimes committed by women.

A.0266 Rafter-Hahn, Nicole (1989, January-March). Crime and the family. *Socialist Review, 19*(1), 123-129. Discusses causes of female crime relating to poverty and the family.

A.0267 Rafter-Hahn, Nicole, & Natalizia, E. (1981, January). Marxist feminism: Implications for criminal justice. *Crime and Delinquency, 27*(1), 81-98. Examines sexist bias in criminal justice from a Marxist perspective. Discusses problems encountered by women.

A.0268 Rans, Laurel (1978, March). Women's crime: Much ado about...? *Federal Probation, 42*, 45-49. Discusses whether or not "women's crime" really exists.

A.0269 Rasche, Christine (1975). The female offender as an object of criminological research. In A. Brodsky (Ed.), *The female offender* (pp. 9-28). Newbury Park, CA: Sage Publications. Traces historical approach to the female offender through correctional literature of the past century.

A.0270 Rasche, Christine (1974). The female offender as an object of criminological research. *Criminal Justice and Behavior, 1*(4), 301-320. Discusses the need for more criminological research on women offenders.

A.0271 Reckless, Walter (1957, January). Female criminality. *National Probation and Parole Association Journal, 3*, 1-68. Early discussion of female criminality.

A.0272 Renzetti, Claire (1993). On the margins of the malestream (Or, they still don't get it, do they?): Feminist analysis in criminal justice education. *Journal of Criminal Justice Education, 4*(2), 219-234. Critical review of the Fall, 1992 issue of the *Journal of Criminal Justice* on women in criminal justice education.

A.0273 Richards-Ekeh, Kaylene (1994) *Racial ethnic women correctional officers.* Paper presented at the ACJS Annual Meeting, 1994, Chicago, IL. Assesses the extent to which racial ethnic women are employed as correctional officers. Data from two prison systems.

A.0274 Rietz, John (1991, Summer). Criminal Ms-representation: Moll Flanders and female criminal biography. *Studies in the Novel, 23*(2), 185-195. Critiques Daniel Defoe's ideas of the relationship between femininity and criminality.

A.0275 Rison, Richard (1994). Women as high-security officers. *Federal Prisons Journal, 3*(3), 19-23. Explores gender-neutral employment in high-security prisons.

A.0276 Robinson, Mary (1988). Women and the law in Ireland. *Women's Studies International Forum, 11*(4), 351-354. Discusses how women are viewed in Irish law.

A.0277 Rodmell, S. (1981). Men, women, and sexuality: A feminist critique of the sociology of deviance. *Women's Studies International Quarterly, 4*(2), 145-155. Discusses deviance from the feminist perspective.

A.0278 Rolison, Garry (1993). Toward an integrated theory of female criminality and incarceration. In B. Fletcher et al. (Eds.), *Women prisoners: A forgotten population* (pp. 135-146). Westport, CT: Praeger. A theoretical framework for understanding women's experiences with crime and incarceration.

A.0279 Rosenbaum, Jill, & Chesney-Lind, Meda (1994, April). Appearance and delinquency: A research note. *Crime and Delinquency, 40*(2), 250-261. Discusses how standards of attractiveness are used to determine how women are treated in various aspects of their lives as well as in the criminal justice system.

A.0280 Rosenbaum Jill (1989, January). Women and crime. *Crime and Delinquency, 35*(1), [complete issue]. Essays on various aspects of women and crime.

A.0281 Rosenblum, K. E. (1975). Female deviance and the female sex role: A preliminary investigation. *British Journal of Sociology, 26*(2), 173-178. Discusses what is/was considered deviant for women due to sex role stereotyping.

A.0282 Ryan, Karen (1994, Fall). Mad or bad? Women and the forensic psychiatric process. *Masters Abstracts International, 32*(3), 863. Explores the social control of mentally disordered female inmates by the forensic psychiatric system. Compares forensic processing of males and females.

A.0283 Sandhu, Harjit, & Allen, D. (1969, May). Female delinquency: Goal obstruction and anomie. *Canadian Review of Sociology and Anthropology, 6*(2), 107-110. Discussion of female delinquency.

A.0284 Schur, E. (1984). *Labelling women deviant: Gender, stigma and social control.* New York, NY: Random House. Theoretical discussion of female deviance.

A.0285 Schweber, Claudine, & Feinman, Clarice (1984, Fall). Criminal justice politics and women: The aftermath of legally mandated change. *Women and Politics, 4*(1). 133. Discusses legal changes that have affected women.

A.0286 Scott, Edward (1982). Delinquent females: In-depth therapy and some theoretical opinions. *International Journal of Offender Therapy and Comparative Criminology, 26*(3), 215-222. Discusses theories of female delinquency and the use of therapy.

A.0287 Scott H., Wilma (1975). Feminism and the fallen woman. In A. Brodsky (Ed.), *The female offender* (pp. 77-82). Newbury Park, CA: Sage Publications. Defines a feminist approach to planning for female offenders.

A.0288 Scutt, Jocelynne (1979, February). The myth of the "chivalry factor" in female crime. *Australian Journal of Social Issues, 14*(1), 3-20. Discusses the idea of chivalry towards women criminals.

A.0289 Scutt, Jocelynne (1978, February). Toward the liberation of the female offender. *International Journal of Criminology and Penology, 6*(1), 5-18. Discusses new theories of female criminality.

A.0290 Scutt, Jocelynne (1977). Psychiatry and the creation of female criminality. *Australian Journal of Forensic Science, 9*(2), 64-75. Discusses the idea of the female offender as a sick woman.

A.0291 Scutt, Jocelynne (1976). Role conditioning theory: An explanation for disparity in male and female criminality. *Australian and New Zealand Journal of Criminology (Melbourne), 9*(1), 25-35. Discusses the differences in expectations of male and female offenders.

A.0292 Shacklady-Smith, L. (1978). Sexist assumptions and female delinquency. In C. Smart & B. Smart (Eds.), *Women, sexuality and social control.* London: Routledge & Kegan Paul. Discusses pervasive sexism in theories of female delinquency.

A.0293 Shepherd, Judith (1980, December). *Female delinquency: A control perspective.* Dissertation, University of California, Berkeley. Discussion of theories of female delinquency.

A.0294 Shield, Deanna, & Moyer, Imogene (1994). *HERSTORY: Frances Alice Kellor, 1873-1952.* Paper presented at the ACJS Annual Meeting, 1994, Chicago, IL. Presents the life of feminist criminologist, Frances Alice Kellor known for her anthropological laboratories.

A.0295 Simon, Rita (1994). Female criminality. In *The Encyclopedia of Criminology.* New York, NY: Macmillan. Discusses theories of female criminality.

A.0296 Simon, Rita (1993). Women, crime, and justice. In. B. Forst (Ed.), *The socio-economics of crime and justice* (pp. 121-154). Armonk, NY: M.E. Sharpe. Discusses causes of female criminality and women in the criminal justice system.

A.0297 Simon, Rita, et al. (1980). Contemporary theories of deviance and female delinquency: An empirical test. *Research on Crime and Delinquency, 17*(1), 42-57. Analyzes data on traditional theories of deviance and self-reported delinquency for both males and females.

A.0298 Simon, Rita, & Benson, Michael (1980). Evaluating changes in female criminality. In M. Klein & K. Teilman (Eds.), *Handbook of criminal justice evaluation* (pp. 549-571). Newbury Park, CA: Sage. Interprets current data (1980's) on female criminality and proposes new research.

A.0299 Simon, Rita (1975). *The contemporary woman and crime: Crime and delinquency issues, a monograph series.* Washington, DC: U.S. Government Printing Office. Reviews characteristics of female offenders in the criminal justice system over a twenty year period.

A.0300 Simpson, Sally (1991, February). Caste, class, and violent crime: Explaining differences in female offending. *Criminology, 29*(1), 115-135. Examines, neo-Marixism, power-control theory and, socialist feminist theory, for intragender/racial inclusivity.

A.0301 Simpson, Sally (1994, Fall). Is gender subordinate to class? An empirical assessment of Colvin and Pauly's structural Marxist theory of delinquency. *Journal of Criminal Law & Criminology*, *85*(2), 453-480. Examines the role of social class and gender in the prevalence of delinquency.

A.0302 Simpson, Sally (1989, November). Feminist theory, crime, and justice. *Criminology*, *27*(4), 605-631. Discusses the influence of feminist research on criminology, and the criminal justice processing of female offenders.

A.0303 Singh, M. (1981, October). Women and crime phenomenon. *Indian Journal of Social Work*, *42*(3), 281-292. Discusses theories of female criminality.

A.0304 Smart, Carol (1990). Feminist approaches to criminology or postmodern woman meets atavistic man. In L. Gelsthorpe & A. Morris (Eds.), *Feminist perspectives in criminology* (pp. 70-84). Milton Keynes: Open University Press. Discusses feminist approaches to criminology.

A.0305 Smart Carol (1989). *Feminism and the power of law*. London: Routledge. Discusses the intersection of feminism and the law.

A.0306 Smart, Carol (1986). Feminism and law: Some problems of analysis and strategy. *International Journal of the Sociology of Law*, *14*(1), 109-123. Discusses the intersection of feminism and the law.

A.0307 Smart, Carol (1979a, January). The new female criminality: Reality or myth? *British Journal of Criminology*, *19*(1), 50-59. Assesses the relationship between women's liberation and increases in criminal acts by women.

A.0308 Smart, Carol (1979b). *Women, sexuality and social control*. London: Routledge & Kegan Paul. Discusses societal attitudes towards deviance in women.

A.0309 Smart, Carol (1977). *Women, crime, and criminology: A feminist critique*. London: Routledge & Kegan Paul. Investigates criminology and sociology of deviance by examining female crime from a feminist perspective.

A.0310 Smart, Carol (1977, March). Criminological theory: Its ideology and implications concerning women. *British Journal of Sociology*, *28*(1), 89-100. Discusses attitudes about the nature of female criminality that affect the treatment of female offenders. Outlines major works.

A.0311 Snider, Laureen (1990). The potential of the criminal justice system to promote feminist concerns. *Studies in Law, Politics, and Society*, *10*, 143-172. Argues that the criminal justice system promotes illusion regarding feminist problems with the patriarchy.

A.0312 Sohoni, Neera (1994, Spring). Correlates of female crime. *Feminist Issues*, *14*(1), 25-35. Discusses female crime in the context of Western and Indian literature.

A.0313 South, Scott, & Messner, Steven (1987). The sex ratio and women's involvement in crime: A cross-national analysis. *Sociological Quarterly*, *28*(2), 171-188. Hypothesizes that sex ratio is linked to women's involvement in crime, both as victims and as offenders.

A.0314 Spatz, Cathy, & Ames, Ashley (1988). Biology and female crime. In T. Moffitt & A. Mednick (Eds.), *Biological contributions to crime causation. NATO advanced science institutes series D: Behavioral and social science* (pp. 308-331). Netherlands: Martinus Nijhoff Publishing. Discusses biological theories of crime.

A.0315 Spence, C., & Phillips, M. (1990). Women, values, and the law: Women teaching and learning about gender, ideology, and law. *Social Justice 17*(3), 189-194. Discusses feminist methodologies in law.

A.0316 Stang-Dahl, T. (1987). *Women's law: An introduction to feminist jurisprudence.* Oslo, NO: Norwegian University Press. Discusses feminist jurisprudence.

A.0317 Steffensmeier, Darrell, et al. (1989). Development and female crime: A cross national test of alternative explanations. *Social Forces, 68*(1), 262-283. Tested 4 alternative explanations of the relationship between development and female crime using Interpol data from 69 countries.

A.0318 Steffensmeier, Darrell (1980). Sociocultural vs. biological/sexist explanations of sex difference in crime: A survey of American criminology textbooks, 1918-1965. *The American Sociologist, 15*(4), 246-255. Reviews criminology textbooks for gender-specific discussions.

A.0319 Strosnider, Christine (1978). Leadership by women in criminal justice: There is room at the top. *Dissertation Abstracts International, 40*(4), 2283-A. Practical informative guide for women entering the field of criminal justice.

A.0320 Szockyj, E. (1989, July). Working in a man's world: Women correctional officers in an institution for men. *Canadian Journal of Criminology, 31*(3), 319-328. Discusses the experiences of staff and prisoners at a provincial pre-trial center in Western Canada.

A.0321 Terry, R. M. (1979, Summer). Trends in female crime. A comparison of Adler, Simon, & Steffensmeier. *California Sociologist, 2*(2), 200-212. Discusses studies of Adler & Simon, and Steffensmeier.

A.0322 Thomas, Suzie, & Stein, Nancy (1990, Summer). Criminality, imprisonment & women's rights in the 1990's. *Social Justice, 17*, 5-135. Discussion of the criminality of women in the 1990's.

A.0323 Thornton, W. E. (1977). *Gender roles and delinquency from a social control perspective.* Dissertation, University of Tennessee. Discusses the social control perspective in criminology.

A.0324 Van Der Westhuizen, J., et al. (1979). Female criminality: Two views. *South African Journal of Criminal Law and Criminology*, 252-260. Two articles from South Africa that present opposing views on female criminality.

A.0325 Viccia, Antoinette (1985). Women, crime, and criminal justice: The United Nations search for fairness. In P. R. David (Ed.), *Crime and criminal policy* (pp. 729-734). Milan, Italy: UN Social Defense Research Institute. Discusses human rights issues for women.

A.0326 Vitaliano, P., et al. (1981, November). Sexuality of deviant females: Adolescent and adult correlates. *Social Work*, 468-472. Suggests an association between negative sexual experiences in adolescents, low self-image, and subsequent deviant adult life styles.

A.0327 Walters, Stephen (1993). Changing the guard: Male correctional officers' attitudes toward women as co-workers. *Journal of Offender Rehabilitation, 20*(1-2), 47-60. Results of surveying male correctional officers at four correctional facilities.

A.0328 Walters, Stephen (1992). Attitudinal and demographic differences between male and female corrections officers: A study in three Midwestern prisons. *Journal of Offender Rehabilitation, 18*(2), 173-179. Explores relationships between gender differences and other variables in correctional officer environment in three prisons.

A.0329 Weisberg, D. K. (1980). *Women and the law, Vol.1.* Boston, MA: Schenkman. Discussions of women and the law.

A.0330 Weisheit, Ralph, & Mahan, Sue (1988). *Women, crime and criminal justice.* Cincinnati, OH: Anderson. Examines major research on female criminality, criminal justice processing, incarceration, and women in criminal justice occupations.

A.0331 Weisheit, Ralph (1984, October). Women and crime: Issues and perspectives. *Sex Roles, 11*(7-8), 567-581. Examines key issues in the study of female criminality from the structural, individual, and small group perspectives.

A.0332 Widom, Cathy, & Stewart, A. J. (1986). Female criminality and the status of women. *International Annals of Criminology, 24,* 137-162. Examines the relationship between female crime rates and the status of women using statistics for 1971 & 1972 from 43 countries.

A.0333 Widom, Cathy (1979, December). Female offenders: Three assumptions about self-esteem, sex-role identity, and feminism. *Criminal Justice and Behavior, 6*(4), 365-382. Investigated the validity of assumptions about self-esteem, sex-role identity, and feminism in female offenders.

A.0334 Widom, Cathy (1978a). Toward an understanding of female criminality. In B. Maher (Ed.), *Progress in experimental personality research* (pp. 245-308). New York, NY: Academic Press. Discusses female criminality.

A.0335 Wilbanks, W. (1981). A test of Verkko's static and dynamic "laws" of sex and homicide. *International Journal of Women's Studies, 4*(2), 173-180. Discusses Verkko's study, in Copenhagen in 1951 testing women's crime rates across and within countries over time.

A.0336 Williams, Yvonne (1982). *Structural aspects of female criminality in the United States: Aggregate analysis and policy implications.* Dissertation, Case Western Reserve University. Presents statistical evidence of ecological and societal influences on women's criminality.

A.0337 Wilson Nanci (1983). An international perspective on women and criminology. In E. Johnson (Ed.), *International handbook of contemporary developments in criminology: General issues and the Americas* (pp. 99-118). Westport, CT: Greenwood Press. Discusses criminology and women from an international perspective.

A.0338 Wilson, Nanci (1982). Women in the criminal justice professions: An analysis of status conflict. In N. Rafter-Hahn & E. Stanko (Eds.), *Judge, lawyer, victim thief: Women, gender roles and criminal justice* (pp. 359-374). Boston, MA: Northeastern University Press. Discusses the meaning of status, particularly as "woman" and as "criminal justice professional."

A.0339 Wilson, Nanci, & Rigsby, Constance (1975). Is crime a man's world? Issues in the exploration of criminality. *Journal of Criminal Justice, 3,* 131-140. Discusses the development of theories of female criminality.

A.0340 Windschuttle, Elizabeth (1981). Women, crime and punishment. In S. Mukherjee & J. Scutt (Eds.), *Women and crime* (pp. 31-50). Winchester, MA: Allen & Unwin. Discusses historical sociological mindset regarding women and crime and women penal reformers.

A.0341 Wonders, Nanci, & Caufield, Susan (1993). Women's work? The contradictory implications of courses on women and the criminal justice system. *Journal of Criminal Justice Education, 4,* 79-100. Discusses issues with teaching courses on women in criminology.

A.0342 Wright, Kevin (1994). *A feminist critique of fifty years of corrections research.* Paper presented at the ACJS Annual Meeting, 1994, Chicago, IL: Critiques existing research on the extent to which feminist theory and methodology are incorporated in paradigm construction.

A.0343 Wright, Richard (1992, Fall). From vamps to tramps to teases and flirts: Stereotypes of women in criminology textbooks, 1956-1965 and 1981-1990. *Journal of Criminal Justice Education, 3*(2), 223-236. Discusses images of women in criminology textbooks.

A.0344 Wright, Richard (1987a, January). Incorporating women and crime topics into criminology classes: Assignments, exercises, and projects. *Teaching Sociology, 15*(1), 95-98. Recommends what to incorporate in criminology classes to compensate for the lack of women & crime topics.

A.0345 Wright, Richard (1987b, October). Are "sisters in crime" finally being booked? The coverage of women and crime in journals and textbooks. *Teaching Sociology, 15*(4), 418-422. Indicates that criminology texts show little improvement in the coverage of women & crime over the years.

A.0346 Yotopoulow-Marangopoulos, Alice (1992). *The peculiarities of female criminality and their causes: A human rights perspective.* London: Esperia. Analyzes characteristics of female crime in light of sex-roles. Suggests taking into account social, economic, and cultural factors.

A.0347 Zaitow, Barbara (1991, July). Toward an integrated explanation of female criminality: The deprivation-compensation model. *Dissertation Abstracts International, 52*(1), 304. Presents a theoretical explanation for female crime.

A.0348 Zedner, Lucia (1989, July). The criminality of women and its control in England, 1850-1914. *Dissertation Abstracts International, 50*(1), 265-A. Discusses the social control of women in England, 1850-1914.

A.0349 Zimmer, Lynn (1989). Solving women's employment problems in corrections. *Women & Criminal Justice, 1*(1), 55-79. Explores the occupational problems faced by women correctional officers who work in male institutions.

A.0350 Zupan, Linda (1992, July). Men guarding women: An analysis of the employment of male correction officers in prisons for women. *Journal of Criminal Justice, 20*(40, 297-309. Assesses male officers employed in women's prisons, their jobs, and inmates reactions.

2

CRIMES

Fetal Abuse; Substance Abuse; Women Who Kill

B.0001 Abelson, Elaine (1989a). *When ladies go a-thieving.* New York, NY: Oxford University Press. Historical study of shoplifting by middle-class women. Explores the development of late 19th century consumer culture.

B.0002 Abelson, Elaine (1989b). The invention of kleptomania. *Signs: Journal of Women in Culture and Society, 15*(1), 123-143. Uses the shoplifting case of Ella Castle in 1896 to illustrate the development of social, medical and legal thought on kleptomania in the late 19th century USA.

B.0003 Adam, H. C. (1912). *Women and crime.* London: T.W. Laurie. Early discussion of female criminality.

B.0004 Adams, S. G. (1978). *The female offender: A statistical perspective.* Ottowa, Canada: Ministry of the Solicitor General. Discusses the types of crimes women in Canada were charged with in the ten-year period from 1965-1975.

B.0005 Adelberg, Ellen (1985). *Women in conflict with the law: A forgotten minority.* Ottawa, Ontario: Canadian Association of Elizabeth Fry Societies. An overview of female offenders and female prison inmates of Canada.

B.0006 Adler, Freda (1981a). *The incidence of female criminality in the contemporary world.* New York, NY: New York University Press. Addresses the nature of female criminality and the status of female offenders in the United States, Europe, Africa, Latin America, and elsewhere.

B.0007 Adler, Freda (1981b). International concern in light of the American experience. In F. Adler (Ed.), *The incidence of female criminality in the contemporary world* (pp. 1-13). New York, NY: New York University Press. Discusses 1975 as a focal point for change in addressing women and crime internationally.

B.0008 Adler, Freda (1975). *Sisters in crime: The rise of the new female criminal.* New York, NY: McGraw-Hill. Adler's theory of female criminality.

B.0009 Adler, Freda (1971). *The female offender in Philadelphia.* Dissertation, University of Pennsylvania. Empirical research on crimes by women in Philadelphia.

B.0010 Adler, Jeffrey (1992, Summer). Streetwalkers, degraded outcasts, and good-for-nothing huzzies: Women and the dangerous class in Antebellum St. Louis. *Journal of Social History, 25*(4), 737-755. Discusses police protection of prostitutes in the mid-19th century and the arrests of women for drunkeness or homelessness.

B.0011 Ahuja, R. (1970, October). Female murderers in India: A sociological study. *Indian Journal of Social Work, 31*(3), 271-284. Study of 136 female murderers in India.

B.0012 Alexander, Shana (1983). *Very much a lady: The untold story of Jean Harris and Dr. Herman Tarnower*. Boston, MA: Little Brown. Story of Jean Harris.

B.0013 Allen, Craig, & Pothast, Henry (1994). Distinguishing characteristics of male and female child sex abusers. *Journal of Offender Rehabilitation, 21*(1-2), 73-88. Explores the relationship of gender and need in adult relationships of child sexual abusers and nonabusers.

B.0014 Allen, Craig, & Chung, Lee (1992). Family of origin structure and intra/extrafamilial childhood sexual victimization of male and female offenders. *Journal of Child Sexual Abuse, 1*(3), 31-45. Data from 25 adult female offenders and 25 adult male offenders classified as child abusers.

B.0015 Allen, Craig (1990). Women as perpetrators of child sexual abuse. In A. Horton et al. (Eds.), *From incest perpetrator: A family member no one wants to treat* (pp. 99-107). Newbury Park, CA: Sage Publications. Discusses barriers to recognition of child sexual abuse by female perpetrators.

B.0016 Allen, Judith (1990). *Sex and secrets: Crimes involving Australian women since 1880.* Melbourne, Australia: Oxford University Press. Discusses crimes committed by women in Australia.

B.0017 Allen, Thomas (1994, February). An assessment of factors related to the continued criminal behavior of female felons. *Dissertation Abstracts International, 84*(8), 3210-3211. Assessed factors related to the repetition of crime by rural women offenders.

B.0018 American Journal of Nursing (1995, May). Fetal harm greater from cigarettes than cocaine. *American Journal of Nursing, 95*(5), 56. Reviews two large studies on the correlation of use of cocaine with low birth weight and preterm delivery.

B.0019 Anderson, Camilla (1967, November-December). The female criminal offender. *American Journal of Corrections, 29,* 7-9. Discusses crimes committed by women.

B.0020 Anderson, Carole (1981, May). A self-concept study of white women addicted to heroin. *Dissertation Abstracts International, 41*(11), 4249. Data collected from four groups of women incarcerated at Las Colinas Women's Detention Facility in San Diego.

B.0021 Anderson, Cerisse (1995, March 13). Judge bars a commitment to aid fetus. *National Law Journal, 17*(28), ALL. Reviews case of New York judge who ruled that the state may not involuntarily commit a mentally ill pregnant woman to protect her fetus.

B.0022 Anglin, M. D., & Hser, Yih-Ing (1987). Addicted women and crime. *Criminology, 25*(2), 359-397. Examines the relationship between women's narcotics use and crime. Data collected from 328 Anglo and Chicana female methadone maintenance clients in California between 1976-1978.

B.0023 Antilla, I. (1984). Female criminality in Finland: What do statistics show? In F. Adler (Ed.), *The incidence of female criminality in the contemporary world* (pp. 64-83). New York, NY: New York University Press. Presents tables detailing female criminality in Finland over 75 years.

B.0024 Appel, Deborah (1992, Fall). Drug use during pregnancy: State strategies to reduce the prevalence of prenatal drug exposure. *University of Florida Journal of Law and Public Policy, 5*, 103-148. Discusses the criminalization of drug use during pregnancy.

B.0025 Argeriovi, M., & Paulina, Donna (1976, May). Women arrested for drunken driving in Boston: Social characteristics and circumstance of arrest. *Journal of Studies on Alcohol, 37*(5), 648-658. Review of police records of women arrested for drunk-driving in Boston.

B.0026 Aris, Brenda, et al. (1992). Women and crime. *Southern California Review of Law and Women's Studies, 2*(1), 1-425. 13 articles on women, crime and criminal justice.

B.0027 Arizona Law Review (1991). Prosecuting pregnant addicts for dealing to the unborn. *Arizona Law Review, 33*, 221-237. Discusses the criminalization of prenatal drug abuse.

B.0028 Ashbrook Debra, & Solley, Linda (1979). *Women and heroin abuse: A survey of sexism in drug abuse administration.* Palo Alto, CA: R & E Research Associates. Discusses the treatment of women addicts.

B.0029 Ashley, Michele (1994, Fall). An examination of the effects of the Life Activities Inventory of a female DUI offender: A social cognitive approach. *Masters Abstracts International, 32*(3). Assesses the use of social cognitive theory to explain women driving under the influence.

B.0030 Augustine, Rene (1991). Pregnancy and addiction: Eliminating the saint-sinner motif. *Wisconsin Women's Law Journal, 6*, 151-172. Discusses issues surrounding the criminalization of drug abuse during pregnancy.

B.0031 Aultman, M. G. (1980). Group involvement in delinquent acts: A study of offense types and male-female participation. *Criminal Justice and Behavior, 7*, 185-192. Discusses crimes committed by males and females in collaboration.

B.0032 Austin, Roy (1993). Recent trends in official male and female crime rates: The convergence controversy. *Journal of Criminal Justice, 21*(5), 447-466. Examines the proposition that male and female crime rates have not converged in recent years.

B.0033 Awad, G., & Harrison, S. (1976). A female fire-setter: A case report. *Journal of Nervous and Mental Disease, 163*(6), 432-437. Discusses arson in women.

B.0034 Bailey, Deborah (1992, Spring). Maternal substance abuse: Does Ohio have an answer. *University of Dayton Law Review, 17*, 1019-1053. Discusses Ohio's solution to maternal substance abuse.

B.0035 Bader, Eleanor (1990, July). Fetal protection proposals: Pregnant drug users get jail, not treatment. *Women's Health Journal, 19*, 51-53. Discusses the criminalization of addicted pregnancy.

B.0036 Ball, J. C., et al. (1975). Pretreatment criminality of male and female drug abuse patients in the United States. *Addictive Diseases: An International Journal, 1*(4), 481-489. Discusses criminal activity of male and female drug abusers prior to treatment.

B.0037 Banning, A. (1989). Mother-son incest: Confronting prejudice. *Child Abuse & Neglect, 13*(4), 563-570. Examines the proposition that the incidence of child abuse by female perpetrators is underestimated.

B.0038 Barnard, G. W., et al. (1982, Fall). Til' death do us part: A study of spouse murder. *Bulletin of the American Academy of Psychiatry and the Law, 10*(2), 271-280. Analyzes data on 11 women and 23 men charged with spousal murder who underwent pretrial psychiatric evaluation.

B.0039 Barrett, Mary (1993, Fall). Mother's role in incest: Neither dysfunctional women nor dysfunctional theories when both are explored in their entirety. *Journal of Child Sexual Abuse, 2*(3), 99-101. Discusses maternal incest.

B.0040 Barry, Ellen (1991, Winter). Pregnant, addicted, and sentenced. *Criminal Justice, 5*(4), 22-27. Discusses the criminalization of drug use during pregnancy.

B.0041 Barry, Ellen (1981). *Pregnant, substance-dependent women: Debunking the myth of incarceration.* San Francisco, CA: Legal Services for Prisoners. Discusses the criminalization of drug abuse during pregnancy.

B.0042 Bartholomew, A., & Bonnici, A. (1965). Infanticide: A statutory offense. *Medical Journal of Australia, 52*(25), 1018-1021. Discusses infanticide and the law.

B.0043 Baskin, Deborah ,& Sommers, Ira (1993). Females initiation into violent street crime. *Justice Quarterly, 10*(40, 559-583. Examines when and how women become involved in violent street crime. Data collected from women arrested for violent street crimes in New York City.

B.0044 Bauman, Norman (1995, September 4). Breast-feeding murder prosecution draws fire. *National Law Journal, 18*(1), 6. Case of Karen Henderson convicted of felony child endangerment and sentenced to six years in prison for taking methamphetamines while breast-feeding her two-month-old son, who died.

B.0045 Baunach, Phyllis (1977, Fall). Women offenders: A commentary. Current conceptions on women in crime. *Quarterly Journal of Corrections, 1*(4), 14-18. Discusses women's perceived violations of traditional norms and role expectations.

B.0046 Bauschard, Louise, & Kimbrough, Mary (1986). *Voices set free: Battered women speak from prison.* St. Louis, MO: Women's Self-Help Center. Battered women discuss abusive relationships that led to murder.

B.0047 Beattie, J. M. (1975a). The criminality of women in eighteenth century England. In D. K. Weisberg (Ed.), *Women and the Law: A social historical perspective.* Cambridge, MA: Schenkman Publishing Co, Inc. Discusses types of crimes committed by women.

B.0048 Beattie, J. M. (1975b, Summer). The criminality of women in eighteenth century England. *Journal of Social History, 8*(4), 81-116. Analysis of judicial records reveals patterns of offense in crimes against property (robbery, burglary, theft) and crimes against person (murder, assault).

B.0049 Bembenek, Laurencia (1992). *Woman on trial.* New York, NY: Harper Collins. Case of a policewoman accused and tried for murder of her husband's ex-wife.

B.0050 Benda, B. B. (1990). Crime, drug abuse and mental illness: A comparison of homeless men and women. *Journal of Social Service Research, 13*(3), 39-60. Discusses the criminalization of homelessness.

B.0051 Benedek, Elissa (1982). Women and homicide. In B. L. Danto et al. (Eds.), *The human side of homicide* (pp. 150-164). New York, NY: Columbia University Press. Discusses women murderers and current thinking about women who murder their husbands.

B.0052 Benson, Margaret (1973). *Adult female offenders: An examination of the nature of their offenses.* Toronto, Canada: Elizabeth Fry Society. Looks at adult female offenders, the crimes they commit, and the criminal justice process.

B.0053 Berenson, Edward (1992). *The trial of Madame Caillaux.* Berkeley, CA: University of California Press. The 1914 case of the wife of a French diplomat who shot the editor of the French newspaper, *Le Figaro.*

B.0054 Bhanot, M., & Surat, M. (1981). Criminality amongst women in India: A study of female offenders and female convicts. In F. Adler (Ed.). *The incidence of female criminality in the contemporary world* (pp. 228-258). New York, NY: New York University Press. Discusses the nature and patterns of female criminality in India.

B.0055 Biggers, Trisha (1979, Spring). Death by murder: A study of women murderers. *Death Education, 3*(1), 1-9. Data collected from interviews with 135 convicted female murderers.

B.0056 Birch, Helen (1994). *Moving targets: Women, murder, and representation.* Berkeley, CA: University of California Press. Collection of ten essays on representations of women who murder.

B.0057 Birch, Helen (1994). If looks could kill: Myra Hindley and the iconography of evil. In H. Birch (Ed.), *Moving targets: Women, murder and representation* (pp. 32-61). Berkeley, CA: University of California Press. Case of Myra Hindley who took part in the murders of five children with her lover, Ian Brady.

B.0058 Biron, Louise, et al. (1995, January-March). The issue of drugs and crime among a sample of incarcerated women. *Deviant Behavior, 16*(1), 25-43. Data collected from 94 female prisoners (aged 18-64 yrs) in Quebec. Investigates drug use and abuse and its relation to crime.

B.0059 Biron, Louise, et al. (1987). Violent female offender. In J. MacLatchie (Ed.), *Insights into violence in contemporary Canadian Society* (pp. 132-134). Ontario, Canada: John Howard Society of Canada. Data collected from 19 Canadian women convicted of a crime.

B.0060 Blackman, Julie (1989). *Intimate violence.* New York, NY: Columbia University Press. Discusses spousal abuse and homicide.

B.0061 Blank, Robert (1993, March). Maternal-fetal relationship: The courts and social policy. *Journal of Legal Medicine, 14,* 73-92. Discusses legal ramifications of drug use during pregnancy

B.0062 Bledsoe, Jerry (1994, June). *Before he wakes: A true story of money, marriage, sex, and murder.* New York, NY: Dutton. Story of Barbara Stager, a woman accused of killing her first and second husbands, who was convicted and sentenced to life in prison.

B.0063 Blinder, Martin (1985a). *Lovers, killers, husbands, and wives.* New York, NY: St. Martin's Press. Discusses violence and murder among intimates.

B.0064 Blinder, Martin (1985b). The domestic homicide. *Family Therapy, 12*(1), 1-24. Interviews with two convicted killers, one a woman who killed her husband. Discusses dependent relationships

B.0065 Block, Alan (1977, January). Aw! Your mother's in the Mafia: Women criminals in progressive New York. *Contemporary Crises, 1*(1), 5-22. Focuses on female criminals who operated within the Jewish underworld in New York's Lower East Side during the 1910's.

B.0066 Block, K. J. (1990). Age-related correlates of criminal homicides committed by women: A study of Baltimore. *Journal of Crime and Justice, 13*(1), 42-65. Discusses data of homicides commited by 294 women in Baltimore from 1974 to 1986.

B.0067 Blount, William, et al. (1994, Winter-Spring). Alcohol and drug use among abused women who kill, abused women who don't, and their abusers. *Journal of Drug Issues, 24*(1-2), 165-177. Comparative study of drug & alcohol use among 52 women with abuse histories who killed their husbands & 59 women with similar abuse histories who had not killed their husbands.

B.0068 Blount, W. R., et al. (1991, Spring). Influence of substance use among adult female inmates. *Journal of Drug Issues, 21*(2), 449-467. Data collected from a 90% sample of women (1,076) incarcerated in Florida in August, 1985

B.0069 Blum, A., & Fisher, G. (1978). Women who kill. In I. Kutash et al. (Eds.), *Violence: Perspectives on murder and aggression* (pp. 187-197). San Francisco: Jossey-Bass. Discusses why women commit murder.

B.0070 Blumenthal, W. H. (1962). *Brides from Bridewell: Female felons sent to colonial America.* Rutland, VT: Charles E. Tuttle. 1993 reprint. Discussion of the practice of sending women criminals to America as a punishment for their crimes.

B.0071 Boockvar, K. (1994, Winter). Beyond survival: The procreative rights of women with HIV. *Boston College Third World Law Journal, 14,* 1-42. Discusses issues with HIV pregnancies.

B.0072 Bonger, William (1979). The criminality of women. In F. Adler & R. Simon (Eds.), *The criminology of deviant women* (pp. 14-21). Statistics on crimes committed by women in various countries. Tables.

B.0073 Bopp, James, & Gardner, Deborah (1991, Summer). AIDS babies, crack babies: Challenges to the law. *Issues in Law and Medicine, 7,* 3-5. Discusses fetal abuse.

B.0074 Boston College Law Review (1991, May). The constitutionality of punishing pregnant substance abusers under drug trafficking laws: The criminalization of a bodily function. *Boston College Law Review, 32,* 629-662. Discusses fetal abuse and women's constitutional right to procreate.

B.0075 Boudouris, J. (1971). Homicide and the family. *Journal of Marriage and the Family, 33,* 667-676. An analysis of 6,839 homicides in Detroit from 1927-1968. Statistics on male and female perpetrated homicide in Detroit.

B.0076 Bourget, D., & Bradford, J. (1990, April). Homicidal parents. *Canadian Journal of Psychiatry, 35*(3), 233-238. Data collected from 13 cases of parents (ages 17-50) who killed their children. Sixty-nine per cent of the perpetrators were mothers.

B.0077 Bourget, D., & Bradford, J. (1989). Female arsonists: A clinical study. *Bulletin of the American Academy of Psychiatry and the Law, 17*(3), 293-300. Looks at the high prevalence of behavior disorders in female arsonists.

B.0078 Bourget, D., & Bradford, J. (1987, April). Affective disorder and homicide: A case of familial filicide: Theoretical and clinical considerations. *Canadian Journal of Psychiatry, 32*(3), 222-225. The case of a 43-year-old woman who murdered her children.

B.0079 Bowker, Lee (1981). *Women and crime in America.* New York, NY: Macmillan. Essays on the criminality of women and the crimes women commit.

B.0080 Bowker, Lee (1978b, March-April). The incidence of female crime and delinquency: A comparison of official and self-report statistics. *International Journal of Women's Studies, 1*(2), 178-192. Looks at women and crime between 1972-1978.

B.0081 Boyd, Carol. (1993, September). The antecedents of women's crack cocaine abuse: Family substance absue, sexual abuse, depression and illicit drug use. *Journal of Substance Abuse Treatment, 10*(5), 433-438. Discusses correlations of family drug use, sexual abuse, and age of first illicit drug use. Data from a sample of 105 primarily African American women.

B.0082 Broskowski, Anthony, et al. (1971). Actuarial assessment of criminality in women. *Criminology, 9,* 166-184. Comparative personality study. Discusses crimes committed by women.

B.0083 Brown, Arnold (1991). *Lizzie Borden: The legend, the truth, the final chapter.* Nashville, TN: Rutledge Hill Press. Life of Lizzie Borden.

B.0084 Brown, Joyce Ann (1990). *Joyce Ann Brown: Justice denied.* Chicago, IL: Noble Press. Details one woman's experience of being accused, convicted, and imprisoned falsely.

B.0085 Brown, Marjorie, et al. (1990) *Women who rape.* Boston, MA: Examines characteristics of rapes in which a female is the offender. Data obtained from records of 20 females charged with rape in Massachusetts.

B.0086 Browne, Angela, & Williams, Kirk (1993). Gender, intimacy and lethal violence: Trends from 1976 through 1987. *Gender & Society, 7*(1), 78-98. Documents patterns of homicide between opposite gender relational partners from 1976-1987.

B.0087 Browne, Angela, & Williams, Kirk (1989, February). Exploring the effect of resource availability and the likelihood of female-perpetrated homicides. *Law & Society Review, 23*(1), 75-94. Considers gender-specific rates of partner homicide in the United States for 1976-1979 and 1980-1984, and legal and extralegal resources for abused women.

B.0088 Browne, Angela (1988). Family homicide: When victimized women kill. In V. V. Hasselt, et al. (Eds.), *Handbook on family violence.* New York, NY: Plenum Press. Discusses battered women who kill.

B.0089 Browne, Angela (1987). *When battered women kill.* New York, NY: The Free Press. Addresses the question of why some women in abusive relationships kill their partners and others do not.

B.0090 Browne, Angela (1986). Assault and homicide: When battered women kill. In M. Saks & L. Saxe (Eds.), *Advances in applied social psychology, Vol. 3* (pp. 57-79). Hillsdale, NJ: Lawrence Erlbaum Associates, Inc. Investigates severely abusive relationships from the perpectives of the women involved in them.

B.0091 Browne, W. J., & Palmer, A. J. (1975). A preliminary study of schizophrenic women who murdered their children. *Hospital and Community Psychiatry, 26,* 71-75. Discusses infanticide.

B.0092 Brownstein, Henry, et al. (1994). Changing patterns of lethal violence by women: A research note. *Women and Criminal Justice, 5*(2), 99-118. Cases of 9 women incarcerated for homicide.

B.0093 Brozovsky, M., & Falit, H. (1971, October). Neonaticide: Clinical and psychodynamic considerations. *Journal of the American Academy of Child Psychiatry, 10*(4), 673-683. Discusses psychological aspects of killing one's newborn.

B.0094 Bruck, Connie (1975, December). Women against the law. *Human Behavior, 4,* 25+. Discusses women criminals.

B.0095 Bruinsma, G. J., et al. (1984). Female criminality in the Netherlands. In F. Adler (Ed.), *The incidence of female criminality in the contemporary world* (pp. 14-63). New York, NY: New York University Press. Reviewed data from the Netherlands on female criminality from 1962-1976.

B.0096 Brumberg, Joan (1984). "Ruined" girls: Changing community responses to illegitimacy in upstate New York. *Journal of Social History, 18*(2), 247-272. Case of 18-year-old Nettie Mayers, who ran away from the Elmira, New York, home for unwed mothers and killed her child.

B.0097 Brummit, H. (1963). Observations on drug addicts in a house of detention for women. *Corrective Psychiatry and Journal of Social Therapy, 9*(2), 62-70. Discusses addiction in women.

B.0098 Bryant, T. (1990, Spring). Oya-ko shinju: Death at the center of the heart. *UCLA Pacific Basin Law Review, 8*(1), 1-31. Analyzes parent-child suicide by discussing two cases of mothers killing their children.

B.0099 Bryson, John (1987). *Evil angels.* New York, NY: Summit Books. Discusses infanticide.

B.0100 Bucove, A. D. (1968). A case of prepartum psychosis and infanticide. *Psychiatric Quarterly, 42,* 263-270. Discusses causes of infanticide.

B.0101 Cahalone, D. K. (1989). Court-ordered confinement of pregnant women. *New England Journal on Criminal and Civil Confinement, 15*(2), 203-223. Considers the duties of the physician and the rights of the fetus, as well as the right of the state to compel treatment.

B.0102 Callahan, Joan, & Knight, James (1992). Prenatal harm as child abuse? *Women and Criminal Justice, 3*(2), 5-33. Legal sanctions for use against pregnant women who take drugs.

B.0103 Campbell, Anne (1986, January). Self-report of fighting by females. *The British Journal of Criminology, 26*(1), 28-46. British girls and women were surveyed on aggressive experiences.

B.0104 Carlen, Pat, et al. (1985a). *Criminal women: Autobiographical accounts.* New York, NY: Basil Blackwell. Based on the oral histories of 39 women's criminal careers in Great Britain.

B.0105 Carlen, Pat (1985b). *Women, crime and poverty.* Philadelphia, PA: Open University Press. Oral histories of 39 women criminals in Great Britain. Discusses the relationship between socioeconomic status and women's crime.

B.0106 Carlisle, Marcia (1992, July/August). What made Lizzie Borden kill? *American Heritage, 43*(4), 66-72. Another look at the acquittal of Lizzie Borden.

B.0107 Carpozi, George (1972). *Ordeal by trial: The Alice Crimmins case.* New York, NY: Walker. Case of Alice Crimmins accused of murdering her two children in 1965.

B.0108 Cassity, J. H. (1941). Socio-psychiatric aspects of female felons. *Journal of Criminal Psychopathology, 3,* 597-604. Discusses why women commit crimes.

B.0109 Castellucci, John (1986). *The big dance.* New York, NY: Dodd, Meade & Co. Story of Kathy Boudin and the Brink's robbery murders.

B.0110 Caufield, Sueann (1993, Autumn). Getting into trouble: Dishonest women, modern girls, and women-men in the conceptual language of *Vida Policial*, 1925-1927. *Signs: Journal of Women in Culture and Society, 19*(1), 146-176. Chronicles women criminals in Rio de Janeiro, Brazil in the late 1920's using accounts from the weekly police journal "Vida Policial".

B.0111 Chamberlain, Lindy (1991). *Through my eyes: An autobiography.* Sydney, Australia: Mandarin Paperbacks. Personal memoir of a woman convicted and imprisoned for killing her child.

B.0112 Chambers, C., & Inciardi, James (1971). *Criminal careers of female narcotic addicts.* New York, NY: New York State Narcotic Addiction Control Commission. Data collected in face-to-face interviews with a nationwide sample of 168 female addicts.

B.0113 Chan, Louise (1993, Fall). S.O.S. from the womb: A call for New York legislation criminalizing drug use during pregnancy. *Fordham Urban Law Journal, 21,* 199-237. Discusses the criminalization of drug use during pregnancy.

B.0114 Chandler, Susan, & Kassebaum, Gene (1994, Summer). Drug-alcohol dependence of women prisoners in Hawaii. *Affilia: Journal of Women and Social Work, 9*(2), 157-170. Discusses drug-alcohol use of incarcerated women in Hawaii.

B.0115 Chase, Beverly (1989). In S. Johann & F. Osanka (Eds.), *Representing battered women who kill* (Introduction). Springfield, IL: Charles C. Thomas. Introduction by Beverly Chase, a battered woman who killed her husband.

B.0116 Chasnoff, I., & Schnoll, S. (1987). Consequences of cocaine and other drug use in pregnancy. In A. Washton & M. Gold (Eds.), *Cocaine: A clinician's handbook* (pp. 241-251). New York, NY: Guilford. Discusses medical ramifications of drug use during pregnancy.

B.0117 Chavkin, D. F. (1992). For their own good: Civil commitment of alcohol and drug-dependent pregnant women. *South Dakota Law Review, 37,* 224-288. Discusses legality of incarcerating pregnant drug abusers.

B.0118 Chavkin, Wendy, et al. (1993, September). Psychiatric histories of drug using mothers: Treatment implications. *Journal of Substance Abuse Treatment, 19*(5), 445-448. Data collected from 146 crack/cocaine using mothers in New York City.

B.0119 Chavkin, Wendy (1992). Women and fetus: The social construction of conflict. *Women and Criminal Justice, 13*(2), 71-80. Discusses the concept of mothers as antagonists to fetus if they deviate from medically, socially, or legally sanctioned behavior.

B.0120 Chavkin, Wendy (1991, September 18). Mandatory treatment for drug use during pregnancy. *Journal of the American Medical Association, 266*(11), 1556-1561. Assessment of mandatory treatment for crack-addicted pregnant women and whether it should be social policy.

B.0121 Chavkin, Wendy (1990, April). Drug addiction and pregnancy: Policy crossroads. *American Journal of Public Health, 80*(4), 483-487. Discusses the needs of pregnant mothers addicted to drugs and the conflict with drug policy. Some policy options presented.

B.0122 Chesler, Phyllis (1993, Fall-Winter). A woman's right to self-defense: The case of Aileen Carol Wuornos. *St. John's Law Review, 66,* 933-977. Discusses the case of Aileen Wuornos who is on Florida's death row for murder.

B.0123 Cheung, P. T. (1986). Maternal filicide in Hong Kong, 1971-1985. *Medicine, Science and the Law, 26*(3), 185-192. Discusses rates of filicide in Hong Kong.

B.0124 Chimbos, P. D. (1978). Marital violence: A study of interspousal homicide. *Dissertation Abstracts International, 37*(9), 6081-A. Exploratory study of husband/wife homicides in a Canadian cultural setting. Investigated early life experience and family processes.

B.0125 Chunn, Dorothy, et al. (1989). Women and crime in Canada. In M. Jackson & C. Griffiths (Eds.), *Canadian criminology* (pp. 275-314). Canada: Harcourt, Brace & Jovanavich. Discusses several aspects of women and crime in Canada including crimes rates and incarceration policies.

B.0126 Cianciulli, J. M. (1993, Fall). The outpatient forensic substance abuse profile. *International Journal of Offender Therapy and Comparative Criminology, 37*(3), 231-237. Data collected from a sample of parolees and probationers included 18 women.

B.0127 Cicchetti, Concetta (1988). *New Female offender.* Boston, MA: Massachusetts Trial Court Office of Commissioner of Probation. Discussion of crimes women commit.

B.0128 Clecker, Patricia (1978). Jive, dope fiend, whores: In the street and in rehabilitation. In J. Hochsmita & A. Spring (Eds.), *Women in ritual and symbolic roles* (pp. 269-285). New York, NY: Plenum Press. Discusses drugs, addiction, prostitution, and treatments for women.

B.0129 Clifford, W. (1976). *Crime control in Japan.* Lexington, MA: Lexington Books. Looks at the numbers of male and female offenders in Japan since the pre-WWII era committing murder.

B.0130 Climent, Carlos, et al. (1974). Biological, psychological, and social correlates of drugs and addiction. *International Journal of Addictions, 9*(2), 345-350. Data collected from women prisoners.

B.0131 Closen, Michael, & Isaacman, Scott (1990, December). Criminally pregnant: Are AIDS-transmission laws encouraging abortion? *American Bar Association Journal, 76,* 76-78. Discusses HIV criminalization statutes of several states which make it a criminal offense to become pregnant if HIV infected.

B.0132 Cohen, A. I. (1994, Winter). Challenging pregnancy discrimination in drug treatment: Does the ADAMHJA reorganization Act provide an answer? *Yale Journal of Law and Feminism, 6,* 91-142. Discusses the practice of excluding pregnant women from drug treatment programs.

B.0133 Cohn, H. (1966). Uxoricides. *Journal of Offender Therapy, 10*(2), 42-45. Discusses spousal murder.

B.0134 Cole, K. E., et al. (1968). Women who kill: A sociopsychological study. *Archives of General Psychiatry, 19*(1), 1-8. Data collected from 112 female homicide offenders to determine personality style and behavior patterns.

B.0135 Coleman, B. I. (1974). Helping women addicts in New York City. *International Journal of Offender Therapy & Comparative Criminology, 18*(1), 82-85. Discusses treatment programs for women addicts in New York City.

B.0136 Congressional Quarterly Researcher (1993, February 26). Battered women who kill. *Congressional Quarterly Researcher, 3*(8), 1056-2036. Discusses statistics of battered women who kill and legal sanctions.

B.0137 Connor, W. (1973). Criminal homicide, USSR/USA. *Journal of Criminal Law and Criminology, 64*, 111-117. Study looks at female murderers and female victims in the USSR and in the USA.

B.0138 Cooper, H. H. (1979). Woman as terrorist. In F. Adler & R. Simon (Eds.), *The criminology of deviant women*. Boston, MA: Houghton Mifflin. Discusses the participation of women in international terrorist activities.

B.0139 Cottle, Thomas (1994, May-June). Women who kill. *The North American Review, 279*(3), 4 - 10. Discusses two women who used the battered wife self-defense argument in court and the events that led to the killing of their husbands.

B.0140 Craik, Jennifer (1987). The Azaria Chamberlain case and questions of infanticide. *Australian Journal of Cultural Studies, 4*(2). Case of Lindy Chamberlain, an Australian woman, accused of murdering her daughter, Azaria, while on a camping trip.

B.0141 Cramer, Mary Jane, & Blacker, E. (1966, Winter). Social class and drinking experience of female drunkenness offenders. *Journal of Health and Human Behavior, 7*(4), 276-284. Data collected from 54 white females assigned to the alcoholic section of a state reformatory.

B.0142 Cramer, Mary Jane, & Blacker, E. (1963, Winter). "Early" and "late" problem drinkers among female prisoners. *Journal of Health and Human Behavior, 4*(4), 282-290. Explores the hypothesis that early alcohol experience may relate to accelerated onset of problem drinking.

B.0143 Cristen, Ken (1987). *The Crown vs. Chamberlain, 1980-1987*. Sutherland: Albatross. Case of Lindy Chamberlain, an Australian woman, acccused of murdering her daughter, Azaria.

B.0144 Crites, Laura (1976). Women offenders: Myth vs. reality. In L. Crites (Ed.), *The female offender* (pp. 33-43). Toronto: DC Heath. Discusses the truth of three popular beliefs about women's crimes.

B.0145 Cuskey, W. R., et al. (1979). Survey of opiate addiction among females in the United States between 1850-1970. In F. Adler & R. Simon (Eds.), *The criminology of deviant women* (pp. 223-247). Boston, MA: Houghton Mifflin. Discusses historical studies that have consistently shown higher numbers of women addicted than men.

B.0146 Dabbs, J. M., et al. (1988). Saliva testosterone and criminal violence among women. *Personal and Individual Differences, 9*(2), 269-275. Tested levels of saliva testosterone in women accused of violent crimes.

B.0147 Daly, Kathleen (1989, November). Gender and varieties of white-collar crime. *Criminology, 27*, 769-794. Discusses differences in types of white-collar crimes committed by women and men.

B.0148 Daly, Martin, & Wilson, Margo (1990). Killing the competition: Female/female and male/male homicide. *Human Nature, 1*(1), 81-107. Data collected from records of sex & age specific rates of killing unrelated persons of one's own sex in Canada, England and the U.S.

B.0149 Daniel, Anasseril, & Kashani, J. H. (1983a, September). Women who commit crimes of violence. *Psychiatric Annals, 13*(9), 697-713. Discusses characteristics and contributory factors.

B.0150 Daniel, Anasseril (1983b). A study of female check offenders referred for pretrial psychiatric evaluation. *American Journal of Forensic Psychology, 1*(2), 21-29. Compared 19 female check offenders with 54 other female offenders on four variables.

B.0151 Daniel, Anasseril, & Harris, Phillip (1982). Female homicide offenders referred for pre-trial psychiatric examination: A descriptive study. *Bulletin of the American Academy of Psychiatry and the Law, 10*(4), 261-269). Study of 22 women charged with homicide and 44 women charged with other crimes who underwent psychiatric interviews.

B.0152 Datesman, Susan (1981). Women crime, and drugs. In J. Inciardi (Ed.), *The drugs-crime connection* (pp. 85-104). Beverly Hills, CA: Sage. Discusses the intersection of drugs and crime in the cirminality of women.

B.0153 Datesman, Susan (1980). The criminality of female heroin users. *Dissertation Abstracts International, 40*(12-Pt. 1), 6435-A. Explores two aspects of the relationship between heroin use and the nature and extent of criminality among female heroin users.

B.0154 Datesman, Susan, et al. (1979). Female heroin use, criminality and prostitution. *Contemporary Drug Problems, 8*(4), 455-474. Discusses crimes women commit to maintain drug habits.

B.0155 David, Jay (1980). *The Scarsdale murder.* New York, NY: Leisure. Case of Jean Harris.

B.0156 Davin, Patricia (1994, January). The best kept secret: A study of female sex offenders. *Dissertation Abstracts International, 54* (7), 3849. Study of 76 incarcerated female sex offenders.

B.0157 Dawson, T. B. (1991, Spring). A feminist response to unborn child abuse: Contemplating legal solution. *Canadian Journal of Family Law, 9,* 157-176. Discusses drug use during pregnancy.

B.0158 Deadman, W. J. (1964). Infanticide. *Canadian Medical Association Journal, 91*(10), 558-560. Discusses infanticide.

B.0159 DeBettencourt, Kathleen (1990, July). The wisdom of Solomon: Cutting the cord that harms. *Children Today, 19*(4), 17-20. Discusses efforts to criminalize fetal abuse.

B.0160 De Castro, Lola (1981). Venezuelan female criminality: The ideology of diversity and marginality. In F. Adler (Ed.), *The incidence of female criminality in the contemporary world* (pp. 215-227). New York, NY: New York University Press. Discusses role expectations of women in Venezuela and gives statistical data regarding crimes women commit.

B.0161 Decker, Scott, et al. (1993, March). A woman's place is in the home: Females and residential burglary. *Justice Quarterly, 10*(1), 143-161. Examines women's involvement in residential burglary by comparing the characteristics of female burglars with those of male burglars.

B.0162 DeGrave, Kathleen (1989). "Swindler,Spy, Rebel": The confidence woman in nineteenth century America. *Dissertation Abstracts International, 50*(10): 3226. Discusses the different types of "confidence women" in 19th-century America.

B.0163 De la Torre, Lilian (1955). *The truth about Belle Gunness.* New York, NY: Gold Medal Books. Known as the "Lady Bluebeard" because of the murders attributed to her which involved a number of male suitors and her three children.

B.0164 DeLeon, G., & Jainchill, N. (1979, April). *Are female drug abusers more deviant?* Paper presented at the Eastern Psychological Association, Philadelphia, 1979. Considered previous research that female drug abusers reveal more signs of psychological disturbance than males.

B.0165 Del Olmo, Rosa (1990, Summer). The economic crisis and the criminality of Latin American women. *Social Justice, 17,* 40-53. Analyzes the changing nature of female criminality in Venezuela in the context of t he growing economic crisis in Latin America.

B.0166 Dembo, Richard (1994). Drugs and crime revisted. *Journal of Drug Issues, 24*(1-2), 1-360. Presents life histories of some women arrested for drugs.

B.0167 Denison, G. T. (1920). *Recollections of a police magistrate.* Toronto: Musson. Includes the case of Clara Ford who was charged with murder.

B.0168 Denys, R. G. (1969). Lady paperhangers. A study of the relationship of lady paperhangers to five social institutions. *Canadian Journal of Corrections, 11*(3), 165-192. A paperhanger is a professional who passes worthless checks. This study involved twenty-six female paperhangers.

B.0169 de Rhram, Edith (1969). *How could she do that? A study of the female criminal.* London: Clarkson Potter. Discusses what the author considers 7 "typical cases" of women with criminal histories. Includes the case of Carole Tregoff.

B.0170 Dickinson Law Review (1993, Winter). From mother to child, a criminal pregnancy: Should criminalization of the prenatal transfer of AIDS/HIV be the next step? *Dickinson Law Review, 97*, 383-409. Discusses AIDS-HIV and pregnancy.

B.0171 Dickson, Abigail (1975). A descriptive study of male and female murderers. *Dissertation Abstracts International, 36*(6), 4053-A. Investigated the causes of murder as well as characteristic behaviors of individuals who commit murder.

B.0172 Dickson, Marcia (1987). The destructive mother in twentieth-century American drama. *Dissertation Abstracts International, 48*(2), 388. Explores mothers who kill as portrayed in various plays by different playwrights.

B.0173 Ding, L. K., & Chan, L. Y. (1970). A study of ex-prisoner female narcotic addicts in Hong Kong. *Bulletin of Narcotics* (Hong Kong), *22*(2), 7-11. Discusses drug abuse by women in Hong Kong.

B.0174 Dobkins, Dwight, & Hendricks, Robert (1973). *Winnie Ruth Judd: The trunk murders.* New York, NY: Grosset & Dunlap. 1931 case of Winnie Ruth Judd accused of killing two women friends.

B.0175 Dobson, Tracy, & Eby, Kimberly (1992, Spring). Criminal liability for substance abuse during pregnancy: The controversy of maternal vs. fetal rights. *Saint Louis University Law Journal, 36*, 655-694. Discusses substance abuse during pregnancy.

B.0176 Doody, Margaret (1984, Autumn). Those eyes are madeso killing: Eighteenth-century murderesses and the law. *Princeton University Library Chronicle, 46*(1), 49-80. Discusses the treatment of murder by women in 18th century law.

B.0177 D'Orban, P. T. (1990, March). Female homicide. *Irish Journal of Psychological Medicine, 7*(1), 64-70. Discusses the incidence, characteristics, and patterns of female homicide reported in annual criminal statistics for the UK and Wales, 1980-1988.

B.0178 D'Orban, P. T. (1979). Women who kill their children. *British Journal of Psychiatry, 134*, 560-571. Looks at 89 women who were charged with killing their children (1970-1975).

B.0179 D'Orban, P. T. (1976, July). Child stealing: A typology of female offenders. *British Journal of Criminology, 16*(3), 275-281. Discusses kidnapping by women.

B.0180 D'Orban, P. T. (1973). Female narcotic addicts: A follow-up study of criminal and addiction careers. *British Medical Journal* (London), *4*(5888), 345-347. Discusses crimes committed by female narcotic addicts.

B.0181 D'Orban, P. T. (1972a). Baby stealing. *British Medial Journal, 2*(5814), 635-639. Discusses the crime of kidnapping by male and female perpetrators.

B.0182 D'Orban, P. T. (1972b). Female crime. *Criminologist, 7*(23), 29-51. Discusses crimes committed by women.

B.0183 D'Orban, P. T. (1970, May). Heroin dependence and delinquency in women: A study of heroin addicts in Holloway prison. *British Journal of Addictions, 65,* 67-78. Discusses drug addiction in women in England.

B.0184 Dorczak, Anita (1991, Spring). Unborn child abuse: Contemplating legal solution. *Canadian Journal of Family Law, 9,* 133-156. Discusses the use of drugs during pregnancy as fetal abuse.

B.0185 Dorn, N., et al. (1992). *Women, HIV, drugs: Criminal justice issues.* London, England: Institute for the Study of Drug Dependence. Discusses treatment of women offenders in England who are drug users and/or HIV positive. Articles by practitioners and academics.

B.0186 Dorsey, L. C. (1987). *The significance of jealous and addictive love in acts of homicide among black women.* Dissertation, Washington, DC: Howard University. Discusses motives for homicide in black women.

B.0187 Dougherty, J. (1992). Women's violence against their children: A feminist perspective. *Women and Criminal Justice, 4*(2), 91-114. Indicates that the feminist perspective is the key to unlocking the secrets of maternal child abuse.

B.0188 Dreher, Melanie (1984, Spring). Marijuana use among women: An anthropological view. *Advances in Alcohol and Substance Abuse, 3*(3), 51-64. Discusses women's use of marijuana.

B.0189 Duggan, Lisa (1993, Summer). The trials of Alice Mitchell: Sensationalism, sexology, and the lesbian subject in turn-of-the-century America. *Signs, 18*(4), 791-814. Case of Alice Mitchell, who was charged with the murder of her 17-year-old lover Freda Ward in 1892.

B.0190 Duncan, Meredith (1993, May). Battered women who kill their abusers. *Harvard Law Review, 106*(7), 1574+. Discusses battered women who kill.

B.0191 Duncan, Meredith (1992, Winter). Battered women who kill their abusers and a new Texas law. *Houston Law Review, 29,* 963-990. Discusses the law concerning battered women who kill in Texas.

B.0192 Dunlap, Eloise, et al. (1994, January-March). A successful female crack dealer: Case study of a deviant career. *Deviant Behavior, 15*(1) 1-25. Describes the life of a successful female crack dealer in Harlem .

B.0193 Dutton, Mary Ann, et al. (1994, October). Traumatic responses among battered women who kill. *Journal of Traumatic Stress, 7*(4), 549-564. A comparison between battered women charged with a violent crime and battered women seeking mental health clinic services.

B.0194 Easteal, Patricia (1994). Homicide between adult sexual intimates in Australia: Implications for prevention. *Studies on Crime and Crime Prevention, 3,* 24-40. Data collected from 150 homicides between adult sexual intimates in Australia from 1989 to 1990.

B.0195 Easteal, Patricia (1993a). Homicide between adult sexual intimates: A research agenda. *Australian and New Zealand Journal of Criminology, 26*(1), 3-18. Study provides insight into marital homicide in Australia.

B.0196 Easteal, Patricia (1993b). *Killing the beloved: Homicide between adult sexual intimates.* Canberra, Australia: Australian Institute of Criminology. Data collected over a two year period, 1989-1990 and 1990-1991. Focuses on the characteristics of homicides and prevention.

B.0197 Ebner, Lorraine (1981, March). The battered wife's dilemma: To kill or to be killed. *Hastings Law Journal, 32*(4), 895-931. Discusses circumstances that may lead to murder in cases of battered women.

B.0198 Edwall, Glenace, et al. (1989). Females incarcerated for assaultive crimes: Differential personality and demographic variables. *American Journal of Forensic Psychology, 7*(4), 49-57. Delineates between those who assault significant others vs. those who assault relative strangers.

B.0199 Egginton, Joyce (1989). *From cradle to grave: The short lives and strange deaths of Marybeth Tinning's nine children.* New York, NY: Morrow. Case of Marybeth Tinning who stood trial for the death of one child, Tami Lynne, whom she admitted killing. She was sentenced in 1987.

B.0200 Einsele, H. (1981). *Female criminality in the Federal Republic of Germany.* Strasbourg: Council of Europe. Statistics on crimes committed by women in Germany.

B.0201 El Ashmawi, A. W. (1981). Female criminality in Egypt. In F. Adler (Ed.), *The incidence of female criminality in the contemporary world* (pp. 176-187). New York, NY: New York University Press. Discusses the status of women in Egyptian society as a reason for the unpopularity of the concept of female criminality in Egypt.

B.0202 Eldred, Carolyn, & Washington, Mabel (1975, February). Female heroin addicts in a city treatment program: The forgotten minority. *Psychiatry, 38*(1), 75-85. Discusses the DC narcotics treatment administration.

B.0203 Elkind, Peter (1989). *The death shift: The true story of nurse Genene Jones and the Texas baby murders.* New York, NY: Viking. Known as the "death nurse." Case of Genene Jones who was found guilty and convicted of the deaths of several infants at a hospital in Kerrville, TX.

B.0204 Ellis, A. (1951). A young woman convicted of manslaughter. *Case Reports in Clinical Psychology, 2*(1), 9-34. Discusses murder from the psychological perspective.

B.0205 Emory Law Journal. (1990, Fall). Solving the problem of prenatal substance abuse: An analysis of punitive and rehabilitative approaches. *Emory Law Journal, 39*, 1401-1441. Discusses the criminalization of drug abuse during pregnancy.

B.0206 Englade, Ken (1990). Beyond reason. New York, NY: St. Martin's Press. Story of Elizabeth Haysom accused and found guilty of the murder of her parents.

B.0207 English, Kim (1993, December). Self-reported crime rates of women prisoners. *Journal of Quantitative Criminology, 9*(4), 351-382. Self-reports of 128 female prisoners. Participation in crime was defined as activity in one or more of eight crime types.

B.0208 Epps, P. (1961). Women shoplifters in Holloway. In T. C. Gibbens & J. Prince (Eds.), *Shoplifting.* London: Institute for the Study and Treatment of Delinquency. Study of women incarcerated for shoplifting in England.

B.0209 Evenson, M. (1964). Research with female drug addicts at the prison for women (Kingston). *Canadian Journal of Corrections, 6*(1), 21-27. Discusses preliminary research on crime and drug abuse in women in Canada.

B.0210 Fagan, Jeffrey (1994, Spring). Women and drugs revisited: Female participation in the cocaine economy. *Journal of Drug Issues, 24*(1-2), 179-225. Examines female participation in the cocaine economy of New York City in the late 1980's.

B.0211 Faller, K. C. (1987, Winter). Women who sexually abuse children. *Violence and Victims, 2*(4), 263-276. Describes a clinical sample of 40 women who sexually abused a total of 63 children.

B.0212 Farr, Kathryn-Ann (1995, April). Fetal abuse and the criminalization of behavior during pregnancy. *Crime and Delinquency, 41*(2), 235-245. Argues that criminal prosecution of women who use drugs during pregnancy discourages them from seeking treatment.

B.0213 Farrell, Michael (1994, December 24). Adelaide Bartlett and the Pimlico mystery. *British Medical Journal (International), 309*(6970), 1720-1723. Discusses the 1886 murder trial of Adelaide Bartlett who was accused of killing her husband.

B.0214 Feinstein, H. M., et al. (1964). Group therapy for mothers with infanticidal impulses. *American Journal of Psychiatry, 120*(9), 882-886. Discusses the use of therapy to prevent infanticide.

B.0215 Fenne, T. (1984, May 28). Premenstrual shoplifting. *Alberta Report 11,* 30. Discusses incidents of shoplifting among women that occured prior to menstruation.

B.0216 Field, Martha (1993). Pregnancy and AIDS. *Maryland Law Review, 52,* 402-436. Discusses the issue of fetal rights when the mother has AIDS.

B.0217 File, Karen, et al. (1974). Narcotics involvement and female criminality. *Addictive Diseases: An International Journal, 1*(2), 177-188. Data collected from 7,883 arrests made in a 90-day period in Philadelphia.

B.0218 Finch, R. (1992). *Crimes of passion: Women who kill for love, money or their lives.* Boca Raton, FL: Globe Communications. Discusses the legal concept of crimes of passion in crimes women commit.

B.0219 Finkelhorn, D., & Russell, D. (1984). Women as perpetrators: Review of the evidence. In D. Finkelhorn (Ed.), *Child sexual abuse: New theory and research* (pp. 171-181). New York, NY: The Free Press. A four-factor model with psychological variables to explain child sexual abuse.

B.0220 Fishbain, David, et al. (1985, October). Female homicide-suicide perpetrators: A controlled study. *Journal of Forensic Science, 30*(4), 1148-1156. Examination of the files of the Dade County, Florida, Medical Examiners files for 1957-1981 produced 133 homicide-suicide cases.

B.0221 Fisher, Amy (1993). *Amy Fisher: My story.* New York, NY: Pocket Books. Autobiographical account of attempted murder by and incarceration of Amy Fisher.

B.0222 Fisher, Robert (1987). *Sample of 1986 female new commitments for controlled substance convictions involving "crack."* Albany, NY: State of New York Dept. of Correctional Services. Discusses the number of female convictions in New York state in 1986 for drug abuse.

B.0223 Fiume, Giovanna (1994). *The old vinegar lady: or, the judicial modernization of the crime of witchcraft.* Baltimore, MD: Johns Hopkins University Press. Discusses current ideas about what constitutes witchcraft or the criminalization of difference.

B.0224 Flannery, M. T. (1991/1992). Court-ordered prenatal intervention: A final means to the end of gestational substance abuse. *Journal of Family Law, 39*, 519-604. Discusses incarceration of women for using drugs during pregnancy.

B.0225 Flynn, C. P. (1990). Relationship violence by women. *Family Relations, 39*(2), 194-198. Examines violence by women in intimate relationships.

B.0226 Fontanesi, M. (1980). *Womens' criminality in Italy.* Strasbourg: Council of Europe. Discusses crimes committed by women in Italy.

B.0227 Forrest, T. (1974). The family dynamics of maternal violence. *Journal of the American Academy of Psychoanalysis, 2*, 215-230. Discusses the causes and effects of maternal violence.

B.0228 Fortune, Eddyth, et al. (1980). A study of female robbers in a Southern correctional institution. *Journal of Criminal Justice, 8*(5), 317-325. Data collected from 33 female robbers incarcerated at a Florida correctional institute.

B.0229 Foster, Lynne, et al. (1989). Factors present when battered women kill. Special issue: Family violence. *Issues in Mental Health Nursing, 10*(3-4), 273-284. Data collected from 12 women imprisoned for killing their abusive male partners.

B.0230 Frank, Cheryl (1984, December). Driven to kill: Battered women strike back. *American Bar Association Journal, 70*, 26-28. Discusses battered women who kill.

B.0231 Franklin, Alice (1979). Criminality in the workplace: A comparison of male and female offenders. In F. Adler & R. Simon (Eds.), *The criminology of deviant women* (pp. 167-179). Boston, MA: Houghton Mifflin. Discusses theft in the workplace and differences between male and female employees who commit workplace theft.

B.0232 Frankfort, Ellen (1984). *Kathy Boudin and the dance of death.* New York, NY: Stein & Day. Discusses the case of Kathy Boudin.

B.0233 Freudenberger, H. J. (1962). A discussion of kleptomania. *Journal of Offender Therapy, 6*(3), 56-57. Study of four female kleptomaniacs.

B.0234 Gallagher, Mike (1993). *Lovers of deceit: Carolyn Warmus and the "fatal attraction" murder.* New York, NY: Doubleday. Discusses the 1989 case of a New York schoolteacher who had an affair with a fellow teacher, which ended when she went to his home and shot his wife.

B.0235 Garcia, Sandra (1992, June). Drug addiction and mother/child welfare. *Journal of Legal Medicine, 13*, 129-203. Discusses the effects of maternal drug abuse.

B.0236 Garcia, Sandra, & Segalman, R. (1991, Spring). The control of perinatal drug abuse: Legal, psychological, and social imperatives. *Law and Psychology, 15*, 19-64. Discusses medical ramifications of perinatal drug abuse and how it can be prevented.

B.0237 Geis, G., & Soler, J. (1971). Response of female homicide offenders to press coverage of their trials. *Journalism Quarterly, 48*, 558-560. Discussion with women who have committed murder.

B.0238 Genteel, Tina Marie (1994, January). Treatment needs of women offenders with substance abuse histories: A Delphi study. *Dissertation Abstracts International, 54*(7), 3852. Data collected from 25 therapists working primarily with women.

B.0239 Gibbens, T. C. (1981). Female crimes in England & Wales. In F. Adler (Ed.), *The incidence of female criminality in the contemporary world* (pp. 102-121). New York, NY: New York University Press. Interprets statistics on female crime in England and Wales, 1963-1977.

B.0240 Gibbens, T. C., et al. (1971, September). Mental health aspects of shoplifting. *British Medical Journal, 3*(5775), 612-615. A ten-year follow-up of 886 shoplifters.

B.0241 Gibbens, T. C., et al. (1963). *Shoplifting.* London: Institute for the Study and Treatment of Delinquency. Looks at 532 female shoplifters arrested in London between 1959-1960.

B.0242 Gibbs, Jewelle (1982, April). Psychosocial factors related to substance abuse among delinquent females: Implications for prevention and treatment. *American Journal of Orthopsychiatry, 52*(2), 261-271. Looks at psychosocial profiles of women who abuse drugs.

B.0243 Gilfus, Mary (1992). From victims to survivors to offenders: Women's routes of entry and immersion into street crime. *Women and Criminal Justice, 4*(1), 93-99. Explores the patterns by which women enter into criminal activity. Data collected from 20 female offenders.

B.0244 Gillies, H. (1976, February). Homicide in the West of Scotland. *British Journal of Psychiatry, 128,* 105-107. Study included 33 females accused of murder in Glasgow between 1953 and 1974.

B.0245 Girouard, Daniel (1988). Women incarcerated for robbery. *Canadian Journal of Criminology, 30*(2), 121-134. Investigated the role of women in robberies. Data collected from interviews with 13 women prisoners.

B.0246 Glueck, Sheldon, & Glueck, Eleanor (1934). *Five hundred delinquent women.* New York, NY: Alfred A. Knopf. Early detailed study of the Massachusetts Reformatory for Women and the crimes committed by women who were incarcerated there.

B.0247 Goetting, Ann (1989, Autumn). Patterns of marital homicide: A comparison of husbands and wives. *Journal of Comparative Family Studies, 20*(3), 341-354. Study indicates marital homicide is the most frequent type of intrafamily victim-offender relationship.

B.0248 Goetting, Ann (1988a, June). When females kill one another: The exceptional case. *Criminal Justice and Behavior, 15*(2), 179-189. Data collected from 15 females arrested for killing other women in Detroit, Michigan, during 1982-1983.

B.0249 Goetting, Anne (1988b, March). Patterns of homicide among women. *Journal of Interpersonal Violence, 3*(1), 3-20. Analyzes offenders and victims demographic and social characteristics. Data collected from 136 women arrested for homicide in Detroit, Michigan, during 1982-1983.

B.0250 Goetting, Ann (1987, September). Homicidal wives: A profile. *Journal of Family Issues, 8*(3), 332-341. Data collected from 56 women arrested for killing their husbands in Detroit, Michigan, during 1982-1983.

B.0251 Goldstein, P.J., et al. (1991). Volume of cocaine use and violence: A comparison between men and women. *Journal of Drug Issues, 21*(2), 345-367. Discusses violence and cocaine use in males and females.

B.0252 Goldstein, P. J. (1987). Drugs and violence among women. In B. Foster & J. Solloway (Eds.), *Chemical bonds: The socio-cultural matrix of alcohol and drug use.* Wadsworth Health Sciences. Discusses the intersection of drugs and violence in women.

B.0253 Goldstein, P. J. (1981). Getting over: Economic alternatives to predatory crime among street drug users. In J. Inciardi (Ed.), *The drugs-crime connection* (pp. 67-84). New York, NY: Narcotic & Drug Research, Inc. Data collected from 51 participants (8% female) in 1978-1979 in East Harbor, NY.

B.0254 Gora, Jeanne (1979). A longitudinal analysis of female crime trends in an American city. *Sociological Abstracts, 27*(94), 10980. Results of a longitudinal study on female crime.

B.0255 Gossop, M. (1978, September). Drug dependence, crime and personality among female addicts. *Drug and Alcohol Dependence, 3*(5), 359-364. Looks at incidence of crime among female addicts.

B.0256 Gostyla, J. F. (1993). The needle or the baby spoon? Termination of the parental rights of a drug-abusing mother in Connecticut. *The Connecticut Probate Law Journal, 7,* 279-309. Discusses legal sanctions of the mother in cases of drug-abuse.

B.0257 Graham, Nanette, & Wish, Eric (1994, Winter-Spring). Drug use among female arrestees: Onset, patterns and relationship to prostitution. *Journal of Drug Issues, 24* (1-2), 315-329. Data collected from a sample of 164 female arrestees in Manhattan, NY.

B.0258 Grant, Bernadette, & Curry, David (1993, January). Women murderers and victims of abuse in a southern state. *American Journal of Criminal Justice, 17*(2), 75-83. Examined the hypothesis that abused women who kill their abusers are not socially different from other abused women.

B.0259 Grant, Bernadette (1983). "Til death do us part": A social, psychosocial analysis of women who kill their spouses. *Dissertation Abstracts International, 44*(3), 871. Explores spousal homicides committed by females, using a life course sequence model of marital conflict resolution.

B.0260 Grayson, J. (1989). *Female sex offenders.* Denver, CO: National Center for the Prevention and Treatment of child abuse and neglect. Discusses characteristics of female sex offenders.

B.0261 Greenberg, H. R. (1966). Pyromania in a woman. *Psychoanalytic Quarterly, 35,* 256-262. Discusses female arsonists.

B.0262 Gribble, Leonard (1988). *Such lethal ladies.* New York, NY and London: Chivers Press. Discusses cases of women who committed murder.

B.0263 Grier, Priscilla, et al. (1993, December). Comparative study of personality traits of female sex offenders. *Psychological Reports, 73*(3, Pt. 2), 1378. Data collected from 11 incarcerated white adult female sex offenders and 11 matched nonoffenders.

B.0264 Gross, Kenneth (1975). *The Alice Crimmins case.* New York, NY: Alfred A. Knopf. Case of Alice Crimmins accused and found guilty of murdering her two children in New York in 1965.

B.0265 Gustavsson, Nora, & Rycraft, J. R. (1994). Chemically dependent mothers and their children. *Journal of Social Science Research, 20*(1-2), 55-71. Discusses problem areas with drug addicted mothers, including criminal activity, delinquency, and aggressiveness.

B.0266 Gustavsson, Nora (1991, Summer). Pregnant, chemically dependent women: The new criminals. *Affilia: Journal of Women and Social Work, 6*(2), 61-73. Analyzes recent court cases establishing the rights of the fetus over the rights of the mother.

B.0267 Haigh, W. H. (1851). *The trial of Mrs. Ann K. Simpson, charged with the murder of her husband.* New York, NY: A. S. Barnes. Account of the indictment, trial, and jury verdict.

B.0268 Hamberger, L. K., & Potente, T. (1994). Counseling heterosexual women arrested for domestic violence: Implications for theory and practice. *Violence and Victims, 9*(2), 125-137. Community intervention with women arrested for domestic violence referred to court-mandated treatment.

B.0269 Hanawalt, Barbara (1980). Women before the law: Females as felons and prey in fourteenth-century England. In D. K Weisberg (Ed.), *Women and the law* (pp. 165-195). Boston, MA: Schenkman. Discusses women in 14th-century England as both felons and prey.

B.0270 Hanawalt, Barbara (1976). The female felon in fourteenth century England. *Viator(5),* 253-278. Discusses female felons in 14th-century England.

B.0271 Hanke, Penelope (1993, October). She kills everyone: A research note on homicide victims. *Sociological Focus, 26*(4), 365-368. Data on 679 women imprisoned in Alabama's Tutwiler Prison for homicide, 1929-1985.

B.0272 Hansen, Mark (1993, February). Bembenek freed. *American Bar Association Journal, 79,* 25. Information regarding the case of Laurencia Bembenek.

B.0273 Hardesty, Constance, & O'Shea, Kathleen (1994, March). *Profile of women incarcerated in Oklahoma for murder.* Paper presented at the Annual Meeting of the ACJS, Chicago. Focuses on profiles of women incarcerated for murder in Oklahoma.

B.0274 Harmon, R. B., et al. (1985). Women and arson: A demographic study. *Journal of Forensic Science, 30*(2), 467-477. Describes women accused of setting fires in New York City who were evaluated between 1980 and 1983.

B.0275 Harris, Ruth (1985, August). Murder under hypnosis. *Psychological Medicine, 15*(3), 477-505. Discusses the trial of a 22-year-old woman accused of murder whose defense was that she acted unconsciously under the hypnotic influence of her lover.

B.0276 Hartman, Mary (1977). *Victorian murderesses: A true history of thirteen respectable French and English women accused of unspeakable crimes.* New York, NY: Schocken Books. Discusses thirteen nineteenth-century English and French women who were accused of being murderesses.

B.0277 Hartman, Mary (1974). Crime and the respectable woman: Toward a pattern of female criminality in nineteenth-century France and England. *Feminist Studies, 2,* 138-156. Discusses female criminality in England.

B.0278 Hartman, Mary (1973). Murder for respectability: The case of Madeleine Smith. *Victorian Studies, 16,* 381-400. Discusses the case of Madeleine Smith.

B.0279 Harvard Civil Rights-Civil Liberties Law Review (1991, Summer). Regulating women's bodies: The adverse effect of fetal rights theory on childbirth decisions and women of color. *Harvard Civil Rights-Civil Liberties Law Review, 26,* 523-548. Discusses the effects of the fetal rights theory for women of color.

B.0280 Harvard Law Review (1988, March). Maternal rights and fetal wrongs: The case against the criminalization of "fetal abuse." *Harvard Law Review, 101*(5), 994-1012. Case of People vs Stewart involving charges of fetal abuse.

B.0281 Hassard, A. R. (1926). *Not guilty and other trials.* Toronto: Lee Collins. Case of Clara Ford.

B.0282 Hastings Constitutional Law Quarterly (1991a, Fall). Legislation punishing drug use during pregnancy: Attack on women's rights in the name of fetal protection. *Hastings Constitutional Law Quarterly, 19*, 197-234. Discusses the mother vs. fetus legal controversy.

B.0283 Hastings Constitutional Quarterly (1991b, Fall). Order in the court: Challenging judges who incarcerate pregnant, substance dependent defendants to protect fetal health. *Hastings Constitutional Quarterly, 19*, 235-259. Discusses legal rights of pregnant women.

B.0284 Hatch, Alison, & Faith, Karlene (1989/1990). The female offender in Canada: A statistical profile. *Canadian Journal of Women and the Law, 3*(2), 432-456. Looks at crimes women commit in Canada.

B.0285 Haustater, Glenn, & Hardy, Sarah (1984). *Infanticide: Comparative and evolutionary perspectives.* New York, NY: Aldine. Historical perspective on infanticide.

B.0286 Heidensohn, Frances (1991). Women and crime in Europe. In F. Heidensohn & M. Farrell (Eds.), *Crime in Europe.* New York, NY: Routledge. Discusses female criminality in Europe.

B0287 Heilbrun, A. B. (1982, September). Female criminals: Behavior and treatment within the criminal justice system. *Criminal Justice and Behavior, 9*(3), 341-351. Crimes committed by black and white females were compared with crimes by black and white males.

B.0288 Heidkamp, Bettina (1994). Angels of death: The Lainz hospital murders. In H. Birch (Ed.), *Moving targets: Women, murder, and representation* (pp. 218-240). Berkeley, CA: University of California Press. Case of four female assistant nurses convicted of killing twenty elderly and feeble patients with lethal drug overdoses or by forcing water into their lungs.

B.0289 Hewitt, John (1985). Patterns of female criminality in Middletown: 1900 to 1920. *Indiana Social Studies Quarterly, 38*(2), 49-59. Uses a representative community, Muncie, Indiana, to assess crime among women in the early 1900's.

B.0290 Hicks, R. (1992). *The vampire killer: A journey into the mind of Tracey Wigginton.* Sydney: Bantam Books. Tracey Wigginton was tried for murder and became infamous because she was accused of and believed to be a vampire.

B.0291 Higginbotham, Ann (1989, Spring). "Sin of the age:" Infanticide and illegitimacy in Victorian London. *Victorian Studies, 32*(3), 319-337. A study of court cases involving infanticide in the 19th century. Cases are discussed in terms of Victorian ideas about fallen women.

B.0292 Hoffer, P. C. (1984). *Murdering mothers: Infanticide in England and New England, 1558-1803.* New York, NY: New York University Press. Traces the emergence of modern law on infanticide in England and New England. Focuses on the period between 1558-1893.

B.0293 Hohnecker, Laura (1995, September). Traumatic effects among battered women who kill: An examination of a contextual model of battered women's responses to violence. *Dissertation Abstracts International, 56*(3), 1700. Examined differences between a group of battered women who assaulted their abusers and a clinical group of battered women who did not.

B.0294 Holmes, S. T. (1991, Spring). Women who kill: An exploratory study of the other case. *Masters Abstracts International, 29*(1), 58. Data collected from females incarcerated for homicide in Kentucky from December 22, 1976 through October 1, 1986.

B.0295 Holmes, S. T., et al. (1991, December). Female serial murderesses: Constructing differentiating typologies. *Journal of Contemporary Criminal Justice, 7*(4), 245-256. Discusses known cases of serial murders by women.

B.0296 Holmlund, Christine (1994). A decade of deadly dolls: Hollywood and the woman killer. In H. Birch (Ed.), *Moving targets: Women, murder and representation* (pp. 127-151). Berkeley, CA: University of California Press. Looks at female murderers in Hollywood films.

B.0297 Hooper, Columbus, & Moore, Johnny (1990, January). Women in outlaw motorcycle gangs. *Journal of Contemporary Ethnography, 18*(4), 363-387. Discusses the place of women in motorcycle gangs. Compares biker women to street gang girls.

B.0298 Howard, Clark (1993). *Love's blood.* New York, NY: Crown. Case of Patricia Colombo, accused and sentenced for the murder of her parents and little brother on May 7, 1976.

B.0299 Howard, Margaret (1986, Winter). Husband-wife homicide: An essay from a family law perspective. *Law and Contemporary Problems, 49*(1), 63-88. Debate on gun-control literature is examined in the light of spousal homicides.

B.0300 Hser, Yih-Ing, et al. (1990, June). The criminality of female narcotics addicts: A causal modeling approach. *Journal of Quantitative Criminology, 6*(2), 207-228. Data collected 1976-1979 from 328 Anglo and Chicana women in a methadone maintenance clinic in California.

B.0301 Hubbard, Eleanor (1993). "Of course I fight back": An ethnography of women's use of violence in intimate relationships. *Dissertation Abstracts International, 54*(2), 695. Data collected from in-depth interviews with two groups of battered women.

B.0302 Hull, N. E. H. (1987). *Female felons: Women and serious crime in Colonial Massachusetts.* Champaign, IL: University of Illinois Press. Attemps to determine the frequency and experience of women accused and tried for serious crimes in colonial Massachusetts.

B.0303 Hunt, G., et al. (1989, June). Wretched, hatless, and miserably clad: Women and the inebriate reformatories of 1900-1913. *British Journal of Sociology, 40*(2), 144-270. Discusses early reformatories for the treatment of alcoholic women.

B.0304 Hunt, Peter (1950). *The Madeleine Smith affair.* London: Carroll & Nicholson. Case of Madeleine Smith.

B.0305 Hussain, S. A., & Annasseril, Daniel (1984). A comparative study of filicidal and abusive mothers. *Canadian Journal of Psychiatry, 29*(7), 596-598. Study of 8 filicidal mothers and 52 abusive mothers referred for pretrial psychiatric evaluation.

B.0306 Hussain, Arshad, et al. (1983, March). A study of young-age and mid-life homicidal women admitted to a psychiatric hospital for pre-trial evaluation. *Canadian Journal of Psychiatry, 28*(2), 109-113. Data collected from 16 young female homicidal offenders and 7 middle-aged homicidal women.

B.0307 Iannicola, Dominic (1993, March). Constitutional law/search and seizure/equal protection. *Illinois Bar Journal, 81*, 159-162. Discusses the portion of a corrections statute of Illinois law requiring HIV testing of convicted prostitutes.

B.0308 Iglehart, Alfreda, & Stein, Martha (1985, March). The female offender: A forgotten client? *Social Casework, 66*(3), 152-159. Discusses social work with female offenders.

B.0309 Inciaridi, James, et al. (1993). *Women and crack-cocaine.* Laurel, MD: American Correctional Association. Quotes from four thousand pages of transcripts of interviews with drug-addicted women.

B.0310 Inciardi, James, & Pottieger, Anne (1986, Winter). Drug use and crime among two cohorts of women narcotics users: An empirical assessment. *Journal of Drug Issues, 16*(1), 91-106. Data collected from 286 active women narcotics interviewed on the streets of Miami, Florida.

B.0311 Inciardi, James, et al. (1982). Black women, heroin, and crime: Some empirical notes. *Journal of Drug Issues, 12*(3), 241-250. Discusses results of a study of 63 black female heroin users in Miami, Florida. Most had started using as adolescents.

B.0312 Inciardi, James (1980). Women, heroin and property crime. In F. Scarpitti & S. Datesman (Eds.), *Women, crime and justice* (pp. 214-222). New York, NY: Oxford University Press. Data casts doubt on traditional characterization of the woman heroin addict as a prostitute.

B.0313 Inciardi, James (1979). Heroin use and street crime. *Crime and Delinquency, 25*, 335-346. Data collected 117 women as a part of a study of 356 participants in Miami, Florida.

B.0314 International Management (1991, April). Italy: Godmothers watch over the family. *International Management, 46*, 15+. Discusses the fact that many of the Mafia-style bosses of criminal families in Southern Italy are women.

B.0315 Ishihara, K., & Yui, S. (1981, October). Successful treatment of a foreign prisoner incarcerated for murdering her child, who exhibited mutism. *Japanese Journal of Criminal Psychology, 18*(1-2), 19-24. Case of a 29-year-old Chinese American woman incarcerated for murder.

B.0316 James, Jennifer, et al. (1979). The relationship between female criminality and drug use. *The International Journal of Addictions, 14*(2), 215-229. Study of the relationship between drug use and criminality in women.

B.0317 Jenkins, Elizabeth (1949). *Six criminal women.* London: Sampson Low. Early study on female criminality.

B.0318 John Marshall Law Review (1990, Spring). A proposal to Illinois legislators: Revise the Illinois criminal code to include criminal sanctions against prenatal substance abusers. *The John Marshall Law Review, 23*, 393-424. Advocates criminal sanctions for prenatal drug use.

B.0319 Johnson, B. D., & Preble, E. (1981, June). *The criminal behavior of street heroin and cocaine users.* Paper presented at the International Institute on the Prevention of Drug Dependence, Vienna, Austria. Data collected from 51 participants in East Harlem, New York from 1978-1979. Eight percent of the participants were female.

B.0320 Johnson, Diane (1984). From fairy to witch: Imagery and myth in the Azaria case. *Australian Journal of Cultural Studies, 2*(2). Case of Lindy Chamberlain.

B.0321 Johnson, E. A. (1985). Women as villians and criminals: Female homicide and criminality in imperial Germany, 1873-1914. *Criminal Justice History, 6*, 151-176. Discusses homicide by women in Germany, 1873-1914.

B.0322 Johnson, J. L. (1978). *Descriptive profile of seventy-three women convicted of murder in Texas.* Masters Thesis, Sam Houston State University. Data collected from prison records of 73 female inmates held in the Goree Unit of the Texas Department of Corrections.

B.0323 Johnson, Norma (1977). Special problems of the female offender. *Juvenile Justice, 28,* 3. Considers problems of female delinquents.

B.0324 Johnson, P. E. (1990). The ACLU philosophy and the right to abuse the unborn. *Criminal Justice Ethics, 9*(1), 48-51. Discusses criminal prosecution and the ACLU's philosophy of protecting the pregnant mother as answers to fetal abuse.

B.0325 Jones, Anne (1985a). *Everyday death: The case of Bernadette Powell.* New York, NY: Holt, Rinehart & Winston. Discusses the case of Bernadette Powell.

B.0326 Jones, Anne (1985b). Women who kill their batterers. In M. Safir (Ed.), *Women's world: From the new scholarship* (pp. 174-180). New York, NY: Praeger. Discusses battered women who kill.

B.0327 Jones, Anne (1983, Fall). When battered women fight back. *Barrister, 9,* 12-15. Discusses battered women who kill.

B.0328 Jones, Anne (1981). *Women who kill.* New York , NY: Holt, Rinehart & Winston. Women murderers in the U.S. from colonial times to the present. Includes Belle Gunness and Lizzie Borden.

B.0329 Jones, Frank (1992). *Murderous women: True tales of women who kill.* Canada: Key Porter. Presents cases of women who committed murder.

B.0330 Jordan, Jan (1990). *Sex and secrets: Crimes involving Australian women since 1880.* Melbourne: Oxford University Press. Historical overview of crimes committed by women in Australia.

B.0331 Journal of Juvenile Law (1991a). Mother's prenatal drug use: Sufficient grounds for juvenile court jurisdiction. *Journal of Juvenile Law, 12,* 116-119. Discusses legal sanctions for pregnant women who use drugs.

B.0332 Journal of Juvenile Law (1991b). Regulation of maternal behavior: An attempt to punish pregnant women who use drugs or alcohol. *Journal of Juvenile Law, 12,* 1-15. Discusses legal sanctions for pregnant drug users.

B.0333 Journal of Contemporary Law (1991). Prosecuting mothers of drug-exposed babies: The state's interest in protecting the rights of a fetus versus the mother's constitutional rights to due process, privacy and equal protection. *Journal of Contemporary Law, 17,* 325-344. Discusses mothers rights vs. fetal rights.

B.0334 Jurik, Nancy, & Winn, Russ (1990, Winter). Gender and homicide: A comparison of men and women who kill. *Violence and Victims, 5*(4), 227-242. Compares patterns of homicides committed by men and women.

B.0335 Kalichman, S. C. (1988). MMPI profiles of men and women convicted of domestic homicide. *Journal of Clinical Psychology, 44*(6), 847-853. Study investigates the psychological characteristics of men and women convicted of domestic homicide.

B.0336 Kandall, S. R., & Chavkin, Wendy (1992, March). Illicit drugs in America: History, impact on women and infants and treatment strategies for women. *The Hastings Law Journal, 43,* 615-643. Discusses women's use of drugs.

B.0337 Kasamatsuri, H., et al. (1985). Homicidality in a woman with a 47XXX karyotype. *Journal of Clinical Psychiatry, 46*, 346-347. Discusses the predisposition to murder in women.

B.0338 Kasal, Charlotte (1990). Female perpetrators of sexual abuse: A feminist view. In M. Hunter (Ed.), *The sexually abused male, Vol. 1: Prevalence, impact, and treatment* (pp.259-274). Lexington, MA: DC Heath and Company. Discusses sexual abuse by women.

B.0339 Kasinsky, R. G. (1994). Child neglect and "unfit mothers": Child savers in the Progressive Era and today. *Women and Criminal Justice, 6*(1), 97-129. Examines the movement against child abuse and the campaign against pregnant women who use drugs.

B.0340 Katz, Elaine (1978a). Tracking a legend. In E. Katz (Ed.), *Folklore for the time of your life* (pp. 205-214). Birmingham, AL: Oxmoor House. Details the lore surrounding Hazel Farris who in 1905 shot and killed her husband and four policemen in Louisville, Kentucky.

B.0341 Katz, Elaine (1978b, Winter). Variation as relative perception in the legend of Hazel Farris. *Mid-South Folklore, 6*(3), 55-64. Background on Farris who committed suicide the year after committing five murders.

B.0342 Kearney, Margaret, et al. (1994, January). Mothering on crack cocaine: A grounded theory analysis. *Social Science Medicine, 38*(2), 351-361. Analyzed 68 interviews with cocaine-using mothers to explore idea that women on crack cocaine are neglectful and uncaring mothers.

B.0343 Keeney, Belea, & Heide, Kathleen (1994, September). Gender differences in serial murderers: A preliminary analysis. *Journal of Interpersonal Violence, 9*(3), 383-398. Uses data on 14 female serial murderers in the U.S. to construct a profile to compare to male serial murderers.

B.0344 Kennedy, Mary (1991, Spring). Maternal liability for prenatal injury arising from substance abuse during pregnancy. *Duquesne Law Review, 29*, 533-578. Discusses legal sanctions for drug abusing pregnant women.

B.0345 Kent, David (1993). *Slaughter on second street: Lizzie Borden.* London: King Philip. Case of Lizzie Borden.

B.0346 Kent, David (1992). *Forty whacks: New evidence in the life and legend of Lizzie Borden.* London: Yankee Books. Case of Lizzie Borden.

B.0347 Kent, J. N. (1981). Argentine statistics on female criminality. In F. Adler (Ed.), *The incidence of female criminality in the contemporary world* (pp. 188-214). New York, NY: New York University Press. Presents statistical findings for 1973-1977 on female criminality in Argentina. Tables.

B.0348 Kertzer, D. I. (1994). Patrizia Guarnieri: A case of child murder: Law and science in nineteenth-century Tuscany. *Social History of Medicine, 7*(2), 1-331. Discusses infanticide.

B.0349 Ketner, Linda (1979-1980). Homicide, sex role differences and role relationships. *Omega: Journal of Death and Dying, 10*(4), 379-387. Study, based on Palmer's theory of role reciprocity investigates similarities and differences between male and female homicide offenders.

B.0350 Kimmel, H. (1993, Winter). In re Valerie D. [613 A.2d 748 (CT. 1992)]: Prenatal conduct an insufficient basis for termination of parental rights. *New England Law Review, 28*, 483-513. Discusses the use of drugs during pregnancy and legal sanctions for pregnant women.

B.0351 Kirkpatrick, John (1984). The lives of criminally violent women. *Dissertation Abstracts International, 45*(2), 652. Looks at the life experiences of 76 women convicted of homicide who were at the North Carolina Correctional Center for Women.

B.0352 Kirkpatrick, John, & Humphrey, John (1989). Stress in the lives of female criminal homicide offenders in North Carolina. In J. Humphrey (Ed.), *Human stress: Current selected research, Vol. 3* (pp. 109-120). New York, NY: AMS Press, Inc. Data collected from 76 women incarcerated in North Carolina for criminal homicide or voluntary manslaughter.

B.0353 Knopp, Fay, & Lackey, Lois (1987). *Female sexual abusers: A summary of data from 44 treatment providers.* Orwell, VT: Safer Society Program. Investigates treatment of female sex abusers. Data from 44 helping professionals who treated 220 females between 1986-1988.

B.0354 Knudson, B. (1968). *Career patterns of female misdemeanant offenders.* Dissertation, University of Minnesota, 1968. Discusses criminality in women beginning as teenagers and continuing into adulthood.

B.0355 Kocsis, Mary (1991). Pregnant women abusing drugs: A medical-legal dilemma. *Medical Trial Technique Quarterly, 37*, 496-532. Discusses the issue of mothers rights vs. fetal rights.

B.0356 Kolman, Anita, & Wasserman, Claudia (1991, March). Theft groups for women: A cry for help. *Federal Probation, 55*(1), 48-54. Data from 164 females in group counseling, 1985-1987.

B.0357 Koprowski, Elizabeth (1977). *Women who kill: A study of violent behavior.* Dissertation, George Washington University. Study of women who commit murder.

B.0358 Korbin, Jill (1989). Fatal maltreatment by mothers: A proposed framework. *Child Abuse and Neglect: The International Journal, 13*(4), 481-489. Explores patterns of child abuse prior to a fatality. Data collected from nine women incarcerated for the death of a child.

B.0359 Korbin, Jill (1987). Incarcerated mothers' perceptions and interpretations of their fatally maltreated children. *Child Abuse and Neglect: The International Journal, 11*(3), 397-407. Maternal interpretations of children's actions that might lead to abuse.

B.0360 Korbin, Jill (1986). Childhood histories of women imprisoned for fatal child maltreatment. *Child Abuse and Neglect, 10,* 331-338. Investigates the presence of abuse in childhoods of women incarcerated for murdering a child.

B.0361 Kord, Susanne (1993, Spring). Women as children, women as child-killers: Poetic images of infanticide in eighteenth-century Germany. *Eighteenth Century Studies, 26*(3), 449-466. Explores why infanticide was a popular theme in late 18th-century German literature by men.

B.0362 Kowalski, Gregory, & Faupel, Charles (1990, January-March). Heroin use, crime, and the "main hustle." *Deviant Behavior, 11*(1), 1-16. Examined the "main hustle" hypothesis which predicts that heroin users have certain crimes at which they are skilled and on which they rely for income.

B.0363 Kowalski, Gregory, et al. (1985, Fall). The female murderer: Alabama 1929-1971. *American Journal of Criminal Justice, 10*(1), 75-90. Looks at incidences of murder by women in Alabama, 1929-1971.

B.0364 Kromm, Jane, et al. (1982). Occupational therapy in the assessment of women accused of murder. *Psychiatric Quarterly, 54*, 85-96. Case of alleged matricide involving a 17-year-old female.

B.0365 Krouse, A., & Peters, Margot (1975, Spring). Why women kill. *Journal of Communication, 25*(2), 98-104. Looks at Agatha Christie's female murderesses.

B.0366 Kruttschnitt, Candace (1995). Violence by and against women: A comparative and cross-national analysis. In R. Ruback & N. Weiner (Eds.), *Interpersonal violent behaviors: Social and cultural aspects* (pp. 89-108). New York, NY: Springer Publishing Co., Inc. Exploration of women's involvement in violent crime, using data at the individual and aggregate levels.

B.0367 Kruttschnitt, Candace (1993, Fall). Violence by and against women: A comparative and cross-national analysis. Special issue: Social and cultural aspects of interpersonal violent behaviors. *Violence and Victims, 8*(3), 253-270. Current knowledge on women's violent offending.

B.0368 Kruzicki, J. (1987, August). Dispelling a myth: The facts about female alcoholics. *Corrections Today, 49*(5), 110-115. Identifies differences in alcoholism patterns between men and women.

B.0369 Kuhns, J. B., et al. (1992, November). Substance use/misuse among female prostitutes and female arrestees. *International Journal of Addictions, 27*(11), 1283-1292. Investigates the correlation between prostitution and drug use/misuse. Data from female prostitutes and arrestees.

B.0370 Kunci, T. (1985). *Ladies who kill.* New York, NY: Pinnacle. Case of Velma Barfield.

B.0371 Kydd, J. W. (1992). Abandoning our children: Mothers, alcohol and drugs. *Denver University Law Review, 69, 359-479.* Looks at the rights of children of addicted women.

B.0372 LaChance, Andre (1981). Women and crime in Canada in the early eighteenth century. In L. Knafla (Ed.), *Crime and criminal justice in Europe and Canada* (pp. 157-177). Waterloo: Wilfred Laurier University. Historical overview of women and crime in Canada.

B.0373 Ladwig, Gail, & Andersen, Marcia (1992). Substance abuse in women: Relationship between chemical dependency of women and past reports of physical and/or sexual abuse. In C. Sampselle (Ed.), *Violence against women: Nursing research, education, and practice issues* (pp. 167-180). New York, NY: Hemisphere Publishing. Histories of 118 incarcerated female felons who were chemically dependent prior to their convictions.

B.0374 Ladwig, Gail, & Andersen, Marcia (1989). Substance abuse in women: Relationship between chemical dependency of women and past reports of physical and/or sexual abuse. *International Journal of Addictions, 24*(8), 739-754. Discusses personal histories of abuse in addicted women.

B.0375 Lake, Elise (1993, Spring). An exploration of the violent victim experiences of female offenders. *Violence Victim (AYT), 8*(1), 41-51. Examined the possibility of linkages between victimization and offending. Data from 83 female inmates.

B.0376 Landesco, J. (1936, March). The woman and the underworld. *Journal of Criminal Law and Criminology, 26,* 891-902. Early look at women in the underworld.

B.0377 Landon, Elizabeth (1986). Female crime in Calgary, 1914-1941. In L. Knafla (Ed.), *Law and justice in a new land: Essays in Western Canadian legal history* (pp. 293-309). Waterloo: Wilfred Laurier University. Examines police court records to assess the incidence of female crime during 1914-1941.

B.0378 Lane, Christopher (1993, Summer). The delirium of interpretation: Writing the Papin affair. *Differences, 5*(2), 24-61. Discusses various interpretations of the murder of Mme Lancelin and her daughter by Christine and Lea Papin.

B.0379 Langlois, Janet (1985). *Belle Gunness: The lady bluebeard.* Bloomington, IN: Indiana University Press. Belle Gunness was accused of murdering her husbands and several suitors.

B.0380 Langlois, Janet (1983, Summer). Belle Gunness: The lady bluebeard: Symbolic inversion in verbal art and American culture. *Signs, 8,* 617-634. Discusses the life of Belle Gunness.

B.0381 Lawrence, Sally (1994, August). Women on the edge: The social economic marginalization of women offenders. *Dissertation Abstracts International, 55*(2), 381. Data collected from 152 adult women prisoners on self-reported drug use and criminal behavior.

B.0382 Leboutte, R. (1991, October). Offense against family order: Infanticide in Belgium from the fifteenth through the early twentieth centuries. *Journal of the History of Sexuality, 2*(2), 159-185. Discusses infanticide in Belgium.

B.0383 Legal Services of Prisoners with Children (1991, Spring). *Battered women in prisons and jails.* San Francisco: Legal Services of Prisoners with Children. Advocacy materials regarding battered women particularly those who have been convicted of killing or assaulting their abusers.

B.0384 Leng, Roger (1992, February 28). Imprisonment for prostitutes. *New Law Journal, 142,* 270+. Discusses the imprisonment of prostitutes.

B.0385 Leslie, Genevieve (1974). Domestic service in Canada, 1880-1920. In J. Acton (Ed.), *Women at work: Ontario 1850-1930* (pp. 71-126). Toronto: Women's Educational Press. Case of Carrie Davies, a woman domestic who was convicted of murder.

B.0386 Lester, David (1992, December). The murder of babies in American states: Association with suicide rates. *Psychological Reports, 71,* 1202. Discusses incidence of infanticide in the U.S.

B.0387 Lester, David (1986a). *The murderer and his murder: Review of research.* New York, NY: AMS Press, Inc. Includes several studies involving women.

B.0388 Lester, David (1986b, February). The relation of twin infanticide to status of women, societal aggression and material well-being. *The Journal of Social Psychology, 126,* 57-59. Discusses infanticide.

B.0389 Lester, David (1973). Murder: A review. *Corrective and Social Psychiatry and Journal of Applied Behavior Therapy, 19*(4), 40-50. Studies of murders including parents who kill their children, women who kill, and several theories of murder.

B.0390 Letcher, M. (1979). Black women and homicide. In H. Rose (Ed.), *Lethal aspects of urban violence* . Lexington, MA: Lexington Books. Examines patterns of involvement in homicides among black women. Data from Detroit, Michigan, police department records.

B.0391 Levit, H. I. (1985). The battered woman. *American Journal of Forensic Psychology, 3*(2), 9-14. Characteristics associated with battered women who kill their husbands/lovers.

B.0392 Lewin, Tamara (1979). When victims kill. *National Law Journal, 2(7), 24+.* Discusses abuse and murder.

B.0393 Lewis, Jeannete (1992, Fall). Realigning maternal/fetal interests in the battle against substance abuse. *St. Thomas Law Review, 5,* 275-292. Discusses the mothers rights vs. fetal rights controversy.

B.0394 Lewis-Collins, E. (1982, September-October). Psychiatric diagnostic predispositions to alcoholism. *Comprehensive Psychiatry, 23*(5), 451-461. Data from 66 females on probation or parole, 100 female addicts in a public health facility, and 70 psychiatrically hospitalized females.

B.0395 Lex, Barbara, et al. (1991, July-August). Putative Type II alcoholism characteristics in female third DUI offenders in Massachusetts: A pilot study. *Alcohol, 8*(4), 283-287. Indicates that the onset of women's alcohol problems before age 25 predicts greater severity of alcohol problems.

B.0396 Livsey, Clara (1980). *The Manson women: A "family" portrait.* New York, NY: R. Marek. Details the lives of the women who were followers of Charles Manson in the 60's.

B.0397 Lloyd, Chris (1987, February). Working with the female offender: A case study. *British Journal of Occupational Therapy, 50*(2), 44-46. Describes the types of offenses for which women are most often convicted and suggests uses of occupational therapy for normalization.

B.0398 Logaipa, Susan (1990, October-December). Suffer the little children: The ancient practice of infanticide as a modern moral dilemma. *Issues in Comprehensive Pediatric Nursing, 13*(4), 241-251. Historical overview of the practice of infanticide.

B.0399 Logli, Paul (1992, March). The prosecutor's role in solving the problems of prenatal drug use and substance abused children. *The Hastings Law Journal, 43,* 559-567. Discusses legal sanctions for women who use drugs during pregnancy.

B.0400 Logli, Paul (1990, Winter-Spring). Drugs in the womb: The newest battlefield in the war on drugs. *Criminal Justice Ethics, 9*(1), 23-30. Argues for the use of criminal law in cases of fetal abuse.

B.0401 Lomis, M. J. (1986). Maternal filicide: A preliminary examination of culture and victim sex. *International Journal of Law and Psychiatry, 9*(4), 503-506. Explores infanticide and cultural factors. Data from 15 women in Canada forensically evaluated for murder of a biological child.

B.0402 Losco, Joseph (1989, June). Fetal abuse: An exploration of emerging philosophic, legal, and policy issues. *Western Political Quarterly, 42*(2), 265-286. Focuses on California court cases about fetal abuse and neglect.

B.0403 Loughton, M. (1973). The need to steal. *New Society, 23*(544), 540-541. Discussion of female shoplifters.

B.0404 Lowman, John, & Matthews, Roger (1992, Winter). Street prostitution control: Some Canadian reflections on the Finsbury Park experience. *British Journal of Criminology, 32*(1), 1-22. Discusses the decriminalization of prostitution.

B.0405 Lowry, Susan (1992). The growing trend to criminalize gestational substance abuse. *Journal of Juvenile Law, 13,* 133-143. Discusses legal sanctions for women who use drugs during pregnancy.

B.0406 Lyons, Gene (1993). *Widow's web.* New York, NY: Simon & Schuster. Case of Mary Lee Orsini of Little Rock, Arkansas.

B.0407 MacClure, V. (1935). *She stands accused: Being a series of accounts of the lives and deeds of notorious women, murderesses, drawn from authenticated sources.* Philadelphia, PA: Lippincott. Early account of female murderers.

B.0408 MacIntyre, Martha (1978). "Desperately Wicked": A study of Jane Cameron, female convict. *Women's Studies International Quarterly, 1*(1), 39-46. Historical account of Jane Cameron.

B.0409 Mack, Linda (1989). *Battered women and battered women who kill: An evaluation review.* Dissertation, Indiana State University. Study of battered women discusses why some women kill.

B.0410 MacMillan, Jane, & Baldwin, S. (1993, July). A pilot study of an alcohol education course for young women offenders: What's good for the goose? *Alcohol and Alcoholism, 28*(4), 499-504. Used data from female participants in a pilot alcohol education course for drink related offending, to explore the usefulness of the course.

B.0411 Madden, Robert (1993, March). State actions to control fetal abuse: Ramifications for child welfare practice. *Child Welfare, 72*(2), 129-140. Examines recent case law and surveys state statutes to illustrate strategies regarding infants born addicted to alcohol or other drugs.

B.0412 Maden, A., et al. (1990). Women in prison and use of illicit drugs before arrest. *British Medical Journal, 301*(6761), 1133. Study of the incidence of drug use in incarcerated women.

B.0413 Mahan, Barbara (1991, September). Till death do us part. *California Lawyer, 11*, 42-48. Study of battered women who kill.

B.0414 Mahan, Sue (1994, March). *How women support a crack-cocaine habit.* Paper presented at the Annual Meeting of the ACJS, Chicago. Examined the relationship between prostitution and crack cocaine. Data on women in residential treatment.

B.0415 Maher, Lisa (1992). Punishment and welfare: Crack cocaine and the regulation of mothering. *Women and Criminal Justice, 3*(2), 35-70. Uses dominant cultural norms regarding femininity and motherhood to look at crack pregnancies.

B.0416 Maher, Lisa, & Curtis, R. (1992, November). Women on the edge of crime: Crack cocaine and the changing contexts of street-level sex work in New York City. *Crime Law and Social Change, 18*, 221-258. Discusses crimes women commit to support addiction.

B.0417 Maher, Lisa (1990). Criminalizing pregnancy: The downside of a kinder, gentler nation. *Social Justice, 17*(3), 111-135. Discusses the criminal prosecution of cocaine-using pregnant mothers as child abusers.

B.0418 Maier, Susan (1994, May). "Bandit queen" free. *World Press Review, 41*(5), 23. Discusses Phoolan Devi, a modern day Robin Hood in India, who served 11 years in prison before being released.

B.0419 Mair, George (1993). *Lethal ladies.* New York, NY: Windsor Publishing. Women who commit murder.

B.0420 Mann, Coramae (1996). *When women kill.* Ithaca, NY: State University of New York Press. Profiles women who murder using data collected from 296 females arrested for homicide in six urban areas between 1979-1983.

B.0421 Mann, Coramae (1992). Female murderers and their motives: A tale of two cities. In E. D. Viano (Ed.), *Intimate violence: Interdisciplinary perspectives* (pp. 73-81). New York, NY: Hemisphere Publishing. Exploratory study of women murderers in Chicago & Houston, 1979-1983.

B.0422 Mann, Coramae (1990a). Female homicide and substance use: Is there a connection? *Women and Criminal Justice, 1*(2), 87-109. Compares two groups of women arrested for homicide in six urban areas. Looks at those who had taken drugs and those who had not before the crime.

B.0423 Mann, Coramae (1990b, June). Black female homicide in the United States. *Journal of Interpersonal Violence, 5*(2), 176-201. Data collected from 296 women arrested for murder.

B.0424 Mann, Coramae (1990c). Black women who kill their loved ones. In R. L. Hampton (Ed.), *Black family violence: Current research and theory* (pp. 129-146). Lexington, MA: DC Heath. Discusses African American women who kill intimates or family members.

B.0425 Mann, Coramae (1989a). Getting even? Women who kill in domestic encounters. In S. Johann & F. Osanka (Eds.), *Representing battered women who kill* (pp. 8-26). Springfield, IL: Charles C. Thomas. Explores female homicide offenders and the nature of their crimes.

B.0426 Mann, Coramae (1988, March). Getting even? Women who kill in domestic encounters. *Justice Quarterly, 5*(1), 33-51. Research in six US cities with the highest murder rates in the country. Explores female criminal homicide offenders and the circumstances of their crimes.

B.0427 Mann, Coramae (1987). Black women who kill. In R. Hampton (Ed.), *Violence in the Black family* (pp. 157-186). Lexington, MA: Lexington Books. Profile of the black woman homicide offender based on previous research by the author.

B.0428 Mann, Coramae (1986). The black female criminal homicide offender in the United States. In report of the *Secretary's Task Force on Black and Minority Health, Vol. V.: Homicide, suicide, and unintentional injuries.* Washington, DC: U.S. Government Printing Office.

B.0429 Mann, Jessica (1981). *Deadlier than the male: Why are respectable English women so good at murder?* New York, NY: Macmillan. Study of women who murder.

B.0430 Marcotte, Paul (1989, August). Crime & pregnancy. *American Bar Association Journal, 75,* 14-16. Discusses mother's legal obligation to her baby and fetal abuse.

B.0431 Marcus, Julie (1989, June). Prisoner of discourse: The dingo, the dog, and the baby. *Anthropology Today, 5*(3), 15-19. Discusses the murder trial of Lindy Chamberlain.

B.0432 Mariner, Wendy, et al. (1990, Winter-Spring). Pregnancy, drugs, and the perils of prosecution. *Criminal Justice Ethics, 9*(1), 30-40. Examines the assumptions that underlie prosecution of pregnant women who use drugs.

B.0433 Marks, N., & Kumar, R. (1993). Infanticide in England and Wales. *Medicine, Science, and the Law, 33*(4), 329-339. Explored the incidence of infanticide in England and Wales from 1981-1988.

B.0434 Martin, Dianne (1993). Casualties of the criminal justice system: Women and justice under the war on drugs. *Canadian Journal of Women and the Law, 6,* 305-327. Discusses women involved in the buying and selling of drugs and what happens when they are caught.

B.0435 Martin, Ronald, et al. (1985, January). Alcohol misuse and depression in women criminals. *Journal of Studies on Alcohol, 46*(1), 65-71. Examines the interaction of alcohol misuse and major depressive syndromes. Data collected from 66 female criminals.

B.0436 Martin, Ronald, et al. (1982a, November-December). The natural history of somatization and substance abuse in women criminals: A six year follow-up. *Comprehensive Psychiatry, 23*(6), 528-537. Study of history of substance abuse in women criminals.

B.0437 Martin, Ronald, et al. (1982b, October). Alcoholism and female criminality. *Journal of Clinical Psychiatry, 43*(10), 400-403. Data collected from 66 female felons of whom 47% were diagnosed as alcoholic.

B.0438 Marvasti, J. (1986). Incestuous mothers. *American Journal of Forensic Psychiatry, 7*(4), 63-69. Discusses incest by mothers.

B.0439 Marzagao, L. R. (1972). Systematic desensitization treatment of kleptomania. *Journal of Behavior Therapy and Experimental Psychiatry, 3*(4), 327-328. Case of a 24-year-old female with a 12-year history of kleptomania.

B.0440 Mather, Victoria (1992). A scary tale: Battered women who kill their abusers. *Ohio Northern University Law Review, 18*, 601-622. Discusses battered women who kill.

B.0441 Mathews, Ruth (1990). Female sexual offenders. In M. Hunter (Ed.), *The sexually abused male: Prevalence, impact and treatment* (pp. 275-293). Lexington, MA: Lexington Books. Discusses three types of female sexual offenders, teacher/lover, the predisposed offender, and the male-coerced offender.

B.0442 Mathieu, Nicole (1979). Biological paternity, social maternity: On abortion and infanticide as unrecognized indicators of the cultural character for maternity. In M. Harris (Ed.), *The sociology of the family: New directions for Britain* (pp. 232-240). Totowa, NJ: Rowman and Littlefield. Study of abortion and infanticide.

B.0443 Matthew, Jane, et al. (1991). Female sexual offenders: A typology. In M. Patton (Ed.), *Family sexual abuse: Frontline research and evaluation* (pp. 199-219). Newbury Park, CA: Sage Publications. Profiles of female sex offenders.

B.0444 Matthew, Jane (1964). The female criminal sexual psychopath. *Corrective Psychiatry and Journal of Social Therapy, 10*(3), 156-158. Discusses sex crimes by women.

B.0445 Mayer, Adele (1992). *Women sex offenders*. Holmes Beach, FL: Learning Publications. Discusses sex crimes committed by women.

B.0446 Mayer, J., & Green, M. (1967). Group therapy of alcoholic women ex-prisoners. *Quarterly Journal of Studies on Alcohol, 28*(3), 493-504. Discusses a group therapy initiative of the Alcoholism Clinic of Boston's Peter Ben Brigham Hospital for alcoholic women ex-offenders.

B.0447 Mayer, J., et al. (1967, October). Treatment of the female alcoholic: The former prisoner. *American Journal of Orthopsychiatry, 37*(5), 932-937. Discusses post-incarceration treatment for female ex-offenders.

B.0448 McBride, Timothy (1993, Spring). Criminal law: Should states criminally prosecute mothers for delivering drugs to their newborns during the birthing process. *Suffolk University Law Review, 27*, 251-260. Discusses legal sanctions for women who use drugs during pregnancy.

B.0449 McCaldon, R. J. (1967). Lady paperhangers. *Canadian Journal of Corrections, 9*, 243-256. Discusses women and forgery.

B.0450 McCarty, L. M. (1986). Mother-child incest: Characteristics of the offender. *Child Welfare, 65*(5), 447-458. Data collected from 26 mothers who participated in a three-year incest treatment program to present a profile of the sexually abusive mother.

B.0451 McClain, Paula (1982a). Black females and lethal violence: Has time changed the circumstances under which they kill? *Omega: Journal of Death and Dying, 13*(1), 13-25. Explores whether social changes in American society have impacted murders by black females.

B.0452 McClain, Paula (1982b, Fall). Black female homicide offenders and victims: Are they from the same population? *Death Education, 6*(3), 265-278. Survey data on female offenders gathered through the Black Homicide and Large Urban Environments Project.

B.0453 McClain, Paula (1981, Fall). Social and environmental characteristics of black female homicide offenders. *Western Journal of Black Studies, 5*(3), 224-230. Discusses black women who kill.

B.0454 McCoy, Virginia, et al. (1995, Fall). Women, crack, and crime: Gender comparisons of criminal activity among crack cocaine users. *Contemporary Drug Problems, 22*(3), 435-451. Results of interviews with 387 Miami adults (female & male) whose primary drug was crack cocaine.

B.0455 McCreary, C. P. (1976). Trait and type differences among male and female assaultive and non-assaultive offenders. *Journal of Personality Assessment, 40*(6), 617-621. Data collected from 506 offenders at the Los Angeles Legal Psychiatric Clinic.

B.0456 McCullough, M. K. (1968, October 10). Society at work: Some women criminals. *New Society, 12*(315), 522-523. Descriptive study based on data collected from a sample of 27 women on probation for acquisitive offenses.

B.0457 McDermott, N. J. (1985). *Female offenders in New York state.* Albany, NY: N.Y. State Division of Criminal Justice Services. Examined trends and patterns in female criminality and criminal justice processing in New York State between 1970 & 1984.

B.0458 McNall, S. G. (1986, Spring). It was a plot got up to convict me: The case of Henrietta Cook v. the state of Kansas, 1876. *Qualitative Sociology, 9*(1), 26-47. Case of a Kansas woman who was tried and found guilty of poisoning her husband .

B.0459 Memphis State University Law Review (1991, Fall). Fetal protection: An overview of recent state legislative response to crack cocaine abuse by pregnant women. *Memphis State University Law Review, 22,* 119-134. Discusses legal sanctions for pregnant women who use drugs.

B.0460 Mercy, James, & Saltzman, Linda. (1989, May). Fatal violence among spouses in the United States, 1976-1985. *American Journal of Public Health, 79*(5), 595-599. Looks at patterns and trends in homicides between marriage partners or lovers from 1976-1985.

B.0461 Merkle, C. (1911). *Crime among women in Oklahoma.* Dissertation, University of Oklahoma. Early discussion of crimes women were incarcerated for in Oklahoma.

B.0462 Merrick, Janna (1993, March). Maternal substance abuse during pregnancy: Policy implications in the United States. *Journal of Legal Medicine, 14,* 57-71. Discusses legal sanctions for women who use drugs during pregnancy.

B.0463 Meyers, Laura (1983). Battered wives, dead husbands. In A. Skolnick & J. Skolnick (Eds.), *Family in transition* (pp. 345-352). Boston, MA: Little Brown. Discusses battered women who kill.

B.0464 Middendorf, Wolf, & Middendorf, Dorothea (1984). Changing patterns of female criminality in Germany. In F. Adler (Ed.), *The incidence of female criminality in the contemporary world* (pp. 122-131). New York, NY: New York University Press. Discusses types of crimes committed by women in Germany and presents ideas about female aggression.

B.0465 Mieczkowski, Tom (1994, Winter-Spring). The experiences of women who sell crack: Some descriptive data from the Detroit Crack Ethnography Project. *Journal of Drug Issues, 24*(1-2), 227-248. Examines the role of women in crack sales.

B.0466 Mier y Teran, Carmen (1974). Drug abuse among the inmates of a women's prison in Mexico City. *Addictive Diseases: An International Journal, 1*(2), 153-175. Interview data collected from 24 Mexican female narcotics addicts on family backgrounds and drug abuse histories.

B.0467 Miller, Betty (1974). Male vs. female criminality: A comparative analysis of three male respondent groups. *Dissertation Abstracts International, 35*(11), 7416-A. Explored social distance and negative reactions toward male and female felons convicted of violent crimes.

B.0468 Miller, Brenda (1981, July-September). Drug and crime interrelationships among women in prison. *Journal of Psychoactive Drugs, 13*(8). Discusses the number of women incarcerated for drug-related offenses.

B.0469 Miller, Brenda (1980). Illegal drug use among women in detention. *Dissertation Abstracts International, 41*(4), 1784. Focuses on three major areas of illegal drug use among incarcerated women.

B.0470 Miller, E. M. (1986). *Street woman.* Philadelphia, PA: Temple University Press. Data collected from 64 interviews with female con artists, petty thieves, and prostitutes in Milwaukee, WI.

B.0471 Miller, Jody (1993, November). "Your life is on the line every night you're on the streets": Victimization and resistance among street prostitutes. *Humanity and Society, 17*(4), 422-446. Interview data from 16 female prostitutes in a midwestern city jail.

B.0472 Miller, Richard (1984, October-December). Nationwide profile of female inmate substance involvement. *Journal of Psychoactive Drugs, 16*(4), 319-326. Data from the U.S. Bureau of Census state prison survey which included 2,255 female inmates.

B.0473 Miloslavich, E. L. (1951, September-October). Uncommon criminal methods of infanticide. *The Journal of Criminal Law, Criminology, and Police Science, 42*(3), 414-416. Early discussion of infanticide.

B.0474 Miner, M., & Gorta, A. (1987, March). Heroin use in the lives of women prisoners in Australia. *Australian and New Zealand Journal of Criminology, 20*(1), 3-15. Compares characteristics and experiences of women heroin users with incarcerated women non-users.

B.0475 Moinat, Sheryl, & Snortum, J. R. (1976, March). Self-management of personal habits by female drug addicts: A feasibility study. *Criminal Justice & Behavior, 3*(1), 29-40. Tested a 9-week program for training incarcerated female drug addicts in the use of self-management techniques.

B.0476 Moller, J. (1979, February). Female offender. *Liason (Ontario, Canada), 5*(2), COMPLETE ISSUE. Articles on various aspects of female offending.

B.0477 Monahan, Florence (1941). Women who kill. In F. Monahan (Ed.), *Women in crime* (pp. 260-275). New York, NY: Ives Washington, Inc. Early discussion of women who commit murder.

B.0478 Montague, D. H., & McLauchlin, S. E. (1992, Summer). Drug exposed infants: En ventre sa mere--and in need of protection. *Baylor Law Review, 44,* 485-527. Discusses legal sanctions for pregnant women who use drugs.

B.0479 Moon, Dreama, et al. (1993). Patterns of substance use among women in prison. In B. Fletcher et al. (Eds.), *Women prisoners: A forgotten population* (pp. 45-54). Westport, CT: Praeger. Discusses substance use and abuse among women in prison.

B.0480 Moore, Joan (1990). Mexican American women addicts: The influence of family background. In R. Glick & J. Moore (Eds.), *Drug use in Hispanic communities.* New Brunswick, NJ: Rutgers University Press. Study on drug use among Mexican American women.

B.0481 Moore, Joan, & Devitt, Mary (1989, March). The paradox of deviance in addicted Mexican American mothers. *Gender and Society, 3*(1), 53-70. Analysis of data from 1980/1981 of 58 addicted Chicana mothers focused on using drugs during pregnancy.

B.0482 Morris, Allison (1993). Rocking the cradle: Mothers who kill their children. In H. Birch (Ed.), *Moving targets: Women, murder, and representation* (pp. 198-217). Berkeley, CA: University of California Press. Discusses infanticide and the social expectations of "woman" and "mother."

B.0483 Morris, Allison (1989). Interspousal violence: A review of research. *The Cambrian Law Review, 20,* 7-16. Discussion of research on women who kill.

B.0484 Morris, Allison (1980). *Women and crime: Papers presented to the Cropwood Round-table Conference, December, 1980.* Eight papers and discussions from a 1980 conference held in England on crimes committed by women, explanations for it, the law, and women and the penal system.

B.0485 Morris, Virginia (1983, Autumn). Arsenic and blue lace: Sayers' criminal women. *Modern Fiction Studies, 29*(3), 485-495. Discusses the way women criminals are depicted in novels.

B.0486 Moseley, Kathryn (1986, March). The history of infanticide in Western society. *Issues in Law & Medicine, 1,* 345-361. Discusses infanticide.

B.0487 Moss, Debra (1988, November 1). Pregnant? Go directly to jail. *American Bar Association Journal,* 20(1), 74. Discusses legal sanctions for women who use drugs during pregnancy.

B.0488 Moss, Kary (1991, Winter). Forced drug or alcohol treatment for pregnant and postpartum women: Part of the solution or part of the problem. *New England Journal on Criminal and Civil Confinement, 17,* 1-16. Discusses legal sanctions for women who use drugs during pregnancy.

B.0489 Moss, Kary (1990, Spring). Substance abuse during pregnancy. *Harvard Women's Law Journal, 13,* 278-299. Discusses legal sanctions for women who use drugs during pregnancy.

B.0490 Muraskin, Roslyn, & Alleman, Ted (1993). *It's a crime: Women and justice.* Englewood Cliffs, NJ: Prentice Hall. Discusses the crimes women commit and their treatment in the criminal justice sytem.

B.0491 Myers, C. J. (1987, Fall). A visitor from another planet: The case of D. J. *Journal of Psychiatry and Law, 15*(3), 373-416. Case of a young adult woman diagnosed with paranoid schizophrenia who killed a 4-year-old black child because of racial prejudice.

B.0492 Myers, J. E. (1991). A limited role for the legal system in responding to maternal substance abuse during pregnancy. *Notre Dame Journal of Law, Ethics, & Public Policy, 5*, 747-781. Discusses legal sanctions for women who use drugs during pregnancy.

B.0493 Narcotics Control Digest (1993, March 17). Court reinstates cocaine possession charges against mother. *Narcotics Control Digest, 23*(6), 6+. Discussion of drug use by mothers.

B.0494 Narcotics Demand Reduction Digest (1994, October). Five percent of pregnant women used illegal drugs. *Narcotics Demand Reduction Digest, 6*(10), 9-10. Study of self-reported drug use during pregnancy.

B.0495 Narcotics Demand Reduction Digest (1993, May). Pregnant drug abusers. *Narcotics Demand Reduction Digest, 5*(5), 6. Discusses mother's use of drugs during pregnancy.

B.0496 Neiheisel, Cynthia (1987). A descriptive and comparative study of female homicide offenders incarcerated in the state of Kentucky. *Dissertation Abstracts International, 26*(2), 209. Study provides information on women convicted of homicide in Kentucky from 1979-1986.

B.0497 Neil, John (1991). *Battered women who have killed: A critical literature review.* Dissertation, Nova University. Research on battered women who kill.

B.0498 Nerney, M. (1987). *Battered women and criminal justice.* New York. NY: Committee on Domestic Violence and Incarcerated Women. Analysis of issues of battered women incarcerated for killing their abusers and for other violent crimes.

B.0499 Neustadter, R. (1994). Fetal attraction: Legal, ethical, and sociological considerations in the criminalization of pregnancy. *Journal of Crime and Justice, 17*(2), 107-131. Discusses charges against pregnant women who use drugs, such as, criminal neglect and child abuse.

B.0500 Neville, M. (1930, May). Ladies of the gang: A study in feminine deportment, underworld species. *Police 13-13*(Chicago), 5, 10-11. Early discussion of women in Chicago's criminal underworld.

B.0501 New England Journal on Criminal and Civil Confinement (1991, Winter). Criminalizing substance abuse during pregnancy. *New England Journal on Criminal and Civil Confinement, 17*, 69-106. Dsicusses the criminalization of drug use during pregnancy.

B.0502 New England Law Review (1991, Summer). A cracked image of my mother/myself? The need for a legislative directive proscribing maternal drug abuse. *New England Law Review, 25*, 1325-1361. Discusses legal sanctions for women who use drugs during pregnancy.

B.0503 New York Department of Correctional Services (1990). *Female drug commitment population, 1987-1989.* Albany, NY: N.Y. Department of Correctional Services. Profiles the female new court commitment population in New York from January 1, 1985 through December 21, 1989.

B.0504 New York Law School Journal of Human Rights (1991, Spring). Criminal sanctions for drug abuse during pregnancy: The antithesis of fetal health. *New York Law School Journal of Human Rights, 8*, 415-459. Discusses the use of legal sanctions for women who abuse drugs during pregnancy.

B.0505 Noblit, George, & Burcart, Janie (1976). Women and crime: 1960-1970. *Social Science Quarterly, 56*(4), 650-657. Looks at crime committed by women in 1960 and 1970. Documents trends in female perpetrated crime and offers explanations for observed patterns.

B.0506 Nolan, Kathleen (1990, Winter-Spring). Protecting fetuses from prenatal hazards: Whose crimes? What punishment? *Criminal Justice Ethics, 9*(1), 13-22. Considers changes in criminal law to prosecute women who engage in activity that may be harmful to the fetus.

B.0507 Northern Illinois University Law Review (1990). When self abuse becomes child abuse: The need for coercive prenatal government action in response to the cocaine baby problems. *Northern Illinois University Law Review, 11,* 73-117. Discusses the use of legal sanctions for women who abuse drugs during pregnancy.

B.0508 Oberman, Michelle (1992a, March). Sex, drugs, pregnancy, and the law: Rethinking the problems of pregnant women who use drugs. *The Hastings Law Journal, 43,* 505-548. Discusses the use of drugs during pregnancy.

B.0509 Oberman, Michelle (1992b). The control of pregnancy and the criminalization of femaleness. *Berkeley Women's Law Journal, 7,* 1-12. Discusses the use of legal sanctions for women who abuse drugs during pregnancy.

B.0510 O'Brien, Patricia (1984, Fall). The kleptomania diagnosis: Bourgeois women and theft in late nineteenth century France. *Journal of Social History, 17,* 475-498. Discusses a body of case studies of kleptomania perpetrated by women who were diagnosed as stealing out of compulsion.

B.0511 O'Brien, R. M. (1988, February). Exploring the intersexual nature of violent crimes. *Criminology, A Interndisciplinary Journal, 26*(1), 151-170. Analyzed data to determine the extent to which violent crimes occurred within or between the sexes.

B.0512 O'Connor, Art (1987). Female sex offenders. *British Journal of Psychiatry, 150,* 615-620. Data collected from 19 women convicted of indecency and 62 women convicted of other sex offenses.

B.0513 Odem, Mary (1992, Spring). Fallen women and thieving ladies: Historical approaches to women and crime in the United States. *Law and Social Inquiry, 17,* 351-361. Historical overview of crimes committed by women in the United States.

B.0514 O'Donnell, E. (1930). *Women bluebeards.* London: Stanley Paul. Early account of women who murder.

B.0515 Oloruntiemehin, Olufunmilayo (1992). Crime and control in Nigeria: Female criminality. In H. Heiland et al. (Eds.), *Crime and control in comparative perspectives* (pp. 171-176). Discusses crimes, sentencing and imprisonment of women in Nigeria.

B.0516 Oloruntiemehin, Olufunmilayo (1981). A preliminary study of female criminality in Nigeria. In F. Adler (Ed.), *The incidence of female criminality in the contemporary world* (pp. 158-169). New York, NY: New York University Press. Discusses crimes by women in Nigeria and suggests areas for further research.

B.0517 Osborne, Judith (1987, Summer). The crime of infanticide: Throwing out the baby with the bathwater. *Canadian Journal of Family Law, 6*(1), 46-59. Discusses the reluctance to find a mother guilty of murder of an infant reflected in the Canadian Criminal Code.

B.0518 Owens, Robert, & Harms, Laura (1993). Differential responses of female forgers to MMPI items. *Journal of Offender Rehabilitation, 19*(3-4), 165-171. A comparison of MMPI items for 128 females convicted of forgery with 128 females of an age-matched normative sample.

B.0519 Palmer, Stuart, & Humphrey, J. A. (1982). Familial and other relationships in criminal homicide in North Carolina. *Journal of Family Issues, 3*(3), 301-318. Looked at increased number of homicides by women against their husbands Data from 985 criminal homicide offenders.

B.0520 Paltrow, Lynn (1990, Winter-Spring). When becoming pregnant is a crime. *Criminal Justice Ethics, 9*(1), 41-47. Reviews 30 cases of pregnant women arrested for behavior that may potentially harm the fetus.

B.0521 Panaro, Lydia (1982, January). Desperate women: Murderers and suicides in nine modern novels. *Dissertation Abstracts International, 42*(7), 3150. Looks at reasons underlying the destructive behavior of heroines in nine novels.

B.0522 Parker, Elizabeth (1974). The victims of mentally disordered female offenders. *British Journal of Psychiatry, 125*, 51-59. Reviews case records of 55 victims of 47 female offenders who committed murder, manslaughter, attempted murder, or wounding.

B.0523 Parker, Linda (1992). Murderous women and mild justice: A look at female violence in pre-1910 San Diego, San Luis Obispo and Tuolumne counties. *Journal of San Diego History, 38*(1), 22-49. Specific cases of murder by women in three California counties from 1850 to 1910.

B.0524 Parker, Robert, & Toth, Allison (1990). Family, intimacy, and homicide: A macro-social approach. *Violence and Victims, 5*(3), 195-210. A study of violence among sexual intimates and family members using the macro-social tradition.

B.0525 Parker, Tony (1967). *Women in crime: Five revealing cases.* New York, NY: Delacorte Press. Discusses the cases of five criminal women.

B.0526 Parness, J. A. (1992, November). Arming the pregnancy police: More outlandish concoctions? *Louisiana Law Review, 53*, 427-448. Discusses legal sanctions for pregnant women.

B.0527 Payne, Jennifer (1992, Winter). Risk factors for infant homicide: A case-control study. *Masters Abstracts International, 30*(4), 1137. Data on infant homicide during the period 1980-1989 collected from computer-linked birth and death records for the state of Washington.

B.0528 Peak, Ken, & Del Papa, Frankie (1993). Criminal justice enters the womb: Enforcing the right to be born drug-free. *Journal of Criminal Justice, 21*(3), 245-263. Discusses the legal and ethical dilemma over whose "rights" should prevail -- those of the fetus or the mother's.

B.0529 Peckham, Audrey (1985). *A woman in confinement.* London: Fontana. Personal experience of a woman taken into custody for "incitement to murder."

B.0530 Pelka-Slugooki, M. D., & Slugooki, L. (1979). Alcoholism and female crime in Poland. *International Journal of Offender Therapy and Comparative Criminology, 21*(2), 174-183. Examines data of 365 incarcerated women to determine whether drinking is a cause of crime.

B.0531 Peluso, Emanuel, & Putnam, Nicholas (1996, January). Case study: Sexual abuse of boys by females. *Journal of the American Academy of Child & Adolescent Psychiatry, 35*(1), 51-54. Discusses the cases of two boys who experienced sexual abuse by females.

B.0532 Peters, Roger, & Schonfeld, Lawrence (1993, Winter). Determinants of recent substance abuse among jail inmates referred for treatment. *Journal of Drug Issues, 23*(1), 101-117. Study included 38 females referred for treatment at a metropolitan jail.

B.0533 Petrie, Carol, & Garner, Joel (1990). Is violence preventable? In D. Besharov (Ed.), *Family violence: Research and public policy issues* (pp. 164-184). Washington, DC: AEI Press. Includes an analysis of family violence. Urges continued research in the area of female offending.

B.0534 Pettiway, L. E. (1987, August). Participation in crime: Partnerships by female drug users: The effects of domestic arrangements, drug use, and criminal involvement. *Criminology, 25*(3), 741-766. Discusses women who assist other women in drug addiction and crime.

B.0535 Petrow, Julie (1991). Addicted mothers, drug-exposed babies: The unprecedented prosecution of mothers under drug-trafficking statutes. *New York Law School Law Review, 36*, 573-607. Discusses legal sanctions for drug abuse during pregnancy.

B.0536 Piers, Maria (1978). *Infanticide.* New York, NY: W. W. Norton. Discusses infanticide.

B.0537 Pittel, S. M., et al. (1979). Reentry concerns of incarcerated substance abusers. *American Journal of Drug and Alcohol Abuse, 6*(1), 59-71. Data collected from 110 female and male offenders to obtain information for the creation of aftercare programs for substance abusers.

B.0538 Plass, Peggy (1993, June). African American family homicide: Patterns in partner, parent, and child victimization, 1985-1987. *Journal of Black Studies, 23*(4), 515-540. Examines the incidence of family homicide in African-American families.

B.0539 Plenska, Danuta (1981). The criminality of women in Poland. In F. Adler (Ed.), *The incidence of female criminality in the contemporary world* (pp. 134-144). New York, NY: New York University Press. Discusses crimes of women in Poland in light of socioeconomic status.

B.0540 Plenska, Danuta (1980). Female criminality in Poland. *Canadian Journal of Criminology, 22*(4), 465-575. Discusses crimes committed by women in Poland.

B.0541 Pollak, O. (1950). The ways women commit murder. In O. Pollack (Ed.), *The criminality of women* (pp. 16-28). Philadelphia, PA: University of Pennsylvania Press. Discusses women who kill.

B.0542 Pollock, Philip, & Kear-Colwell, John (1994, March). Women who stab: A personal construct analysis of sexual victimization and offending behavior. *British Journal of Medical Psychology, 67*(1), 13-22. Data collected from 2 women with histories of sexual abuse.

B.0543 Price, Ray (1977). The forgotten female offender. *Crime and Delinquency, 23*(2), 101-108. Discusses dramatic increases in female crime and suggests ways of reforming the criminal justice system.

B.0544 Priest, L. (1992). *Women who killed: Stories of Canadian female murderers.* Toronto: McClelland & Stewart. Discusses women murderers in Canada.

B.0545 Pucci, Idanna (1996). *The trials of Maria Barbella: The true story of a 19th century crime of passion.* New York, NY: Four Walls Eight Windows. Discusses the life and trials of Maria Barbella.

B.0546 Radish, K. (1992). *Run, Bambi, run.* New York, NY: Seal. Case of Laurencia Bambenek.

B.0547 Rani, M. B. (1981, January). The pattern and nature of female criminality in Andhra Pradesh. *Indian Journal of Social Work, 41*(40), 393-401. Discusses major classes of offenses represented among female criminals in India. Includes murder, assault, theft, and prostitution.

B.0548 Rasche, Christine (1990). Early models for contemporary thought on domestic violence and women who kill their mates: A review of the literature from 1895-1970. *Women and Criminal Justice, 1*(2), 31-53. Reviews the literature on women and domestic homicide, 1895-1970.

B.0549 Rasko, Gabriella (1981). Crimes against life committed by women in Hungary. In F. Adler (Ed.), *The incidence of female criminality in the contemporary world* (pp. 145-156). New York, NY: New York University Press. Disucsses "crimes against life" by women in Hungary.

B.0550 Ray, Crace (1972). *Wily women of the West.* San Antonio, TX: Naylor. Discusses female outlaws of the pioneer days.

B.0551 Ray, Joseph, et al. (1983, September). First offender adult shoplifters: A preliminary profile. *Journal of Clinical Psychology, 39*(5), 769-770. Data collected by administering a battery of psychological tests to 94 adult 1st offender shoplifters in Texas.

B.0552 Raynes, A., et al. (1974). Factors related to imprisonment in female heroin addicts. *International Journal of the Addictions, 9*(1), 145-150. Comparisons are made with data from 49 female addicts in a detoxification program and incarcerated female addicts.

B.0553 Renzetti, Claire (1992). *Violent Betrayal: Partner abuse in lesbian relationships.* Newbury Park, CA: Sage. Discusses abuse and murder in lesbian relationships.

B.0554 Resnik, Judith (1970, April). Murder of the newborn: A psychiatric review of neonaticide. *American Journal of Psychiatry, 126*(1), 1414-1420. Discusses the killing of a newborn.

B.0555 Resnik, Judith (1969, September). Child murder by parents: A psychiatric review of filicide. *American Journal of Psychiatry, 126*(3), 325-334. Discusses incidents of child murder.

B.0556 Reston, James (1977). *The innocence of Joan Little: A Southern mystery.* New York, NY: Times Books. Discusses the case of Joan Little, a black woman imprisoned in a North Carolina county jail who killed her white male jailer in self-defense against sexual assault.

B.0557 Rhode, John (1928). *The case of Constance Kent.* New York, NY: Scribner. A study of 88 mothers and 43 fathers who had murdered children over the age of one day.

B.0558 Riccio, R. (1992, July). Street crime strategies: The changing schemata of streetwalkers. *Environment and Behavior, 24*(2), 555-570. Data obtained via field observations, police arrest records, and interviews with 37 imprisoned streetwalkers in San Diego, California.

B.0559 Rich, Kim (1993). *Johnny's girl: A daughter's memoir of growing up in Alaska's underworld.* New York, NY: Morrow. Personal memoir.

B.0560 Rivera Dominquez, R. (1976). Considerations on female participation in the combined crime incidence picture in Panama. In *Criminology: First National Seminar* (pp. 72-79). Panama. Analysis of the incidence and patterns of female delinquency in Panama over a five year period.

B.0561 Roberts, Dorothy (1991, May). Punishing drug addicts who have babies: Women of color, equality, and the right of privacy. *Harvard Law Review, 104,* 1419-1482. Discusses the legality of harsh sanctions for pregnant women addicts.

B.0562 Roberts, Dorothy (1990, April). Drug-addicted women who have babies. *Trial, 26*(4), 56-61. Discusses legal sanctions and drug addicted pregnancies.

B.0563 Roberts, Virginia (1985). The women was too tough. *Journal of Arizona History, 26*(4), 395-414. Examines the lives of Arizona frontier women including women murderers.

B.0564 Roberts, Y. (1990). Missing baby. *New Statesman and Society, 3*(84), 16-17. Discusses research on women involved in kidnapping.

B.0565 Roberts, Y. (1989). To the slaughter. *New Statesman and Society, 2*(71), 10-11. Considers the exploitation of women incarcerated in Great Britain who were hired drug carriers.

B.0566 Robertson, John, & Paltrow, Lynn (1989, August). Fetal abuse. *American Bar Association Journal, 75,* 38-39. Robertson argues the case for recognizing fetal abuse as a crime. Paltrow argues the case against recognizing fetal abuse as a crime.

B.0567 Robertson, R. G., et al. (1987, December). The female offender: A Canadian study. *Canadian Journal of Psychiatry, 32*(9), 749-755. Profile of women offenders in Canada. Includes personal history, family background, psychological factors and mental health.

B.0568 Robinson, B. F. (1961). Criminality among narcotic addicts in the Illinois state reformatory for women. *Illinois Medical Journal, 119,* 320-326. Study of the incidence of crime among incarcerated women narcotic addicts

B.0569 Robinson, Michael (1993, May). Unnatural wives and pitiless mothers: Images of murderesses in English society, 1550-1650. *Masters Abstracts International, 32*(3), 840. Examines murderesses in English society (1550-1650) and the roles of women.

B.0570 Rodenburg, M. (1971). Child murder by a depressed mother: A case report. *Canadian Psychiatric Association Journal, 16*, 49-53. Discusses murder of a child by the mother.

B.0571 Rodriguez, S., et al. (1995, January-March). Intimate homicide: Victim-offender relationship in female perpetrated homicide. *Deviant Behavior, 16*(1), 45-57. Discusses conditions under which women would be likely to commit homicide against male partners.

B.0572 Romenesko, K., & Miller, E. (1989, January). The second step in double jeopardy: Appropriating the labor of female street hustlers. *Crime and Delinquency, 35*(1), 109-135. Data collected from 14 Milwaukee female street hustlers ages 18-25.

B.0573 Roper, Mary (1992, Spring). Reaching the babies through the mothers: The effects of prosecution on pregnant substance abusers. *Law and Psychology Review, 16,* 171-188. Discusses legal sanctions against pregnant substance abusers.

B.0574 Rose, Lionel (1986). *The massacre of the innocents: Infanticide in Britain, 1800-1939.* London: Routledge & Kegan Paul. Discusses the economic and social pressures on women to rid thenselves of unwanted babies by criminal means in late 19th century.

B.0575 Rosenbaum, M. (1990, August). The role of depression in couples involved in murder-suicide and homicide. *American Journal of Psychiatry, 147*(8), 1036-1039. Comparison of 12 couples in cases of murder-suicide with 24 couples in cases of homicide during 1978-1987.

B.0576 Rosenbaum, Marsha (1981). *Women on heroin.* New Brunswick, NJ: Rutgers University Press. Discusses heroin addiction in women.

B.0577 Rosenblatt, Ellen, & Greenland, C. (1974, April). Female crimes of violence. *Canadian Journal of Criminology and Corrections, 16*(2), 173-180. Data collected from case studies of 2 groups of violent offenders during 1970-1971 in Ontario, Canada.

B.0578 Rosenbluth, Jean (1993, March). Abortion as murder: Why should women get off? *Southern California Law Review, 66,* 1237-1271. Discusses abortion as murder.

B.0579 Rosenzweig, S., et al. (1942). The psychodynamics of uxorcide. *American Journal of Orthopsychiatry, 12,* 283-294. Early discussion of spousal murder.

B.0580 Rosner, R., et al. (1985, July). Forensic psychiatric evaluations of women accused of felonies: A three year descriptive study. *Journal of Forensic Sciences, 30*(3), 721-729. Study of psychological factors affecting the incidence of crime in women.

B.0581 Rowan, Edward, et al. (1990). Women who molest children. *Bulletin of the American Academy of Psychiatry and the Law, 18*(1), 79-83. Case studies of 9 women (aged 20-65 yrs) identified through sex offender evaluations of 600 convicted child molesters.

B.0582 Rowan, Edward (1988a). Pedophilia. *Journal of Social Work and Human Sexuality, 7*(1), 91-100. Includes a discussion of female incest perpetrators and child molesters.

B.0583 Rowan, Edward, et al. (1988b). Female pedophiles. *Corrective and Social Psychiatry and Journal of Behavior Technology Methods and Therapy, 34*(3), 17-20. Examines the backgrounds of female child molesters.

B.0584 Rowe, G. S. (1985). Women's crime and criminal administration in Pennsylvania, 1763-1790. *Pennsylvania Magazine of History and Biography, 109*(3), 335-368. Examines the types of crimes committed by women during the 18th century in Pennsylvania.

B.0585 Rudin, Margaret (1994, March). The relationship among characteristics of child sexual abuse victims and perpetrator gender. *Dissertation Abstracts International, 54*(9), 4932. Looks at female offenders who sexually abuse children.

B.0586 Ruggiero, K. (1992, August). Honor, maternity, and the disciplining of women: Infanticide in late nineteenth-century Buenos Aires. *Hispanic American Historical Review, 72*(3), 353-373. Discusses infanticide as a crime against motherhood.

B.0587 Ruhle, Nancy (1992, March). Perinatal substance abuse: Personal triumphs and tragedies. *The Hastings Law Journal, 43,* 549-558. Discusses legal sanctions for drug abusing pregnant women.

B.0588 Rule, Anne (1991). *If you really loved me: A true story of desire and murder.* New York, NY: Simon & Schuster. Case of a man who coerced his 14-year-old daughter into murdering his 23-year-old wife.

B.0589 Rule, Anne (1987). *Small sacrifices: A true story of passion and murder.* Ontario: New American Library. Case of Diane Downs, who shot her three children.

B.0590 Russell, M. (1978). Groups of women who shoplift. *Journal of Criminology, 20*(1), 73-74. Discusses women who shoplift.

B.0591 Ryterski, Louise (1991, October/November). "Till death do us part." *Journal of the Missouri Bar, 47,* 577-584. Discusses battered women who kill.

B.0592 Saltstone, Robert, et al. (1994, September-October). A multivariate evaluation of the Michigan Alcoholism Screening Test in a female offender population. *Addictive Behaviors, 19*(5), 455-462. Study using two alcohol screening tests with 615 incarcerated women.

B.0593 Sanchez, J. E., & Johnson, B. D. (1987, April-June). Women and the drugs-crime connection: Crime rates among drug abusing women at Rikers Island. *Journal of Psychoactive Drugs, 19*(2), 205-216. Examines the relationship between crime rates and extent and type of drug abuse in a 1983 study of 175 female inmates of the Rikers Island Correctional Facility in New York.

B.0594 Sangree, Suzanne (1993, Spring). Control of childbearing by HIV-positive women: Some responses to emerging legal policies. *Buffalo Law Review, 41,* 309-349. Discusses legal sanctions of pregnancy in HIV positive women.

B.0595 Sarrel, P. M., & Masters, W. H. (1982). Sexual molestation of men by women. *Archives of Sexual Behavior, 11*(2), 117-131. Reviews case studies that contradict the belief that it is impossible for men to respond when sexually molested by women.

B.0596 Sasaki, Y. (1988). Pathological problems of mother-child relation. *Japanese Psychological Review, 31*(1), 146-157. Discusses views on mother-child suicide and infanticide in Japan.

B.0597 Sato, K. S. (1981). Emancipation of women and crime in Japan. In F. Adler (Ed.), *The incidence of female criminality in the contemporary world* (pp. 258-271). New York, NY: New York University Press. Discusses role of women in Japanese society and gives statistics for crimes committed by women in 1943 and 1972.

B.0598 Saunders, Daniel (1986, Spring). When battered women use violence: Husband-abuse or self-defense? *Violence and Victims, 1*(6), 47-60. Discusses battered women who kill.

B.0599 Saunders, Daniel, & Browne, Angela (1991). Domestic homicide. In R. T. Ammerman & M. Hersen (Eds.), *Case studies in family violence* (pp. 379-402). New York, NY: Plenum Press. Describes domestic homicide and patterns and dynamics of male and female perpetrators.

B.0600 Saunders, Edward (1989, July-August). Neonaticides following "secret" pregnancies: Seven case reports. *Public Health Reports, 104,* 368-372. Discusses neonaticide.

B.0601 Saxena, Rekha (1994). *Women and crime in India: A study in socio-cultural dynamics.* New Delhi: Inter-India Publishers. A study of crimes committed by women in India.

B.0602 Scarpitti, Frank, & Datesman, Susan (1980). *Women, crime and justice.* New York, NY: Oxford University Press. Essays on crimes women commit and the treatment of women in the criminal justice system

B.0603 Schmall, Lorraine (1993, Spring). Addicted pregnancy as a sex crime. *Northern Illinois University Law Review, 13,* 263-334. Discusses legal sanctions against pregnant drug abusers.

B.0604 Schofield, Ann (1993a). Constructing Lizzie Borden: History, feminism, and American culture. *Australian Cultural History, 12,* 1-13. Explores the persistent attraction of the story of Lizzie Borden, accused and acquitted of the 1892 axe murder of her father and stepmother.

B.0605 Schofield, Ann (1993b). Lizzie Borden took an axe: History, feminism and American culture. *American Studies, 34*(1), 91-103. Examines the story of Lizzie Borden in popular culture.

B.0606 Schroedel, Jean, & Peretz, Paul (1994, Summer). A gender analysis of policy formations: The case of fetal abuse. *Journal of Health Politics, Policy and Law, 19*(2), 335-360. Discusses the value of a feminist perspective on policy issues in areas such as fetal abuse.

B.0607 Schultz, C. G. (1973). Sociopathic and non-sociopathic female felons. *Dissertation Abstracts International, 34*(11), 7357A. A study of sociopathy in female felons.

B.0608 Schweber, Claudine (1981, Spring). Criminalization and incarceration: The Federal government's response to drug addiction among women, 1914-1934. *George Mason University Law Review, 4,* 71-98. Discusses early legal sanctions against women addicts.

B.0609 Scott, Elsie (1978). *Black women, crime, and crime prevention.* Paper presented at the National Conference of Black Political Scientists, 1978, Jackson, MS. Discusses how crimes committed by black women differ from crimes committed by black men.

B.0610 Scott, H. (1993, Summer). The female serial killer: A well-kept secret of the "gentler sex." *Masters Abstracts International, 31*(2), 654. Investigation based on the premise that women, as perpetrators of serial murder, have been ignored. Documents case studies of thirteen women.

B.0611 Seese, Robin, et al. (1994, March). *Fight or flight: Characteristics of abusive situations for female homicide offenders and women in a battered women's shelter.* Paper presented at the Annual Meeting of the ACJS, Chicago, IL. Interview data from 9 women in three crisis shelters and 35 women incarcerated for homicide of an intimate partner.

B.0612 Seldin, B. E. (1980). *A comparison of selected personality variables among assaultive and non-assaultive female offenders with varying sex-role orientations.* Dissertation, The Catholic University of America. Study on assaultive behavior in female offenders.

B.0613 Sethna, M. J. (1952). Women offenders. In M. J. Sethna (Ed.), *Society and the criminal* (pp. 113-114). Bombay, India: Leaders Press. Discusses socialization of women in India as a reason for so few crimes by women.

B.0614 Sexton, Patricia (1993, Spring). Imposing criminal sanctions on pregnant drug users: Throwing the baby out with the bath water. *Washburn Law Journal, 32,* 410-430. Discusses legal sanctions for pregnant drug abusers.

B.0615 Shapiro, Ann-Louise (1991, Fall). Love stories: Female crimes of passion in Fin-de-Siecle Paris. *Differences: A Journal of Feminist Cultural Studies, 3*(3), 45-68. Discusses why female crimes, particularly crimes of passion, attracted so much attention in turn-of-the century Paris.

B.0616 Sharma, Shridhar (1985, January). Mass murder by women. *Indian Journal of Criminology, 13,* 11-15. Discusses 228 women convicted of murder in India's two most populous states in 1981-1983. Six of these were mass murderers. One case of a female gang mass murder is detailed.

B.0617 Sheppard, Anthony (1991, Spring). The Supreme Court of Canada and criminal evidence reform: Recent cases on sexual abuse of children and spousal murder. *Canadian Journal of Family Law, 9,* 11-27. Discusses reform in the Canadian legal system to deal with crimes such as child abuse and spousal homicide.

B.0618 Sherman, Rorie (1992, February 24). Split rulings for fetal abuse cases. *National Law Journal, 14*(25), 3, 10. Discusses case of the first woman jailed for "prenatal child abuse" which was overturned by a Kentucky court of appeals.

B.0619 Shoop, Julie (1992, May). States cannot punish pregnant women for "fetal abuse" courts say. *Trial, 28*(5), 11-14. Appellate courts in two states held that women who abuse drugs while pregnant cannot be prosecuted for endangering the life of the fetus.

B.0620 Shoop, Julie (1992, October). Fetal abuse conviction overturned in Florida. *Trial, 28*(10), 16-17. The Florida Supreme Court ruled that pregnant women cannnot be sued under the state's drug laws for passing drugs to fetuses. Implications are discussed.

B.0621 Shore, Elsie, et al. (1988, January). Arrests of women for driving under the influence. *Journal of Studies on Alcohol, 49*(1), 7-10. Reviewed police records (1980-1985) of DUI arrests in Wichita, Kansas, to determine whether female arrests increased or decreased.

B.0622 Showalter, R. C., et al. (1980). The spousal homicide syndrome. *International Journal of Law and Psychiatry, 3*, 117-141. Discusses battered women who kill.

B.0623 Silverman, I. J., et al. (1993). The female murderer. In A. V. Wilson (Ed.), *Homicide: The victim/offender connection.* Cincinnati, OH: Anderson Publishing. Discusses women who kill.

B.0624 Silverman, I. J. (1982, Spring). Women, crime and drugs. *Journal of Drug Issues, 12*(2), 167-183. Research on the relationship between substance abuse among women and patterns of crime.

B.0625 Silverman, Robert, & Kennedy, Leslie (1988, Summer). Women who kill their children. *Violence and Victims, 3*(2), 113-127. Looks at ways in which killing of children by women differs from spousal murders in terms of circumstances, motivation, and characteristics.

B.0626 Silverman, Robert, & Kennedy, Leslie (1987, December). *The female perpetrator of homicide in Canada.* Paper presented to the Annual Meeting of the American Society for Criminology. Describes homicides committed by women in Canada. Analyzes data from 1961-1983.

B.0627 Silverman, Robert, & Mukherjee, S. K. (1986). Intimate homicide: An analysis of violent social relationships. *Behavioral Sciences and the Law, 5*(1), 37-47. Discusses women who kill.

B.0628 Simon, Rita (1993). *Rabbis, lawyers, immigrants, thieves: Exploring women's roles.* Westport, CT: Praeger. Study on women's roles.

B.0629 Simon, Rita, & Landis, J. (1991). *Crimes women commit: The punishments they receive.* Lexington, MA: Lexington Books, DC Heath. Discusses the relationship between social, economic, and environmental factors and types and frequency of crime among women.

B.0630 Simon, Rita, & Sharma, Navin (1978, September-October). Women and crime: Does the American experience generalize? *Humanist, 38*(5), 32-33. Cross-cultural comparison of female criminals in the United States, Japan, and Israel.

B.0631 Simon, Rita (1977). Women and crime in Israel. In S. Landau & L. Sebba (Eds.), *Criminology in perspective: Essays in honor of Israel Drapkin.* Lexington, MA: Lexington Books. Discusses crimes committed by women in Israel.

B.0632 Simon, Rita (1976a, January). American women and crime. *Annals of the American Academy of Political Science, 423*(31), 281-292. Discusses crimes committed by women in America.

B.0633 Simon, Rita (1976b). Women and crime revisited. *Social Science Quarterly, 56*(4), 658-663. Critiques article by Noblit & Burcart examining trends and patterns in crimes committed by women from 1960-1970.

B.0634 Simon, Rita (1975a). *Women and crime.* Lexington, MA: DC Heath. Discusses incidences of crime committed by women in the U.S.

B.0635 Simon, Rita (1975b, August). Criminal Behavior among Israeli women. *Crime and Social Deviance, 3*(3). Discusses crime by women in Israel.

B.0636 Singh, Myriam (1993, August). *Colonial state, women victims and criminals: The Northwestern provinces of Oudh* (India), 1870-1910. Dissertation, Temple University. Study of women's experiences as victims and as criminals in the Northwestern provinces of colonial India.

B.0637 Skrapec, Candice (1994). The female serial killer: An evolving criminality. In H. Birch (Ed.), *Moving targets: Women, murder, and representation* (pp. 241-268). Berkeley, CA: University of California Press. Looks at the case of Aileen Wuornos.

B.0638 Smith, David (1995). *Beyond all reason: My life with Susan Smith.* New York, NY: Kensington Books. Case of Susan Smith convicted of murdering her two children by drowning, from the point of view of her former husband.

B.0639 Smith, George (1988-1989). Fetal abuse: Culpable behavior by pregnant women or parental immunity? *Journal of Law and Health, 3*, 223-235. Discusses legal sanctions for drug abusing pregnant women.

B.0640 Smith, P. (1989, July 7). Perfect murderers. *New Statesman and Society, 2*(57), 14-16. Interviews with 18 individuals, including 4 women, who committed murder.

B.0641 Smith, Ronald, et al. (1988). Social cognitions about adult male victims of female sexual assault. *Journal of Sex Research, 24,* 101-112. Compares male and female victims in testing the hypotheses concerning social cognitions that are assumed to underlie male rape.

B.0642 Smitten, Richard (1990). *The Godmother.* New York, NY: Pocket Books. Story of Griselda Blanco, a Colombian criminal.

B.0643 Sommers, Ira, et al. (1994, April-June). Getting out of the life: Crime desistance by female street offenders. *Deviant Behavior, 15*(2), 125-149. Examines methods used by 30 women with histories of criminal involvement to change their lives.

B.0644 Sommers, Ira, & Baskin, Deborah (1993, May). The situational context of violent female offending. *Journal of Research in Crime and Delinquency, 30*(2), 136-162. Examines motive, victim precipitation, victim-offender relationship and precipitating circumstances.

B.0645 Song, Lin, et al. (1993). *Female sex offenders in Washington State.* Olympia, Washington: Washington State Institute for Public Policy. Reviews female sex offenders in general and convicted female sex offenders in Washington state, in particular.

B.0646 Soothill, K. L., & Pope, P. J. (1973). Arson: A twenty-year cohort study. *Medicine, Science and the Law, 13*(2), 127-138. Women included in the study.

B.0647 Southern California Law Review (1991, May). The efficacy and constitutionality of criminal punishment for maternal substance abuse. *Southern California Law Review, 64*, 1103-1141. Discusses legal sanctions for addicted pregnant women.

B.0648 Southern California Law Review (1987, May). Maternal substance abuse: The need to provide legal protection for the fetus. *Southern California Law Review, 60,* 1209-1238. Discusses legal sanctions for pregnant drug abusers.

B.0649 Sparrow, Gerald (1970). *Women who murder.* New York, NY: Abelard-Schuman. Discusses women who kill.

B.0650 Spelman, Elizabeth, & Minow, Martha (1992, Summer). Outlaw women: An essay on Thelma & Louise. *New England Law Review, 26,* 1281-1296. Discusses the concept of outlaw women.

B.0651 Spiering, Frank (1984). *Lizzie.* New York, NY: Random House. Case of Lizzie Borden.

B.0652 Sprintz, Heather (1993, Summer). The criminalization of perinatal AIDS transmission. *Health Matrix, 3,* 495-537. Discusses AIDS transmission in pregnancy.

B.0653 Stanford, Rosemary, et al. (1982, Summer). A study of the female forger. *Journal of Offender Counseling, Serivices and Rehabilitation, 6*(4), 71-81. Data collected from 32 females involved in forgery and passing bad checks on family background and attitudes toward criminality.

B.0654 Stark, E. (1990). Rethinking homicide: Violence, race, and the politics of gender. *International Journal of Health Services, 20*(1), 3-26. Examines family dynamics, highlighting the intense social engagement aspects of battering in intersexual and child homicides.

B.0655 Steele, B. F. (1978). Psychology of infanticide resulting from maltreatment. In M. Kohl (Ed.), *Infanticide and the value of life.* Buffalo, NY: Prometheus. Discusses infanticide.

B.0656 Steffensmeier, Darrell (1987, June). The invention of the "new" senior citizen criminal: An analysis of crime trends of elderly males and elderly females, 1964-1984. *Research on Aging, 9*(2), 281-311. Examines claims of rising levels of larceny-theft and DUI by the elderly.

B.0657 Steffensmeier, Darrell (1982). Trends in female crime: It's still a man's world. In B. Price & N. Sokoloff (Eds.), *The criminal justice system and women.* New York, NY: Clark Boardman Co. Discusses trends and patterns in crimes committed by women.

B.0658 Steffensmeier, Darrell (1981). Crime and the contemporary women: An analysis of changing levels of female property crime, 1960-1975. In L. Bowker (Ed.), *Women and crime in America* (pp. 35-39). New York, NY: MacMillan. Discusses changes in female crimes.

B.0659 Steffensmeier, Darrell, et al. (1979). Trends in female violence, 1960-1977. *Sociological Focus, 12*(3), 217-228. Discusses trends of violence perpetrated by women., 1960-1977.

B.0660 Steffensmeier, Darrell (1978a, December). Crime and the contemporary women: An analysis of changing levels of female property crime, 1960-1975. *Social Forces, 57*(2), 566-584. Data collected from Uniform Crime Reports examines female property crime between 1960-1978.

B.0661 Steffensmeier, Darrell (1978b, Spring). Changing patterns of female crime in rural America, 1962-1975. *Rural Sociology, 43*(1), 87-102. Examines data concerning increased violence and property crime in rural female offenders as compared to increased larceny for urban women.

B.0662 Steffensmeier, Darrell, et al. (1977, September). Violence and the contemporary woman: An analysis of changing levels of female violence, 1960-1975. Paper presented at the 72nd Annual Meeting of the American Sociological Association, Chicago, IL, 1977. Examines violent crimes committed by women and changes since 1960.

B.0663 Steinmetz, S. K., & Lucca, J. S. (1988). Husband battering. In V. Van Hasselt, et al. (Eds.), *Handbook of family violence* (pp. 233-246). New York, NY: Plenum Press. Discusses husband battering as a significant underdocumented social problem.

B.0664 Stewart, Lynn (1993, August). Profile of female firesetters: Implications for treatment. *British Journal of Psychiatry, 163,* 248-256. Examines psychological and situational antecedents to firesetting from 28 female arsonists and 28 female controls incarcerated in Holloway Prison.

B.0665 Stout, Karen, & Brown, Patricia (1995, Summer). Legal and social differences between men and women who kill intimate partners. *Affilia: Journal of Women and Social Work, 10*(2), 194-205. Studies differences between men and women who were convicted of partner homicide.

B.0666 Stout, Karen (1991, Winter). Women who kill: Offenders or defenders? *Affilia: Journal of Women and Social Work, 6*(4), 8-22. Data collected from interviews with 18 women incarcerated in Missouri for killing their male partners.

B.0667 Stovall, Marcy (1993, Summer). Looking for a solution: In re Valerie D. [613 A.2d 748 (Conn. 1992)] and state intervention in prenatal drug abuse. *Connecticut Law Review, 25*, 1265-1300. Discusses legal sanctions for pregnant addicted women.

B.0668 Sullenger, T. E. (1937, January-February). Female criminality in Omaha. *Journal of Criminal Law and Crimonology, 27*, 706-711. Discusses incidence of crime committed by women in Omaha, NE.

B.0669 Sun, Xingzhong (1993, July-August). A survey of 217 women murderers. *Chinese Education and Society, 26*, 7-13. Discusses women who kill.

B.0670 Sutker, Patricia, et al. (1978, October). Female criminal violence and differential MMPI characteristics. *Journal of Consulting and Clinical Psychology, 46*(5), 1141-1143. Data collected on MMPI and profiles of 22 female murderers and 40 female nonviolent offenders.

B.0671 Suval, E. M., & Brisson, R. C. (1974). Neither beauty nor beast: Female criminal homicide offenders. *International Journal of Criminology and Penology, 2*, 23-34. Discusses women who kill.

B.0672 Swenson, Victoria, & Crabbe, Cheryl (1994). Pregnant substance abusers: A problem that won't go away. *St. Mary's Law Journal, 25*, 623-673. Discusses legal sanctions against pregnant drug abusers.

B.0673 Tahourdin, Betty (1977b). Women and violence throughout history. *International Journal of Offender Therapy and Comparative Criminology, 21*(3), 234-236. Historical overview of women who kill.

B.0674 Tamura, Masayuki (1983, December). Changes in the patterns of criminal homicide for recent three decades. *Reports of National Research Institute of Police Sciences, 24*(2), 149-161. Includes statistics for females involved in murder and infanticide.

B.0675 Tariz, Anila (1993, December). Marital maladjustment and the crime of murder among Pakistani female criminals. *International Journal of Psychology, 28*(6), 809-819. Data from 70 Pakistani female convicts (aged 15-51 yrs) on variables indicating marital maladjustment.

B.0676 Temkin, Jennifer (1986, November). Prenatal injury, homicide and the Draft Criminal Code. *The Cambridge Law Journal, 45*, 414-429. Discusses legal sanctions for pregnant women abusers.

B.0677 Tennent, T. G., et al. (1971, November). Female arsonists. *British Journal of Psychiatry, 119*(522), 497-502. Discusses arson committed by women.

B.0678 Thompson, Tommy (1990). Feeblemindedness, criminal behavior, and women: A turn of the century case study. *Palimpsest, 71*(3), 132-145. Case of Bettie Libbecke, an Iowa woman whose purported mental instability and documented criminal behavior led to her incarceration.

B.0679 Totman, Jane (1978). *The murderess: A psychosocial study of criminal homicide.* Palo Alto, CA: R. & E. Research Associates. Historical overview of women and murder.

B.0680 Totman, Jane (1971). The murderess. *Police, 15*(6), 16-22. Discussion of women who kill.

B.0681 Townes, B. D., et al. (1981). Criminal involvement of female offenders: Psychological characteristics among four groups. *Criminology, 18,* 471-480. Data collected from 271 female offenders. Identified addicts, prostitutes, addicts-prostitutes, and non-addicts-non-prostitutes.

B.0682 Trent, B. (1988, April). Why do women commit arson? *Canadian Medical Association Journal, 138*(8), 745-747. Discusses why women commit arson.

B.0683 Trilling, Diana (1981). *Mrs. Harris, the death of the Scarsdale diet doctor.* New York, NY: Harcourt, Brace and Jovanovich. Case of Jean Harris.

B.0684 Trumble, A. (1882). *The female sharpers of New York: Their haunts and habits, their wiles and victims.* New York, NY: Fox. Early discussion of crimes by women in New York City.

B.0685 Tucker, L. S., & Cornwall, T. P. (1977, October). Mother-son folie a deux: A case of attempted patricide. *American Journal of Psychiatry, 134*(10), 1146-1147. Case of a mother and 10-year-old son who plotted and attempted the murder, by arson, of the husband/father.

B.0686 Tuteur, W., & Glotzer, J. (1966). Further observations on murdering mothers. *Journal of Forensic Science, 11,* 373-383. Discusses women who murder their children.

B.0687 Tuteur, W., & Glotzer, J. (1959). Murdering mothers. *American Journal of Psychiatry, 116,* 447-452. Early studies on women who murder their children.

B.0688 Uhnak, Dorothy (1977). *The investigation.* New York, NY: Simon & Schuster. Fictionalized version of the Alice Crimmins case.

B.0689 University of Illinois Law Review (1991). The prosecution of maternal fetal abuse: Is this the answer? *University of Illinois Law Review,* 533-580. Discusses legal sanctions for pregnant drug abusers.

B.0690 University of Pennsylvania Law Review (1990, December). Prosecution of mothers of drug-exposed babies: Constitutional and criminal theory. *University of Pennsylvania Law Review, 139,* 505-539. Discusses legal sanctions of pregnant drug abusers.

B.0691 Vandor, Maria, et al. (1991). Women and illegal drugs. In P. Roth (Ed.), *Alcohol and drugs are women's issues, Vol 1, A review of the issues* (pp. 155-160). Metuchen, NJ: Women's Action Alliance & The Scarecrow Press. Discusses drug abuse by women.

B.0692 Van Waters, Miriam (1951, May). Rehabilitation of women sex offenders. *Journal of Social Hygiene, 37*(5), 218-222. Early discussion on rehabilitating prostitutes.

B.0693 Van Waters, Miriam (1944, March-April). The woman offender of today: Aims of classification. *Prison World, 6*(2), 8, 26. Discusses classification of the female offender by the courts.

B.0694 Vega, M., et al. (1977). Female felon. In H. Allen & N. Beran (Eds.), *Reform in Corrections.* New York, NY: Praeger. Describes the nature of female criminality and trends in female crime. Data collected from the Florida prison system.

B.0695 Verhoeven, Deb (1994). Biting the hand that breeds: The trials of Tracey Wigginton. In H. Birch (Ed.), *Moving targets: Women, murder, and representation* (pp. 95-126). Case of Tracey Wigginton who became infamous because she was accused of, and believed to be, a vampire.

B.0696 Versele, S. C. (1969). Study of female shoplifters in a department store. *International Journal of Police, 24,* 66-70. Discussion of female shoplifters.

B.0697 Victor, Sarah (1887). *The life story of Sarah M. Victor, for sixty years.* Cleveland, OH: Williams. Convicted of murdering her brother. Story told by herself.

B.0698 Visher, J. S. (1960, Winter). Successful therapy in a case of infanticide. *Archives of Criminal Psychodynamics, 4*(1), 76-90. Discussion of therapy for women who commit infanticide.

B.0699 Wahl, C. W. (1960, August). The psychodynamics of consummated maternal incest. *Archives of General Psychiatry,* 188-193. Early studies on maternal incest.

B.0700 Walker, Lenore (1989). *Terrifying love: Why battered women kill and how society responds.* New York, NY: Harper & Row. Stories of battered women who killed abusive husbands with whom the author worked to secure justice in the courts.

B.0701 Walker, Lenore (1984, October). Battered women, psychology, and public policy. *American Psychologist, 39,* 1178-1182. Discussion of battered women who kill and public policy.

B.0702 Wallace, Marjorie (1986). *The silent twins.* London: Chatto & Windus. Discusses black female twins born in England who never spoke to anyone but each other and eventually turned to crime. Both were writers and were incarcerated in Broadmoor.

B.0703 Wallace, W. S. (1931). *Murders and mysteries: A Canadian series.* Toronto, Canada: MacMillan. Examines the case of Clara Ford.

B.0704 Ward, David, & Ward, Renne (1980). Crimes of violence by women. In S. Datesman & F. Scarpitti (Eds.), *Women, crime and justice* (pp. 171-191). New York, NY: Oxford University Press. Discusses violent crime by women.

B.0705 Ward, David, et al. (1979). Crimes of violence by women. In F. Adler & R. Simon (Eds.), *The criminology of deviant women* (pp. 114-138). Boston, MA: Houghton Mifflin. Discusses violent crimes women commit.

B.0706 Ward, David (1969). Crimes of violence by women. In *Crimes of violence: A staff report submitted to the National Commission on the Causes and Prevention of Violence* (pp. 843-907). Washington, DC: U.S. Government Printing Office. Statistical summary of crimes committed by women.

B.0707 Ward Jouve, Nicole (1994). An eye for an eye: The case of the Papin sisters. In H. Birch (Ed.), *Moving targets: Women, murder, and representation* (pp. 7-31). Berkeley, CA: University of California Press. Case of the Papin sisters, two French maids who committed a double murder.

B.0708 Warren, Marguerite, & Rosenbaum, Jill (1986, December). Criminal careers of female offenders. *Criminal Justice and Behavior, 13*(4), 391-418. Examines criminal careers of 159 females committed to the California Youth Authority during the 1960's.

B.0709 Warren, Marguerite (1979). The female offender. In H. Toch (Ed.), *Psychology of crime and criminal justice* (pp. 444-469). Prospect Heights, IL: Waveland Press. Discusses various aspects of offending by women.

B.0710 Washington Law Review (1990, April). Gestational substance abuse: A call for a thoughtful legislative response. *Washington Law Review, 65,* 377-396. Discusses legal sanctions for pregnant substance abusers.

B.0711 Wayne Law Review (1991, Summer). The use of deadly force by women against rape in Michigan: Justifiable homicide? *Wayne Law Review, 37,* 1969-1987. Discusses women who kill in self defense.

B.0712 Wayne Law Review (1990, Spring). Fetus vs. mother: Criminal liability for maternal substance abuse during pregnancy. *Wayne Law Review, 36,* 1285-1318. Discusses legal sanctions against women substance abusers.

B.0713 Weidensall, Clara (1916). *The mentality of the criminal woman: A comparative study of the criminal woman, the working girl, and the efficient working woman in a series of physical tests.* Baltimore, MD: Warwick & York. Early investigation comparing women at the Bedford Hills Reformatory with responses of women at the Bureau of Vocational Guidance in Cincinnati, Ohio.

B.0714 Weinberg, K. (1973, March). Female delinquency in Ghana, West Africa: A comparative analysis. *International Review of Modern Sociology, 3*(1), 65-73. Discusses crimes committed by women in Ghana, West Africa.

B.0715 Weinberg, L., & Eubanks, W. (1987). Italian women terrorists. *Terrorism: An International Journal, 9*(3), 241-262. Discusses the role of women in Italian terrorist groups. Based on biographical information of 451 women who were active in terrorist organizations.

B.0716 Weisheit, Ralph (1988, October). When mothers kill their children. *Social Science Journal, 23*(4), 439-448. Looks at 460 female homicide offenders admitted to a state prison form 1940-1983. Thirty-nine were institutionalized for killing their children.

B.0717 Weisheit, Ralph (1984). Female homicide offenders: Trends over time in an institutionalized population. *Justice Quarterly, 1*(4), 471-489. Discusses trends in homicides by women.

B.0718 Weissman, J. C., & File, Karen (1976). Criminal behavior patterns of female addicts: A comparison of findings in two cities. *International Journal of Drug Issues, 11*(6), 1063-1077. Study of crimes committed by female addicts.

B.0719 Weitzel, Susan, & Blount, William (1982, Summer). Incarcerated female felons and substance abuse. *Journal of Drug Issues, 12*(3), 259-273. Data from a proportional random sample by offense and race from a woman's prison (N=176).

B.0720 Wellisch, Jean, et al. (1993, Winter). Numbers and characteristics of drug-using women in the criminal justice system. *Journal of Drug Issues, 23*(1), 7-30. Surveys of 2,094 female arrestees administered by the Drug Use Forecasting Program operating nationwide in 24 sites.

B.0721 Wellman, M. W. (1954). *Dead and gone: Classic crimes of North Carolina.* Chapel Hill, NC: University of North Carolina Press. Reviews ten murders that occurred in North Carolina between 1808 and 1914 including two committed by women, Ann Simpson and Ida Warren.

B.0722 West Virginia Law Review (1991, Summer). Maternal drug use during pregnancy as child neglect or abuse. *West Virginia Law Review, 93,* 1083-1100. Discusses legal sanctions for pregnant women who abuse drugs.

B.0723 White, Katherine (1990, Fall). Precedent to process: The impending crisis of fetal rights. *Women and Language, 13,* 47-49. Discusses legal sanctions against pregnant women who abuse drugs.

B.0724 Wilbanks, William (1983). The female homicide offender in Dade County, Florida. *Criminal Justice Review, 8*(2), 9-14. Examines a population of female offenders from one jurisdiction to test a claim of more severe treatment of female offenders.

B.0725 Wilbanks, William (1983, September-October). Female homicide offenders in the U.S. *International Journal of Women's Studies, 6*(4), 302-310. Examines patterns of homicide offenses committed by women in the U.S. in 1980.

B.0726 Wilbanks, William (1982). Murdered women and women who murder: A critique of the literature. In N. Rafter-Hahn & E. Stanko (Eds.), *Judge, lawyer, victim, thief* (pp. 151-180). Boston, MA: Northeastern University Press. Historical patterns in homicides committed by women.

B.0727 Wilczynski, Ania, & Morris, Allison (1993, January). Parents who kill their children. *The Criminal Law Review,* 31-36. Discusses patterns of murder by parents.

B.0728 Wilczynski, Ania (1991). Images of women who kill their infants: The mad and the bad. *Women and Criminal Justice, 2*(2), 71-88. Examines two predominant images of infanticidal women, the mad and the bad and gives examples of each.

B.0729 Wilkins, A. J. (1985, February). Attempted infanticide. *British Journal of Psychiatry, 146,* 206-208. Discussion of infanticide and attempted infanticide.

B.0730 Williams, Joyce, et al. (1980). *Lizzie Borden: A case book of family and crime in the 1890's.* Bloomington, IN: T.I.S. Publications. Case of Lizzie Borden.

B.0731 Williamson, W. H. (1930). *Annals of crime: Some extraordinary women.* London: Routledge. Early discussion of crimes by women.

B.0732 Willis, Andrew (1986, July). Criminal women. *Journal of Social Policy, 15,* 405-407. Discusses crimes committed by women.

B.0733 Wilson, C., & Pitman, Patricia (1962). *Encyclopedia of murder.* New York, NY: G. P. Putman. Includes story of Ada LeBoeuf and her lover who were hanged for the murder of Ada's husband on February 1, 1929.

B.0734 Wilson, Margo, & Daly, Martin (1993, Spring). Spousal homicide risk and estrangement. *Violence and Victims, 8*(6), 13-16. Reports on frequencies of homicide victimization of wives and of husbands while cohabitating and when estranged.

B.0735 Wilson, Margo, & Daly, Martin (1992, May). Who kills whom in spouse killings: On the exception of sex ratio of spousal homicides in the United States. *Criminology, 30*(2), 189-215. Investigates the larger sex ratio of killing in the U.S. vs. other Western countries.

B.0736 Wilson, Nanci (1993). Gender interaction in criminal homicide. A. V. Wilson (Ed.), *Homicide: The victim/offender connection.* Cincinnati, OH: Anderson Publishing Co. Discusses gender variations in criminal homicide.

B.0737 Wilson, Stephen (1988, October). Infanticide, child abandonment, and female honour in nineteenth-century Corsica. *Comparative Studies in Society and History, 30,* 762-783. Historical account of infanticide.

B.0738 Windle, M., & Miller, B. A. (1989). Alcoholism and depressive symptomatology among convicted DWI men and women. *Journal of Studies on Alcohol, 50*(5), 406-413. Data collected from 461 convicted DWI offenders for presence of depressive symptomatology.

B.0739 Winifred, Mary (1993, June). Women sex offenders: Treatment and dynamics. *Corrections Today, 55*(3), 112. Discusses treatment of women sex offenders.

B.0740 Winnik, H. (1963). The psychopathology of infanticide: A case study. *Israel Annals of Psychiatry and Related Disciplines, 1*(2), 293-309. Discusses the case of a woman who committed a double infanticide.

B.0741 Winnik, H., & Horovitz, M. (1961-1962). The problem with infanticide. *The British Journal of Criminology, 2*, 40-52. Discusses infanticide.

B.0742 Winter, Barry (1993). *Female offenders and their victims.* Thesis, Wichita State University. Discusses the victims of female crime.

B.0743 Wolfgang, Marvin (1957). Victim precipitated criminal homicide. *Journal of Criminal Law, Criminology and Police Science, 48*, 1-11. Early data regarding women who kill abusive husbands.

B.0744 Wolfgang, Marvin (1956). Husband-wife homicides. *Journal of Social Therapy, 2*(4), 263-271. Analysis of 588 criminal homicides in Philadelphia from Jan. 1, 1948 to Dec. 3, 1952, 100 of these were husband-wife homicides.

B.0745 Woo, Deborah (1989, November). The people vs. Fumiko Kimura: But which people? *International Journal of the Sociology of Law, 17*(4), 403-428. Case of a Japanese woman who tried to commit "oyako-shinjii" or "parent-child suicide."

B.0746 Wood, Briar (1994). The trials of motherhood: The case of Azaria and Lindy Chamberlain. In H. Birch (Ed.), *Moving targets: Women, murder, and representation* (pp. 62-94). Berkeley, CA: University of California Press. Case of Lindy Chamberlain.

B.0747 Woodside, M. (1961, January). Women drinkers admitted to Holloway prison during February, 1960: A pilot survey. *British Journal of Criminology, 1*, 221-235. Discusses alcoholism in incarcerated women.

B.0748 Worth, D. (1991). Women and polydrug abuse. In P. Roth (Ed.), *Alcohol and drugs are women's issues* (pp. 1-9). Metuchen, NJ: Women's Action Alliance & The Scarecrow Press. Discusses women who abuse multiple drugs.

B.0749 Wright, Julie (1991). *The angel of death.* Sydney, Australia: Allen & Unwin. Story of Australia's most wanted female criminal in her own words.

B.0750 Wulffen, Erich (1934). *Woman as sexual criminal.* New York, NY: American Ethnological Press. Early study on prostitution.

B.0751 Yadav, R. A. (1976, September). Women who kill: An exploratory study of the institutionalized homicide female offender. *Indian Journal of Clinical Psychology, 3*(2), 121-123. Data collected from 50 female homicide offenders ranging from 25-50 years.

B.0752 Yale Law & Policy Review (1991). Prosecuting maternal substance abusers: An unjustified and ineffective policy. *Yale Law & Policy Review, 9*, 130-160. Discusses sanctions for pregnant drug abusers.

B.0753 Young, Vernetta (1981, November). Patterns of female criminality. *Dissertation Abstracts International, 42*(5), 2309. Examines the phenomenon of female criminality as it is perceived and reported by victims.

B.0754 Young, Vernetta (1975). Victims of female offenders. In W. H. Parsonage (Ed.), *Perspectives on victimology* (pp. 73-87). Beverly Hills, CA: Sage. Research on the victims of female offenders.

B.0755 Yu, Jiang, et al. (1992, June). DWI/DWAI offenders and recidivism by gender in the eighties: A changing trend? *International Journal of the Addictions, 27*(6), 637-647. Reviewed files of New York drivers convicted of driving while intoxicated , 1978-1988.

B.0756 Zahn, Margaret, & Ball, J. C. (1974). Patterns and causes of drug addiction among Puerto Rican females. *Addictive Diseases: An International Journal, 1*(2), 203-213. Examines drug addiction patterns in 12 addicted and formerly addicted Puerto Rican females living in Puerto Rico.

B.0757 Zietz, Dorothy (1981). *Women who embezzle or defraud: A study of convicted felons.* New York, NY: Praeger. Compared typologies of 100 women incarcerated at the California Institution for women for embezzlement or fraud with male offenders who had committed crimes of fraud.

B.0758 Zimring, F., et al. (1983). Intimate violence: A study of intersexual homicide in Chicago. *University of Chicago Law Review, 50*, 910-930. Discusses spousal homicide.

3

ARREST, PROSECUTION, SENTENCING

Alternative Sentencing; Battered Woman's Syndrome; Death Penalty; Race and Gender

C.0001 Abell, Jennie (1992, Spring). Women, violence, and the criminal law: "It's the fundamentals of being a lawyer that are at stake here." *Queen's Law Journal, 17,* 147-143. Discusses woman's place in the courts and criminal law.

C.0002 Adams, K. (1986, August). Gender differences in court processing: A methodological comment. *Journal of Research in Crime and Delinquency, 23*(3), 305-317. Looks at gender differences in the court processing of male and female offenders.

C.0003 Aderibigbe, Y., et al. (1996, March). Reflections on the sociodemographic and medicolegal profiles of female criminal defendants. *International Journal of Offender Therapy and Comparative Criminology, 40*(1). Medical and economic profiles of female defendants.

C.0004 Akron Law Review (1989, Summer). State v. Steward [763 P.2d 572 (Kan)]: Self-defense and battered women: Reasonable perception of danger or license to kill. *Akron Law Review, 23,* 89-104. Discusses use of the battered woman's syndrome for women who kill their abusers.

C.0005 Alabama Law Review (1975). A study of differential treatment accorded female defendants in Alabama criminal courts. *Alabama Law Review, 27,* 676-746. Discusses discriminatory practices in Alabama courts.

C.0006 Allen, Hilary (1989). Fines for women: Paradoxes and paradigms. In P. Carlen & D. Cook (Eds.), *Paying for crime.* London: Milton Keynes: Open University Press. Discusses the practice of fining women in English courts.

C.0007 Allen, Hilary (1987a). *Justice unbalanced: Gender, psychiatry, and judicial decisions.* Philadelphia, PA: Open University Press. Examines reasoning behind medical and judicial decisions to deal with women on trial medically rather than through correctional means.

C.0008 Allen, Hilary (1987b). Rendering them harmless: The professional portrayal of women charged with serious violent crimes. In P. Carlen & A. Worrall (Eds.), *Gender, crime and justice* (pp. 81-94). Discusses how female offenders and their crimes are portrayed in the courtroom.

C.0009 Allen, Hilary (1984). At the mercy of her hormones: Premenstrual tension and the law. *Male/Female, 9,* 19-44. Cases of two English women guilty of homicide who used extreme premenstrual tension as a defense.

C.0010 Allstetter, Billy (1991, May). Compulsory contraception. *American Health, 10*(4), 32-34. Case of Darlene Johnson and the ACLU challenging a ruling that Johnson have the Norplant contraceptive implanted until she stopped mistreating her children.

C.0011 Amato, D. A. (1979). Admissibility of evidence of a homicide victim's character where the defendant pleads self-defense. *Suffolk University Law Review, 13,* 1135-1149. Discusses cases of battered women who plead self-defense.

C.0012 American Bar Association (1992). *Defending battered women in criminal cases.* Chicago: American Bar Association. Discusses the use of the battered woman's defense.

C.0013 American Criminal Law Review. (1973, Winter). Women and criminal law: A symposium. *The American Criminal Law Review, 11*(2). Looks at the treatment of women in criminal law.

C.0014 American Society of Criminology (1981). *Comparing female and male offenders.* Newbury Park, CA: Sage Publications. Compares female offenders with male offenders in crime and delinquent behavior, processing in the system, and explanations for deviant behavior.

C.0015 Andersen, E. (1992). Constitutional dimensions of the battered woman syndrome. *Ohio State Law Journal, 53*(9), 363-411. Covers the constitutionality of the battered woman's defense.

C.0016 Anderson, Etta (1976). The chivalrous treatment of the female offender in the arms of the criminal justice system: A review of the literature. *Social Problems, 23*(3), 350-357. Discusses chivalry in the criminal justice system.

C.0017 Anderson, J. (1990, March). Continuity in crime: Sex and age differences. *Journal of Quantitative Criminology, 6*(1), 85-100. Discusses sex and age as variables in criminal behavior.

C.0018 Angell, S. (1979, September). Death row women. *Prison Law Monitor, 2,* 101. Discusses women on death row .

C.0019 Apodaca, L., & Fink, L. (1987). Pre-menstrual syndrome in the courts. In S. Johann & F. Osanka (Eds.), *Representing battered women who kill* (pp. 113-127). Springfield, IL: Charles C. Thomas Publishers. Discusses the use of premenstrual syndrome as a defense for murder.

C.0020 Archer, Dane, & McDaniel, Patricia Anne (1989). *Violence and gender: Differences and similarities across societies.* Paper presented at the American Sociological Association 84th Annual Meeting, August 9-13, San Francisco, CA. Analysis of male and female differences in aggression and violence.

C.0021 Arditi, R., et al. (1973a). The sexual segregation of American prisons. *Yale Law Journal, 82,* 1229-1273. Discusses reasons for separating males and females in the prison system.

C.0022 Arditi, R., & Goldberg, F. (1973b, September). Sexual segregation of American prisons. *Mental Health Digest, 5*(9), 18-26. Discusses reasons for the separation of males and females in prison.

C.0023 Arizona Law Review (1990). Limitations on expert testimony on the battered woman syndrome in homicide cases. *Arizona Law Review, 32,* 665-689. Discusses the limitations of expert testimony in trials of battered women who kill.

C.0024 Armstrong, Gail (1977). Females under the law - protected but unequal. *Crime and Delinquency, 23*(2), 109-120. Examines the double standard of morality in statutes and sentencing practices.

C.0025 Aron, C. (1993, Fall). In defense of battered women: Is justice blind? *Human Rights (ABA). 20*(4), 14-17. Discusses the use of the battered woman's defense.

C.0026 Arthur, O. (1855). *The three sisters: The life, confession, and execution of Amy, Elizabeth, and Cynthia Halzingler.* New York, NY: Orton. Discusses the execution of three sisters.

C.0027 Arthur, Stacey (1992, October). The Norplant prescription: Birth control, woman control, or crime control? *UCLA Law Review, 40,* 1-101. Discusses the use of Norplant as a punitive measure in the courts.

C.0028 Austin, J. B., et al. (1992). *Female offenders in the community: An analysis of innovative strategies and programs.* Washington, DC: U.S. Department of Justice. Looks at community alternatives to incarceration for female offenders.

C.0029 Avery, C. K. (1952). *Official court record of the trial, conviction and execution of Frances Silvers, first woman hanged in North Carolina.* Morgantown, NC. Historical review of the case of Frances Silvers.

C.0030 Aylward, Anna, & Thomas (1984, June). Quiescence in women's prison litigation: Some exploratory issues. *Justice Quarterly, 1*(2), 253-276. Considers litigation involving incarcerated women.

C.0031 Backhouse, Constance (1991). *Petticoats and prejudice: Women and law in 19th century Canada.* Toronto: Women's Press. Historical overview of women and the law in Canada.

C.0032 Backhouse, Constance (1984, Fall). Desperate women and compassionate courts: Infanticide in nineteenth-century Canada. *University of Toronto Law Journal, 34,* 447-478. Looks at court dispositions regarding women found guilty of infanticide.

C.0033 Bacon, Wendy, & Landsdowne, Robyn (1982). Women who kill husbands: The battered wife on trial. In C. O'Donnell & J. Craney (Eds.), *Family violence in Australia* (pp. 67-94). Sydney: Longman Cheshire Ltd. Considers the battered woman's syndrome.

C.0034 Baer, Judith (1991). Nasty law or nice ladies? Jurisprudence, feminism, and gender difference. *Women and Politics, 11*(1), 1-31. Examines premises of feminist jurisprudence and reviews some basic works in the field.

C.0035 Baker, L. A., et al. (1989). Sex differences in property crime in a Danish adoption cohort. *Behavior Genetics, 19*(3), 355-370. Looks at male and female property crimes in Denmark.

C.0036 Baker, Scott (1994, Spring). Deaf justice? Battered women unjustly imprisoned prior to the enactment of Evidence Code Section 1107. *Golden Gate University Law Review, 24,* 99-130. Looks at the situation of battered women who were imprisoned before the Evidence Code.

C.0037 Baldwin, Janice (1983, Spring-Summer). The effects of women's liberation and socialization on delinquency and crime. *Humboldt Journal of Social Relations: Special Issue: The study of women: New challenges, new directions, 10*(2), 90-111. Examines how early socialization affects male and female criminals.

C.0038 Bandalli, Susan (1994, Fall). Women, spousal homicide and the doctrine of provocation in English criminal law. *Masters Abstracts International, 32*(2), 845. Discusses the cases of three battered women who killed their husbands and were convicted of murder.

C.0039 Barfield, Velma (1985). *Woman on death row.* Nashville, TN: Oliver-Nelson Books. Autobiography of Velma Barfield, convicted of murder and executed in North Carolina in 1984 for poisoning four people including her mother and fiancee.

C.0040 Barnett, E. (1969). *The woman offender: Sentence, treatment, resettlement.* Sydney, Australia, Australian Crime Prevention. Presents the history of the female offender in Australia.

C.0041 Barnhorst, S. (1978). Female delinquency and the role of women. *Canadian Journal of Family Law, 1*(2), 254-273. Addresses judicial bias in Canadian Criminal Codes in terms of the stereotypical roles of women in society.

C.0042 Baskin, Deborah, & Sommers, Ira (1990). The gender question in research on female criminality. *Social Justice, 17*(2), 148-156. Discusses the issue of gender in criminological research.

C.0043 Baskin, Deborah, et al. (1989, September). Role incongruence and gender variation in the provision of prison mental health services. *Journal of Health and Social Behavior, 30*(3), 305-314. Examines the disproportionate placement of female inmates in mental health facilities.

C.0044 Belchamber, Janet (1988). *Women, poverty, and crime: Sentencing options and their implications: A report.* Norwood, S. Australia: Norwood Community Legal Services. A report of a seminar on women, poverty, and crime at the Universtiy of Adelaide, February 3, 1988.

C.0045 Benedek, Elissa (1985). Premenstrual syndrome: A new defense. In J. Gold (Ed.), *The psychiatric implications of menstruation.* Washington, DC: American Psychiatric Press. Considers the use of premenstrual syndrome as a defense for women accused of a crime.

C.0046 Benn, Melissa (1993). Body talk: The sexual politics of PMT. In H. Birch (Ed.), *Moving targets: Women, murder and representation* (pp. 152-171). Berkeley, CA: University of California Press. Discussion of PMS as a defense for murder. Gives case examples.

C.0047 Benn, Melissa (1990). Every month a crisis. *New Statesman & Society, 3*(130), 20-22. Discusses the use of PMS as a defense for women who commit serious crimes.

C.0048 Benson, Margaret (1973). *Fines imposed on women in the provincial courts, Toronto.* Toronto, Ontario: Elizabeth Fry Society. Looks at court dealings with women in Canadian provinces.

C.0049 Benson, Margaret (1962). *From arrest to trial for female offenders appearing in the former magistrates courts in Toronto from September 1961 to February 1962.* Examines the nature of female offenders' crimes, the criminal process, and service patterns in Toronto.

C.0050 Berkman, A. S. (1980, November). The state of Michigan versus a battered wife: A case study. *Bulletin of the Menninger Clinic, 44*(6), 603-616. Presents the case of a woman who killed her spouse and used the battered woman's syndrome as a defense.

C.0051 Bernat, Frances (1984, Fall-Winter). Gender disparity in the setting of bail: Prostitution in Buffalo, NY, 1977-1979. *Journal of Offender Counseling, Services, and Rehabilitation, 9*(1-2), 21-47. Pretrial release decisions of Buffalo Criminal Court from January 1977 to December, 1979 were examined for gender disparity.

C.0052 Bernstein, I., et al. (1979). Defendant's sex and criminal court decisions. In R. Alvarez & K. Lutterman (Eds.), *Discrimination in organizations.* San Francisco, CA: Josey-Bass. Discusses how gender influences court decisions.

C.0053 Bershad, L. (1985, March). Discriminatory treatment of the female offender in criminal justice. *Boston College Law Review, 26,* 389-483. Looks at ways in which women are discriminated against in the criminal justice system.

C.0054 Berzins, Lorraine, & Cooper, Sheelagh (1982, October). The political economy of correctional planning for women: The case of the bankrupt bureaucracy. *Canadian Journal of Criminology, 24*(2), 399-416. Reports on discrepancy between the facilities and services available to women inmates and those available to men in Canada.

C.0055 Bickle, G., & Peterson, R. (1991, August). The impact of gender-based family roles on criminal sentencing. *Social Problems, 38*(3), 372-394. Examined how and why family roles influence criminal justice decisions. Data collected from 124 female and 390 males convicted of forgery.

C.0056 Bigelow, Paige (1992). Guilty of survival: State v. Strieb [790 p.2d 98 (Kansas) 1990] and battered women who kill in Utah. *Utah Law Review,* 979-1019. Discusses court dispositions regarding battered women in Utah.

C.0057 Bilionis, Louis (1991, Summer). Moral appropriateness, capital punishment, and the Lockett [Lockett v. Ohio, 98 S. Ct. 2954] doctrine. *The Journal of Criminal Law & Criminology, 82,* 283-333. Discusses the case of Sandra Lockett who was given the death penalty.

C.0058 Binford, Jessie (1927, November). Police and women offenders. *Policewoman's International Bulletin, 3,* 2-3. Discusses attitudes of police officers when arresting women.

C.0059 Binkley-Jackson, Deborah, et al. (1991). African American women in prison. In B. Fletcher et al. (Eds.), *Women prisoners: A forgotten population* (pp. 65-73). Westport, CT: Praeger. Discusses racism and sexism in prisons and focuses on the number of African-American women incarcerated in Oklahoma.

C.0060 Bishop, Donna, & Frazier, C. (1984, Summer). The effects of gender on charge reduction. *The Sociological Quarterly, 25*(3), 385-396. Discusses how courts discriminate in considering offenses committed by women.

C.0061 Black, C. L. (1977). Death penalty now. *Tulane Law Review, 51,* 429-445. Case of Sandra Lockett of Ohio who refused a negotiated plea and was sentenced to death. The Lockett case is used to demonstrate the arbitrariness of the death penalty.

C.0062 Blackman, Julie, & Brickman, Ellen (1984, Fall). The impact of expert testimony on trials of battered women who kill their husbands. *Behavioral Science and the Law, 2*(4), 413-422. Discusses the use of expert testimony in battered women's murder trials.

C.0063 Blair, S. (1979). Making the legal system work for battered women. In D. Moore (Ed.), *Battered women.* Beverly Hills, CA: Sage Publications. Discusses the battered woman's defense in court.

C.0064 Blankenship, Estelle, & Hewitt, J. D. (1976, May). *The relationship of women to criminal law: The case of differential sentencing.* Paper presented at the 1976 Annual Meeting of the Northcentral Sociological Association: Louisville, Kentucky, May 1976. Examines differential sentencing on the basis of sex and other biases against women in the criminal justice system.

C.0065 Bluestone, Harvey, & McGahee, Carl (1962). Reaction to extreme stress: Impending death by execution. *The Journal of Psychiatry, 119,* pp. 393-396. A study of 18 men and 1 woman under the sentence of death in New York. Documents efforts to cope with the stresses of death row.

C.0066 Bochnak, Elizabeth (1981). *Women's self-defense cases: Theory and practice.* Charlottesville, VA: Michie Company. Discusses the use of self-defense for women who commit murder.

C.0067 Boland, Beth (1994, Spring). Battered women who act under duress. *New England Law Review, 28,* 603-635. Discusses what battered women do under duress, including murder.

C.0068 Bonnie, Richard, et al. (1980). The spousal homicide syndrome: Legal implications. *Bulletin of the American Academy of Psychiatry and Law, 8*(4), 432-444. Discusses use of the battered woman syndrome as a defense for murder.

C.0069 Boritch, Helen (1992, August). Gender and criminal court outcomes: An historical analysis. *Criminology, 10*(3), 293-325. Historical overview of how gender has influenced court decisions.

C.0070 Boritch, Helen, & Hagan, John (1990, November). A century of crime in Toronto: Gender, class, and patterns of social control: 1859-1955. *Criminology, 28*(4), 567-599. Looks at structures of social control and female arrest rates in Toronto from 1859-1955.

C.0071 Bowker, Lee (1981). Gender differences in prisoner subcultures. In L. Bowker (Ed.), *Women and crime in America* (pp. 409-419). New York, NY: Macmillan. Looks at nine important differences between subcultures in male and female correctional institutions.

C.0072 Bowman, Mary Jean (1939, May-June). Causes of arrest of women committed to the Massachusetts State Reformatory. *Journal of Criminal Law and Criminology, 30,* 77-82. Early look at why women were arrested and incarcerated in Massachussetts.

C.0073 Brahams, D. (1983). Pre-menstrual tension and criminal responsibility. *The Practitioner, CCXXVII,* 807-813. Looks at premenstrual syndrome as a criminal defense.

C.0074 Brennan, Pauline (1994, March). *A critical reveiw of research on female case processing.* Paper presented at the 1994 ACJS Annual Meeting, Chicago, IL. Reviews empirical literature on female case processing and identifies factors that predict sentencing disparity.

C.0075 Brennan, Sheila (1992, Winter). Popular images of American women in the 1950's and their impact on Ethel Rosenberg's trial and conviction. *Women's Rights Law Reporter, 14,* 43-63. Discusses what may have influenced court's decision in the trial of Ethel Rosenberg.

C.0076 Bresler, L., & Lewis, D. (1983, Autumn-Winter). Black and white women prisoners: Differences in family ties and their programmatic implications. *Prison Journal, 63*(2), 116-123. Discusses why black female inmates are more likely to have closer contact with children and other relatives than white female inmates.

C.0077 Bricker, Denise (1993, Winter). Fatal defense: An analysis of battered woman's syndrome expert testimony for gay men and lesbians who kill abusive partners. *Brooklyn Law Review, 58,* 1379-1437. Discusses battering and murder in homosexual relationships.

C.0078 Broad, Lewis (1952). *The innocence of Edith Thompson.* London: Hutchison. Edith Thompson was found guilty of murdering her husband and was sentenced to death and hung on January 9, 1923 at Holloway prison.

C.0079 Brockman, J., & Chunn, D. (1993). *Investigating gender bias: Law, courts, and the legal profesion.* Toronto, Canada: Thompson. Looks at gender discrimination in the courts in Canada.

C.0080 Brodsky, Annette (1979). Female offenders. *Counseling Psychologist, 8*(1), 43-44. Contrasts views of male and female offenders and discusses the lack of rehabilitation services for women.

C.0081 Brodsky, D. (1987). Educating juries: The battered woman defense in Canada. *Alberta Law Review, 25*(3), 461-476. Discusses the need to educate juries when the battered woman syndrome is used as a defense.

C.0082 Brophy, J., & Smart, Carolyn (1981). From disregard to disrepute: The position of women in family law. *Feminist Review, 9,* 12. Discusses where women stand according to the law.

C.0083 Brown, E., & Adler, D. (1989). *Public justice, private mercy: A governor's education on death row.* Death penalty decisions by Governor Brown, including the case of Elizabeth Duncan.

C.0084 Brown, Pamela (1990, Summer). Justifiable homicide: Battered women, self-defense and the law. *Affilia: Journal of Women and Social Work, 5*(2), 106-109. Discusses using the battered woman's syndrome as a defense in criminal court cases.

C.0085 Brown, W. (1963). *Women who died in the chair.* New York, NY: Collier. Stories of several women who were executed.

C.0086 Buda, M. A., & Burler, T. L. (1985). The battered wife syndrome: A backdoor assault on domestic violence *Social Action and the Law, 10*(3), 63-71. Factors considered in defining battered wife syndrome include a woman's psychological paralysis and a feeling of helplessness.

C.0087 Burke, A. (1982, Spring). Determinants of delinquency in female West Indian migrants. *The International Journal of Social Psychiatry, 28*(1), 28-34. Study of crime in Indian women.

C.0088 Burkhart, Kathryn (1973). Eva Dugan. In K. Burkhart (Ed.), *Women in prison* (pp. 273-275). New York, NY: Doubleday. Eva Dugan was the last person hanged in Arizona.

C.0089 Burns, Legerie (1980). Expert testimony relating to subject matter of battered women admissible on issue of self-defense. *Seton Hall Law Review, 11,* 255-264. Discusses the use of experts in criminal courts where battered woman's syndrome is the defense.

C.0090 Butler, Anne (1989, February). Still in chains: Black women in Western prisons, 1865-1910. *Western Historical Quarterly, 20*(1), 19-35. Historical overview of early incarceration of black women.

C.0091 Byrne, James, & Taxman, Faye (1994, April-June). Crime control policy and community corrections practice: Assessing the impact of gender, race, and class. *Evaluation and Program Planning, 17*(2), 227-233. Reviews bias and disparity in the criminal justice system with regard to race, gender, and class.

C.0092 Caldwell, Paulette (1991, April). A hair piece: Perspectives on the intersection of race and gender. *Duke Law Journal,* 365-396. Discusses how race and gender are viewed according to the law.

C.0093 Campbell, C., et al. (1988, August). The female inmate: Gender, schema and institutional career phase. *Psychological Reports, 63,* 177-178. Discusses the place of gender in decisions regarding incarcerated women.

C.0094 Campbell, C., et al. (1987, June). Female offenders: Criminal behavior and gender-role. *Psychological Reports, 60*(3) 867-873. Discusses gender specific crimes.

C.0095 Campbell Law Review (1989). Criminal law: Battered woman syndrome: The killing of a passive victim: A perfect defense or a perfect crime? *Campbell Law Review, 11,* 263-278. Discusses State v. Norman [366 S.E.2d 586 (NC)].

C.0096 Campbell, Ruth (1984, May). Sentence of death by burning for women. *Journal of Legal History, 5,* 44-59. Historical discussion of the death penalty.

C.0097 Canadian Association of Elizabeth Fry Societies (1988). *Women and sentencing workshop proceedings.* Ottawa, Ontario: Canadian Association of Elizabeth Fry Societies. Discussions on women and sentencing and the causes of female criminality.

C.0098 Cannici, J. P., et al. (1989). Ego-strength changes associated with incarceration in males and females. *Journal of Offender Counseling Services and Rehabilitation, 14*(1), 31-35. Study of imates at a coeducational correctional facility to determine differences in ego-strength changes.

C.0099 Carlen, Pat (1990). *Alternatives to women's imprisonment.* Bristol, PA: Open University Press. Discusses cases of female inmates who might be suitable for noncustodial sentences.

C.0100 Carlen, Pat (1989). *Paying for crime.* Milton Keynes: Open University Press. Discusses sentences women receive, including fines.

C.0101 Carlen, Pat, & Worrall, Ann (1987). *Gender, crime and justice.* Philadelphia, PA: Open University Press. Essays on the intersection of gender, crime, and justice in criminal justice cases involving women offenders.

C.0102 Carlen, Pat (1985). Law, psychiatry, and women's imprisonment: A sociological view. *British Journal of Psychiatry, 146,* 618-621. Analyzes conditions by which the concept of psychopathic personality disorder is repeatedly used to imprison female offenders in England.

C.0103 Cazenave, Noel, & Zahn, Margaret (1992). Women, murder, and male domination: Police reports of domestic violence in Chicago and Philadelphia. In E. Viana (Ed.), *Intimate violence: Interdisciplinary perspectives,* (pp. 83-97). New York, NY: Hemisphere Publishing. Explores whether domestic homicides involving male victims and female victims are the same.

C.0104 Cernkovich, S., & Giordano, P. (1979). Criminology, delinquency, opportunity and gender. *Journal of Law and Criminology, 70*(2), 145-151. Examines the place of gender in criminology.

C.0105 Chamblin, M. H. (1979). *Effect of sex on the imposition of the death penalty.* Paper presented at a symposium entitled "Extra legal attributes affecting death penalty sentencing," New York, NY, September, 1979. Analyzed 829 individuals indicted for murder in Florida in terms of the state's death penalty legislation and in terms of the differential treatment of male and female offenders.

C.0106 Chan, Wendy (1994). A feminist critique of self-defense and provocation in battered women's cases in England and Wales. *Women and Criminal Justice, 6*(1), 39-65. Examines the law of self-defense and provocation in cases where battered women kill their partners.

C.0107 Chesney-Lind, Meda (1987). Female offenders: Paternalism reexamined. In L. Crites & W. Hepperle (Eds.), *Women, the courts, and equality* (pp. 114-139). Newbury Park, CA: Sage Publications. Discusses how the criminal justice system operates to enforce women's obedience to traditional gender roles at all ages.

C.0108 Chesney-Lind, Meda (1986, January). Sexist juvenile research: A continuing international problem. *Resources for Feminist Research, 14,* 7-10. Discusses sexism in research involving juveniles on a global scale.

C.0109 Chesney-Lind, Meda (1978). Chivalry reexamined: Women and the criminal justice system. In L. Bowker (Ed.), *Women, crime, and the criminal justice system* (pp. 197-219). Discusses how women are arrested, tried and sentenced in the criminal justice system.

C.0110 Chilton, R., & Datesman, Susan (1987, June). Gender, race, and crime: An analysis of urban arrest trends, 1960-1980. *Gender and Society, 1*(2), 152-171. Looks at urban arrests rates for certain crimes focusing on issues of gender and race.

C.0111 Chunn, Dorothy, & Menzies, R. J. (1989). *Female follies: The forensic assessment of women defendants.* West Coast Law and Society Group Symposium, Vancouver, BC, March 31, 1989. Papers on how women are arrested, charged, and sentenced for various crimes.

C.0112 Cipparone, Rocco (1987, January). The defense of battered women who kill. *University of Pennsylvania Law Review, 135*(2), 427-452. Explores the legal defense of battered women who kill their abusers.

C.0113 Clements, M.C. (1972). Sex and sentencing. *Southwestern Law Journal, 26,* 890-904. Discusses the influence of gender on sentencing practices.

C.0114 Cohen, W. (1985). Justice Douglas and the Rosenberg case: Setting the record straight. *Cornell Law Review, 70,* 211-252. Discusses Justice Douglas' role in the Supreme Court's refusal to halt the executions of Ethel and Julius Rosenberg.

C.0115 Comack, Elizabeth (1993). *Feminist engagement with the law: The legal recognition of the battered woman's syndrome.* Ottawa: Canadian Research Institute for the Advancement of Women. Discusses the factors that led to the recognition of the battered woman's syndrome as a legal defense.

C.0116 Comack, Elizabeth (1987). Women defendants and the battered wife syndrome: A plea for the sociological imagination. *Crown Counsel's Review, 5*(11), 15-16. Discusses the battered woman's syndrome as a legal defense.

C.0117 Connecticut Law Review (1982, Fall). The admissibility of expert testimony on the battered woman syndrome in support of a claim of self-defense. *Connecticut Law Review, 15,* 121-139. Discusses the circumstances under which the battered woman's syndrome could be used.

C.0118 Conway, Zanthia (1989). Factors predicting verdicts in cases where battered women kill their husbands. *Law and Human Behavior, 13*(3), 253-269. Looks at factors that influence jury verdicts in cases involving battered women who kill.

C.0119 Cook, Beverly (1993, November-December). Moral authority and gender difference: Georgia Bullock and the Los Angeles Women's Court. *Judicature, 77,* 144-155. Discusses the question of morality as it plays out in court decisions involving female offenders.

C.0120 Cook, Thomas (1991). *Early graves: The shocking true-crime story of the youngest woman ever sentenced to death row.* New York, NY: Onyx. Case of Judith & Alvin Neelley.

C.0121 Coombs, Mary (1992, January). Foreword: Gender and justice. *University of Miami Law Review, 46,* 503-510. Discusses the intersection of gender and justice in the law.

C.0122 Coontz, Phyllis (1983, Autumn-Winter). Women under sentence of death: The social organization of waiting to die. *Prison Journal, 63*(2), 88-98. Interviews with four women on death row in the summer of 1983 explored the experience of daily life on death row.

C.0123 Coontz, Phyllis (1982, August). *Ethnographic study of women on death row.* Paper presented at the 1982 World Congress of the International Sociological Association, Mexico City, DF, August 16-21, 1982. Data collected on 10 women who were on death row in 1982. Information given by the women themselves in interviews.

C.0124 Copemann, Chester, & Shaw, Paula (1976, June). Effects of contingent management of addicts expecting commitment to a community based treatment program. *British Journal of Addiction, 71*(2), 187-191. Looks at female and male addicts in alternative sentencing and incarceration treatment programs.

C.0125 Corrections Digest (1994, July 13). NCCD studying alternatives to imprisoning women offenders. *Corrections Digest, 25*(14), 1-3. Discusses alternatives to incarceration for women.

C.0126 Coughlin, Anne (1994, January). Excusing women. *California Law Review, 82*(1), 1-93. Examines and discusses the battered woman syndrome as a defense for a variety of crimes.

C.0127 Coulter, E. M. (1973). Hanging as a socio-penal institution in Georgia and elsewhere. *Georgia Historical Quarterly, 57*(1), 17-55. Discusses Georgia murderers and hangings including the execution of Alice Riley (1735), Anna Hunt (1874), and Susan Eberhart (1873).

C.0128 Cousins, M. (1980). Mens rea: A note on sexual difference, criminology and the law. In P. Carlen and M. Collison (Eds.), *Radical issues in criminology* (pp. 109-122). Oxford: Martin Robertson. Looks at gender and the law.

C.0129 Covington, Jeanette (1988, June). Crime and heroin: The effects of race and gender. *Journal of Black Studies, 18*(4), 486-506. Examines race and gender differences as explanations for variations in crime levels among black and white male and female heroin addicts.

C.0130 Covington, Jeanette (1985, November). Gender differences in criminality among heroin users. *Journal of Research in Crime and Delinquency, 22*(4), 329-353. Discusses crimes committed by male and female heroin addicts.

C.0131 Creach, D. L. (1982, February). Partially determined imperfect self-defense: The battered wife kills and tells why. *Stanford Law Review, 34*, 615-638. Discusses the use of the battered woman's syndrome as a defense in criminal homicide cases.

C.0132 Crew, B. K. (1991, March). Sex differences in criminal sentencing: Chivalry or patriarchy? *Justice Quarterly*, 59-84. Discusses differences in the sentencing of male and female offenders.

C.0133 Crites, Laura, & Hepperle, Winifred (1987). *Women, the courts and equality.* Newbury Park, CA: Sage Publications. Anthology of 10 papers on women offenders and overcoming gender bias in the courts.

C.0134 Crites, Laura (1978). Women in the criminal court. In L. Crites & W. Hepperle (Eds.), *Women in the courts* (pp. 160-175). Williamsburg, VA: National Center for State Courts. Discusses discrimination against women in criminal courts.

C.0135 Crocker, Phyllis (1989, Spring). The meaning of equality for battered women who kill men in self-defense. *Harvard Women's Law Journal, 8*(1), 121-153. Discusses the use of the battered woman's syndrome as a defense.

C.0136 Crowe, Patricia (1981, Fall). Ideological components of jury deliberation: Expectations of good mothers and ordinary women. *Quarterly Journal of Ideology, 5*(3), 46-51. Discusses how social expectations of women influence jury deliberations.

C.0137 Crowe, R. R. (1972, November). Adopted offspring of women criminal offenders: A study of their arrest records. *Archives of General Psychiatry, 27*(5), 600-603. Data collected on 41 female inmates born between 1925 and 1956. Compared arrest records with controls.

C.0138 Cuffaro, Sara (1979, March). A discriminant analysis of sociocultural, motivation, and personality differences among Black, Anglo and Chicana female drug abusers in a medium security prison. *Dissertation Abstracts International, 39,* (9-B), 4572-4573. Study of drug use.

C.0139 Cummings, Patricia (1979). The single mother as criminal defendant: A practitioner's guide to the consequences of incarceration. *Golden Gate University Law Review, 9,* 507-552. Discusses what the incarceration of a single mother means for the family.

C.0140 Curran, Debra (1983, February). Judicial discretion and defendant's sex. *Criminology, 21*(1), 41-58. Discusses the influence of gender socialization on criminal court decisions.

C.0141 Dalton, Katharina (1990). *Premenstrual syndrome goes to court.* Droitwich: Peter Andrew. Discusses the use of premenstrual syndrome as a criminal defense.

C.0142 Dalton, Katharina (1987). Should premenstrual syndrome be a legal defense? In B. E. Ginsburg & B. Carter (Eds.), *Premenstrual syndrome: Ethical and legal implications* (pp. 287-300). New York, NY: Plenum Press. Proposes that before premenstrual syndrome can be considered a legal defense a single definition of what it is must be recognized, understood, and followed.

C.0143 Dalton, Katharina (1961). Menstruation and crime. *British Medical Journal, 2,* 1752-1753. Discusses whether or not menstruation is a predictor of criminal activity in women.

C.0144 Daly, Kathleen (1994). *Gender, crime, and punishment.* New Haven, CT: Yale University Press. Explores whether men and women are prosecuted differently for similar crimes. Analyzes criminal cases that are routinely processed in felony courts in New Haven, CT.

C.0145 Daly, Kathleen (1989a, January). Neither conflict nor labeling nor paternalism will suffice: Intersections of race, ethnicity, gender and family in criminal court decisions. *Crime and Delinquency, 35*(1), 136-168. Examines sentencing and pre-trial release decisions for black, white and Hispanic women and men. Data from New York City and Seattle criminal courts.

C.0146 Daly, Kathleen (1989b). Rethinking judicial paternalism: Gender, work-family relations, and sentencing. *Gender and Society, 3*(1), 9-36. Used data from male and female judges to determine what factors judges consider when sentencing females and males.

C.0147 Daly, Kathleen (1987a, Summer). Structure and practice of familial-based justice in a criminal court. *Law and Society Review, 21*(2), 267-290. Discusses the consideration of the family in criminal court decisions.

C.0148 Daly, Kathleen (1987b, September). Discrimination in the criminal courts: Family, gender, and the problem of equal treatment. *Social Forces, 66*(1), 152-175. Examines the disposition of certain criminal cases where women are more likely to receive lenient treatment than men.

C.0149 Daly, Kathleen (1987c). *Order in the court: Gender and justice.* Washington, DC: National Institute of Justice. Discusses the influence of gender in criminal court decisions

C.0150 Dart, H. P. (1923, October). Trial of Mary Glass for murder, 1780. *Louisiana Historical Quarterly, 6*(4), 591-654. Discusses the trial of Mary Glass, a free quadroon, who was accused of murdering a white girl and was hanged on July 26, 1781.

C.0151 Davis, Natalie, et al. (1993). *A history of women in the West, V. III: Renaissance and enlightenment paradoxes.* Boston, MA: Harvard University Press. Discusses women who did not fit into societies norms, such as witches, prostitutes, criminals, and activists, 16th-19th centuries.

C.0152 DeConstanzo, Elaine, & Scholes, Helen (1988, June). Women behind bars: Their numbers increase. *Corrections Today, 50*(3), 104-108. Discusses alternatives to incarceration for some women offenders.

C.0153 Decrow, Karen (1974). *Sexist justice.* New York, NY: Random House. Discusses sexism in the justice system.

C.0154 Del Teste, Doris (1980, November). The battered spouse syndrome as a defense to a homicide charge under the Pennsylvania crimes code. *Villanova Law Review, 26*(1), 105-134. Describes battered spouse syndrome and discusses its use as a defense.

C.0155 D'Emilio, Joann (1985). Battered woman's syndrome and premenstrual syndrome: A comparison of the possible use as defenses to criminal liability. *St. John's Law Review, 59,* 558-587. Discusses the use of battered woman's syndrome as a criminal defense.

C.0156 Dergan, Bridget (1876). *The life and confession of Bridget Dergan.* Evanston, IN: Northwestern University Gary Law Library. Full confession and an account of the execution of Bridget Dergan who murdered Mrs. Ellen Doriell.

C.0157 Derr, A. R. (1973). Criminal justice: A crime against women? *Trial* (Cambridge, MA), *9*(6), 24-26. Discusses how women are treated differently than men in court.

C.0158 DeSouza, Joan (1991). *An exploratory study of criminal violence among male and female offenders from a social learning and developmental perspective.* Dissertation, Wayne State University. Discusses differences in types of criminal violence committed by women and men.

C.0159 Diaz-Cotto, Juanita (1996). *Gender, ethnicity, and the state: Latina and Latino prison politics.* Albany, NY: State University of New York Press. Discusses how gender and ethnicity influence prison politics at the state level.

C.0160 Diaz-Cotto, Juanita (1993, July). Imprisonment and the state: The political dynamics of Latino men and women in New York State Prisons, 1971-1987. *Dissertation Abstracts International, 54*(1), 300. Compares male and female maximum security prisons between 1971-1987.

C.0161 Dickinson Law Review (1990, Winter). Criminal law: Battered women and self-defense. *Dickinson Law Review, 94,* 553-560. Discusses expert evidence on battered woman syndrome. Uses Commonwealth v. Stonehouse, [555 A.2d 772 (Pa.)].

C.0162 DiGennaro, Judith (1983, Spring). Sex-specific characteristics as defenses to criminal behavior. *Criminal Justice Journal, 6*(2), 187-203. Discusses the influence of gender-specific defenses in the criminal court.

C.0163 Dion, Susan (1986). Women in the Boston Gazette, 1755-1775. *Historical Journal of Massachusetts, 14*(2), 87-102. Discusses gender-defined roles as exhibited in the Boston Gazette in the 1700's.

C.0164 Dobash, Rebecca, et al. (1995). *Gender and crime.* University of Wales Press. Examines societal views of women criminals and crimes committed against women.

C.0165 Dominelli, L. (1984). Differential justice: Domestic labour, community service and female offenders. *Probation Journal, 3*(3), 100-103. Discusses the influence of gender in criminal court dispositions against women.

C.0166 Donovan, James (1991, April). Infanticide and the juries in France, 1825-1913. *Journal of Family History, 16*(2), 157-176. Examines attitude changes in French juries toward persons accused of infanticide from 1825-1913.

C.0167 D'Orban, P. T. (1985, August). Psychiatric aspects of contempt of court among women. *Psychological Medicine, 15*(3), 597-607. Examined the records of 72 women admitted to prison for contempt of court between 1979 and 1983 in England and Wales.

C.0168 D'Orban, P. T. (1974). Court sentences of female narcotic addicts. *British Journal of Addiction, 69*(2), 167-172. Discusses court sanctions against women who abuse drugs.

C.0169 Dowd, M. (1992, Spring). Dispelling the myths about the "battered woman's defense": Towards a new understanding . *Fordham Urban Law Journal, 19*(1), 567-583. Discusses what the battered woman's defense is and what it is not.

C.0170 Douglas, Mary Ann (1987). The battered woman syndrome. In D. Sonkin (Ed.), *Domestic violence on trial.* New York, NY: Springer Publishing. Discusses the use of the battered woman's syndrome as a criminal defense.

C.0171 Drause, Katherine (1974, August). Denial of work release programs to women: A violation of equal protection. *Southern California Law Review, 47*(1). Discusses discrimination against female inmates in the denial of equal programming.

C.0172 Dresser, Rebecca (1995, January). Long-term contraceptives in the criminal justice system. *Hastings Center Report, 25*(1), S15-S18. Discusses ethical dilemmas surrounding the use of long-term contraceptives in criminal sentencing.

C.0173 Dubec, B. (1982). *Native women in the criminal justice system: An increasing minority.* Thunder Bay: Ontario Native Women's Association. Discusses the over-representation of native women in Canadian women's prisons.

C.0174 Dubinsky, Karen, & Iacovetta, Franca (1991, December). Murder, womanly virtue, and motherhood: The case of Angelina Napolitano. *Canadian Historical Review, 72*(4), 505-532. The case of Angelina Napolitano who was tried for the murder of her husband and given the death penalty in Canada in 1911.

C.0175 Duffy, Clinton, & Hirshberg, A. (1962). *88 men and 2 women.* Garden City, NY: Doubleday. Stories of men and women who were executed at San Quentin during the time Clinton Duffy was warden of that institution. Stories told by Warden Duffy.

C.0176 Duffy, Clinton (1950). *The San Quentin story.* New York, NY: Doubleday. Warden Clinton Duffy writes of the criminals he knew while he was at San Quentin. The story of one female criminal on death row is included.

C.0177 Dunn, S. (1981, Spring-Summer). Prison women: Sex discrimination in Canada's only federal prison for women. *Perception, 4*, 33-36. Discusses gender discrimination in the Canadian prison system.

C.0178 Dvoskin, J. (1978). Legal alternatives for battered women who kill their abusers. *Bulletin of the American Academy of Psychiatric Law, 6*, 335-354. Discusses the use of battered woman's syndrome as a legal defense.

C.0179 Easteal, Patricia (1993, September). Sentencing those who kill their sexual intimates: An Australian study. *International Journal of the Sociology of Law, 21*(3), 189-218. Analysis of backgrounds & dispositions in 76 cases of homicide between adult sexual intimates in Australia.

C.0180 Eastwood, Mary (1971). The double standard of justice: Women's rights under the Constitution. *Valparaiso University Law Review, 5,* 281-282. Discusses equality as it exists in the Constitution.

C.0181 Eaton, Mary (1987). The question of bail: Magistrates responses to applications for bail on behalf of men and women defendants. In P. Carlen & A. Worrall (Eds.), *Gender, crime, and justice* (pp. 95-107). Philadelphia, PA: Open University Press. Discusses sexism in the courts manifested in disparate treatment of male and female defendants.

C.0182 Eaton, Mary (1986). *Justice for women?: Family, court, and social control.* Philadelphia, PA: Open University Press. Discusses discrimination against women in the courts

C.0183 Edwards, Anne (1989). Sex/Gender, sexism and criminal justice: Some theoretical considerations. *International Journal of the Sociology of Law, 17*(2), 165-184. Examines sexism in the criminal justice system and the confusion about the terms "sex" and "gender."

C.0184 Edwards, Susan (1992, October 2). Battered woman syndrome. *New Law Journal, 142,* 1350-1351. Discusses the use of the battered woman's syndrome as a criminal defense.

C.0185 Edwards, Susan (1990, October 5). Battered women who kill. *New Law Journal, 140,* 1380-1381. Argues that the scope of provocation should be widened and "heat of the moment" redefined in cases of battered women who kill.

C.0186 Edwards, Susan (1985). A socio-legal evaluation of gender ideologies in domestic violence assault and spousal murder. *Victimology, 10*(1-4), 186-205. Notes how provocation, is more accessible to husbands who kill their wives than to wives who kill their husbands.

C.0187 Edwards, Susan (1985). *Gender, sex and the law.* London: Croom Helm. Discusses how gender influences various aspects of the practice of law.

C.0188 Edwards, Susan (1984). *Women on trial: A study of the female suspect, defendant, and offender in the criminal law and criminal justice system.* Manchester: Manchester University Press. Discusses the hypotheses that women are treated in accordance with the extent to which their criminal behavior deviates from what is expected in their "proper" gender role.

C.0189 Edwards, Susan (1981). *Female sexuality and the law: A study of constructs of female sexuality as they inform statute and legal procedure.* Oxford: Robertson. Discusses the influence of gender in the making and practice of law.

C.0190 Eich, W. (1986, April-May). Gender bias in the courtroom: Some participants are more equal than others. *Judicature, 69*(6), 339-343. Discusses discrimination against women in the courts.

C.0191 Eisenberg, Alan, & Dillon, David (1980). Medico-legal aspects of representing the battered women. In S. Johann & F. Osanka (Eds.), *Respresenting battered women who kill* (Chaper 3). Springfiled, IL: Charles C. Thomas. Details investigative techniques for determining if a woman has been battered and proving it.

C.0192 Eisenberg, Alan, & Seymour, E. (1978). Self-defense plea and battered women. *Trial, 15*(8), 28-31. Discusses the use of self-defense as a defense in the trials of battered women who kill.

C.0193 Elliot, R. G. (1940). *Agent of death: The memoirs of an executioner.* New York, NY: Dutton. Includes execution of two women in his memoirs.

C.0194 Emmerichs, Mary Beth (1993). Trials of women for homicide in nineteenth-century England. *Women & Criminal Justice, 5*(1), 99-109. Looks at murder trials of women from 1845-1900 in England.

C.0195 Erickson, N. S. (1974). Women and the Supreme Court: Anatomy is destiny. *Brooklyn Law Review, 41*(2), 209-282. Examines early birth control, abortion, and maternity leave cases.

C.0196 Espy, Watt, & Smykla, John (1987). *Executions in the United States, 1608-1987: The Espy file.* Tuscaloosa, Alabama: Inter-University Consortium for Political and Social Research. Extensive records of executions in America, includes women.

C.0197 Evans, Moncia (1993, Summer). Stealing away: Black women, outlaw culture and the rhetoric of rights. *Harvard Civil Rights-Civil Liberties Law Review, 28*, 263-298. Discusses the treatment of black women in the law.

C.0198 Ewing, Charles (1990, December). Psychological self-defense: A proposed justification for battered women who kill. *Law and Human Behavior, 14*(6), 579-594. Argues that under certain circumstances the law should recognize psychological self-defense as a just defense.

C.0199 Ewing, Charles (1987). *Battered women who kill: Psychological self-defense as legal justification.* Lexington, MA: Lexington Books. Advocates the acceptance of psychological self-defense as justification for homicide by battered women.

C.0200 Faigman, D. L. (1987). Review essay: Discerning justice when battered women kill. *Hastings Law Journal, 39,* 207-227. Discusses the use of the battered woman's syndrome as a defense.

C.0201 Faith, Karlene, et al. (1990, Fall). Native women in Canada: A quest for justice. *Social Justice, 17*(3), 167-188. Discusses the treatment of native women in Canadian courts.

C.0202 Farnworth, Margaret, et al. (1988, June). Aggregation effects on male-to-female arrest rate ratios in New York state, 1972 to 1984. *Journal of Quantitative Criminology, 4*(2), 121-135. Discusses data on female and male adult arrests in New York over a 13-year period.

C.0203 Farren, Denise (1988). The trial of Ruth Ellis. *Studies in Sexual Politics, 24*(1), 1-109. Uses the official trial transcript of the last female to be hanged in Great Britain.

C.0204 Farrington, D., & Morris, Allison (1983, July). Sex, sentencing, and reconviction. *British Journal of Criminology, 23*(3), 229-248. Discusses the influence of gender in sentencing and reconviction.

C.0205 Feinman, Clarice (1979). Sex role stereotypes and justice for women. *Crime and Delinquency, 25*(1), 87-94. Investigated whether the sex of the defendant was related to the severity of sentencing and the likelihood of reconviction.

C.0206 Feinman, Clarice (1977, July). Afro-American experience: The women in New York City's jail. *Afro-Americans in New York Life and History, 1*(2), 201-210. Reviews treatment programs instituted between 1932-1975 for Afro-American women incarcerated in New York City.

C.0207 Female Offenders Program of Western Pennsylvania (1979). *Programs for women offenders: How to start, fund, maintain.* Pittsburgh, PA: Female Offenders Program of Western Pennsylvania. Handbook on how to start, fund and maintain a community services project for women offenders.

C.0208 Fenster, Carol (1981, Summer). Societal reactions to male-female co-defendants: Sex as an independent variable. *California Sociologist, 4*(2), 219-232. Discusses the influence of societal norms for women on court decisions.

C.0209 Fenster, Carol (1979a). Partners in crime: A study of the legal processing of male-female criminal co-defendants. *Dissertation Abstracts International, 40*(12-Pt 1), 6435-A. Focuses on the court's treatment of male-female co-defendants.

C.0210 Ferguson, Sandra (1994, Summer). Women and drug policy: Implications of normalization. *Affilia: Journal of Women and Social Work, 9*(2), 29-44. Discusses adverse effects of punitive drug policies on women, such as the prosecution of pregnant drug users.

C.0211 Fersch, Ellsworth (1982). Law and psychiatry: A case in the district court and at the community mental health center. *International Journal of Offender Therapy and Comparative Criminology, 26*(2), 157-165. Discusses the case of a white female arrested for threatening to shoot her aunt.

C.0212 Feyerharm, W. (1981). Measuring gender differences in delinquency: Self reports versus police contact. In M. Warren (Ed.), *Comparing female and male offenders.* Beverly Hill, CA: Sage Publications. Comparison of arrest rates of male and female offenders.

C.0213 Figueira-McDonough, J. (1985, May). Gender differences in informal processing: A look at charge bargaining and sentence reduction in Washington, DC. *Journal of Research in Crime and Delinquency, 22*(2), 101-133. Investigates how women defendants fare compared to men in the plea bargaining process.

C.0214 Fiora-Gormally, Nancy (1978). Battered wives who kill: Double standard out of court, single standard in? *Law and Human Behavior, 2*(2), 133-165. Explores sociocultural definitions of "woman" and "wife" and the battered wife syndrome.

C.0215 Flavin, Jeanne (1994, March). *A better model for bad women: The utility of a structural-contextual approach in explaining gender differences in judicial outcomes.* Paper presented at the 1994 ACJS Annual Meeting, Chicago, IL. Looks at various approaches to explaining the differences in judicial outcomes for male and female offenders.

C.0216 Foley, L., & Rasche, C. (1979). The effect of race on sentence, actual time served and final disposition of female offenders. In J. Conley (Ed.), *Theory and research in justice.* Cincinatti, OH: Anderson. Discusses racial discrimination in the processing and incarceration of female offenders.

C.0217 Follingstad, Diane, et al. (1989, September). Factors predicting verdicts in cases where battered women kill their husbands. *Law and Human Behavior, 13*(3), 253-269. Used 338 college students giving a fictitious legal case involving a battered woman who killed her husband.

C.0218 Frankel, Lois (1973, Winter). Sex discrimination in criminal law: The effect of the Equal Rights Amendment. *American Criminal Law Review, 11,* 469-473. Discusses disparate attitudes towards males and females incorporated in criminal law.

C.0219 Frazier, C. E., et al. (1983, Spring). The role of probation officers in determining gender differences in sentencing severity. *The Sociological Quarterly, 24*(2), 305-318. Data collected from presentence investigation reports of 309 criminal cases. Thirty-five percent of the cases involved females.

C.0220 French, Laurence (1983, Autumn-Winter). Profile of the incarcerated black female offender. *Prison Journal, 63*(2), 80-87. Reviews research literature on black female delinquents and black female adult offenders. Discusses over-representation in the criminal justice system.

C.0221 French, Laurence (1978a, March). The incarcerated black female: The case of social double jeopardy. *Journal of Black Studies, 8*(3), 321-335. Discusses discrimination against black female offenders in the courts and prison systems.

C.0222 French, Laurence (1978b). *Women, crime and the male dominated criminal justice system.* Washington, DC: U.S. Department of Health, Education, and Welfare. Discusses the double standard of justice for male and female offenders.

C.0223 French, Laurence (1977, Winter). An assessment of the black female prisoner in the South. *Signs, 3*(2), 483-488. Addresses the over representation of black females in Southern correctional centers, particularly North Carolina.

C.0224 Fry, Lincoln, & Glaser, Daniel (1987, Fall-Winter). Gender differences in work adjustment of prison employees. *Journal of Offender Counseling Servicies and Rehabilitation, 12*(10), 39-52. Discusses fieldwork and survey data from a study of staff in 3 California prisons.

C.0225 Garvey, Jane (1984, May-June). Securing the female offender: Special treatment required? *Campus Law Enforcement Journal, 14*(3), 16-17. Discusses the process of arresting women.

C.0226 Gates, D. (1975). *Theft and the status of women: The question of chivalry and equal treatment of men and women in the criminal justice system of Riverside county, California from 1960 through 1971.* Dissertation, University of Hawaii. Discusses female arrests and treatment.

C.0227 Gavigan, S. (1989-1990). Petit treason in eighteenth century England: Women's inequality before the law. *Canadian Journal of Women and the Law, 3, 335-374.* Discusses discrimination against women in English Courts in the 18th century.

C.0228 Gebhart, Fred (1993, April 19). Women prisoners allege drugging during their trials. *Drug Topics, 137*(8), 54-57. Discusses cases of forty-four California women prisoners who claim they were improperly medicated with antipsychotic drugs during their trials.

C.0229 Gehlert, Susan, & Lickey, Sarah (1995, June). Social and health policy concerns raised by the introduction of the contraceptive Norplant. *Social Service Review, 69*(2), 323-337. Discusses health policy concerns regarding Norplant's use as a social remedy.

C.0230 Gelsthorpe, Lorraine (1986, May). Towards a skeptical look at sexism. *International Journal of the Sociology of Law, 14*(2), 125-152. Looks at sexism in the law.

C.0231 Ghali, M., & Chesney-Lind, Meda (1986). Gender bias and the criminal justice system: An empirical investigation. *Sociology and Social Research, 70*(2), 164-171. Research on gender discrimination in the criminal justice system.

C.0232 Gillespie, Cynthia (1989). *Justifiable homicide: Battered women, self-defense, and the law.* Columbus, OH. State University Press. Discusses the use of the battered woman's syndrome as a criminal defense.

C.0233 Goetting, Ann (1992, January). Criminology, deviance and law: Abused and battered: Social and legal response to family violence. *Contemporary Sociology, 21*(1), 87. Discusses legal responses to family violence, including battering.

C.0234 Goetting, Ann (1985, September). Racism, sexism, and ageism in the prison community. *Federal Probation, 44*(3), 10-22. Discusses formal and informal prison practices that discriminate against, blacks, women, and the elderly.

C.0235 Golden Gate University Law Review (1993, Summer). Courtroom, code and clemency: Reform in self-defense jurisprudence for battered women. *Golden Gate University Law Review, 23,* 829-862. Discusses the use of the battered woman's defense in criminal courts.

C.0236 Golden, Megan (1991, December). When pregnancy discrimination is gender discrimination: The constitutionality of excluding pregnant women from drug treatment programs. *New York University Law Review, 66,* 1832-1880. Discusses the practice of excluding drug dependent pregnant women from some drug treatment programs.

C.0237 Goldman, Marilyn, et al. (1979). *Job options: First offender women, a pretrial intervention program.* Newton, MA: Education Development Center. Describes how to set up and operate a pretrial intervention program for female first offenders.

C.0238 Gottheil, Diane (1980). The participation of women and minorities in pretrial diversion programs. *Peace and Change, 6*(3), 49-58. Discusses diversion programs where eligible individuals are provided with counseling and other appropriate human services.

C.0239 Gousie, Monique (1993, Winter). From self-defense to coercion: McMaugh v. State [612 A.2d 725, (R I) 1992]. Use of battered woman's syndrome to defend wife's involvment in third-party murder. *New England Law Review, 28,* 453-481. Discusses other uses of the battered woman's syndrome in criminal cases.

C.0240 Governor's Committee to Study Sentencing and Correctional Alternatives for Women Convicted of Crime (1988). *Governor's Committee to study sentencing and correctional alternatives for women convicted of crime: State of Maryland: Final report.* Annapolis, MD: Governor's Committee. Looks at alternative sentencing.

C.0241 Governor's Commission on Crime Prevention and Control (1974, March). *Community Correction Center for women: A preliminary evaluation report.* St. Paul, MN: Governor's Commission on Crime Prevention and Control. Prelimanry evaluation of a community correction center for women.

C.0242 Graff, Sunny (1988). Battered women, dead husbands: A comparative study of justification and excuse in American and West German Law. *Loyola of Los Angeles International and Comparative Law Journal, 10*(1), 1-55. Discusses the use of the battered woman's syndrome as a defense in criminal law.

C.0243 Grasmick, Harold, et al. (1984a). Sex and criminal court dispositions: The unsolved controversy. *Research on Crime and Delinquency, 21*(3), 213-232. Discusses the influence of gender on criminal court cases.

C.0244 Grasmick, Harold, et al. (1984b, September). Labor force participation, sex-role attitudes and female crime. *Social Science Quarterly, 65*(3), 703-718. Tests the hypothesis that employed females and females with non-traditional sex-roles are similar to males in their illegal behavior.

C.0245 Graydon, Charalee (1992, January). Habilitation: Sentencing of female offenders. *Canadian Journal of Law and Jurisprudence, 5,* 121-141. Discusses the sentencing of female offenders.

C.0246 Greene, Dwight (1991, Fall). Abusive prosecutors: Gender, race & class discretion and the prosecution of drug-addicted mothers. *Buffalo Law Review, 39,* 737-802. Discusses the prosecution of drug-addicted mothers.

C.0247 Greene, E., et al. (1989). Jurors' knowledge of battered women. *Journal of Family Violence, 4*(2), 105-125. Discusses the purpose of expert testimony in the case of a battered woman who has killed her partner.

C.0248 Greene, Helen (1981, Fall). Black women in the criminal justice system. *Urban League Review, 6*(1), 55-61. Presents information on black women in the criminal justice system. Focuses on statistical profiles, unique problems, and future directions for research, and programs.

C.0249 Greene, J. (1989, December). A provocation defense for battered women who kill. *Adelaide Law Review, 12*(2), 145-163. Discusses provocation as a defense for battered women who kill an abusive partner.

C.0250 Greenwald, Mary, & Manning, Mary-Ellen (1994, March). When mercy seasons justice: Commutation for battered women who kill. *Boston Bar Journal, 38*(2), 3. Discusses the commutation of sentences of battered women who have been incarcerated for murder.

C.0251 Greschner, Donna (1992). Aboriginal women: The constitution and criminal justice. *University of British Columbia Law Review: Special edition,* 338-366. Discusses the treatment of aboriginal women in the Canadian criminal justice system.

C.0252 Grosman, Alan (1991, July-August). The battered woman syndrome. *New Jersey Lawyer, 141,* 30-33. Discusses the use of the battered woman's syndrome as a defense for murder.

C.0253 Gruhl, J., et al. (1984). Women as criminal defendants: A test for paternalism. *Western Political Quarterly, 37*(3), 456-467. Discusses paternalism as it exists in criminal courts.

C.0254 Haines, J. (1981). Women, the law, and provocation. *Australian Nursing Journal, 10,* 1-3. Discusses the use of provocation as a defense for women.

C.0255 Hampton, R. L. (1987). *Violence in the black family: Correlates and consequences.* Lexington, MA: Lexington Books. Overview of violence as it affects African-American families.

C.0256 Hancock, Linda (1986). Economic pragmatism and the ideology of sexism: Prison policy and women. *Women's Studies International Forum, 9*(1), 101-107. Discusses unequal and inadequate treatment of women in prison in Victoria, Australia. Gives examples.

C.0257 Hancock, L. (1980). The myth that females are treated more leniently than males in the juvenile justice system. *Australia and New Zealand Journal of Sociology, 16*(3), 4-13. Discusses the treatment of females in the juvenile justice system.

C.0258 Hancock, Robert (1985). *Ruth Ellis: The last woman to be hanged.* London: Weidenfeld & Nicolson. After deliberating for fourteen minutes, the jury found Ellis guilty of murder and she was hanged on July 13, 1955 at the Holloway Women's Prison in North London.

C.0259 Harris, Jean (1993). Comparison of stressors among female vs. male inmates. *Journal of Offender Rehabilitation, 19*(1-2), 43-56. Results of Prison Environmental Inventory and Prison Preference Inventory of 71 female and 942 male inmates. Addresses Giallombardo, 1966.

C.0260 Harris, Jean (1989, January). Humane and equitable treatment? The case of New York state female and male prisons. *Dissertation Abstracts International, 49*(7), 1970. Discusses discrimination in the New York state prison system.

C.0261 Hart, Cynthia (1995). Gender differences in social support among inmates. *Women and Criminal Justice, 6*(2), 67-88. Examines the relationship between social support and psychological well-being for male and female prisoners. Based on a survey of 117 men and 96 women.

C.0262 Hartjen, A. (1986). Crime and development: Some observations on women and children in India. *International Journal of Criminolgoy (Paris), 24*(1-2), 39-57. Compares arrest frequencies and distributions for 9 serious crimes in the U.S. and India.

C.0263 Harvey, Linda, & Burnham, R. (1992, Spring). Gender differences in criminal justice: An international comparison. *British Journal of Criminology, 32*(2), 208-217. Study shows that males are more suspected, apprehended, prosecuted, convicted, and imprisoned throughout the world.

C.0264 Hawke, Anne (1996, January 15). Alternative sentences: Not just a women's issue. *National Law Journal, 18*(20), A19-A20. Discusses alternative criminal sentencing for non-violent offenders, using a gender-neutral criterion.

C.0265 Hawkes, Ellen (1986). *Feminism on trial: The Ginny Foat case and its meaning for the future of the women's movement.* New York, NY: Morrow. Discusses the case of Ginny Foat.

C.0266 Heggestad, Kay (1980). The devil made me do it: The case against using premenstrual syndrome as a defense in a court of law. *Hamline Law Review, 9,* 155-163. Discusses the use of premenstrual syndrome as a defense for women in criminal courts.

C.0267 Heilbrun, Alfred, & Heilbrun, Mark (1986). The treatment of women in the criminal justice system: An inquiry into the social impact of the women's rights movement. *Psychology of Women Quarterly, 10*(3), 240-251. Discusses the impact of the feminist movement on criminal justice decisions relating to women.

C.0268 Heilbrun, K., et al. (1988, September). Comparing females acquitted by reason of insanity, convicted, and civilly committed in Florida. *Law and Human Behavior, 12*(3), 295-311. Compares criminal and psychiatric histories of females acquitted by reason of insanity, convicted of comparable offenses, and those involuntarily hospitalized without criminal involvement.

C.0269 Helfield, R. (1990). Female prisoners of the 19th century: A study of gender bias in the application of the law. *Osgoode Hall Law Journal, 28*(10, 53-101. A study of discriminatory sentencing.

C.0270 Henry, M. D. (1932). Ballads and folk-songs from the Southern Highlands. *Journal of American Folklore, 45,* 60-65. Contains folk song account of the case of Frances Silver who was hung at Morgantown, WV, on July 12, 1883 for the murder of her husband, Charles.

C.0271 Hepperle, Winifred, & Crites, Laura (1978). *Women in the courts.* Williamsburg, VA: National Center for State Courts. Examines the question of level of commitment of judiciary in raising female status. Focuses on judiciary attachment to female sex stereotyping.

C.0272 Herbert, Rosemary (1985, April). Women's prisons: An equal protection evaluation. *The Yale Law Journal, 94*(5), 1182-1206. Argues that incarcerated women will have equal access to prison services and rehabilitative programs only if prison facilities are shared with men.

C.0273 Herbig, J. M. (1977). Disparity in sentences recommended for women convicted of felonies: Multivariate analysis programs. *Dissertation Abstracts International, 38*(4), 2357-A. Looked at data for June, 1972 and May, 1975 in the California Institute for Women.

C.0274 Herdman, Teresa (1993, Winter). Criminal law: Marshaling the defense: Indigent defendants guaranteed psychiatric assistance at trial to explain battered woman syndrome [Dunn b. Roberts. 963 F.2d. 308, 1992]. *Washburn Law Journal, 32,* 249-259. Discusses battered woman defense.

C.0275 Hertz, R., & Weisber, R. (1981). In mitigation of the penalty of death: Lockett v. Ohio and the capital defendant's right to consideration of mitigating circumstances. *California Law Review, 69,* 317-376. Case of Sandra Lockett.

C.0276 Hill, Gary, & Crawford, E. (1990, November). Women, race, and crime. *Criminology, 28*(4), 601-626. Discusses the intersection of race and gender in crimes committed by women.

C.0277 Hill, Gary, & Harris, A. R. (1981). Changes in the gender patterning of crime, 1953-1977: Opportunity vs. identity. *Social Science Quarterly, 62*(4), 658-671. Looks at patterns of crime by gender during 1953-1977.

C.0278 Hindelang, Michael (1981). Variations of sex-race-age: Specific incidence rates of offending. *American Sociological Review, 46,* 461-474. Looks at specific incidences of offending according to sex, race, and age variations.

C.0279 Hindelang, Michael (1979, December). Sex differences in criminal activity. *Social Problems, 27*(2), 143-156. Examines data from 1972-1976 surveys to investigate the extent to which it is in accord with Uniform Crime Report arrest data regarding offender's sex.

C.0280 Hodgins, S., et al. (1986). Women declared insane: A follow-up study. *International Journal of Law and Psychiatry, 8*(2), 203-216. A 7-9 year follow-up of 29 women declared incompetent to stand trial by reason of insanity.

C.0281 Hoffman, K. S. (1979). *Variables relating to program outcomes in a community based program for women offenders.* Dissertation, Wayne State University. Discusses outcomes of community based programs for female offenders.

C.0282 Hogue, Carol (1987, March 4). How to book and search a female prisoner and survive. *Corrections Digest, 18*(5), 10. Discusses the arrest of women from the viewpoint of the arresting officer.

C.0283 Holahan, Paulette (1993, December). Women in Louisiana's courts: A study concluded. *Louisiana Bar Journal, 41,* 317-319. Looks at how women are treated in Louisiana courts.

C.0284 Horney, J. (1978). Menstrual cycles in ciminal responsibility. *Law and Human Behavior, 2*(1), 25-36. Discusses the use of PMS as a criminal defense.

C.0285 Humphrey, Elaine (1988). *Female new court commitments, 1976-1987.* Albany, NY: State of New York Department of Correctional Services. Looks at sentencing patterns in New York State, 1976-1987.

C.0286 Human Rights (1993, Summer). Norplant: Miracle drug or threat to women's rights? *Human Rights, 20*(3), 16-17. Discusses Norplant as a threat to women's rights. Focuses on constitutional concerns about its use to regulate behavior.

C.0287 Husbands, R. H. (1979). New direction for capital sentencing or an about-face for the Supreme Court? *American Criminal Law Review, 16,* 317-337. Discusses the case of Sandra Lockett.

C.0288 Hustak, A. (1987). *They were hanged.* Toronto: James Lorimer. Accounts of hangings of women in Canada up to 1953.

C.0289 Hutton, Chris, et al. (1989, Summer). I fought the law and the law won: A report on women and disparate sentencing in South Dakota. *New England Journal on Criminal and Civil Confinement, 15,* 177-201. Discusses one woman's case.

C.0290 Iacovetta, Frances, & Velarde, Mariana (1992). *Gender conflicts.* Toronto: University of Toronto Press. Accounts of the trials of Clara Ford and Carrie Davies, both accused of murder.

C.0291 Ireland, Robert (1992). Frenzied and fallen females: Women and sexual dishonor in the nineteenth-century United States. *Journal of Women's History, 3*(3), 95-117. Discusses the unwritten law to avenge sexual dishonor and how it was applied across gender lines.

C.0292 Jenkins, Pamela, & Davidson, Barbara (1990, Spring). Battered women in the criminal justice system: An analysis of gender stereotypes. *Behavioral Sciences and the Law, 8*(2), 161-170. Analyzes ten court cases of battered women charged with the death of their partners. Focuses on the structure of the trial, language of the trial, participants, and the role the defendant played.

C.0293 Jensen, A. (1984). Norwegian women in court. In F. Adler (Ed.), *The incidence of female criminality in the contemporary world* (pp. 84-101). New York, NY: New York University Press. Discusses women offenders in Norway, crimes they commit and how they are punished.

C.0294 Joesting, J., et al. (1975, October). Male and female prison inmates, differences on MMPI scale and revised beta I.Q. *Psychological Reports, 37*(2), 471-474. Discusses results of a comparison of MMPI scores of 272 female and 257 male inmates incarcerated in North Carolina in 1971.

C.0295 Johann, Sara, & Osanka, Frank (1989). *Representing battered women who kill.* Springfield, IL: Charles C. Thomas. Anthology of legal and psychological articles exploring strategies for legal representation of battered women who kill their abusers.

C.0296 Johnson, Justin (1993, Spring). Flotsam on the sea of humanity: A view from the bench on class, race, and gender. *Social Justice, 20*(1-2), 140-149. Discusses several court cases that indicate how race, class and gender distort the U.S. criminal justice system.

C.0297 Johnston, Janet, et al. (1987, March). Gender differences in the sentencing of felony offenders. *Federal Probation, 51*(1), 29-55. Examines gender differences in sentencing. Data collected from females and males found guilty of serious crimes in Arizona between 1979-1983.

C.0298 Kamps, Celia Ann (1988, October). Determinants of sentencing for black and white women in state correctional facilities, 1979. *Dissertation Abstracts International, 49*(4), 959-A. Discusses variables that affect the sentencing of women.

C.0299 Kandel, Minouche (1993, August). Women who kill their batterers are getting battered in court. *Ms., 4*(1), 88-89. Discusses the California landmark case People v. Valorie Jean Day where a woman convicted of killing her batterer had her conviction overturned.

C.0300 Kandel, Minouche (1992, Spring). Whores in court: Judicial processing of prostitutes in the Boston Municipal Court in 1990. *Yale Journal of Law and Feminism, 4,* 329-352. Discusses the disposition of Boston's court system regarding prostitutes in 1990.

C.0301 Kasian, Marilyn, et al. (1993, June). Battered women who kill: Jury simulation and legal defenses. *Law and Human Behavior, 17*(3), 289-312. Assesses acquittal rates using mock jurors in cases involving a battered woman charged with killing her husband.

C.0302 Katzenelson, Susan (1978). The female defendant in Washington, DC. In D. Szabs and S. Katzenelson (Eds.), *Offenders and corrections.* New York, NY: Praeger. Discusses sentencing practices in Washington, DC.

C.0303 Kaubin, B. J. (1974). Sexism shades the lives and treatment of female addicts. *Contemporary Drug Problems, 3,* 193-197. Discusses sexism in the treatment of female addicts.

C.0304 Keating, Hope (1993, Winter). Battered women in Florida: Will justice be served? *Florida State University Law Review, 20,* 679-695. Discusses the use of the battered woman's syndrome as a defense in Florida's courts.

C.0305 Kellermann, A., & Mercy, J. (1992). Men, women, and murder: Gender specific differences in rates of fatal violence and victimization. *The Journal of Trauma, 33*(1), 27-32. Discusses differences in murder by men and murder by women.

C.0306 Kempinen, Cynthia (1983). Changes in the sentencing patterns of male and female criminal defendants. *The Prison Journal, 63*(2), 3-11. Discusses discriminate sentencing of male and female offenders.

C.0307 Kendall, Kathy (1992). Sexual difference and the law: Premenstrual syndrome as legal defense. In D. H. Currie & V. Raoul (Eds.), *Anatomy of gender: Women's struggle for the body* (pp. 130-146). Ottawa: Carleton University Press. Discusses the use of premenstrual syndrome as a defense in Canadian criminal courts.

C.0308 Kermode, Jennifer, & Walker, Garthine (1994). *Women, crime and the courts in early modern England.* Chapel Hill, NC: University of North Carolina Press. Discusses the treatment of women in English criminal courts.

C.0309 Ketner, Linda, & Humphrey, J. A. (1979). Homicide, sex role differences and role relationships. *Omega: Journal of Death and Dying, 10*(4), 379-387. Investigates similarities and differences between female and male homicide offenders.

C.0310 Kieviet, T. G. (1978). The battered wife syndrome: A potential defense to a homicide charge. *Pepperdine Law Review, 6,* 213-239. Discusses the use of the battered woman's syndrome as a defense for homicide.

C.0311 Kjervik, Diane (1992). A legal analysis of domestic violence against women. In C. M. Sampselle (Ed.), *Violence against women: Nursing research, education and practice issues* (pp. 33-43). New York, NY: Hemisphere Publishing Corp. Reviews ethical questions and legal problems of the battered woman's syndrome as a defense for battered women who kill.

C.0312 Klock, E. (1990). Criminality and gender in Leiden, 1678-1794. *Criminal Justice History, 11,* 1-30. Discusses gender-specific crimes in Leiden, 1678-1794.

C.0313 Kneeland, J. C. (1947). *Life and confession of Mary Runkle who was condemned and sentenced to be executed at Whitesboro, Oneida Co., NY on the 9th day of November 1847 for the murder of her husband, John Runkle.* Troy, NY: J. C. Kneeland. Life of Mary Runkle.

C.0314 Kramer, John, & Steffensmeier, Darrell (1977, July-October). Reactions of male inmates to male and female offenders: Sex bias in prison? *International Journal of Contemporary Sociology, 14*(3-4), 169-184. Explores inmates ideas about appropriate punishments for male and female offenders. Data collected from 100 students of criminology and 75 inmates.

C.0315 Kratz, Althea (1940). *Prosecutions and treatment of women offenders and the economic crisis: Philadelphia, 1925-1934.* Philadelphia, PA: University of Pennsylvania Press. Discusses the treatment of women in Philadelphia courts, 1925-1934.

C.0316 Krause, Katherine (1974, August). Denial of work release programs to women: A violation of equal protection. *Southern California Law Review, 47*(4), 1453-1490. Discusses the discriminatory nature of denying work-release programs to women.

C.0317 Kritzer, H., & Uhlman, T. (1977, April). Sisterhood in the courtroom: Sex of judge and defendant in criminal case disposition. *The Social Science Journal, 14*(2), 77-88. Discusses how women judges treat women defendants in the courtroom.

C.0318 Krohn, M., et al. (1983). Is chivalry dead? An analysis of changes in police dispositions of males and females. *Criminology, 21*(3), 417-437. Data suggested that police frequently respond to female offenders in a paternalistic manner.

C.0319 Kruttschnitt, Candace, & McCarthy, D. (1985a). Gender, criminal sentences, and sex role stereotypes. *Windsor Yearbok of Access to Justice, 5,* 306-323. Discusses sex role stereotyping in sentencing practices.

C.0320 Kruttschnitt, Candace (1985b, September). Legal outcomes and legal agents: Adding another dimension to the sex-sentencing controversy. *Law and Human Behavior, 9*(3), 287-303. Discusses the outcomes of sentencing where gender is a variable.

C.0321 Kruttschnitt, Candace (1985c). Female crimes or legal labels? The effect of deviance processing agents on our understanding of female criminality. In I. Moyer (Ed.), *The changing roles of women in the criminal justice system: Offenders, victims, and professionals* (pp. 76-94). Prospect Heights, IL: Waveland Press. Examined arrest and conviction data for female offenders to see what factors affect officially recorded crimes.

C.0322 Kruttschnitt, Candace (1984a, February). Sentencing recommendations and women offenders: The biopsychological model and the treatment of female offenders. *Law and Inequality, 2,* 97-120. Discusses the affect of gender in recommendations for female criminal sentencing.

C.0323 Kruttschnitt, Candace, & Green, Donald (1984b, August). The sex-sanctioning issue: Is it history? *American Sociological Review, 49*(4), 541-551. Discusses gender-based leniency.

C.0324 Kruttschnitt, Candace (1984c, August). Sex and criminal court dispositions: The unresolved controversy. *Journal of Research in Crime and Delinquency, 21*(3), 213-232. Discusses gender as a factor in sentencing practices.

C.0325 Kruttschnitt, Candace (1983, October). Race relations and the female inmate. *Crime and Delinquency, 29*(4), 577-592. Explores the extent of racial tension in women's prisons using questionnaire data obtained from inmates of the Minnesota Correctional Institute for Women.

C.0326 Kruttschnitt, Candace (1982a, February). Women, crime, and dependency: An application of the theory of law. *Criminology, 19*(4), 495-513. Explores the expectation that sentencing disparaties within offense categories can be predicted.

C.0327 Kruttschnitt, Candace (1982b). Respectable women and the law. *Sociological Quarterly, 23*(2), 221-234. Data on female defendants processed in an adult probation department in Northern California during 1972-1976. Supports Black's contention that the lower a woman's respectability the more likelihood of a severe sentence.

C.0328 Kruttschnitt, Candace (1980-1981, Winter). Social status and sentences of female offenders. *Law and Society Review, 15*(2), 247-265. Discusses the affect of class on sentencing practices with female offenders.

C.0329 Kruttschnitt, Candace (1979). The social control of women offenders: A study of sentencing in a criminal court. *Dissertation Abstracts International, 40*(6), 3548-A. Examines how female defendants are processed through the criminal court system in America.

C.0330 Kuhl, Ann (1986). Implications of justifiable homicide verdicts for battered women. *Response to the Victimization of Women and Children, 9*(2), 6-10. Discusses the implications of the justifiable homicide defense when invoked on behalf of battered women.

C.0331 La Beff, Emily (1981, May). Race, sex, and prison sentence disparity. *Free Inquiry in Creative Sociology, 9*(1), 35-38. Tested for effects of race and sex on sentence disparity and controlled for seriousness of offense and recidivism in five crime categories.

C.0332 Lampe, P. E. (1982). Sex differences in the perception of crime and criminals. *International Journal of Womens Studies, 5*(5), 413-422. Examines the role of social status in determining the type of criminal court disposition a woman receives.

C.0333 Lancaster, Jennie (1992). Management issues for female inmates on death row. In American Correctional Association *Female offenders: Meeting the needs of a neglected population* (pp. 89-93). Laurel, MD: American Correctional Association. Gives guidelines regarding mangement issues with female inmates on death row.

C.0334 Lancaster, Jennie (1988, Fall). Corrections staff are "silent actors" in executions. *National Prison Project Journal, 17.* Discusses the execution of Velma Barfield in North Carolina in 1984.

C.0335 Landon, Elizabeth (1986). Female crime in Calgary, 1914-1941. In L. Knafla (Ed.), *Law and justice in a new land: Essays in Western Canadian legal history* (pp. 293-309). Examines police court records to assess the incidence of female crime during the 1914-1941 era.

C.0336 Langan, Patrick (1995). *Spouse murder defendants in large urban counties: Executive summary.* Washington, DC: Bureau of Justice statistics. Statistics on spousal murders in criminal courts in the U.S.

C.0337 Lansdowne, R. (1990). Infanticide: Psychiatrists and the plea-bargaining process. *Monash University Law Review, 16*(1), 41-63. Discusses the role of psychiatrists in cases of infanticide.

C.0338 Laster, Kathy (1994) Arbitrary chivalry: Women and capital punishment in Victoria, Australia, 1842-1967. *Women and Criminal Justice, 6*(1), 67-95. Study of the death penalty for women in Victoria, Australia. Concludes that politics rather than law influenced sentencing outcomes.

C.0339 Laurie, B. (1932). *The Newgate calendar of malefactors' bloody register.* New York, NY: G. P. Putnam. Narratives of the lives, as well as pre-death speeches, of the most notorious criminals of both sexes who suffered death punishment in Great Britain and Ireland.

C.0340 Lawrence, Sally (1994, March). *Racial differences in criminogenic influences among women offenders.* Paper presented at the 1994 ACJS Annual Meeting, Chicago, IL. Discusses race in current theories of female crime.

C.0341 Lays, Julie (1992, May). Babies behind bars. *State Legislatures, 18*(5), 44-46. Discusses alternative sentencing for female offenders that allows mothers and babies to stay together.

C.0342 Leader-Elliott, K. (1993, December). Battered but not beaten: Women who kill in self defense. *The Sydney Law Review, 15*(4), 403-460. Discusses the use of the battered woman's syndrome as a defense in criminal cases.

C.0343 Leonard, Eileen (1983, October). Judicial decisions and prison reform: The impact of litigation on women prisoners. *Social Problems, 31*(1), 45-58. Discusses prison reform, prison litigation, and sex discrimination in U.S. women's prisons.

C.0344 Levanthal, G., & Krate, R. (1977). Physical attractiveness and severity of sentencing. *Psychological Reports, 40*(1), 315-318. Study of sentences of 48 women.

C.0345 Levinson, Betty (1986, Fall). Using expert testimony in the Grand Jury to avoid a homicide indictment for a battered woman: Practical considerations for defense counsel. *Women's Rights Law Reporter, 9*(3-4), 239-244. Discusses how expert testimony is used in cases of battering.

C.0346 Levit, H. I. (1991). Battered women: Syndrome versus self-defense. *American Journal of Forensic Psychology, 9*(1), 29-25. Differentiates between acts of violence committed as a result of battered woman-syndrome and acts of violence in self-defense.

C.0347 Lewin, Tamara (1980). Battered women and the doctrine of self-defense: A reevaluation of the meaning of deadly force. *Student Lawyer, 8,* 10-12. Discusses the use of battered woman's syndrome as self-defense.

C.0348 Lewis, Diane (1981b). Black women offenders and criminal justice. In M. Warren (Ed.), *The sex role system* (pp. 89-105). London: Sage. Discusses the treatment of black women in the criminal justice system.

C.0349 Lewis, James (1990, October). Premenstrual Syndrome as a criminal defense. *Archives of Sexual Behavior, 19*(5), 425-441. Discusses criteria for using PMS as a criminal defense.

C.0350 Lowry, Beverly (1992). *Crossed over: A murder, a memoir.* New York, NY: Alfred A. Knopf. A biographical account of the case of Karla Faye Tucker, a woman on death row in Texas.

C.0351 Madden, Allison (1993, Winter). Clemency for battered women who kill their abusers: Finding a just forum. *Hastings Women's Law Journal, 4,* 1-86. Discusses the use of the battered woman's syndrome as a criminal defense.

C.0352 Madden, Allison, et al. (1992, Spring). The ethnic origin of women serving a prison sentence. *British Journal of Criminology, 32*(2), 218-221 Survey of 1988 figures in Great Britain indicated the presence of many foreign women, specifically women from West Africa, in British prisons.

C.0353 Maguigan, Holly (1991, December). Battered women and self-defense: Myths and misconceptions in current reform proposals. *University of Pennsylvania Law Review, 140*(2), 379-486. Discusses redefinitions of legal rules regarding self-defense.

C.0354 Maher, Lisa, & Waring, E. (1990, Spring). Beyond simple differences: White collar crime, gender, and workforce. *Phoebe, 2*(1), 44-54. Discusses women and white-collar crime.

C.0355 Maier-Katkin, D. (1991, March). Postpartum psychosis, infanticide and the law. *Crime, Law, and Social Change, 15*(2), 109-123. Discusses the use of postpartum psychosis as a defense for women who kill their children.

C.0356 Mann, Coramae (1993). *Unequal Justice: A question of color.* Bloomington, IN: Indiana University Press. Discusses racial discrimination in the justice system.

C.0357 Mann, Coramae (1989, Winter). Minority and female: A criminal justice double bind. *Social Justice, 16*(4), 95-114. Considers status of nonwhite women from arrest to incarceration since the 1970's, noting the "double discrimination" they face.

C.0358 Mann, Coramae (1984, March-April). Race and sentencing of female felons: A field study. *International Journal of Women's Studies, 7*(2), 160-172. Examined race and sentencing by tracking women arrested in Atlanta, Georgia, during September, 1981. Total, 217.

C.0359 Marholin, D., et al. (1975, June). Mobilization of the community through a behavioral approach: A school program for adjudicated females. *Criminal Justice and Behavior, 2*(2), 130-145. Discusses community education of women offenders.

C.0360 Martinez, T. A. (1994). Embracing the outlaws: Deviance at the intersection of race, class, and gender. *Utah Law Review, 1994,* 193-207. Discusses the intersection of race, gender and the criminal justice system.

C.0361 Massachusetts Bar Association (1993). *Two cutting-edge defenses: Diminished capacity & battered woman syndrome.* Boston, MA: Massachusetts Bar Association. Discusses use of the battered woman's syndrome as a criminal defense.

C.0362 Massachussetts Supreme Judicial Court (1989). Gender bias study of the court system in Massachussetts. Boston, MA: Massachussetts Supreme Judicial Court. Investigated the extent, nature, and consequences of gender bias in Massachussetts courts over a 3-year period.

C.0363 McClellan, Dorothy (1994, March). Disparity in the discipline of male and female inmates in Texas prisons. *Women and Criminal Justice, 5*(2), 71-97. Compared disciplinary practices in two prisons housing Texas female inmates to those found in the Texas prisons for men.

C.0364 McColgan, Aileen (1993, Winter). In defense of battered women who kill. *Oxford Journal of Legal Studies, 13*(4), 508-529. Argues that self-defense should be considered more often for battered women because self-defense more adequately represents the reality of their situation.

C.0365 McCord, J., & Otten, L. (1983, March). A consideration of sex roles and motivations for crime. *Criminal Justice and Behavior, 10,* 3-12. Discusses gender-specific crimes.

C.0366 McCorkle, Richard (1995). Gender, psychopathology, and institutional behavior: A comparison of male and female mentally ill prison inmates. *Journal of Criminal Justice, 23*(1), 53-61. Examines the relationship between mental disorder and disruptiveness in correctional institutions by comparing male and female inmate populations.

C.0367 McGillivray, A. (1987). Battered women: Definition, models, a prosecutorial policy. *Canadian Journal of Family Law, 6,* 1545. Discusses use of the battered woman's syndrome as a defense.

C.0368 McKanna, C. (1987). The nameless ones: The ethnic experience in San Quentin, 1851-1880. *Pacific Historian, 31*(1), 20-33. Analyzes prison records for the first 30 years of San Quentin's existence for ethnicity, crime type, age, and disposition. Records show 33 women prisoners during that time.

C.0369 McKerracher, D., et al. (1966, September). A comparison of the behavior problems presented by male and female abnormal offenders. *British Journal of Psychiatry, 112*(490), 891-897. Discusses gender-specific behavior problems in an incarcerated population.

C.0370 McKinnie, Karen (1989). The use of expert testimony in the defense of battered women. In S. Johann & F. Osanka (Eds.), *Representing battered women who kill* (pp. 212-217). Springfield, IL: Charles C. Thomas. Defines psychological autopsy and discusses its use as a trial strategy.

C.0371 Meerpol, Michael (1994). *The Rosenberg letters: A complete edition of the prison correspondence of Ethel and Julius Rosenberg.* New York, NY: Garland. Letters presented by one of their sons, Michael Meeropol.

C.0372 Menzies, Robert, et al. (1992). Female follies: The forensic psychiatric assessment of women defendants. *International Journal of Law and Psychiatry, 15,* 179-193. Discusses use of psychiatric assessments for female offenders.

C.0373 Messner, S. F. (1986). Sex differences in arrest rates for homicide: An application of the general theory of structural strain. *Comparative Social Research, 8,* 187-201. Looks at male and female arrests for homicide.

C.0374 Meyer, Cheryl (1994, March). *Postpartum syndromes and the legal system.* Paper presented at the 1994 ACJS Annual Meeting, Chicago, IL. Explains three types of postpartum syndromes. Focuses on the overlap of postpartum syndromes as insanity defenses for criminal behavior.

C.0375 Miller, Alan (1986, November). The physical attractiveness of physiques in determining certainty of guilt, recommended punishment, and rehabilitative potential of defendants. *Dissertation Abstracts International, 47*(5), 2230. Discusses physical attractiveness, determination of guilt, recommended prison sentence, and rehabilitative potential of defendants.

C.0376 Miller, E. E. (1977). The woman offender and community corrections. In E. Miller & M. Montilla (Eds.), *Corrections in the community.* Reston, VA: Reston Publishing Co. Looks at alternative sentencing.

C.0377 Miller, J. L., et al. (1986). Perceptions of justice: Race and gender differences in judgements of appropriate prison sentences. *Law and Society Review, 20,* 314-334. Looks at race and gender as variables in sentencing.

C.0378 Mitchell, Marilyn (1978). Does wife abuse justify homicide? *Wayne Law Review, 24*(5), 1705-1731. Discusses battered women who kill.

C.0379 Mitchell, Tom (1993,Winter). Blood with the taint of Cain: Immigrant labouring children, Manitoba politics, and the execution of Emily Hilda Blake. *Journal of Canadian Studies, 28,* 49-71. Discusses the execution of Emily Blake in Canada.

C.0380 Mohr, Renate (1990, July). Sentencing as a gendered process: Results of a consultation. *Canadian Journal of Criminology, 32*(3), 479-485. Explores sentencing reform from a feminist perspective. Discusses criminal sentencing as discriminatory and gender-specific.

C.0381 Morash, Merry, et al. (1994, April). A comparison of programming for women and men in U.S. prisons in the 1980s. *Crime and Delinquency, 40*(2), 197-221. Discusses how prison experiences for women do not assist in overcoming marginalization from the workforce.

C.0382 Morash, Merry, et al. (1986, February). Gender, peer group experiences, and seriousness of delinquency. *Journal of Research in Crime and Delinquency, 23*(1), 43-67. Discusses gender and peer group as variables in types of crime.

C.0383 Morgan-Sharp, Etta, & Jackson, Angela (1994, March). *Men, morals and murder.* Paper presented at the 1994 ACJS Annual Meeting, Chicago, IL. Examines the affect of gender and class on the trials and sentencing of twin sisters in a murder-for-hire.

C.0384 Morris, Allison (1988, March). Sex and sentencing. *Criminal Law Revue(London),* 163-171. Explores the idea that women are treated more leniently than men in the criminal justice system.

C.0385 Morris, Amy (1993, July), Insanity defense: Gender differences. *Dissertation Abstracts International, 54*(1), 504. Addresses differences between female and male insanity defendants.

C.0386 Morse, S. J. (1990, December). The misbegotten marriage of soft psychology and bad law: Psychological self-defense as a justification for homicide. *Law and Human Behavior, 14*(6), 595-618. Discusses "psychological self-defense" as an excuse for battered women who kill.

C.0387 Moulds, Elizabeth (1980). Chivalry and paternalism: Disparities of treatment in the criminal justice system. In S. Datesman & F. Scarpitti (Eds.), *Women, crime and justice* (pp. 277-299). New York, NY: Oxford University Press.

C.0388 Moyer, Imogene (1982, December). Police responses to women offenders in a Southeastern city. *Journal of Police Science and Administration, 10*(4), 376-383. Tested hypotheses that police are less inclined to arrest women than men unless they exhibit traditionally masculine behavior.

C.0389 Moyer, Imogene (1981a). Demeanor, sex, and race in police processing. *Journal of Criminal Justice, 9*(3), 235-246. Assesses the processing of females by police. Reports the results of a study that took place between September-December, 1978.

C.0390 Moyer, Imogene, & White, G. F. (1981b). Police processing of female offenders. In L. Bowker (Ed.), *Women and crime in America.* New York, NY: Macmillan. Discusses the treatment of female offenders in the arrest process.

C.0391 Moyer, Sharon (1992, July). Race, gender, and homicide: Comparisons between aboriginals and other Canadians. *Canadian Journal of Criminology, 34*(3-4), 387-402. Analyzes homicide data for 1962-1984. Discusses the relationship between race and gender of victims and suspects.

C.0392 Mudd, Susan (1990, August). Convicted women and magistrates: Assessing theory and practice. *Dissertation Abstracts International, 51*(2), 643-A. Discusses gender in the courts.

C.0393 Murphy, J., et al. (1992). *In the decade of the child: Addicted mothers, imprisonment, and alternatives.* Albany, NY: New York State Coalition for Criminal Justice. Examines programs and policies for drug abusing female offenders and their children in the state of New York.

C.0394 Naffine, Ngaire (1995). *Gender, crime, and feminism.* Dartmouth Publishing Co. Discusses gender and crime from a feminist perspective.

C.0395 Naffine, Ngaire, & Gale, Fay (1989, Spring). Testing the nexus: Crime, gender, and unemployment. *Journal of Criminology, 29*(2), 144-156. Examines the relationship between gender, crime, and unemployment using South Australia as a case study.

C.0396 Nagel, Ilene, & Johnson, Barry (1994, Summer). The role of gender in a structured sentencing system: Equal treatment, policy choices, and the sentencing of female offenders under the United States sentencing guidelines. *Journal of Criminal Law & Criminology, 85*(1), 181-221. Challenges claim that adoption of gender-neutral sentencing guidelines treats women unfairly.

C.0397 Nagel, Ilene, & Hagan, John (1983). Gender and crime: Offense patterns and criminal court sanctions. In M. Tonry & N. Morris (Ed.), *Crime and justice: An annual review of research* (pp. 91-144). Chicago IL: University of Chicago Press. Discusses the relation of gender to case processing decisions in criminal court.

C.0398 Nagel, Ilene, et al. (1982). Sex differences in the processing of criminal defendants. In D. K. Weisberg (Ed.), *Women and the law*. Cambridge, MA: Schenkman Publishing. Discusses discriminatory processing of criminal defendants.

C.0399 Nagel, S., & Weitzman, Lenore (1971, November). Women as litigants. *The Hastings Law Journal, 23,* 171-198. Discusses how the treatment of female litigants differs from the treatment of male litigants.

C.0400 Naish, Camille (1991). *Death comes to the maiden: Sex and execution, 1431-1933.* London: Routledge. Discusses the execution of women historically.

C.0401 Nance, L. (1988, April). *Women in crime: The sentencing of female defendants.* Sacramento, CA: California Department of Justice. Discusses data from 1978-1987 which indicated that 15% of over 2 million adult felony dispositions involved female defendants in California courts.

C.0402 National Coalition to Abolish the Death Penalty (1992, March). *Women on death row.* Washington, DC: National Coalition to Abolish the Death Penalty. A listing of women on death row according to date of sentencing and crimes committed.

C.0403 Neville, M. (1929, May). Our laws and the ladies. Does justice discriminate against sex? *Police 13-13, 4,* 16-17. Early discussion of discrimination in the courts.

C.0404 New England Law Review (1990, Spring). Postpartum depression defense: Are mothers getting away with murder? *New England Law Review, 24,* 953-989. Discusses the use of postpartum depression as a defense in criminal cases involving women who kill their infants.

C.0405 New Jersey Committee on Sex Discrimination in the Statutes (1985). *Public hearing on sex discrimination in criminal justice and correctional institutions, November 19, 1985.* Trenton, NJ: New Jersey Committee on Sex Discrimination in the Statutes.

C.0406 New York Law School Review (1987). Battered woman syndrome testimony and the jury: The question of admissibility. *New York Law School Law Review, 32,* 79-109. Discusses educating juries to understand the battered woman's syndrome.

C.0407 New York State Unified Court System (1987). *Report of the Committtee to Implement Recommendations of the New York Task Force on Women in the Courts.* Albany, NY: New York State Unified Court System. Task force concluded that gender bias against women as litigants, attorneys, and court employees was pervasive in New York State.

C.0408 Nodland, I. B. (1992). Defending battered women: Everything she says may be used against them. *North Dakota Law Review, 68,* 131-144. Discusses the defense of battered women who have killed their abusers.

C.0409 Norton, Mary Beth (1991). *Gender, crime, and community in seventeenth-century Maryland.* New York, NY: Alfred A. Knopf. Discusses the affect of gender on ideas about crime in Maryland.

C.0410 Ochie, Charles (1993). *Female offenders and the criminal justice system: Examining patterns of differential treatment of female offenders in Oklahoma.* Dissertation, Oklahoma State University. Discussses discriminatory practices with female offenders in Oklahoma.

C.0411 O'Donnell, Bernard (1956). *Should women hang?* London: W. H. Allen. Discussion of the death penalty for women.

C.0412 Offen, L. (1986). Female offender and psychiatric referral: The medicalization of female deviance. *Medicine and Law, 5*(4), 339-348. Discusses court psychiatric referrals of women.

C.0413 Ortega, Suzanne, & Burnett, Cathleen (1987). Age variation in female crime: In search of the new female criminal. *Journal of Criminal Justice, 10*(1), 133-169. A study of police arrests in Kansas City, MO(1962-1980). Considered the convergence of male and female crime rates.

C.0414 Osborne, Judith (1989, Fall). Perspectives on premenstrual syndrome: Women, law, and medicine. *Journal of Family Law, 8*(1), 165-184. Discusses whether a PMS defense might set precedent for discrimination against women in other areas.

C.0415 Osgoode Hall Law Journal (1990, Spring). Female poisoners of the nineteenth century: A study of gender bias in the application of the law. *Osgoode Hall Law Journal, 28,* 53-101. Looks at court disposition towards women.

C.0416 O'Shea, Kathleen (1994). Till death do us part: Women on death row. *Nemesis: A Journal of Women and the Law, 10*(2), 54-57. Discusses the situation of women on death row in the United States.

C.0417 O'Shea, Kathleen (1993). Women on death row. In B. Fletcher et al. (Eds.), *Women prisoners: A forgotten population* (pp. 75-91). Wesport, CT: Greenwood Press. Historical background on the death penalty as applied to women and current status of women on death row in the U.S.

C.0418 Owen, C. E., & Bell, J. (1977). Black women: Income and incarceration. In C. Owen & J. Bell (Eds.), *Blacks and criminal justice* (pp. 85-92). Lexington, MA: Lexington Books, DC Heath. Discusses socio-enconomic influences in decisions to incarcerate black women.

C.0419 Oxford Journal of Legal Studies (1993, Winter). In defense of battered women who kill. *Oxford Journal of Legal Studies, 13,* 508-529. Discusses the battered woman's syndrome as a defense.

C.0420 Palmer, Stuart (1980). Sex differences in criminal homicide and suicide in England and Wales and the United States. *Omega: Journal of Death and Dying, 11*(3), 255-270. Discusses the possibility of a subculture of violence in England and Wales.

C.0421 Panton, James (1975). Personality differences between male and female inmates measured by the MMPI. In A. Brodsky (Ed.), *The female offender* (pp. 40-47). Beverly Hills, CA: Sage. Compared MMPI profiles of male and female offenders.

C.0422 Panton, James (1974, December). Personality differences between male and female prison inmates measured by the MMPI. *Criminal Justice and Behavior, 1*(4), 332-339. Compared MMPI profiles of 128 female and 128 male prisoners.

C.0423 Parisi, Nicolette (1982). Are females treated differently? A review of the theories and evidence on sentencing and parole decisions. In N. Rafter Hahn & E. Stanko (Eds.), *Judge, lawyer, victim, thief* (pp. 205-220). Boston, MA: Northeastern University Press. Outlines major differences between male and female defendants in court dispositions.

C.0424 Parliament, House of Commons (1820, June 29). *A bill to repeal an act passed in the 57th year of the reign of his late Majesty King George the Third: Entitled "An act to abolish the punishment of public whipping of female offenders," and to make further provisions in lieu thereof.* London: Parliament, House of Commons.

C.0425 Pattullo, P. (1983). *Judging women.* London: National Council for Civil Liberties. Discusses factors that influence court cases involving women defendants.

C.0426 Paulus, Paul, & Dzindolet, Mary (1993, June). Reactions of male and female inmates to prison confinement: Further evidence for a two-component model. *Criminal Justice and Behavior, 20*(2), 149-166. Inmates were contacted at the beginning of their confinement and 4 months later for their reactions to incarceration.

C.0427 Pearson, Rose (1976). Women defendants in magistrates courts. *British Journal of Law and Society, 2*(3), 265-273. Discusses women as defendants in English courts.

C.0428 Pennsylvania Program for Women and Girl Offenders (1977). *Courts and the woman offender: a report on judicial views, proceedings, and sentencing of women in Pennsylvania in 1975.* Philadelphia, PA: Pennsylvania Program for Women and Girl Offenders.

C.0429 Phillips, D., & DeFleur, Lois (1982, November). Gender ascription in the stereotyping of deviants. *Criminology, 20*(3-4), 431-448. Tested 3 hypotheses on deviant stereotypes, gender roles, and female crime using data from a Washington statewide survey of adults.

C.0430 Phillipson, Ilene (1988). *Ethel Rosenberg: Beyond the myths.* New York, NY: Franklin Watts. Biography of Ethel Roseberg executed for treason in 1953 at the age of 38. Author focuses on who Ethel Rosenberg was to her family.

C.0431 Pollock-Byrne, Joycelyn (1986). *Sex and supervision: Guarding male and female inmates.* New York, NY: Greenwood Press. Examined supervision problems in working with female and male inmates to evaluate the belief that women prisoners are more difficult to supervise.

C.0432 Popiel, Marianne (1979, Fall-1980, Winter). Sentencing women: Equal protection in the context of discriminatory decision making. *Women's Rights Law Reporter, 6,* 85-106. Discusses discrimination against women in the legal system.

C.0433 Potter, Joan (1979). Women's work? The assault on sex barriers in prison job training. *Corrections Magazine, 5,* 43-46, 48-49. Discusses the types of jobs women are typically trained for in prison programs.

C.0434 Preising, Keith (1994, December). Self-defense and the battered woman syndrome: A moment in time. *Masters Abstracts International, 32*(6), 1555. Discusses problems associated with confrontational and non-confrontational cases of battered women and the self-defense doctrine.

C.0435 Quade, Vicki (1983, August). Sex bias in the courtroom. *American Bar Association Journal, 69,* 1017-1018. Discusses gender discrimination in the practice of criminal law.

C.0436 Quigley, Tim (1991). Battered women and the defense of provocation. *Saskatchewan Law Review, 55,* 223-261. Discusses provocation as a defense in the case of battered women who kill.

C.0437 Quinn, James (1987). Sex roles and hedonism among members of outlaw motorcycle clubs. *Deviant Behavior, 8,* 47-63. Discusses the roles of males and females in motorcycle gangs.

C.0438 Radford, Lorraine (1994). Pleading for time. Justice for battered women who kill. In H. Birch (Ed.), *Moving targets: Women, murder and representation* (pp. 172-197). Berkeley, CA: University of California Press. Discusses the battered woman's syndrome as a defense for spousal homicide.

C.0439 Raeder, Myrna (1993, April). Gender and sentencing: Single moms, battered women, and other sex-based anomalies in the gender-free worlds of the Federal Sentencing Guidelines. *Pepperdine Law Review, 20,* 905-990. Discusses the place of gender in sentencing practices.

C.0440 Rafter-Hahn, Nicole (1992a). Equality or difference? In American Correctional Association *Female offenders: Meeting the needs of a neglected population* (pp. 7-11). Laurel, MD: American Correctional Association. Questions "Should female inmates be treated like male inmates or differently?" when equal treatment often means less adequate care for women.

C.0441 Rafter-Hahn, Nicole (1992b, Spring). Equality or difference? *Federal Prisons Journal: Special issue: Focus on the female offender, 3*(1), 17-19. Addresses the issue of equality in the treatment of female and male offenders.

C.0442 Rafter-Hahn, Nicole (1985). Gender, prisons, and prison history. *Social Science History, 9*(3), 233-248. Discusses gender differentiation in the prison system after 1870 when women prisoners were usually incarcerated for committing crimes against social mores.

C.0443 Rafter, Nicole, & Stanko, Elizabeth (Eds.), *Judge, lawyer, victim, theif: Women, gender roles and criminal justice.* Boston, MA: Northeastern University Press. Fifteen essays on women's involvement with the criminal justice sytem presented in 4 parts.

C.0444 Ramstad, Sheryl (1975). Female offenders: A challenge to courts and the legislature. *North Dakota Law Review, 29,* 530-546. Discusses the affect of gender in the courts and in legislation.

C.0445 Rapaport, Elizabeth (1991). The death penalty and gender discrimination. *Law and Society Review, 25*(2), 367-383. Examines gender discrimination in relation to the death penalty.

C.0446 Recollet, Nancy (1985, December). Native women and the criminal justice system: An increasing minority. *Resources for Feminist Research, 14,* 16-18. Discusses the increase in the number of incarcerated native women.

C.0447 Reed, Jacqueline (1992). *Toward educating minority female offenders: Institutional orientations, academia and vocational stereotyping, Phase I.* Paper presented at the Annual Meeting of the American Education Research Association, San Francisco, CA., April, 1992. First phase of a 3-part model for educational programs for incarcerated minority women.

C.0448 Reske, H. J. (1993, April). License to kill? *American Bar Association Journal, 79,* 37. Discusses the use of self-defense in cases where battered women kill their husbands/abusers.

C.0449 Resnick, Judith (1983). Should prisoners be classified by sex? In J. Doig (Ed.), *Criminal Corrections: Ideals and realities* (pp. 109-123). Lexington, MA: Lexington Books, DC Heath. Historical overview of incarcerating males and females together, then separately.

C.0450 Resnick, Judith (1982, November). Womens prisons and mens prisons: Should prisoners be classified by sex? *Policy Studies Review, 2(2),* 246-252. Examines differences between "women's prisons" and "men's prisons" using data from the 1979.

C.0451 Richards, Pamela, & Tittle, C. R. (1981, June). Gender and percieved chances of arrest. *Social Forces, 59*(4) , 1182-1199. Examines gender differences in perceived chances of arrest for six types of lawbreaking.

C.0452 Richie, Beth (1993, April). Gender entrapment: An exploratory study of the link between gender-identity development, violence against women, race/ethnicity and crime among African American battered women. *Dissertation Abstracts International, 53*(10), 3683. Presents a theoretical model, Gender Entrapment, to examine crime in African American women.

C.0453 Roberts, D. E. (1994). Symposium: Gender issues and the criminal law. Foreword: The meaning of gender equality in criminal law. *Journal of Criminal Law and Criminolgoy, 85*(1), 1-14. A feminist analysis of gender equality in criminal law.

C.0454 Roberts, D. E. (1993). Motherhood and crime. *Iowa Law Reivew, 79*(1), 95-141. Examines how criminal law enforces the subordinating aspects of motherhood and punishes women's resistance.

C.0455 Roberts, Marilyn, & Knoebel, Dixie (1989). National Conference on Gender Bias in the Courts. *State Court Journal, 13*(3), 12. Details proceedings of the National Conference held in May, 1989. Focuses on gender bias in the courts as real and serious.

C.0456 Robinson, Robin (1992). Intermediate sanctions and the female offender. In J. Byrne et al. (Eds.), *Smart sentencing: The emergence of intermediate sanctions* (pp. 245-260). Newbury Park, CA: Sage Publications. Discusses the use of intermediate sanctions with female offenders.

C.0457 Rodash, Polly (1994, March). *An examination of sentencing patterns of female offenders from a critical perspective.* Paper presented at the 1994 ACJS Annual Meeting, Chicago, IL. Examines historical patterns of sentencing female offenders, chivalry, and current sentencing trends.

C.0458 Rogers, J. L., et al. (1983,Winter). Women in Oregon's insanity defense system. *Journal of Psychiatric Law, 11*(4), 515-532. Compared 48 women and 384 men acquitted of crimes by reason of insanity in Oregon from 1978 to 1982.

C.0459 Rose, H., & McClain, Paula (1990). Black females and lethal violence. In H. Rose & P. McClain (Eds.), *Race, place, and risk: Black homicide in urban America.* Albany, NY: State University of New York Press. Discusses black women who commit murder.

C.0460 Rosen, Cathryn Jo (1986, Fall). The excuse of self-defense: Correcting a historical accident on behalf of battered women who kill. *The American University Law Review, 36,* 11-56. Discusses the use of self-defense as a defense for battered women who kill an abuser.

C.0461 Rosen, Richard (1993, January). On self-defense, imminence, and women who kill their batterers. *North Carolina Law Review, 71,* 371-411. Discusses the use of self-defense as a defense for battered women who kill.

C.0462 Rosenbaum, Jill (1988). Age, race, and female offending. *Journals of Contemporary Criminal Justice, 4*(3), 125-130. Examines similarities and differences among white and minority women committed to the California Youth Authority in the 1960's.

C.0463 Roshier, B. (1989). Gender: Women's crime. In B. Roshier (Ed.), *Controlling crime: The classical perspective in criminology* (pp. 110-113). Chicago, IL: Lyceum Books. Discusses gender-specific crimes.

C.0464 Ross, Luana (1994, Fall). Race, gender, and social control: Voices of imprisoned Native American and white women. *WICAZO SA Review, 10*(2), 17-39. Compares the experiences of Native American and white women in prison.

C.0465 Ross, Luana (1993, February). Mothers behind bars: A comparative study of the experiences of imprisoned American Indian and white women. *Dissertation Abstracts International, 53*(8), 3002. Compares experiences of imprisoned American Indian and white mothers.

C.0466 Roudebush, Elizabeth (1994). *Gender differences among juvenile decision-makers.* Paper presented at the ACJS Annual Meeting, March 8-12, 1994, Chicago, IL. Tests the hypothesis that males are more punishment oriented than females.

C.0467 Rowe, A. R. (1983). Sanctions and the aged woman. *Perceptual and Motor Skills, 56*, 427-430. Discusses how women perceive and judge an aging female offender.

C.0468 Rowe, G. S. (1983). Female crime and the courts in revolutionary Lancaster county. *Journal of the Lancaster County Historical Society, 87*(2), 64-70. Considers women's involvement as plaintiffs, defendants, and witnesses in colonial Pennsylvania criminal court cases.

C.0469 Rupert, L. (1980). Woman in North Carolina fights to stay alive. *Southern Coalition Report on Jails and Prisons, 7*, 1-8. Discusses the case of Velma Barfield who was executed in 1984.

C.0470 Ryan, Karen (1994, Fall). Mad or bad? Women and the forensic psychiatric process. *Masters Abstracts International, 32*(3). 863. Explores the role of forensic psychiatry in social control of mentally disordered female offenders.

C.0471 Sachs, A., & Wilson, J. (1978). *Sexism and the law: A study of male beliefs and social bias.* Oxford: Martin Robertson. Explores sexism in the practice of law.

C.0472 Sagatun, Inger (1990). Gender discrimination in criminal justice: Relevant law and future trends. *Women and Criminal Justice, 2*(1), 63-81. Focuses on gender discrimination issues involving persons employed in the criminal justice system.

C.0473 Sagatun, Inger (1989, September). Gender biases in probation officers: Attributions of juvenile delinquency. *International Journal of Offender Therapy & Comparative Criminology, 33*(2), 131-140. Focuses on male and female probation officers' explanations for male and female delinquency.

C.0474 Saitow, Steffani (1993, Summer). Battered woman syndrome: Does the "reasonable batttered woman" exist? *New England Journal on Criminal and Civil Confinement, 19*, 329-371. Discusses the use of the battered woman's syndrome as a defense.

C.0475 Saitow, Steffani (1986, April). The battered woman syndrome and self-defense: A legal and empirical dissent. *Virginia Law Review, 72*, 619-647. Discusses the battered woman's syndrome as a defense.

C.0476 Sangster, Joan (1993, June). Pardon tales from magistrate's court: Women, crime, and the court in Peterborough County, 1920-1950. *Canadian Historical Review, 7*(2), 161-197. Discusses women who appeared before the Magistrate Court in Peterborough county Canada from 1920-1950.

C.0477 Sargent, Georgia (1991, April). Battered woman syndrome gaining legal recognition, *Trial, 27,* 17-20. Discusses the legal recognition of battered woman's syndrome as a defense.

C.0478 Sargent, J. P. (1984, March). The evolution of a stereotype: Paternalism and the female inmate. *The Prison Journal, 64*(1), 37-44. Discusses paternalism in the prison system.

C.0479 Sarri, Rosemary (1989). Unequal protection under the law: Women and the criminal justice system. In J. Figueira-McDonough & R. Sarri (Eds.), *The trapped woman: Catch-22 in deviance and control* (pp. 394-426). Beverly Hills, CA: Sage Publications. Discusses discriminatory practices in the criminal justice system.

C.0480 Sarri, Rosemary (1987). Gender and race differences in criminal justice processing. *Women's Studies International Forum: Special issue: Women and the Law, 9*(1), 89-99. Analysis of court processing of black and white females and characteristics of female offenders.

C.0481 Satterfield, V. (1953, March-April). Criminal responsibility of women. *Journal of Criminal Law, Criminology, and Police Science, 43*(6), 756-763. Discusses criminal responsibility and the law as it applies to women.

C.0482 Saulters-Tubbs, Cecilia (1993, June). Prosecutorial and judicial treatment of female offenders. *Federal Probation, 57*(2), 37-42. Discusses the treatment of female offenders in the courts.

C.0483 Schafran, Lynn (1986, Spring). Educating the judiciary about gender-bias. *Women's Rights Law Reporter, 9*(2), 109-124. Discusses work of the New Jersey Supreme Court Task Force on women in the courts.

C.0484 Scheffler, J. (1990). Ethel Rosenberg's prison letters: An example of women's prison literature in transition. *Women and Criminal Justice, 2*(1), 19-39. A unique insight into the life of a woman on death row and her struggle to adapt to imprisonment in her own words.

C.0485 Schichor, D. (1985). Male-female differences in elderly arrests: An exploratory analysis. *Justice Quarterly, 2*(3), 399-414. Compares crime patterns of elderly males and females.

C.0486 Schneider, Elizabeth (1989). Describing and changing: Women's self-defense work and the problem of expert testimony on battering. In S. Johann & F. Osanka (Eds.), *Representing battered women who kill* (pp. 51-98). Springfield, IL: Charles C. Thomas. Discusses problems that exist in the use of expert testimony on battering.

C.0487 Schneider, Elizabeth (1978, Spring). Representation of women who defend themselves in response to physical or sexual assault. *Women's Rights Law Reporter, 4*(3), 149-163. Discusses the defense of battered women.

C.0488 Schneider, Susan (1978). A Jewish women's community-behind bars. *Lilith, 5,* 10-15. Jewish women in prison describe the double discrimination they face as whites and non-Christians.

C.0489 Schulhofer, S. J. (1990, Spring). The gender question in criminal law. *Social Philosophy, 7*(2), 105-137. Discusses the place of gender in the practice of criminal law.

C.0490 Schuller, Regina (1994a). Applications of battered woman syndrome evidence in the courtroom. In M. Constanzo & S. Oskamp (Eds.), *Violence and the law: Claremont Symposium on Applied Social Psychology* (pp. 113-134). Thousand Oaks, CA: Sage Publications. Examines contributions of social psychologists to the use of battered woman syndrome in trials.

C.0491 Schuller, Regina (1994b). Jurors decisions in trials of battered women who kill: The role of prior beliefs and expert testimony. *Journal of Applied Social Psychology, 24*(4), 316+. Discusses factors that influence jury decisions in trials of battered women who kill.

C.0492 Schuller, Regina (1992, December). The impact of battered woman syndrome evidence on jury decision processes. *Law and Human Behavior, 16*(2), 597-620. Discusses the use of the battered woman's syndrome as a defense and how it influences jury decisions.

C.0493 Schuller, Regina, & Vidmar, N. (1992, June). Battered women syndrome evidence in the courtroom: A review of the literature. *Law and Human Behavior, 16*(3), 273-311. Examination of research on evidence relating to the battered woman syndrome in trials..

C.0494 Schuller, Regina (1990). The impact of battered woman syndrome testimony on jury decision making: Lavalle, V. R. [1 (SC) R.852 (1990)]. *The Windsor Yearbook of Access to Justice, 10,* 105-126. Examines testimony of experts in trials of battered women who murdered their abusers.

C.0495 Scutt, Jocelynne (1992, July). The incredible woman: A recurring character in criminal law. *Women's Studies International Forum, 15*(4), 441-460. Discusses the credibility of a woman offender or victim in the eyes of the law.

C.0496 Scutt, Joycelynne (1981). Sexism in criminal law. In S. Mukherjee & J. Scutt (Eds.), *Women and crime* (pp. 1-21). London: Allen & Unwin. Discusses basic inequalities between men and women according to Australian law.

C.0497 Shacklady-Smith, L. (1978). Sexist assumptions about female delinquency: An empirical investigation. In C. Smart & B. Smart (Eds.), *Women, sexuality, and social control* (pp. 74-86). London: Routledge. Discusses basic sexist assumptions about female delinquency.

C.0498 Sheehy, Elizabeth (1992, December). Defending battered women on trial: The battered woman syndrome and its limitations. *Criminal Law Journal, 16,* 369-394. Discusses the use of the battered woman's syndrome and its limitations in a criminal trial.

C.0499 Sheehy, Elizabeth (1987). *Personal autonomy and the criminal law: Emerging issues for women.* Ottawa: Canadian Advisory Council on the Status of Women. Discusses the status of women in criminal law.

C.0500 Sheppard, Muriel (1935). *Cabins in the Laurel.* Chapel Hill, NC: University of North Carolina Press. Material from the Frances Silvers case. Thirteen stanzas of a ballad she supposedly wrote before her execution as well as "The Quiltin," a poem based on the same case.

C.0501 Shover, Neal, et al. (1979). Gender roles and delinquency. *Social Forces, 58,* 126-175. Discusses gender-specific offenses.

C.0502 Simon, Rita, & Baxter, Sandra (1989). Gender and violent crime. In N. Weiner & M. Wolfgang (Eds.), *Violent crime, violent criminals.* Beverly Hills, CA: Sage Publications. Discusses gender as a variable in the analysis of violent crime.

C.0503 Simon, Rita (1979). Arrest statistics. In F. Adler & R. Simon (Eds.), *Criminology of deviant women* (pp. 101-113). Boston, MA: Houghton Mifflin Company. Discusses arrests, court appearances, and prison statistics of the female offender for the last decade.

C.0504 Simon, Rita, & Sharma, Navin (1978, April). *The female defendant in Washington, DC., 1974-1975.* Washington, DC: Institute for Law and Social Research. Statistics on female crime and arrest rates in Washington, DC.

C.0505 Simon, Marilyn (1994, March). *Day reporting centers: An alternative to the incarceration of women.* Paper presented at the 1994 ACJS Annual Meeting, Chicago, IL. Presents the use of Day Reporting Centers as an alternative to incarceration, particularly for female offenders.

C.0506 Sinden, P. G. (1981, January-March). Offender gender and perceptions of crime seriousness. *Sociological Spectrum, 1*(1), 39-52. Discusses how the perceived seriousness of a crime is related to the gender of the offender.

C.0507 Singh, Udai (1972). Comparative study of attitudes of male and female criminals towards their family, parents and authority. *Journal of the Indian Academy of Applied Psychology, 9*(1), 18-21. Data collected from 82 female and 100 male inmates.

C.0508 Singh, Udai (1970). The self-concept of both criminal male and female: A comparative study. *Psychological Studies, 15,* 101-107. Compares self-concept in male and female offenders.

C.0509 Singleton, Sarah (1990, February). Gender bias skews justice for women. *Trial, 26*(2), 39-41. Discusses gender bias in the courts.

C.0510 Smart, C., & Smart, B. (1979). *Women, sexuality, and social control.* London, Routledge & Kegan Paul. Essays on the socialization of women and gender-specific roles.

C.0511 Smith, Anne (1969). The treatment of women offenders. *British Journal of Criminology, 9*(4), 396-398. Discusses problems of women in prison and alternatives to incarceration.

C.0512 Smith, L. (1988). Images of women: Decision making in courts. In A. Morris & C. Wilkinson (Eds.), *Women and the penal system.* Cambridge: Institute of Criminology. Discusses how gender influences the decision-making process in court.

C.0513 Smith, Stella Mae (1973). Intense experiences of black and white female prisoners. *Dissertation Abstracts International, 34*(10), 51-77. Compares the differences in experiences of black and white female inmates.

C.0514 Smith, Susan (1994, March). Diversifying the judiciary: The influence of gender and race on judging. *University of Richmond Law Review, 28,* 179-204. Discusses how gender and race influence judges.

C.0515 Sobel, Suzanne (1980, April). Women in prison: Sexism behind bars. *Professional Psychology, 11*(2), 331-338. Identifies problems experienced by women incarcerated in the U.S. and compares the availability of occupational and educational programs in prisons for men and women.

C.0516 Solomon, Freda (1983). Factors affecting differing dispositions of urban felony cases: Sex as a critical variable. *Dissertation Abstracts International, 44*(3), 857-858 Discusses the differences in the sentencing of felony cases when gender is a factor.

C.0517 South, Scott, & Messner, Steven (1987, Summer). The sex ratio and women's involvement in crime: A cross-national analysis. *Sociological Quarterly, 28*(2), 171-188. Statistics on female crime across the US.

C.0518 Speigel, A., & Spiegel, M. (1992). Paroxysmal insanity as a murder defense in 1865. *American Journal of Forensic Psychology, 10*(2), 17-34. Discusses the trial and acquittal of Mary Harris in 1865.

C.0519 Speigel, A., & Spiegel, M. (1991, April). Mad doctor vs. common sense doctors in 1865 trial. *Psychiatric Quarterly, 18,* 61-67. Discusses the 1865 trial of a woman for murder, as the first time that expert medical testimony supported a plea of insanity in a murder defense in U.S. history.

C.0520 Spohn, Cassia, & Spears, J. (1994, March). *Gender and case processing decisions.* Paper presented at the 1994 ACJS Annual Meeting, Chicago, IL. Investigates the relationship between gender and criminal justice outcomes.

C.0521 Spohn, Cassia, et al. (1987). The impact of the ethnicity and gender of defendants on the decision to reject or dismiss felony charges. *Criminology, 25*(1), 175-191. Discusses the impact of gender in the courtroom.

C.0522 Spohn, Cassia, et al. (1985, March). Women defendants in court: The interaction between sex and race in convicting and sentencing. *Social Science Quarterly, 66*(1), 178-185. Discusses the interaction of sex and race in sentencing.

C.0523 Steady, Filomina (1981). *The black woman cross-culturally.* Newbury Park, CA: Sage Publications. Black women in prison is one of the topics covered in this overview of black women in Africa, the Caribbean, and North and South America.

C.0524 Steel, Walter, & Sigman, Christine (1991, Winter). Re-examining the doctrine of self-defense to accommodate battered women. *American Journal of Criminal Law, 18,* 169-185. Discusses self defense and the use of the battered woman's syndrome.

C.0525 Steffensmeier, Darrell, et al. (1993, August). Gender and imprisonment decisions. *Criminology, 31*(3), 411-446. Analyzes guideline sentencing data from Pennsylvania for the years 1985-1987 to assess the influence of gender on decisions to imprison.

C.0526 Steffensmeier, Darrell, & Streiffel, Cathy (1991, March). Age, gender, and crime across three historical periods: 1935, 1960, and 1985. *Social Forces, 69*(3), 867-894. Examines the effects of age and gender as predictors of criminal involvement using Uniform Crime Report arrest data for 1935, 1960, and 1985.

C.0527 Steffensmeier, Darrell, & Allan, E. (1990). Gender, age, and crime. In J. Sheley (Ed.), *Handbook of Criminology.* Belmont, CA: Wadsworth. Discusses the intersection of gender, race, and crime as predictors of criminal involvement.

C.0528 Steffensmeier, Darrell, et al. (1989, September). Development and female crime: A cross national test of alternative explanations. *Social Forces, 68*(1), 262-283. Analyzes female arrest rates using INTERPOL arrest data from 69 countries.

C.0529 Steffensmeier, Darrell, & Andersen, Emilia (1988). Sex disparities in arrest by residence, race, and age: An assessment of the gender convergence/crime hypothesis. *Justice Quarterly, 5,* 53-80. Discusses sex disparities in arrest rates.

C.0530 Steffensmeier, Darrell, & Terry, R. (1986). Institutional sexism in the underworld: A view from the inside. *Sociological Inquiry, 56*(3), 304-322. Discusses sexism in the underworld.

C.0531 Steffensmeier, Darrell (1983, June). Organization properties and sex-segregation in the underworld: Building a sociological theory of sex differences in crime. *Social Forces, 61*(4), 1010-1032. Looks at sex-segregation in the underworld.

C.0532 Steffensmeier, Darrell, & Kramer John (1982, April). Sex-based differences in the sentencing of adult criminal defendants: An empirical test and theoretical overviews. *Sociology and Social Research, 66*(3), 289-304. Discusses discriminatory sentencing.

C.0533 Steffensmeier, Darrell (1980a, July). Assessing the impact of the women's movement on sex-based differences in the handling of adult criminal defendants. *Crime and Delinquency, 26*(3), 344-357. Examines five factors that help account for consistent findings of preferential treatment of female offenders.

C.0534 Steffensmeier, Darrell (1980b). Sex differences in patterns of adult crime, 1965-1977: A review and assessment. *Social Forces, 58*(3), 553-564. Looks at patterns of male and female crime.

C.0535 Steffensmeier, Darrell, & Kramer, John (1980c, February). The differential impact of criminal stigmatization on male and female felons. *Sex-Roles, 6*(1), 1-8. Administered questionnaires to assess how sex of convicted felon and sex of subject affect levels of stigmatization.

C.0536 Steffensmeier, Darrell, et al. (1980). World War II and its effects on the sex differential in arrests: An empirical test of the sex-role equality and crime proposition. *Social Quarterly, 21*(3), 403-416. Challenges Pollak's 1950 conclusion that the sex differential in arrests diminished during WW II because of wartime changes in the social and economic roles of women.

C.0537 Steury, Ellen, & Frank, Nancy (1990, September-October). Gender bias and pretrial release: More pieces of the puzzle. *Journal of Criminal Justice, 18*(5), 417-432. Discusses who is granted pre-trial release and how gender influences decision-making.

C.0538 Stewart, J. E. (1980). Defendant's attractiveness as a factor in the outcome of criminal trials: An observational study. *Journal of Applied Social Psychology, 10,* 348-361. Discusses defendants attractiveness and how it influences trial outcome.

C.0539 Stitch, Denise (1993). Alternative sentencing or reproduction control: Should California courts use Norplant to protect future children from child abuse and fetal abuse? *Santa Clara Law Review, 33,* 1017-1055. Discusses the use of Norplant as an alternative to sentencing.

C.0540 Stollman, David (1994, April). Jordan v. Gardner [986 F.2d 152]: Female prisoners rights to be free from random, cross-gender-clothed-body searches. *Fordham Law Review, 62.* 1877-1910. Discusses cross-gender-clothed-body searches of female inmates.

C.0541 Streib, Victor (1992, Summer). Death penalty for battered women. *Florida State University Law Review, 20,* 163-194. Discusses battered women who have been sentenced to death.

C.0542 Streib, Victor (1991, March). *Capital punishment for female offenders: Present female death row inmates and death sentences and executions of female offenders, January 1, 1973 to March 1, 1991.* Cleaveland, OH: Cleveland State University. Discusses the sentencing of females to death and the number of females on death row since 1973.

C.0543 Streib, Victor (1990). Death penalty for female offenders. *University of Cincinnati Law Review, 58*(3), 845-880. Discusses the use of the death penalty for women. Documents female executions, compares male and female executions, and explores gender-bias.

C.0544 Streib, Victor, & Sametz, Lynn (1989). Executing female juveniles. *Connecticut Law Review, 22*(3), 3-59 History of the execution of female juveniles and current specific cases.

C.0545 Streifel, Cathy (1990, November). The status of women and women's involvement in crime: A cross-sectional examination of gender differences in mode of offending. *Dissertation Abstracts International, A.: The Humanities and Social Sciences, 51*(5), 1784. Looks at differences in male and female offending.

C.0546 Stringer, T. (1987). *Sentencing alternatives for Illinois female offenders.* Springfield, IL: Administrative Office of the Illinois Courts. Discusses alternative sentencing for female offenders in Illinois.

C.0547 Suffolk University Law Review (1985, Winter). Expert testimony on battered woman syndrome: Its admissibility in spousal homicide cases. *Suffolk University Law Review, 19,* 877-905. Discusses the use of expert testimony in trials of battered women who kill.

C.0548 Sugar, F., & Fox, L. (1990). Nistum Peyako Seht'wawin Iskwewak: Breaking chains. *Canadian Journal of Women and the Law, 3*(2), 465-482. Discusses the federally sentenced female offenders from the Canadian native cultures.

C.0549 Sundby, Scott (1991, June). The Lockett [Lockett v. Ohio, 98 S. Ct. 2954]: Paradox: Reconciling guided discretion and unguided mitigation in capital sentencing. *UCLA Law Review, 38,* 1147-1208. Discusses the case of Sandra Lockett.

C.0550 Syme, G. J. (1976, November). Paternalism in Australian Courts. *Australian Journal of Social Issues, 11*(4), 287-290. Discusses paternalism in the Australian court system.

C.0551 Tate, K. W. (1974). Title VII: A remedy for discrimination against women prisoners. *Arizona Law Review, 16*(4), 974-1000. Discusses the use of litigation in discriminatory practices.

C.0552 Tauro Law Review (1989, Spring). Postpartum psychosis as a defense to infant murder. *Tauro Law Review, 5,* 287-308. Dsicusses infanticide defense.

C.0553 Taylor, Betty Jean (1983, January). Sexual inequities behind bars: A comparison of male and female prisons. *Dissertation Abstracts International, 43*(7), 2458. Focuses on differences in policies and procedures for incarcerated men and women in California.

C.0554 Taylor, L., & Dalton, K. (1983). Premenstrual syndrome: A new criminal defense? *California Western Law Review, 19*(2), 269-287. Discusses common psychological symptoms of PMS.

C.0555 Temin, Carolyn (1980). Discriminatory sentencing of women offenders. In S. Datesman & F. Scarpitti (Eds.), *Women, crime, and justice* (pp. 255-276). New York, NY: University Press. Discusses discriminatory sentencing practices for women offenders.

C.0556 Temin, Carolyn (1976). Discriminatory sentencing of women offenders: The argument for the ERA in a nutshell. In L. Crites (Ed.), *The female offender* (pp. 49-66). Lexington, MA: Lexington Books. History of discrimination in the courts from the Muncy Act in 1913-1970's.

C.0557 Temin, Carolyn (1973). Discriminatory sentencing of women offenders. The argument for ERA in a nutshell. *American Criminal Law Review, 11,* 355-372. Discusses discriminatory sentencing.

C.0558 Thompson, B. C. (1986, February). Defending the battered wife: A challenge for defense attorneys, *Trial, 22,* 74-80. Discusses defenses used for battered women who kill.

C.0559 Thyfault, Regina, et al. (1987). When battered women kill: Evaluation and expert witness testimony techniques. In D. Sonkin (Ed.), *Domestic violence on trial: Psychological and legal dimensions of family violence* (pp. 71-93). New York, NY: Springer. Discusses the use of expert testimony in trials of battered women who kill.

C.0560 Thyfault, Regina (1984). Self-defense: Battered woman syndrome on trial. *California Western Law Review, 20,* 485-510. Examines legal issues when a battered woman is charged with the murder of her abusive mate. Cites case law.

C.0561 Tishchler, C. A., & Marquart, J. W. (1989, November). Analysis of disciplinary infraction rates among female and male inmates. *Journal of Criminal Justice, 17*(6), 507-513. Compares disciplinary infraction rates of incarcerated men and women.

C.0562 Tittle, C. R. (1969, August). Inmate organization: Sex differentiation and the influence of criminal subcultures. *American Sociological Review, 34*(4), 492-505. Looks at inmate organizational structures where men and women are incarcerated under similar conditions.

C.0563 Tjedan, Patricia, & Tejedan, P. (1981). Differential treatment of the female felon. In M. Warren (Ed.), *Comparing female and male offenders.* Beverly Hills, CA: Sage Publications. Discusses the differential treatment of female felons in the criminal justice system.

C.0564 Tolmie, Julia (1991). Provocation or self-defense for battered women who kill. In S. Heong Yeo (Ed.), *Partial excuses to murder* (pp. 61-79). Sydney, Australia: The Federation Press. Discusses defenses used with battered women who kill.

C.0565 Turnbo, C. (1992). Differences that make a difference: Managing a women's correctional institution. In ACA *Female offenders: Meeting needs of a neglected population* (pp. 12-16). Laurel, MD: American Correctional Association. Warden of an all-female federal correctional institution for women discusses his job.

C.0566 UCLA Law Review (1986, August). Provoked reason in men and women: Heat-of-passion manslaughter and imperfect self-defense. *UCLA Law Review, 33,* 1679-1735. Discussses the defense of provocation.

C.0567 University of Cincinnati Law Review (1992, Winter). Ohio joins the majority and allows expert testimony on the battered woman syndrome: [State v. Koss, 551 N.E.2d 970 (Ohio)]. *University of Cincinnati Law Review, 60,* 877-905. Discusses the use of expert testimony in trials of battered women who kill.

C.0568 University of Kansas Law Review (1989, Fall). Rendering each woman her due: Can a battered woman claim self-defense when she kills her sleeping batterer? *The University of Kansas Law Review, 38,* 169-192. Discusses the definition of self-defense and how it is used.

C.0569 Unversity of Toronto Faculty of Law Review (1990, Spring). Discerning justice for battered women who kill. *University of Toronto Faculty of Law Review, 48,* 229-258. Discusses defenses used with battered women who kill.

C.0570 U.S. Department of Justice (1979). *Seattle, Washington: Women's Community Center exemplary project validation report.* Washington, DC: U.S. Department of Justice. Describes the Women's Community Center of Seattle, Washington, a community-based alternative to incarceration.

C.0571 U.S. General Accounting Office (1980). *Women in prison: Inequitable treatment requires action.* Washington. DC: U.S. General Accounting Office. Report to Congress. Discusses discriminatory prison practices.

C.0572 Van Denburg, Cheryl (1992). The effects of expert testimony on the trials of battered women who kill their batterers. *Dissertation Abstracts International, 54*(4), 22-29. Looks at expert testimony and how it impacts jurors in cases of battered women who kill their abusers.

C.0573 Van Ochten, Marjorie (1992). Legal issues and the female offender. In ACA *Female offenders: Meeting the needs of a neglected population* (pp.31-36). Laurel, MD: American Correctional Association. Discusses the principle areas of litigation by female inmates. Intended primarily to give correctional administrators an understanding of litigation by female prisoners.

C.0574 Vaughn, Elizabeth, & Moore, Maureen (1983). The battered spouse defense in Kentucky. *Northern Kentucky Law Review, 10,* 399-426. Discusses the use of the battered woman's syndrome in Kentucky courts.

C.0575 Velimesis, V. (1975, March). The female offender. *Crime and Delinquency Literature, 7,* 94-112. Discusses discriminatory practices in sentencing, assignments to institutional programs, and parole revocation of female offenders.

C.0576 Veysey, B. M. (1994, June). Gender differences in the adjudication of criminal responsibility: Social pressures for gender role congruity. *Dissertation Abstracts International, 54*(12), 4595. Investigates the effects of gender on the determination of criminal responsibility.

C.0577 Visher, Christy (1983, February). Gender, police arrest decisions, and notions of chivalry. *Criminology, 21*(1), 5-28. Explores chivalrous treatment of female offenders in the initial stages of criminal processing using data collected in 1977.

C.0578 Von Cleve, Elizabeth, & Weis, J. G. (1992). Sentencing alternatives for female offenders. In ACA *Female offenders: Meeting the needs of a neglected population* (pp. 94-99). Laurel, MD: American Correctional Association. Discusses the doubly punitive practice of sentencing female offenders to serve time in locations that are distant from family and friends.

C.0579 Wake Forest Law Review (1989). Ending the continuous reign of terror: Sleeping husbands, battered wives, and the right to self-defense. *Wake Forest Law Review, 24,* 959-993. Discusses the use of battered woman's syndrome as self-defense.

C.0580 Walker, Bill (1961). *The case of Barbara Graham.* New York, NY: Ballantine Books. Case of Barbara Graham who was executed at San Quentin on June 3, 1955.

C.0581 Walker, Lenore (1984). *The battered woman syndrome.* New York, NY: Springer. Defines the battered woman's syndrome and discusses its use as a defense.

C.0582 Walker, Lenore (1982, Spring). Beyond the juror's ken: Battered women. *Vermont Law Review, 7,* 1-14. Discusses educating juries about battered woman's syndrome.

C.0583 Walker, Monica (1985, August). Statistical anomalies in comparing the sentencing of males and females. *Sociology, 19, 446-451.* Reviews statistics on arrest rates for males and females.

C.0584 Wallace, Harvey (1994a, July). Battered woman syndrome: Defendants claims of duress affect prosecution and sentencing. *Law and Order, 42*(7), 82-85. Discusses the use of battered woman's syndrome as a defense.

C.0585 Wallace, Harvey (1994b). The battered woman syndrome: Self-defense and duress as mandatory defenses. *Police Journal, 67*(2), 133-139. Discusses battered women in the courts, the necessity of the self-defense, and the willingness of courts to accept the battered woman syndrome.

C.0586 Wallace, Harvey (1994c). Federal sentencing guidelines and gender issues: Parental responsiblities, pregnancy, and domestic violence. *San Diego Justice Journal, 2*(2), 395-427. Discusses the sentencing of women offenders under the mandatory sentencing ranges of the Federal Sentencing Guidelines.

C.0587 Wallach, A., & Rubin, L. (1971). The premenstrual syndrome and criminal responsibility. *UCLA Law Review, 19*(2), 209-312. Discusses the use of premenstrual syndrome as a defense.

C.0588 Warren, Marguerite (1981a). *Comparing male and female offenders.* Beverly Hills, CA: Sage Publications. Focuses on the comparison of females and males with respect to crime and delinquent behavior and processing in the criminal justice system.

C.0589 Warren, Marguerite (1981b). Gender comparisons in crime and delinquency. In M. Warren (Ed.), *Comparing female and male offenders.* Beverly Hills, CA: Sage Publications. Compares rates of crime by male and female offenders.

C.0590 Washburn Law Journal (1989, Spring). Murder, self-defense, and the battered woman syndrome in Kansas [State v. Stewart, 763 P.2d 572 (Kan.)]. *Washburn Law Journal, 28,* 400-412. Discusses the use of the battered woman's syndrome as a defense in Kansas.

C.0591 Webb, D. (1984, August). More on gender and justice: Girl offenders on supervision. *Sociology, 18*(3), 367-381. Discusses gender and justice in criminal justice system.

C.0592 Weeks, S., et al. (1994). Alone in a crowd: Gender differences in the emotional well-being of Japanese prisoners. *International Journal of Comparative and Applied Criminal Justice, 18*(2), 95-112. Reports on gender differences in the emotional well being of prison inmates.

C.0593 Weir, Susan (1992). Crimes passionnel: Gender differences in perceived justification for murder in the face of marital infidelity. *Irish Journal of Psychology, 13*(3), 350-360. Tested the hypothesis that men who kill because of infidelity might be perceived as more justified than women.

C.0594 Weiss, Norma (1980, January). *Mad or bad: The influence of gender on the defining of deviant behavior.* Dissertation, Rutgers. Discusses gender and what constitutes deviant behavior.

C.0595 Wheeler, Martha (1974, December). The current status of women in prison. *Criminal Justice and Behavior, 1*(4), 374-380. Emphasizes the need for alternatives to incarceration.

C.0596 Wheeler, Patricia, et al. (1989, Spring/Summer). Persephone chained: Parity or equality in women's prisons? *The Prison Journal, 69*(1), 88-102. Discusses discriminatory practices in women's prisons.

C.0597 Whitear, M. (1989, September). Women offenders. *Lay Panel Magazine,* 22, 11-13. Discusses custodial and non-custodial sentencing of women in England.

C.0598 Whitson, Maria, & Hassell, Frances (1994, March). *An historical purview of the black female as offender, victim, and professional in the criminal justice system.* Paper presented at the 1994 ACJS Annual Meeting, Chicago, IL. Discusses how black female offenders are grouped with white females when the issue is gender and with black males when the issue is race.

C.0599 Williams, L., et al. (1984). Women, crimes, and judicial dispositions: A comparative examination of the female offender. *Sociological Spectrum, 4*(2-3), 249-273. Explores issues of the "masculinized" female offender and a "chivalrous" criminal justice system.

C.0600 Wilson, N. K. (1980). Styles of doing time in a coed prison: Masculine and feminine alternatives. In J. Smykla (Ed.), *Coed prison* (pp. 150-171). New York, NY: Human Sciences Press.

C.0601 Wilson, Patrick (1971). *Murderess: A study of the women executed in Britain since 1843.* London: Joseph. Discusses sixty-eight women hanged for murder in the period of Wilson's study.

C.0602 Wilson, T. W. (1986, October). Gender differences in the inmate code. *Canadian Journal of Criminology, 28*(4), 397-405. Investigated gender differences in commitment to the inmate code among 76 male and 24 female inmates of a co-ed prison .

C.0603 Wisconsin Women's Law Journal (1988). An overview of defense of battered women from a postconviction perspective. *Wisconsin Women's Law Journal, 4,* 95-115. Discusses defense of battered women who kill.

C.0604 Wolfe, Nancy, et al. (1984). Describing the female offender: A note on the demographics of arrests. *Journal of Criminal Justice, 12*(5), 483-492. Looked at arrest record data for 2,507 female offenders arrested in a southern city between 1969 and 1975.

C.0605 Wolfe, Nancy (1979, Winter). Victim provocation: The battered wife and legal definition of self-defense. *Sociological Symposium, 25,* 98-118. Discusses legal cases that illustrate the change of sympathy in the 70's for women who committed homicide after being abused.

C.0606 Wolfer, Judith, et al. (1991, July-August). Battered spouse syndrome: Legal reform. *The Maryland Bar Journal, 24,* 29-32. Discusses use of the battered woman's syndrome as a defense.

C.0607 Worrall, Anne (1990a, August). Non-descript women: A study of the judicial construction of female lawbreakers as abnormal women. *Dissertation Abstracts International, 51*(2), 643-A.

C.0608 Worral, Anne (1990b). *Offending women: Female lawbreakers and the criminal justice system.* London: Routledge. Examines reasons English courts and social welfare agencies handle female offenders differently than male offenders.

C.0609 Worrall, Anne (1987). Sisters in law? Women defendants and women magistrates. In P. Carlen & A. Worrall (Eds.), *Gender, crime and justice* (pp. 108-123). Philadelphia, PA: Open University Press. Discusses the interplay of class and gender in the courtroom where "women judges are judging women."

C.0610 Worrall, Anne (1981). Out of place: Female offenders in court. *Probation Journal, 28*(3), 90-93. Discusses discriminatory court practices.

C.0611 Wyrick, E. S., & Owens, O. H. (1977). Black women: Income and incarceration. In C. Owen & J. Bell (Eds.), *Blacks and criminal justice.* Lexington, MA: Lexington Books, DC Heath. Discusses the relationship between income and incarceration for black women.

C.0612 Wylie, Elizabeth (1993, Spring). Birth control for child abusers: Statutory concerns and privacy issues in court-enforced contraception. *The Review of Litigation, 12,* 489-512. Discusses the use of mandatory contraceptives for women convicted of child abuse.

C.0613 Yeo, Stanley (1993). Resolving gender bias in criminal defenses. *Morash University Law Review, 19,* 104-116. Discusses gender bias in courtroom practices.

C.0614 Young, Margot (1995). Reproductive technologies and the law: Norplant and the bad mother. *Marriage & Family Review, 21*(3-4), 259-281. Analyzes the intervention in the reproductive choices of women by the state.

C.0615 Young, Vernetta (1986, September). Gender expectations and their impact on black female offenders and victims. *Justice Quarterly, 3*(3), 305-327. Discusses early application of images of the ideal woman specific to upper class white women to black female offenders.

C.0616 Young, Vernetta (1980, May). Women, race, and crime. *Criminology, 18*(1), 26-34. Examines the interrelationships among women, race, and crime as presented by F. Adler in *Sisters in crime: The rise of the new female criminal.* New York, NY: McGraw Hill. Discusses the intersection of race and crime in the criminal processing of women.

C.0617 Zingraff, Matthew, & Thomson, R. (1984, November). Differential sentencing of women and men in the USA. *Journal of Sociology of Law, 12*(4), 401-413. Discusses sentencing practices in the US.

C.0618 Zingraff, Matthew (1980). Inmate assimilation: A comparison of male and female delinquents. *Criminal Justice and Behavior, 7*(3), 275-292. Compares prison practices in the treatment of male and female inmates.

4

FEMALE JUVENILES

Delinquency; Gangs; Juvenile Prostitution

D.0001 Ajzenstadt, Mimi, & Steinberg, Odeda (1995, Spring). The elasticity of the law: Treating girls in distress in Israel through the shadow of the law. *British Journal of Criminology, 35*(2), 236-247. Focuses on a quasi-legal therapeutic technique used with adolescent girls at risk.

D.0002 Alder, C. (1985). Theories of female delinquency. In P. Borowski & M. Murray (Eds.), *Juvenile delinquency in Australia.* Sydney: Methuen. Reviews research on theories of female juvenile delinquency.

D.0003 Armistead, Lisa, et al. (1992, Summer). Psychopathology in incarcerated juvenile delinquents: Does it extend beyond externalizing problems? *Adolescence, 27*(106), 309-314. Compared 24 incarcerated juvenile nonoffending adolescents on the Revised Behavior Problem Checklist.

D.0004 Bailey-Harris, R., & Naffine, Ngaire (1988). Gender, justice and welfare in South Australia: A study of the female status offender. *International Journal of Law and the Family* (Oxford), *2*(2), 214-233. Discusses the interplay of gender and justice for female juveniles in Australia.

D.0005 Balthazar, Mary, & Cook, Ruall (1984). An analysis of the factors related to the rate of violent crimes committed by incarcerated female delinquents. Special issue: Gender issues, sex offenses, and criminal justice current trends. *Journal of Offender Counseling, Services, and Rehabilitation, 9*(1-2), 103-118. Investigated rate of violent crimes among female juveniles for variance in age, educational level, IQ, family structure, and/or geographic location.

D.0006 Bartek, Sophie, et al. (1993, February). Coping, defending, and the relations between moral judgment and moral behavior in prostitutes and other female juvenile delinquents. *Journal of Abnormal Psychology, 102*(1), 66-73. Administered Kohlberg's Moral Judgement Interview to 20 female juvenile prostitutes, 20 female juvenile non-prostitutes, and 20 same-age controls.

D.0007 Benson, Sheila (1994, June). Girl gangs get their colors. *Interview, 24*(6), 96-97. Discussion of the movie "Mi Vida Loca," about girl gangs.

D.0008 Bergsmann, Ilene (1989, March). The forgotten few: Juvenile female offenders. *Federal Probation, 53*(1), 73-78. Assesses the problems of young women in the Juvenile Justice System. Describes the typical adolescent female offender.

D.0009 Bergsmann, Ilene (1989, August). Adolescent female offenders: Program parity is essential to meeting their needs. *Corrections Today, 51*(5), 98-103. Discusses lack of educational and vocational programs for adolescent female offenders.

D.0010 Bishop, Donna, & Frazier, Charles (1992, Winter). Gender bias in juvenile justice processing: Implications of the JJDP Act. *Journal of Criminal Law and Criminology, 82*(4), 1162-1186. Examines the effects of the Juvenile Justice and Delinquency Prevention Act of 1974 which helped bring about changes in the processing of status offenders regarding gender issues.

D.0011 Bjerregaard, Beth, & Smith, Carolyn (1993, December). Gender differences in gang participation, delinquency, and substance abuse. *Journal of Quantitative Criminolgy, 9*(4), 329-355. Compares male and female juvenile participation in gangs, crime, and drugs.

D.0012 Bour, Daria, et al. (1984, Fall-Winter). A comparison of delinquent prostitutes and delinquent non-prostitutes on self-concept. *Journal of Offender Counseling, Services and Rehabilitation, 9*(1-2), 89-101. Compared sociodemographic statistics for 25 female juvenile prostitutes (aged 13-15 years) and 25 age-matched juvenile nonprostitutes.

D.0013 Bowker, Lee, & Klein, M. (1983, Winter). The etiology of female juvenile delinquency and gang membership: A test of psychological and social structural explanations. *Adolescence, 18*(72), 739-751. Juxtaposes theoretical perspective with social-cultural explanations of both female juvenile delinquency and female gang membership.

D.0014 Bowker, Lee, et al. (1980, Fall). Female participation in delinquent gang activities. *Adolescence, 15*(59), 509-519. Discusses data on female participation in gang and non-gang delinquent activities. Data collected in the mid-60's in Los Angeles county.

D.0015 Bowler, A. C. (1917). Study of seventy-five delinquent girls. *Juvenile Delinquency, 2,* 156-168. Early study of female juvenile delinquency.

D.0016 Boyer, Debra, & James, Jennifer (1982). Easy money: Adolescent involvement in prostitution. In S. Davidson (Ed.), *Justice for young womeñ: Close-up on critical issues* (pp. 73-97). Tucson, AZ: New Directions for Young Women. Discusses female juvenile prostitutes.

D.0017 Bracey, Dorothy (1983). The juvenile prostitute: Victim and offender. *Victomology, 8*(3-4), 151-160. Analyzes the consequences of coming from a background of neglect and abuse for juveniles. Discusses victimization by pimps, customers, and others.

D.0018 Bracey, Dorothy (1979). *Baby pros.* New York, NY: The John Jay Press. Discusses juvenile prostitution.

D.0019 Breckenridge, Sophia, & Abbott, E. (1917). *The delinquent child and the home: A study of the delinquent wards of the juvenile court of Chicago.* New York, NY: The Russell Sage Foundation. Early study of female delinquents in Chicago.

D.0020 Brenzel, Barbara (1980, May). Domestication as reform: A study of the socialization of wayward girls, 1856-1905. *Harvard Educational Review, 50*(2), 196-213. Discusses female juvenile delinquency.

D.0021 Brown, E. J. (1968). *Some psychological differences between neglected and delinquent adolescent girls.* Dissertation, University of Oklahoma. Research on female juvenile delinquency.

D.0022 Brown, M. B. (1978). *Locus of control, self-concept, and level of aspiration in situation-specific institutionalized delinquent girls.* Dissertation, University of Southern California. Discusses possible causes of delinquency in female adolescents.

D.0023 Brown, S. C. (1931, June). Some case studies of delinquent girls described as leaders. *British Journal of Educational Psychology, 1*(2), 162-179. Discusses leadership in female juveniles.

D.0024 Brown, W. (1977). Black female gangs in Philadelphia. *International Journal of Offender Therapy and Comparative Criminology, 21*(3), 221-228. Discusses when and why black females become gang members in Philadelphia and their roles in the gangs.

D.0025 Buckner, J. C., & Chesney-Lind, Meda (1983, June). Dramatic cures for juvenile crime: An evaluation of a prisoner-run delinquency prevention program. *Criminal Justice and Behavior, 10*(2), 227-247. Evaluates a prisoner-run delinquency prevention program at Hawaii's major prison. Discusses results on the delinquent behavior of females.

D.0026 Bunbury, Doris (1931, November). Juvenile delinquency in girls in Colorado. *Colorado University Studies, 18*(4), 215-229. Early study of female juvenile delinquents in Colorado.

D.0027 Burquest, B. (1981). The violent girl. *Adolescence, 16*(64), 749-764. Discusses violence in female adolescents.

D.0028 Burt, C. (1927, February). Causes of sex delinquency in girls. *Journal of Social Hygiene, 13*, 109-114. Early study of prostitution in female juveniles.

D.0029 Butler, E. (1966). An action and research program in a delinquent girls residential treatment program. *Police, 10*(6), 74-81. Looks at a residential treatment program for female juvenile delinquents.

D.0030 Butt, Susan (1972). Psychological styles of delinquency in girls. *Canadian Journal of Behavior Science, 4*, 298-306. Study of the psychological profile of the female juvenile delinquent.

D.0031 Cain, Maureen (1989). *Growing up good: Policing behavior of girls in Europe.* London: Sage. Investigates the ways in which gendered behavior was imposed on girls throughout Europe.

D.0032 Cale, Michelle (1993, June). Girls and the perception of sexual danger in the Victorian reformatory system. *History: The Journal of the Historical Association, 78*(253), 201-217. Discusses how the reformatory sanctioned by the UK parliament dealt with juvenile delinquency, and its role in dealing with sexual delinquency in girls.

D.0033 Calhoun, George, et al. (1993, Summer). The neophyte female delinquent: A review of the literature. *Adolescence, 28*(110), 461-471. Current status of the female juvenile delinquent is assessed focusing on definitional, etiological, and treatment issues.

D.0034 Campbell, Anne (1990). On the invisibility of the female delinquent peer group. *Women & Criminal Justice, 2*(1), 41-62. Examines why peer groups have been ignored in looking at female juvenile delinquents.

D.0035 Campbell, Anne (1990). Female participation in gangs. In C. R. Huff (Ed.), *Gangs in America.* Newbury Park, CA: Sage. Study of female adolescent gang members.

D.0036 Campbell, Anne (1987a). Self-reported delinquency and home life: Evidence from a sample of British girls. *Journal of Youth and Adolescence, 16*(2), 167-177. Examines the correlation between family variables and delinquency in a small sample of British teenage girls.

D.0037 Campbell, Anne (1987b, December). Self-definition by rejection: The case of gang girls. *Social Problems, 34*(5), 451-466. Uses data collected from a 1979-1981 for a participant-observation study of New York City girl gang members to examine their self-representation in social talk.

D.0038 Campbell, Anne (1984a, June). Girls' talk: The social representation of aggression by female gang members. *Criminal Justice and Behavior, 11*(2), 139-156. Analyzes 64 tape-recorded accounts of fights given by female members (aged 15-30 years) of 3 New York street gangs.

D.0039 Campbell, Anne (1984b). *The girls in the gang: A report from New York City.* Oxford: Basil Blackwell. A study of female delinquency in the voices of the girls themselves. Three types of gangs were selected for the study, a street gang, a biker gang and, a religio-cultural gang.

D.0040 Campbell, Anne (1981). *Girl delinquents.* Oxford: Basil Blackwell, New York, NY: St. Martin's. Reviews major theories of female delinquency.

D.0041 Campbell, Anne (1980). Friendship as a factor in male and female delinquency. In H. Foot, et al. (Eds.), *Friendships and the social relations in children.* New York, NY: John Wiley. Discusses the social relationships between male and female juvenile delinquents.

D.0042 Campbell, Anne (1976). *The role of the peer group in female delinquency.* Dissertation, University of Oxford. Study of female juvenile delinquency and peer group relationships.

D.0043 Campbell, B. L. (1978). *Systematic desensitization: An approach to the treatment of black female delinquent adolescents.* Dissertation, California School of Professional Psychology, Berkeley. Study of treatment approach with black female juvenile delinquents.

D.0044 Canter, R. J. (1982, August). Family correlates of male and female delinquency. *Criminology, 20*(2), 149-167. Discusses the family profile of male and female delinquents.

D.0045 Carrington, Kerry (1993). *Offending girls.* St Leonard, Australia: Allen and Unwin. Explores the creation of the female juvenile deliquent by the Australian juvenile justice system.

D.0046 Carrington, Kerry (1990). Aboriginal girls and juvenile justice: What justice? White justice. *Journal for Social Science Studies, 3,* 1-18. Looks at the treatment of aboriginal female delinquents in the Australian juvenile justice system.

D.0047 Carter, B. L. (1972). *On the grounds: Informal culture in a girls' reform school.* Dissertation, Brandeis University. Study of the informal cultural norms of a girls reformatory.

D.0048 Casburn, M. (1979). *Girls will be girls: Sexism and juvenile justice in a London borough.* London: Women's Research and Resources Centre. Study of sexism in English juvenile justice.

D.0049 Caspi, A., et al. (1993). Unraveling girls delinquency: Biological, dispositional, and contextual contributions to adolescent misbehavior. *Developmental Psychology, 29*(1), 19-30. Examines links between biological maturation and delinquency in girls.

D.0050 Chaturvedi, P. L. (1950, November-December). The problem of rehabilitation of female and juvenile ex-convicts. *Penal Reformer, 6*(9-10), 215-218. Early study of rehabilitative approaches with female juvenile delinquents.

D.0051 Chesney-Lind, Meda (1993a, Fall). Judicial enforcement and the female delinquent. *Issues in Criminology, 8*, 51-69. Discusses the place of the judiciary in rehabilitation of female juveniles.

D.0052 Chesney-Lind, Meda (1993b). Girls, gangs, and violence: Anatomy of a backlash. *Humanity and Society, 17*(3), 321-344. Discusses the participation of girls in gangs and suggests that an understanding of girls' gangs that is sensitive to context is needed.

D.0053 Chesney-Lind, Meda, & Shelden, Randall (1992). *Girls, delinquency, and juvenile justice.* Laurel, MD. American Correctional Association. Discusses the nature and extent of female delinquency as well as theories of female delinquency and crime.

D.0054 Chesney-Lind, Meda (1988a, April). Girls in jail. *Crime and Delinquency, 34*(2), 150-168. Profiles female juveniles held in adult jails and lockups in the U.S.

D.0055 Chesney-Lind, Meda (1988b). Girls and status offenses: Is juvenile justice still sexist? *Criminal Justice Abstracts, 20*(1), 144-165. Discusses sexism in the juvenile justice system.

D.0056 Chesney-Lind, Meda (1982). From benign neglect to malign attentions: A critical review of recent research on female delinquency. In S. Davidson (Ed.), *Justice for young women: Close-up on critical issues* (pp. 51-72). Tucson, AZ: National Female Advocacy Project. Review of research on female juvenile delinquents.

D.0057 Chesney-Lind, Meda (1978). Young women in the arms of the law. In L. Bowker (Ed.), *Women, crime and the criminal justice system* (pp. 171-196). Lexington, MA: DC Heath. Reviews reasearch on paternalism and how it affects female juveniles in the criminal justice process.

D.0058 Chesney-Lind, Meda (1977). Judicial paternalism and the female status offender: Training women to know their place. *Crime and Delinquency, 23*(2), 121-130. Presents evidence that girls charged with status offenses are treated more harshly than girls charged with crimes.

D.0059 Chesney-Lind, Meda (1974, July). Juvenile delinquency and the sexualization of female crime. *Psychology Today, 8*(2), 43-46. Discusses the view that female crimes are sex crimes.

D.0060 Chesney-Lind, Meda (1973, Fall). Judicial enforcement of the female sex role: The family court and the female delinquent. *Issues in Criminology, 8*(2), 51-69. Discusses the judicial processing of female juveniles.

D.0061 Cohen, Paz (1978). A double standard of justice: Juvenile courts treat young women differently. *Civil Rights Digest, 10*(3), 10-19. Discusses sexism in the juvenile courts.

D.0062 Cohn, R. R. (1970). *The Tennessee Self-Concept Scale as a differentiator of delinquent female sub-groups.* Dissertation, University of Oklahoma. Study of sub-groups among female juvenile delinquents.

D.0063 Cook, Douglas (1991). The effects of an experimental intervention on juvenile female recidivism and drug relapse. *Dissertation Abstracts International, 51*(9), 3229. Discusses treatment programs for female juvenile offenders.

D.0064 Cowart, Luvenia (1980). An exploratory study: The self-perceived needs and intentions of one population of pregnant adolescents who are involved with the criminal justice system. *Dissertation Abstracts International, 42*(2), 501-A. Presents the results of a study of residents in a state facility designed to explore pregnant adolescents' behavior.

D.0065 Cowie, J., et al. (1968). *Delinquency in girls.* London: Heineman. Study of delinquency in girls in England.

D.0066 Craike, W. (1953). Psychiatric treatment of adolescent delinquent girls. *Howard Journal, 8*(4), 258-262. Early study of psychiatry and the female juvenile delinquent.

D.0067 Crow, Ruth, & McCarthy, Ginny (1981). *Teenage women in the juvenile justice system: Changing values.* Tucson, AZ: New Directions for Young Women. Study of female juvenile delinquency.

D.0068 Cummings, Laura (1994, February). Fighting by the rules: Women street-fighting in Chihuahua, Mexico. *Sex Roles, 30*, 189-198. Study of female delinquents in Mexico.

D.0069 Curry, David, & Foster, Christa (1994, March). *Female gang involvement: Research, services and enforcement.* Paper presented at the Annual Meeting of the Academy of Criminal Justice Sciences, Chicago. Files from gang prevention programs for females revealed 9,029 female gang members in 61 jurisdictions plus 99 independent criminally active female gangs.

D.0070 Cushing, Hazel, & Ruch, G. (1927, February). An investigation of character traits in delinquent girls. *Journal of Applied Psychology, 11*, 1-7. Profiles of personality traits of female juvenile delinquents.

D.0071 D'Angelo, R. Y. (1961). *An evaluation of group psychotherapy with institutionalized delinquent girls.* Dissertation, Fordham University. Looks at the use of psychotherapy with institutionalized female delinquents.

D.0072 Davidson, Sue (1982). *Justice for young women.*Tucson: National Female Advocacy Project. Study of the processing and treatment of female juvenile delinquents.

D.0073 Davies, Jean (1976). Girls appearing before a juvenile court. In N. Goodman et al. (Eds.), *The sentencing of women at the London higher Courts* (pp. 43-111). London: H.M.S.O. Study of court appearances and outcomes of female juveniles in England.

D.0074 Dembo, Richard, et al. (1993, Winter). Gender differences in mental health service needs among youths entering a juvenile detention center. *Journal of Prison and Jail Health, 12*(2), 73-101. Examined the health service needs of 399 youths entering a juvenile detention center.

D.0075 Deutsch, C., et al. (1960). Dominance, aggression and the functional use of space in institutionalized female adolescents. *Aggressive Behavior, 4*, 313-324. Discusses the use of space and aggressive tendencies in female juveniles.

D.0076 Diaz, Amelia, et al. (1994, February). The role of gender in juvenile delinquency: Personality and intelligence. *Personality and Individual Differences, 16*(2), 309-314. Results of questionnaires completed by adolescents in Valencia, Spain.

D.0077 Dill, J. S. (1970). *An experimental comparison of single therapist and multiple therapist group counseling with incarcerated female delinquents.* Dissertation, Ball State University. Study on the use of therapy with institutionalized female juveniles.

D.0078 Donnenwerth, G. V., et al. (1973, June). Cognitive differentiation and self and parents in delinquent and non-delinquent girls. *British Journal of Social and Clinical Psychology, 12*(2), 144-152. Study of relationship to parents and self-concept in female juvenile delinquents

D.0079 Donovan, P. (1983, November-December). Judging teenagers: How minors fare when they seek court authorized abortions. *Family Planning Perspective, 15*(6), 259-267. Discusses Supreme Court decision on unmarried minors who seek abortions.

D.0080 Doorbar, Ruth (1951). Chronic delinquency in a 13-year-old girl. *Clinical Psychology, 2*(1), 35-47. Case study of female delinquency.

D.0081 Dredge, Earl (1974). Development of a model for the prediction of recidivism of female juvenile delinquents. *Dissertation Abstracts International, 34*(12), 7579. Study of recidivism in female juveniles and how it can be predicted.

D.0082 Druckman, Jean (1979, August). A family-oriented policy and treatment program for female juvenile status offenders. *Journal of Marriage and the Family, 41*(3), 627-636. Discusses the family as an integral part of treatment in female juvenile delinquency.

D.0083 D'Souza, N. (1990). Aboriginal children and juvenile justice. *Aboriginal Law Bulletin, 2*(440), 4-5. Looks at the treatment of aboriginal juveniles in the justice system.

D.0084 Duke, D., & Duke, Paula (1978, Winter). The prediction of delinquency in girls. *Journal of Research and Development Education, 11*(2), 18-33. Discussion of ways to predict delinquency in female adolescents.

D.0085 Duke, M., & Fenhagen, E. (1975). Self-parental alienation and locus of control in delinquent girls. *The Journal of Genetic Psychology, 127,* 103-110. Discusses self-concept and family relationships in female juvenile delinquents.

D.0086 Duraj, L. (1982, May). The concept of female juvenile delinquency: A feminist or non-feminist approach. *Juvenile and Family Court Journal, 33*(2), 25-31. A feminist perspective on female juvenile delinquency.

D.0087 Eisen, V. (1956). *An evaluation of several psychological tests for differentiating female delinquents from female nondelinquents.* Dissertation, Fordham University. Early study on female juvenile delinquents.

D.0088 Epps, P. (1954, April). The further study of female delinquents undergoing Borstal Training. *The British Journal of Delinquency, 4*(4), 265-271. Early study of female delinquents in the Borstal system in England.

D.0089 Epps, P. (1950-51, January). A preliminary survey of three hundred female delinquents in Borstal Institutions. *British Journal of Delinquency, 1*(3), 187-197. Early study of English Borstal system and female juvenile offenders.

D.0090 Epstein, E. (1962, June). The self-concept of the delinquent female. *Smith College Studies in Social Work, 32*(3), 220-234. Study of self concept in female juvenile delinquents.

D.0091 Evans, Graham, & Webb, Martin (1993). High profile - but not that high profile: Interviewing of young persons. *Issues in Criminological and Legal Psychology, 18,* 37-45. Examined interviewer behavior in 60 tape-recorded crime interviews with male and female delinquents.

D.0092 Farley, N. B. (1958). *The temporal orientation of the female juvenile delinquent.* Dissertation, University of Oklahoma. Early study on female juvenile delinquency.

D.0093 Farnworth, Margaret (1984, August). Male-female differences in delinquency in a minority group sample. *Journal of Research in Crime and Delinquency, 21*(3), 191-212. Compared delinquency in male and female minority youth.

D.0094 Fehrenbach, Peter, & Monastersky, Caren (1988, January) Characteristics of female adolescent sexual offenders. *American Journal of Orthopsychiatry, 58*(1), 148-152. Study of sex-offenses of female juveniles.

D.0095 Felice, Marianne, & Offord, D. R. (1972, October). Three developmental pathways to delinquency in girls. *British Journal of Criminology, 12*, 375-389. Study of the development of delinquency in female adolescents

D.0096 Felice, Marianne, & Offord, D. R. (1971). Girl delinquency: A review. *Corrective Psychiatry and Journal of Social Therapy, 17*(2), 18-33. Reviews concepts of delinquency in female adolescents.

D.0097 Figueira-McDonough, Josefina (1986, February). School context, gender, and delinquency. *Journal of Youth and Adolescence, 15*(1), 79-98. Discussses variables to be considered in research on juvenile delinquency.

D.0098 Figueira-McDonough, Josefina (1985). Are girls different? Gender discrepancies betweeen delinquent behavior and control. *Child Welfare, 64*(3), 273-284. Study to determine whether the juvenile justice system uses sex-discriminatory criteria in processing juveniles.

D.0099 Figueira-McDonough, Josefina, et al. (1981). Normal deviance: Gender similarities in adolescent subcultures. In M. Q. Warren (Ed.), *Comparing female and male offenders*. Beverly Hills, CA: Sage. Study of deviance and adolescent subcultures.

D.0100 Fiore, B. (1982). *Female delinquency and the double standard of justice in the juvenile justice system*. Dissertation, Rutgers University. Discusses sexism in the juvenile justice system.

D.0101 Firme, T., et al. (1991, October). Adolescent female prostitutes on the streets of Brazil: An exploratory investigation of ontological issues. *Journal of Adolescent Research, 6*(4), 493-504. Study of female juvenile prostitutes in Brazil.

D.0102 Fodor, I. (1972). The use of behavior modification techniques with female delinquents. *Child Welfare, 51*(2), 93-101. Discusses approaches to treatment of female juvenile delinquency.

D.0103 Frank, Susan, & Quinlan, D. (1976, October). Ego development and female delinquency: A cognitive-developmental approach. *Journal of Abnormal Psychology, 85*(5), 505-510. Discusses ego-development in female juveniles

D.0104 Furlong, V. (1971). *Anti-social behavior in youthful female offenders*. Dissertation, University of Northern Colorado. Study of anti-social behavior in female juvenile delinquents.

D.0105 Gaffney, L., & McFall, R. (1981). A comparison of social skills in delinquent and non-delinquent adolescent girls using a behavioral role-playing inventory. *Journal of Consulting and Clinical Psychology, 49*, 959-967. Study of social skills in adolescent females.

D.0106 Gardiner, Muriel (1976). *The deadly innocents: Portraits of children who kill*. New York, NY: Basic Books. Study of children who commit murder.

D.0107 Gibbens, T. C. (1959, October). Supervision and probation of adolescent girls. *British Journal of Delinquency, 10*, 84-103. Discusses probation after institutionalization for female delinquents.

D.0108 Giallombardo, Rose (1974). *The social world of imprisoned girls: A comparative study of institutions for juvenile delinquents*. New York, NY: John Wiley & Sons. Comparative study of the institutional life of female juveniles.

D.0109 Gibbs, Jewelle (1981). Depression and suicidal behavior among delinquent females. *Journal of Youth and Adolescence, 10*(2), 158-168. Discusses depression and suicide in adolescents.

D.0110 Gibbs, Jewelle (1981, April). *Parental psychopathology and female delinquency.* Paper presented at the 61st Annual Meeting of the Western Psychological Association, Los Angeles. Discusses the results of a general social history interview and three psychological instruments given to 48 adjudicated female juvenile delinquents.

D.0111 Gibson, Ainyette, et al. (1988, October). Adolescent female prostitutes. *Archives of Sexual Behavior, 17*(5), 431-438. Study of characteristics of 130 adolescent prostitute and nonprostitute female delinquents.

D.0112 Giordano, Peggy (1978, Spring). Girls, guys and gangs: The changing social context of female delinquency. *Journal of Criminal Law and Criminology, 69*(1), 126-132. Examined the nature and role of peer groups in female delinquency.

D.0113 Giordano, Peggy (1976). *Changing sex roles and females' involvement in delinquency.* Paper presented at the Annual Conference of the Midwestern Sociological Society, St. Louis, MO, April 21-24, 1976. Examines assumptions about female delinquency with in-depth literature review.

D.0114 Gomme, I. (1985, April). Predictors of status and criminal offenses among male and female adolescents in an Ontario community. *Canadian Journal of Criminology, 17*(2), 147-159. Study of predictors of juvenile delinquency in Canada.

D.0115 Goodman, J. (1976, June). The behavior of hypersexual delinquent girls. *American Journal of Psychiatry, 133*(6), 662-668. Discusses hypersexuality in female juvenile delinquents.

D.0116 Goodman, Nancy, et al. (1976). *Further studies of female offenders.* London: H.M.S.O. A descriptive and comparative study of girls sentenced to Borstal and detention center training in 1963. One part of a three piece monograph.

D.0117 Gowdy, Helen (1979). Similarities and differences between juvenile boys and girls in the ability to detect written fallacies in reasoning. *Dissertation Abstracts International, 40*(9), 4979-A. Focuses on differences in abilities to detect written fallacies in reasoning among incarcerated male and female juvenile delinquents.

D.0118 Greene, Nancy, & Esselstyn, T. (1972). The beyond control girl. *Juvenile Justice, 23*, 13-19. Discusses female juvenile delinquency.

D.0119 Griggs, Shirley (1975). *Program for adolescents (male and female) in corrective institutions: Rikers Island.* New York, NY: New York City Board of Education. Discusses a program designed to improve the mathematics skills of 328 males and females at Rikers Island Penitentiary.

D.0120 Gundry, R. (1952, November). Psychotic or delinquent? Case reports of twenty-one girls transferred from training school to state hospitals. *Journal of the American Medical Women's Association, 7*, 403-408. Case histories and results of treatment for 21 girls who were transferred to Maryland State Hospitals from the Montrose Training School for delinquent girls.

D.0121 Hagan, John, & Kay, Fiona (1990, July). Gender and delinquency in white-collar families: A power-control perspective. *Crime and Delinquency, 36*(3), 391-407. Discusses white-collar delinquency by youthful offenders such as copying of videotapes and computer software.

D.0122 Haines, W., & Esser, R. (1950, April). Case history of Ruth Steinhage. *American Journal of Psychiatry, 106*(10), 737-743. Case history of a 19-year-old mentally disordered girl who tried to murder a prominent baseball player.

D.0123 Halleck, S., & Herski, M. (1962). Homosexual behavior in a correctional institution for adolescent girls. *American Journal of Orthopsychiatry, 32,* 911-917. Discusses types of relationships in an institutionalized population.

D.0124 Hampton, R. E. (1979). Sex and sentencing in a children's court. *Australian and New Zealand Journal of Criminology, 12,* 12-32. Looks at the differential sentencing of male and female delinquents in Australia.

D.0125 Hancock, L., & Chesney-Lind, M. (1982). Female status offenders and justice reforms: An international perspective. *Australian and New Zealand Journal of Criminology, 15,* 109-122. Looks at reforms in the justice system that affect female juvenile delinquents.

D.0126 Hanson, K. (1964). *Rebels in the streets: The story of New York's girl gangs.* Englewood Cliffs, NJ: Prentice Hall. Early study of girl gangs.

D.0127 Harris, Mary (1994, February). Cholas, Mexican-American girls and gangs. *Sex Roles, 30,* 289-301. Describes female cliques within male-dominated Latino gangs that operate in the barrios of the San Fernando Valley of Los Angeles, California.

D.0128 Harris, Mary (1988). *Cholas: Latino girls and gangs.* New York, NY: AMS Press. Study of girls in Latino gangs in Los Angeles.

D.0129 Haynes, Jack, & Bensch, Marlene (1983). Female delinquent recidivism and the P-V sign on the WISC. *Journal of Clinical Psychology, 39*(1), 141-144. Examined the Performance-Verbal (P-V) discrepancies on the Wechsler Intelligence Scale for Children.

D.0130 Hennicker, R. (1950, May). Delinquency among female adolescents before and after the Second World War. *International Journal of Sexology, 3,* 247-248. Early study on female delinquency.

D.0131 Higgs, Deborah, et al. (1992, February). Moving from defense to offense: The development of an adolescent female sex offender. *The Journal of Sex Research, 29*(1), 131-140. Discusses prostitution in female adolescents.

D.0132 Hiller, Anne, & Hancock, Linda (1981). The processing of juveniles in Victoria. In S. Mukherjee & J. Scutt (Eds.), *Women and crime* (pp. 92-126). London: Allen & Unwin. Historical look at the court processing of female juveniles in Victoria.

D.0133 Hooper, P. M. (1963). Group work with Borstal girls. *Howard Journal, 11*(2), 119-133. Study of group therapy with institutionalized female juvenile delinquents.

D.0134 Horowitz, Ruth, & Pottieger, Anne (1991, February). Gender bias in juvenile justice handling of seriously crime-involved youths. *Journal of Research in Crime & Delinquency, 28*(1), 75-100. Notes a number of significant differences in male and female juvenile justice outcomes.

D.0135 Huntington, Jane (1982, May). Powerless and vulnerable: The social experiences of imprisoned girls. *Juvenile and Family Court Journal, 33*(2), 33-44. Discusses the vulnerability of institutionalized female adolescents.

D.0136 Inciardi, James (1989). Trading sex for crack among juvenile drug users. *Contemporary Drug Problems, 16*(4), 689-700. Examines characteristics of 27 female drug users, aged 14-17, in Miami, Florida, who trade sex for crack. Data collected 1988-1989.

D.0137 Inciardi, James (1984). Little girls and sex: A glimpse at the world of the "baby pro." *Deviant Behavior, 5*(1-4), 71-78. Interviews with nine 8-12 year old females who admitted involvement in prostitution and/or pornography.

D.0138 Indiana Supreme Court (1986-1989). *Case records: Case of Paula Cooper*. Indianapolis, IN: Indiana Supreme Court. Two boxes of letters and petitions addressed to the Indiana Supreme Court on behalf of Paula Cooper who, at age 15, was sentenced to death for murder.

D.0139 Ito, Fujie (1987, July). A study on female juveniles' sexual misconducts: I. *Reports of National Research Institute of Police Science, 28*(1), 63-71. Part I of two part paper discussing a study of factors that predispose female adolescents to sexual misconduct.

D.0140 Ito, Fujie (1987, July). A study on female juveniles' sexual misconducts: II. An analysis of the background of sexual misconducts. *Reports of National Research Institute of Police Science, 28*(1), 52-71. Study of factors predisposing children to sexual misconduct. Data collected from 623 Japanese female children. Part II of a two-part paper.

D.0141 Joe, Karen, & Chesney-Lind, Meda (1995, August). Just every mother's angel: An analysis of gender and ethnic variation in youth gang members. *Gender and Society, 9*(4), 408-431. Examines differences in boys and girls reasons for joining gangs.

D.0142 Johnson, Cheryl (1990, March). The impact of gender on status offender processing outcomes: A longitudinal analysis. *Dissertation Abstracts International, 50*(9), 3066-A. Study looks at discriminatory practices in the juvenile justice system.

D.0143 Johnson, David, & Scheuble, Laurie (1991, November). Gender bias in the disposition of juvenile court referrals: The effects of time and location. *Criminology, 29*(4), 677-699. Results of testing two models, one predicting more punishment decisions for female offenders and one less.

D.0144 Johnson, Joan (1992). *Teen prostitution*. New York, NY: F. Watts. Discusses teen prostitution.

D.0145 Jurjevich, R. M. (1966). Personality changes concomitant with institutional training of delinquent girls. *Journal of General Psychology, 74*, 207-216. Study of changes in female delinquents after institutional training.

D.0146 Kagan, H. (1969). *Prostitution and sexual promiscuity among adolescent female offenders*. Dissertation, University of Arizona. Study of female juvenile prostitution.

D.0147 Karoly, P. (1975, April). Comparison of "psychological styles" in delinquent and non-delinquent females. *Psychological Reports, 36*(2), 567-570. Study of psychological profiles of female juveniles.

D.0148 Kersten, J. (1990, November). A gender specific look at patterns of violence in juvenile institutions: Or are girls really more difficult to handle? *International Journal of the Sociology of the Law, 18*(4), 473-493. Study of aggessive behavior in institutionalized delinquents.

D.0149 King, Anna Elizabeth (1927). *Changing the delinquent attitude: A study of effective treatment in the cases of forty-four delinquent girls*. Cleveland, OH: Western Reserve University. Early study of female juvenile delinquents.

D.0150 Kohl, E. W. (1937). *Seasonal distribution of girl delinquents in Detroit*. Dissertation, University of Michigan. Early study of female juvenile delinquents in Detroit.

D.0151 Koller, K. M. (1971, March). Parental deprivation, family background, and female delinquency. *British Journal of Psychiatry, 118*(544), 319-327. Discusses family influences in female juveniles.

D.0152 Kopp, M. (1960). *A study of anomie and homosexuality in delinquent adolescent girls.* Dissertation, Saint Louis University. Study of homosexuality in delinquent adolescent girls.

D.0153 Koroki, Jan, & Chesney-Lind, Meda (1985). *Everything just going down the drain: Interviews with female delinquents in Hawaii, Report No. 319.* Manoa: University of Hawaii. Presents and analyzes findings of in-depth interviews with ten delinquent girls in Hawaii.

D.0154 Kosofsky, S., & Ellis, A. (1958). Illegal communication among institutionalized female delinquents. *Journal of Social Psychiatry, 48*, 155-160. Discusses communication among institutionalized adolescent females.

D.0155 Kosofsky, S. (1955, October). Directive therapy with female juvenile delinquents. *Journal of Clinical Psychology, 11*, 357-361. Discusses the use of therapy with female adolescent delinquents.

D.0156 Kratcoski, P. C. (1974). Differential treatment of delinquent boys and girls in juvenile court. *Child Welfare, 53*, 16-22. Discusses discriminatory practices of the juvenile court system.

D.0157 Kratcoski, P. C., & Kratcoski, J. E. (1975). Changing patterns in delinquent activities of boys and girls. *Adolescence, 10*, 83-90. Looks at trends in male and female juvenile delinquency.

D.0158 Kroupa, S. E. (1988, Spring). Perceived parental acceptance and female juvenile delinquency. *Adolescence, 23*(8), 171-185. Compared results of data on adolescent females residing at a Wyoming state training school and females living at home, on perceived parental acceptance.

D.0159 Krueger, Robert, et al. (1994). Personality traits are links to crime among men and women: Evidence from a birth cohort. *Journal of Abnormal Psychology, 103*(2), 328-338. Investigated the association of personality and criminality using a birth cohort of 18 year olds.

D.0160 Lack, C. (1952, July). Observations on the classifying of delinquent adolescent girls. *British Journal of Delinquency, 3*(1), 46-51. Looks at the classification of female juvenile delinquents.

D.0161 Lampman, H. T. (1973). *The wire womb: Life in a girls' penal institution.* Chicago: Nelson-Hall. Study of the daily life of institutionalized female juveniles.

D.0162 Landau, Barbara (1975, April). The adolescent female offender: Our dilemma. *Canadian Journal of Criminology and Corrections, 17*(2), 146-153. Discusses the female juvenile delinquent.

D.0163 Landau, Barbara (1973). The adolescent female offender. *Ontario Psychologist, 5*(2), 56-62. Looks at statistics indicating that girls are more likely than boys to be sent to training school for acts which are not considered a crime.

D.0164 Lang, Deborah, et al. (1976, October). Delinquent females' perceptions of their fathers. *Family Coordinator 25*(4), 475-481. Study of the relationship between female juvenile delinquents and their fathers.

D.0165 Larson, J. H. (1983, February). Rural female delinquents adaptation to institutional life. *Juvenile and Family Court Journal, 34*(1), 83-92. Disccusses the adaptation problems of female juveniles with rural backgrounds to institutional life.

D.0166 Laub, John, & McDermott, Joan (1985, February). An analysis of serious crime by young black women. *Criminology, 23,* 81-98. Looks at types of crimes committed by black female juveniles.

D.0167 Leech, K. R. (1971). *A study of the adjustment of delinquent girls to an institutional setting.* Dissertation, University of Tennessee. Study of adaptation problems for female juveniles.

D.0168 Leve, H. (1972). *Prediction of parolee behavior utilizing the semantic differential and inmate and staff judgements for delinquent girls in a state correctional institution.* Dissertation, Indiana University. Looks at predictors of recidivism in female juvenile offenders on parole.

D.0169 Lewis, D. O., et al. (1982). A comparison of the neuropsychiatric status of female and male incarcerated delinquents: Some evidence of sex and race bias. *Journal of the American Academy of Child Psychiatry, 21*(2), 190-196. Discusses sexism and racism in the juvenile justice system.

D.0170 Li, Congpei, et al. (1993, June-July). Biopsychological, psychosocial characteristics, and family background of girl offenders in a special reform school. *Chinese Mental Health Journal, 7*(3), 111-114. Compared biopsychological, psychosocial, and familial factors of female delinquents and normal girls in 1989.

D.0171 Light, H. (1976). *Highly competent girls and delinquent girls: A comparative study of value-needs and self-concept profiles.* Dissertation, Michigan State University. Study of ego strengths in female juvenile delinquents.

D.0172 Longres, J. F. (1991). An ecological study of parents of adjudicated female teenage prostitutes. *Journal of Social Service Research, 14*(1-2), 113-127. Examined family life from the point of view of 33 parents of adjudicated teenage female prostitutes.

D.0173 Lumpkin, Katharine (1932, September). Parental conditions of Wisconsin girl delinquents. *American Journal of Sociology, 38,* 232-239. Early study of familial profiles of female juveniles.

D.0174 Lumpkin, Katharine (1928). *Factors in the commitment of correctional school girls in Wisconsin.* Dissertation, University of Wisconsin. Early study on girls reformatories.

D.0175 MacVicar, J. (1967). *Homosexual delinquent girls' identification with mother and perception of parents.* Dissertation, Boston University. Study of familial relationships of homosexual female delinquents.

D.0176 Mahoney, A., & Fenster, Carol (1982). Female delinquents in a suburban court. In N. Rafter-Hahan & E. Stanko (Eds.), *Judge, lawyer, victim thief: Women, gender roles and criminal justice* Boston, MA: Northeastern University Press. Explored patterns of male and female delinquency over a ten-year period in a juvenile court.

D.0177 Maiuro, Roland, et al. (1983, April). Sex role differentiation in a female juvenile delinquent population: Prostitute vs. control samples. *American Journal of Orthopsychiatry, 53*(2), 345-352. Results of interviews with 101 female juvenile prostitutes and 78 other female juvenile delinquents (12-17 yrs. old) who completed the Bem Sex-Role Inventory.

D.0178 Mann, Coramae (1979). The differential treatment between runaway boys and girls in juvenile court. *Juvenile and Family Court Journal, 30,* 37-48. Study of discriminatory practices in the juvenile justice system.

D.0179 Mann, Coramae (1972). The juvenile female in the judicial process. *Dissertation Abstracts International, 37*(10), 6782-A. Compares the judicial handling of boys and girls in a midwestern urban area on the basis of the final disposition of their juvenile court cases.

D.0180 Mannarino, A. P., & Marsh, M. E. (1978, Winter). The relationship between sex role identification and juvenile delinquency in adolescent girls. *Adolescence, 13*(52), 643-652. Study of sex-role identification in female juvenile delinquents.

D.0181 Martin, Roger, & Bastian, James (1980, August). Relationship between behavioral indices of aggression and hostile content on the TAT for incarcerated young women. *Perceptual and Motor Skills, 51*(1), 327-332. Investigated the role of fantasy in moderating overt expressions of aggression in 15 incarcerated adolescent women.

D.0182 Maskin, M., & Brookins, E. (1974). The effects of parental composition on recidivism rates in delinquent girls. *Journal of Clinical Psychology, 30*(3), 341-342. Looks at familial influences as predictors of recidivism.

D.0183 Mathur, Sarup (1993, March). Effectiveness of social skills training with female juvenile delinquents. *Dissertation Abstracts International, 53*(9), 3170. Examined the effectiveness of social skills instructions in promoting social competence of female juvenile delinquents.

D.0184 Matthews, J. (1923). A survey of 341 delinquent girls in California. *Journal of Delinquency, 8*, 196-231. Early survey study of female delinquency in California.

D.0185 May, D. (1977). Delinquent girls before the courts. *Medicine, Science, and Law, 17*(3), 203-212. Discusses treatment of female juveniles in the juvenile justice system.

D.0186 McClelland, A. (1982, June). Changing rates or changing roles: Adolescent female delinquency reassessed. *Journal of Adolescence, 5*(2), 85-98. Discusses the complex interaction of factors that account for the rising number of female adolescent delinquents.

D.0187 McDaniel, J. (1976). *A comparative study of extroversion, neuroticism, and self-concept of delinquent and non-delinquent girls.* Dissertation, Ball State University. Compares profiles of female juvenile delinquents with female juvenile non-delinquents.

D.0188 Meichenbaum, D. H., et al. (1968). Modification of classroom behavior of institutionalized female adolescent offenders. *Behavior Research and Therapy, 6*, 343-353. Discusses behavior modification with delinquent juvenile females.

D.0189 Meliksetian, A. S. (1992, February). The social causes of deviant behavior in young women. *Russian Education and Society, 34*, 82-95. Discussion of female juvenile delinquency.

D.0190 Mellor, V. G. (1975). *Becoming a Borstal girl: Assimilation, adjustment and reaction to the environment in two Borstal institutions for girls.* Dissertation, University of London. Discusses the Borstal system for female juveniles in England.

D.0191 Menken, Alice (1926, September). Delinquent girls on parole: A study of girls discharged from Cedar Knolls. *Jewish Social Services Quarterly, 3*, 46-50. Early study of female juveniles after detention.

D.0192 Meyer, Deanna (1994). *The application of female juvenile delinquency theories.* Paper presented at the Academy of Criminal Justice Sciences Annual Meeting, March 8-12, 1994, Chicago, IL. Examines whether existing theories of juvenile delinquency are indicative of trends represented by existing data.

D.0193 Meyers, Wade, et al. (1990). DSM-III diagnoses and offenses in committed female juvenile delinquents. *Bulletin of Psychiatry and the Law, 18*(1), 47-54. Examines the relationship between delinquency and psychiatric disorders. Data collected from 15 female delinquents.

D.0194 Miller, Darcy, et al. (1995, Summer). Adolescent female offenders: Unique considerations. *Adolescence, 30*(118), 429-435. Synthesis of selected characteristics and assessment considerations related to adolescent female offenders.

D.0195 Miller, Walter (1973, November-December). Race, sex, and gangs: The molls. *Trans-Action, 11*(1), 32-35. Discussion of the "molls," eleven "bad girls" of the neighborhood in an Eastern Seaport city who engaged in stealing, playing hookey, drinking, vandalism, and sex offenses.

D.0196 Minkin, N. (1978, June). The analysis, validation, and training of peer criticism skills with delinquent girls. *Dissertation Abstracts International, 38*(12-B), 6122. Study of the use of peer group training with delinquent girls.

D.0197 Mirkin, M. P., et al. (1984, March). Parenting, protecting, preserving: Mission of the adolescent female runaway. *Family Process, 23*(1), 63-74. Delineates a framework for therapy with families of adolescent female runaways.

D.0198 Miser, Martha (1992). Specialization and clinical judgments of social workers in cases involving acting out of delinquent female adolescents. *Dissertation Abstracts International, 53*(12), 4477. Addresses the question of social work specialization and treatment plans formulated for female juvenile delinquents who were exhibiting adolescent depression symptomatology.

D.0199 Moore, Joan (1994). The "chola" life course: Chicana heroin users and the barrio gang. *International Journal of the Addictions, 29*(9), 1115-1126. Study of adolescent Latina girls and factors that lead them to join drug-using gangs.

D.0200 Moore, Joan (1991). *Going down to the barrio: Homeboys and homegirls in change.* Philadelphia: Temple University Press. Study of juvenile delinquency in the Latina community.

D.0201 Morris, Ruth (1964). Female delinquency and relational problems. *Social Forces, 43,* 82-89. Study of factors that influence delinquency in female juveniles.

D.0202 Mortola, D. S. (1970). *Aspects of the self-concept in delinquent girls: Maternal identification and body concept.* Dissertation, Fordham University. Looks at ego-strengths in delinquent girls.

D.0203 Muir, E. (1975). Teaching Borstal girls to relax. *International Journal of Offender Therapy and Comparative Criminology, 19*(3), 237-240. Discussion of relaxation techniques with Borstal girls.

D.0204 Mullins, Ronald, & Hanson, Richard (1983, Winter). Perspective-taking among offender and nonoffender youth. *Adolescence, 18*(72), 831-836. Assessed perspective-taking abilities and compared differences between 64 male and 53 female offenders and nonoffenders.

D.0205 Munger, Elizabeth (1923). A system of classification in the New Jersey state home for girls, Trenton, New Jersey. *Juvenile Delinquency, 8,* 83-98. Early study of classification of female juveniles.

D.0206 Myers, Felicity (1989). Attribution for responsibility for prosocial and anti-social behavior by female juvenile delinquents. *Dissertation Abstracts International, 51*(4), 2116. Investigated prosocial and antisocial behaviors among 67 adjudicated females 12-17 years of age.

D.0207 Naffine, Ngaire (1989). Towards justice for girls: Rhetoric and practice in the treatment of status offenders. *Women and Criminal Justice, 1*(1), 3-19. Examines Australian policies towards young women appearing in court. Data collected from 1958 to 1987 court reports.

D.0208 Narcotics Control Digest (1991, July). Drug-dealing girl gangs crop up in Motown. *Narcotics Control Digest, 21*(14), 4-5. Discussion of girl-gangs in Detroit.

D.0209 Newton-Ruddy, Lara, & Handelsman, Mitchell (1986, Winter). Jungian feminine psychology and adolescent prostitutes. *Adolescence, 21*(84), 815-825. Explores Jungian feminine psychology and its application in the treatment of adolescent prostitutes.

D.0210 Noble, P., et al. (1972, May). Correlates and outcomes of illicit drug use by adolescent girls. *British Journal of Psychiatry, 120*(558), 497-504. Study of drug use by female juveniles.

D.0211 Noble, P. J., & Barnes, G. G. (1971). Drug taking in adolescent girls: Factors associated with progression to narcotic use. *British Medical Journal, 2*, 620-623. Study of long-term drug use in female juvenile delinquents.

D.0212 Nollenberger, H. A. (1981). *A study of attitudes of female delinquents toward the functional and dysfunctional aspects of the school as compared to male juvenile delinquents.* Dissertation, University of Toledo. Results of a study of female juvenile delinquent attitudes towards school.

D.0213 Norcross, B. N. (1977, October). A comparison of sex-role orientation, family ideology, and heterosexual relationships for delinquent and non-delinquent girls. *Dissertation Abstracts International, 38*(4-B), 1894. Study of female juvenile delinquents.

D.0214 Novak, D. F. (1956). *A comparison of vocational interests and aptitudes of delinquent and non-delinquent girls.* Dissertation, Loyola University of Chicago. Looks at vocational interests of female juveniles.

D.0215 Novick, A. G. (1960). The make-believe family: Informal group structure among institutionalized delinquent girls. In Family Service Association (Ed.), *Casework papers from the National Conference on Social Welfare* (pp. 44-59). New York, NY: Family Services Association. Looked at make-believe family group structures in institutions for female juvenile delinquents.

D.0216 Odem, Mary (1995). *Delinquent daughters: Protecting and policing adolescent female sexuality in the United States, 1885-1920.* Chapel Hill, NC: University of North Carolina Press. Historical view of policies and practices with female juvenile delinquents in the United States.

D.0217 Odem, Mary E., & Schlossman, Steve (1991, April). Guardians of virtue: The juvenile court and female delinquency in early 20th century Los Angeles. *Crime and Delinquency, 37*(2), 186-203. Analyzes a policy to discipline female delinquents in early 20th century Los Angeles. Focuses on key institutions which labeled, processed, and punished delinquents.

D.0218 Offord, D. R., et al. (1981). School performance, IQ, and female delinquency. *International Journal of Social Psychiatry, 27*(1), 53-67. Study of school performance of female delinquents.

D.0219 Offord, D. R., et al. (1979, April). Broken homes, parental psychiatric illness, and female delinquency. *American Journal of Orthopsychiatry, 49*(2), 252-264. Looks at psychological factors that may influence delinquency in female juveniles.

D.0220 Offord, D. R., et al. (1968). A study of recidivism among female juvenile delinquents. *Corrective Psychiatry and Journal of Social Therapy, 14*(3), 166-174. Looks at predictors of recidivism in female juvenile delinquents.

D.0221 O'Kelly, E. (1955, March). Some observations on relationships between delinquent girls and their parents. *British Journal of Medical Psychology, 28*, 59-66. Looks at familial factors in female juvenile delinquency.

D.0222 Omodei, Roslyn (1979, March). Delinquency in girls in South Australia. *The Australian and New Zealand Journal of Sociology, 15*(1), 81-85. Study of female juvenile delinquency in Australia.

D.0223 Ordahl, Louise, & Ordahl, G. (1918). A study of delinquent and dependent girls. *Juvenile Delinquency, 3*(2), 41-73. Early study of female juvenile delinquents.

D.0224 Otten, Laura (1986, June). A comparison of male and female delinquents in a birth cohort. *Dissertation Abstracts International, 12*(11), 3869A. Study of similarities and differences in juvenile delinquent behavior in males and females.

D.0225 Patterson, E. J. (1966). *Changes in perceptual field occurring among delinquent adolescent females.* Dissertation, University of Pittsburgh. Study of perceptual changes in female juvenile delinquents.

D.0226 Patterson, Inez (1929, September). Paths of the handicapped delinquent girl. *Minnesota State Board of Control Quarterly, 29*, 16-17. Early study of female juvenile delinquency.

D.0227 Patterson, Richard (1951, April). Psychiatric treatment of institutionalized delinquent adolescent girls. *British Journal of Delinquency, 1*(4), 302-307. Discusses psychiatry and the female juvenile delinquent.

D.0228 Penna-Firme, Thereza, et al. (1991, October). Adolescent female prostitutes on the streets of Brazil: An exploratory investigation of ontological issues. *Journal of Adolescent Research, 6*(4), 493-504. Interviewed 21 female prostitutes (ages 14-26) to develop a profile.

D.0229 Phillips, B. J., et al. (1975, December). Juvenile drug abuse in females: A clinical study. *Australian and New Zealand Journal of Psychiatry, 9*(4), 281-286. Looks at drug abuse patterns in female juveniles.

D.0230 Postlelwaite, M. M. (1975). *The effects of human relations workshops upon the behavior of delinquent adolescent girls.* Dissertation, Columbia University. Studied the use of Human Relations workshops with female juvenile delinquents.

D.0231 Propper, Alice (1982, May). Make-believe families and homosexuality among imprisoned girls. *Criminology, 20*(1). Discusses homosexuality and make-believe families in 4 all-female training schools.

D.0232 Propper, Alice (1976). Importation and deprivation perspectives on homosexuality in correctional institutions. *Dissertation Abstracts International, 37*(1), 6783-A. Examines the relationship of homosexuality to descriptions of self-image.

D.0233 Quicker, J. (1983). *Homegirls: Characterizing Chicano gangs.* San Pedro, CA: International University Press. Study of Latina girl gang members.

D.0234 Quinn, K. M. (1991). Gender issues in the forensic evaluation of adolescents and children. *American Academy of Psychiatry and the Law Newsletter, 16*(2), 52-53. Discusses gender-bias, comorbidity, and stigmatization issues relevant to girls before the court in the United States.

D.0235 Reardon, J. P. (1976). *The effects of rational stage directed therapy on self-concept and reduction of psychological stress in adolescent delinquent females.* Dissertation, Ohio State University. Study of psychological stress in female juvenile delinquents.

D.0236 Redfering, D. L. (1973). Durability of effects of group counseling with institutionalized delinquent females. *Journal of Abnormal Psychology, 82*(1), 85-86. Looks at long-term effects of group counseling for instituionalized female juvenile delinquents.

D.0237 Reese, W. A. (1991, January). Paternalism and the female status offender: Remanding the juvenile justice double standard for desexualization. *The Social Science Journal, 28*(1). An interactionist perspective is used to generate alternative hypotheses of a sexist double standard in juvenile justice.

D.0238 Reitsman-Street, M., & Offord, D. R. (1991, Winter). Girl delinquents and their sisters: A challenge for practice. *Canadian Social Work Review, 8*(1), 11-27. Study of relationships among female juvenile offenders.

D.0239 Riback, Linda (1971). Juvenile delinquency laws: Juvenile women and the double standard of morality. *UCLA Law Review, 19*, 313-342. Looks at discriminatory practices and standards in juvenile justice.

D.0240 Rogers, K. O. (1972, Winter). For her own protection: Conditions of incarceration for female juvenile offenders in the state of Connecticut. *Law and Society Review, 7*(2), 221-246. Contrasts restrictive conditions at the Connecticut School for Girls with those for boys.

D.0241 Rosenbaum, Jill, & Chesney-Lind, Meda (1994). Appearance and delinquency: A research note. *Crime and Delinquency, 40*(2), 250-261. Assesses the effects of physical appearance on the treatment of juvenile females in the criminal justice process.

D.0242 Rosenbaum, Jill (1989, January). Family dysfunction and female delinquency. *Crime and Delinquency, 35*(1), 31-44. Examines family backgrounds of a group of women who, as adolescents in the 1960's, were committed to the California Youth Authority.

D.0243 Rosenthal, L. (1978). *A comparison of social skills in delinquent and non-delinquent adolescent girls using a behavioral role-playing inventory.* Dissertation, University of Wisconsin. Study of social skills in female juvenile delinquents.

D.0244 Ross, R., et al. (1978). Self-mutilation in adolescent female offenders. *Canadian Journal of Criminology, 20*(4), 375-392. Discusses self-cutting in correctional insitutions for adolescent female offenders.

D.0245 Russell, Donald (1985, September). Girls who kill. *International Journal of Offender Therapy and Comparative Criminology, 29*(2), 171-176. Case histories of two juvenile females who committed murder.

D.0246 Sagatun, Inger (1978, September). *Sex differences in attributions of juvenile delinquency.* Paper presented at the 73rd Annual Meeting of the American Sociological Association, San Francisco. An application of attribution theory to the processing of juvenile delinquents in an attempt to understand the differential treatment of female and male juvenile offenders.

D.0247 Sarri, Rosemary (1983, July). Gender issues in juvenile justice. *Crime and Delinquency, 29*(3), 381-397. Looks at discriminatory practices in juvenile justce.

D.0248 Sarri, Rosemary (1976). Juvenile law: How it penalizes females. In L. Crites (Ed.) *The female offender* (pp. 67-79). Lexington, MA: DC Heath. Discusses how female juveniles are dealt with in the courts.

D.0249 Scavo, R. (1984, February). Female adolescent sex offenders: A neglected treatment group. *Social Casework, 70*(2), 114-117. Identifies the societal values and gender bias that contribute to the lack of attention to female offenders. Discusses implications for social casework.

D.0250 Schaffer, Bernie, & DeBlassie, Richard (1984, Fall). Adolescent prostitution. *Adolescence, 19*(75), 689-696. Explores the conditions that lead to female teenaged prostitution and how institutions and the legal system can deal with them.

D.0251 Schlossman, Steven, & Wallach, Stephanie (1978, February). The crime of precocious sexuality: Female juvenile delinquency in the progressive era. *Harvard Educational Review, 48*(1), 65-74. Discusses discriminatory treatment of female delinquents in the early 20th century that resulted from racial prejudice, new theories of adolescence, and movements to purify society.

D.0252 Schwartz, I. M., et al. (1990, October). Federal juvenile justice policy and the incarceration of girls. *Crime and Delinquency, 36*(4), 503-520. Looks at the standards of practice of the Federal juvenile justice policy.

D.0253 Sedlak, Michael (1983). Young women and the city: Adolescent deviance and the transformation of educational policy, 1870-1960. *Historical Educational Quarterly, 23*(1), 1-28. Examines the history of the treatment of pregnant and/or delinquent girls during 1870-1960.

D.0254 Sedlak, Michael (1982). Youth policy and young women, 1870-1972. *Social Service Review, 56*(3), 448-464. Traces the history of social service policy towards delinquent and pregnant adolescents.

D.0255 Sepsi, V. J. (1974, January). Girl recidivists. *Journal of Research in Crime and Delinquency, 11*(1), 70-79. Looks at factors that affect recidivism in female juvenile delinquents.

D.0256 Seymour, Frederick, & Sanson-Fisher, R. W. (1975). Effects of teacher attention on the classroom behavior of two delinquent girls within a token program. *New Zealand Journal of Educational Studies, 10*(2), 111-120. Study of classroom behavior of female juveniles.

D.0257 Seymour, Frederick, & Stokes, Trevor (1976, Spring). Self-recording in training girls to increase work and evoke staff praise in an institution for offenders. *Journal of Applied Behavior Analysis, 9*(1), 41-54. Assessed self-recording procedures used by four 14-18 year old females to increase work in a maximum security institution for offenders.

D.0258 Shanok, S. S., & Lewis, D. O. (1981, February). Medical histories of female delinquents. Clinical and epidemiologic findings. *Archives of General Psychiatry, 38*(2), 211-213. Results of a review of medical records of female juvenile delinquents.

D.0259 Shoemaker, Donald (1994, March). Male-female delinquency in the Philippines: A comparative analysis. *Youth and Society, 25*(3), 299-329. Analyses of self-report data from male and female students in a coastal city in the southern Philippines.

D.0260 Shook, S., & Delaney, H. (1994, March). *Contractural injustice: Historical roots of racism and sexism in the juvenile justice system.* Paper presented at the Annual Meeting of the ACJS, 1994, Chicago, IL. A theoretical exploration into the historically rooted justifications for the differential treatment of female and male offenders by the juvenile justice system.

D.0261 Simons, Ronald, & Whitbeck, Les (1991, September). Sexual abuse as a precursor to prostitution and victimization among adolescent and adult homeless women. *Journal of Family Issues, 12*(3), 361-379. Examined direct and indirect models of the impact of early sexual abuse on prostitution and victimization.

D.0262 Skitka, Linda, et al. (1993). Offense classification and social facilitation in juvenile delinquents. *Social Behavior and Personality, 21*(4), 339-346. Explored the influence of social facilitation on patterns and severity of offenses committed by juvenile delinquents.

D.0263 Slack, Eileen (1974, December). Remedies for wrongs: Updating programs for delinquent girls. *Criminal Justice and Behavior, 1*(4), 381-387. Looks at programs for female juvenile offenders.

D.0264 Smith, Beverly (1989, February). Female admissions and paroles of the Western House of Refuge in the 1880's: An historical example of community corrections. *Journal of Research in Crime and Delinquency, 26*(1), 36-66. Examines records of 75 females admitted in 1885-1886 to the Western House of Corrections, a famous facility for juveniles in the 19th century.

D.0265 Snyder, P. R. (1965). Coordinating residential and community treatment of delinquent girls. *Social Casework, 46*(1), 10-15. Discusses the role of the social worker in working with female juveniles.

D.0266 Sommers, Ira, & Baskin, Deborah (1994, June). Factors related to female adolescent initiation into violent street crime. *Youth and Society, 25*(4), 468-490. Examines when and how adolescent girls become involved in violent street crime.

D.0267 Sorrells, James (1977, July). Kids who kill. *Crime and Delinquency, 23*(3), 312-320. Reviews case records of juveniles charged with homicide January, 1973 through June, 1974.

D.0268 Staples, W. G. (1984, July). Toward a structural perspective on gender bias in the juvenile court. *Sociological Perspectives, 27*(3), 349-367. Looks at discriminatory practices in the juvenile justice system.

D.0269 Steffensmeier, Darrell, & Steffensmeier, Renee (1980, May.). Trends in female delinquency: An examination of arrest, juvenile court, self-report, and field data. *Criminology, 18*(1), 62-85. Evaluates current concepts of the changing nature of female delinquency using national arrest statistics for 1965-1977.

D.0270 Stephens, J. M. (1991). *Parental intactness among female juvenile justice offenders.* Dissertation, Abilene Christian University. Study of familial make-up of female juvenile offenders.

D.0271 Suddick, D. E. (1969). *Female juvenile runaways from home.* Dissertation, University of Northern Colorado. Study of female juvenile runaways.

D.0272 Sullivan-Cosetti, J. (1988, August). An exploratory study of the common and recurring factors present in juvenile female violent offenders referred to juvenile courts nationwide for the crimes of robbery and aggravated assault. *Dissertation Abstracts International, 50*(8), 2660. Study included an integrated theoretical model encompassing developmental theories.

D.0273 Swart, William (1991, Winter). Female gang delinquency: A search for acceptably deviant behavior. *Mid-American Review of Sociology, 15*(1), 43-52. Explores forms of female gang delinquency. Analyzes the deviance norms for females within the gang structure.

D.0274 Tamura, Masayuki (1984, July). A pattern analysis of delinquent gangs: I. On the traits of members' personality. *Reports of National Research Institute of Police Science, 25*(1), 34-41. Investigated the relationship between personality and type of delinquency in 40 delinquents from 10 delinquency groups. Females included in the study.

D.0275 Tappan, P. W. (1947). *Delinquent girls in court.* New York, NY: Columbia University Press. Early study of female juveniles in the juvenile justice system.

D.0276 Taylor, A. J. (1968, April). A search among Borstal girls for the psychological and special significance of their tattoos. *British Journal of Criminology, 8*, 170-185. Discussion of tattooing among female juvenile delinquents.

D.0277 Taylor, A. J. (1967). An evaluation of group psychotherapy in a girl's Borstal. *International Journal of Group Psychotherapy, 17*(2), 168-177. Discussion of group therapy with females.

D.0278 Taylor, A. J. (1965, October). The significance of "darls" or "special relationships" for Borstal girls. *British Journal of Criminology, 5*, 190-196. Study of relationships among Borstal girls.

D.0279 Teilmann, Katherine, & Landry, P. H. (1981, January). Gender bias in juvenile justice. *Journal of Research in Crime and Delinquency, 18*(1), 47-80. Looks at discriminatory practices in the juvenile justice system.

D.0280 Templeton, G. J. (1979). *The impact of the culture of a cottage in a residential treatment center on the implementation of a bibliotherapy program for delinquent girls.* Dissertation, University of North Carolina at Chapel Hill. Discusses the implementation of a bibliotherapy program with institutionalized female juveniles.

D.0281 Tenne, David (1988). Prevention of prostitution among girls in distress. *Crime and Social Deviance, 16*(1-2), 35-49. Analyzes the sexual regression of Afro-Asian girls into prostitution in Israel in the context of intercultural conflict between Afro-Asian immigrants and Israeli society.

D.0282 Thelen, M. H., & Fryrear, J. L. (1971). Imitation of self-reward standards by black and white female delinquents. *Psychological Reports, 29*, 667-671. Discussion of self-rewards among female juvenile delinquents.

D.0283 Thomas, W. I. (1923). *The unadjusted girl.* Boston, MA: Little, Brown. Early study of female juvenile delinquency republished in 1967.

D.0284 Thompson, E. B. (1951, March). Girl gangs of Harlem. *The Negro Digest, 9*, 38-42. Early study of black female gangs in Harlem.

D.0285 Thompson, Robert, & Lozes, Jewell (1976). Female gang delinquency. *Corrective and Social Psychiatry and Journal of Behavior Technology Methods and Therapy, 22*(3), 1-5. Compared delinquent female gang and non-gang members. Reviewed gang incidence between 1967-1974.

D.0286 Tom^sevski, Katarina (1986). *Children in adult prisons: An international perspective.* New York, NY: St. Martin's Press. Looks at the incarceration of children globally.

D.0287 Torstensson, Marie (1990, March). Female delinquents in a birth cohort: Tests of some aspects of control theory. *Journal of Quantitative Criminology, 6*(1), 101-115. Discusses findings of female delinquency and criminality with regard to Control Theory using a birth cohort.

D.0288 Tovar, Christina (1994). *Gender bias in juvenile justice processing: An analysis of four Iowa counties.* Paper presented at the ACJS Annual Meeting, 1994, Chicago, IL. Examines the interaction between gender and decision-making in juvenile justice, using case records.

D.0289 Tracy, Sharon (1989, January). The cracks in the system: A search for the violent female juvenile offender. *Dissertation Abstracts International, A: The Human and Social Sciences, 49*(7), 1972. Study of violence in female juvenile offenders.

D.0290 Truax, C. B., et al. (1966). Effects of group psychotherapy with high accurate empathy and nonpossessive warmth upon female institutionalized delinquents. *Journal of Abnormal Psychology, 71*(4), 267-274. Discussion of group psychotherapy with female juveniles.

D.0291 Vedder, C., & Sommerville, D. (1970). *The delinquent girl.* Springfield, IL: Charles C. Thomas. Study of delinquency in female juveniles.

D.0292 Veldhuizen, J. G. (1971). *The effect of institutional placement on delinquent adolescent girls: An MMPI and CPI sequence testing approach.* Dissertation, Graduate Theological Union. Results of testing on female juvenile delinquents.

D.0293 Viar, J. S. (1976). Differences between obese and non-obese female adolescent delinquents in terms of developmental patterns and psychological variables. *Dissertation Abstracts International, 37*(3-B), 1420. Study of the affects of appearance on female juvenile delinquents.

D.0294 Vitaliano, P. P. (1981). Perceptions of juvenile experience: Females involved in prostitution versus property offenses. *Criminal Justice and Behavior, 8*(3), 325-342. Discusses types of offenses in female juvenile offenders.

D.0295 Walshe, Brennan (1977, Janaury). A socio-psychological investigation of young murderers. *British Journal of Criminology, 17*(1), 58-63. Investigated the number of murders committed by children in England and Wales. One girl included in the study.

D.0296 Ward-Hull, C. I. (1981). *Correlates of female juvenile delinquency.* Dissertation, Indiana University. A study of contributing factors in female juvenile delinquency.

D.0297 Warren, Marguerite (1982). Delinquency causation in female offenders. In N. Rafter-Hahn & E. Stanko (Eds.), *Judge, lawyer, victim, thief: Women, gender roles, and criminal justice* (pp. 181-201). Boston, MA: Northeastern University Press. Discusses theories of crime causation using data from adolescent females.

D.0298 Weisberg, D. K. (1985). *Children of the night: A study of adolescent prostitution.* Lexington, MA: DC Heath. In-depth study of prostitution in adolescents.

D.0299 Widseth, J. C. (1972). *Reported dependent behaviors toward mother and use of alcohol in delinquent girls.* Dissertation, Boston University. Behavioral study of female juvenile delinquents.

D.0300 Wilgosh, L., & Paitich, D. (1978). An examination of sex differences in a clinical sample of juvenile offenders. *Canadian Journal of Criminology, 20*(1), 75-78. Comparative study.

D.0301 Wilkinson, K. R. (1978). *Juvenile delinquency and femininity.* Dissertation, University of Arizona. Study of gender role perception in female juvenile delinquents.

D.0302 Williamson, G. L. (1982). *Commitment decisions in the juvenile justice systems: Results and implications for the female delinquent.* Dissertation, University of Georgia. Study of discriminatory practices in the juvenile justice system.

D.0303 Winfree, L., et al. (1994). Social learning theory, self-reported delinquency, and youth gangs: A new twist on a general theory of crime and delinquency. *Youth and Society, 26*(2), 147-177. Explores the utility of applying selected elements of social learning theory to youth gangs.

D.0304 Wooden, K. (1976). *Weeping in the playtime of others: America's incarcerated children.* New York, NY: McGraw-Hill. Study of incarcerated youth in the United States.

D.0305 Wundersitz, Joy, et al. (1988, November). Chivalry, justice or paternalism?: The female offender in the juvenile justice system. *The Australian and New Zealand Journal of Sociology, 24*(3), 359-376. Compares the treatment of young females and males charged with criminal offenses in South Australia. Uses official statistics from 1979-1984.

D.0306 Zingraff, Matthew, et al. (1980a). Adaptation patterns of incarcerated female delinquents. *Juvenile and Family Court Journal, 31*(2), 35-48. Looks at how female juveniles adapt to incarceration.

D.0307 Zingraff, Matthew (1980b, September). Inmate assimilation: A comparison of male and female delinquents. *Criminal Justice and Behavior, 7*(3), 275-292. Comparative study of adaptation patterns.

D.0308 Zingraff, Matthew (1977, September). *A comparison of male and female delinquents.* Paper presented at the 72nd Annual Meeting of the American Sociological Association, Chicago. Assesses two theoretical models as predictors of juvenile inmate adaptation to confinement.

D.0309 Zingraff, Matthew (1976, November). A comparative study of inmate subcultures and adaptation patterns in correctional institutions of male and female offenders. *Dissertation Abstracts International, 37*(5), 3203-A. A comparative study of inmate subcultures and adaptation patterns in correctional institutions for male and female delinquents.

5

CORRECTIONS

AIDS; Health Issues; Jails; Prisons; Prison programs; Prison Staff

E.0001 Abram, Linda (1981). *Kentucky, locking up the female offender.* Urbana-Champaign, IL: University of Illinois. Discusses the incarceration of women in Kentucky.

E.0002 Ackerman, Helen (1987). *Therapy with women in jail: A manual for the mental health worker.* Washington, DC: American Correctional Health Services. Manual of guidelines for mental health professionals working with women in jail.

E.0003 Ackerman, Helen (1972, July). A staff group in a women's prison. *International Journal of Psychotherapy, 22*(3), 364-373. Discusses counseling for prison staff.

E.0004 Acorn, Linda (1992, June). Elizabeth Fry Center: California program helps women offenders make smooth transition. *Corrections Today, 54*(4), 102. Discusses a transitional program for female offenders.

E.0005 Acorn, Linda (1991, June). Judy Anderson: Warden of the year enjoys leadership role. *Corrections Today, 53*(3), 52. Warden Anderson speaks of her role in a women's prison.

E.0006 Addition, Henrietta (1951). Women's institutions. In P. W. Tappan (Ed.), *Contemporary Corrections* (Chapter 19). New York, NY: McGraw Hill. Study of women's prisons.

E.0007 Additon, Henrietta (1944, March/April). Girls do not learn about crime in prison. *Prison Journal, 6*(2), 20. Discusses the belief of the time that prisons and reformatories were places where girls and women learned about crime.

E.0008 Adler, A. (1977). Rehabilitative programs for women. In D. Bradshaw & P. Ecks (Eds.), *Rehabilitation what part of corrections?* Arlington, VA: Division Institute of Urban Studies. Looks at the place of rehabilitation in prison programs for women.

E.0009 Agan, Ray, & Costley-Oyervides, Betty 1989). *Quest for a career: The female inmate.* Waco, TX: Sam Houston State Unviersity. Discusses female inmates' career education needs according to teachers. Focused on resources, experiences, and coping skills.

E.0010 Ahuja, R. (1969). *Female offenders in India.* Meerut: Meenakshi, Prakashan. Study of female offenders in India.

E.0011 Ahuja, R. (1962). *A case study of the inmates of Nari Nicketan, Delhi: An inquiry into their problems in relation to their rehabilitation program.* Dissertation, Maharaja Sayajirao University, Baroda. Study of a women's prison in India.

E.0012 Aiken, D. V. (1972). *Process of socialization of adult female offenders by inmates into the inmate social system.* Dissertation, Catholic University of America. Washington, DC. Describes the socialization of incarcerated women and adaptation to peer social systems.

E.0013 Alexander, Rudolph, et al. (1993, September). Women offenders incarcerated at the Ohio Penitentiary for men and the Ohio Reformatory for Women from 1913-1923. *Journal of Sociology and Social Welfare, 20*(3), 61-79. Uses qualitative and quantitative data from 1913-1923 to assess legislation passed to suppress prostitution and related behaviors.

E.0014 Alliance on Non-Governmental Organizations on Crime Prevention and Criminal Justice (1987). *Children in prison with their mothers.* New York, NY: Alliance. Reports on children in prison with their mothers based on data collected in 1985-1987 from 70 countries.

E.0015 Al-Mosleh, Hmoud (1994, August). The characteristics of female offenders in Oklahoma: An analysis of high rate of incarceration. *Dissertation Abstracts International, 55*(2), 377. Examines reasons why Oklahoma has highest rate of incarceration per capita of female offenders.

E.0016 Alpert, Geoffrey, & Crouch, Ben (1991, September). Cross-gender supervision, personal privacy and institutional security: Perceptions of jail inmates and staff. *Criminal Justice and Behavior, 18*(3), 304-317. Examines cross-gender supervision in correctional facilities.

E.0017 Alpert, Geoffrey, et al. (1977a, Summer). A comparative look at prisonization: Sex and prison. *Quarterly Journal of Corrections, 1*(3), 29-34. Data collected from 92 female and 241 male inmates on predictors of "prisonization," the taking on of prison folkways, mores and customs.

E.0018 Alpert, Geoffrey, & Wiorkowski, John (1977b, Fall). Female prisoners and legal services. *Quarterly Journal of Corrections, 1*(4), 28-33. Uses data collected from interviews with female offenders to predict who will seek legal aid.

E.0019 Alyonin, Aleksandr (1994, March 6). A lesbian convict tells her story : "My husband's name is Tanya." *Current Digest of the Post-Soviet Press, 46*(7), 15-17. First person account indicates that sexual relations between women convicts in Russian prisons are common.

E.0020 American Bar Association (1975). *Community programs for women offenders: Cost and economic considerations.* Washington, DC: American Bar Association. Examines correctional facilities for women in Washington, DC.

E.0021 American Bar Association (1974). *Women in Detention and statewide jail standards.* Washington, DC: American Bar Association. Offers observations from individual jail studies on the special situation of female defendants and jail standards for female residents.

E.0022 American Correctional Association (1993). *Female offenders: Meeting needs of a neglected population.* Laurel, MD: American Correctional Association. Eighteen articles on managing a women's correctional facility, facility programming, and care of pregnant offenders.

E.0023 American Correctional Association (1990). *The female offender: What does the future hold?* Laurel, MD : American Correctional Association. Essays on the female offender.

E.0024 American Correctional Association (1988). *Tabulation of a nationwide survey of state correctional facilities housing female inmates.* Laurel, MD: American Correctional Association. Results of an 80-question survey of 2,094 adult and juvenile female inmates conducted nationwide in November and December of 1987.

E.0025 American Journal of Corrections (1975, January). Data on women in jail. *American Journal of Corrections, 37*(1), 38+. Data on women serving time in American jails.

E.0026 Anderson, Sally (1991). *A review of Oregon's women offenders and effective corrections programs.* Washington, DC: NCJRS, Report on programs for women offenders in Oregon.

E.0027 Andrews, Brenda (1991). *A training program for pat frisking female inmates for New York City Department of Correction Officers.* Master's Thesis, New York Institute of Technology. Describes training program developed for male correctional officers.

E.0028 Ansay, Sylvia (1994, March). *Inmate perceptions of the prison family as a social entity within a women's prison.* Paper presented at the 1994 ACJS meeting, Chicago, IL. Examines inmate attitudes toward prison family and describes families from the female inmates perspective.

E.0029 Arcaro, T. E. (1984, February). Self identity of female prisoners: The moral career of the inmate. *Humanity and Society, 8*(1), 73-89. Uses Goffman's "moral career" concept to examine the effect of incarceration on female inmates. Ethnographic examples.

E.0030 Arnold, Charlotte (1993, August). Respect, recognition are keys to effective volunteer programs. *Corrections Today, 55*(5), 118-121. Discusses a program for female offenders at a Pittsburgh facility that provides legal help and job training to female offenders.

E.0031 Arnold, Charlotte (1992, January/February). The program for female offenders, Inc.: A community corrections answer to jail crowding. *American Jails,* 36-40. Discusses alternatives to incarceration of women.

E.0032 Arnold, Regina (1984). *Women in prison: Class, criminality, and imprisonment.* Dissertation, Sarah Lawrence College. Study of women in prison.

E.0033 Aron, N. (1981). Legal issues pertaining to female offenders. In *Representing prisoners* (pp. 189-206). New York, NY: Practicing Law Institute. Discusses grounds for litigation in areas where female inmates constitutional rights are violated.

E.0034 Arrigona, N. (1988). *Female offenders in prison: Trends and issues.* Huntsville, TX: Texas Criminal Justice Policy Council. Study of women in prison.

E.0035 Ash, Peter, & Guyer, Melvin (1982). Involuntary abandonment: Infants of imprisoned parents. *Bulletin of the American Academy of Psychiatry and the Law, 10*(2), 103-113. Legal case of an unmarried incarcerated woman who sought custody of her infant.

E.0036 Ashe, Marie (1993, August). Bad mothers, good lawyers, and legal ethics. *The Georgetown Law Journal, 81*, 2533-2566. Discussion of legal rights of incarcerated mothers and their children.

E.0037 Ashley, R. (1990, May/June). Meeting the challenge: Addressing the needs of pregnant women in the District of Columbia Department of Corrections. *American Jails, 4*(1), 24-28. Describes a program for pregnant inmates at DC General Hospital.

E.0038 Ashman, A. (1984, April 4). What's new: Strip searches of women found unconstitutional. *American Bar Association Journal, 70*, 133-134. Discusses strip searches of female inmates.

E.0039 Askins, Billy, & Young, Teresa (1994, March). An action research project to assist incarcerated females to become more effective adult learners. *Journal of Correctional Education, 45*(1), 12-17. Identified learning-style preferences of female inmates for individual counseling.

E.0040 Avallone, Anthony, & Talisano, Richard (1989). *Task force on women, children, and the criminal justice system: Final report.* Hartford, CT: The Commission on the Status of Women. Report and recommendations on incarcerated women and their children.

E.0041 Axon, Lee (1989). *Model and exemplary programs for female inmates: An international review.* Ottawa, Ontario: Ministry of the Solicitor General of Canada. Review of programs for female inmates in several countries.

E.0042 Ayers, K., & Johnson, F. (1987). *Health care of pregnant inmates.* Owensboro, KY: Wesleyan College Criminal Justice Research Center. Discusses the need for better health care for female inmates.

E.0043 Baergen, Elizabeth (1975, April). *The entrance of women into the criminal justice system or, what's a nice girl like you doing in a place like this?* Paper presented at the 38th Annual Meeting of the Southern Sociological Society. Washington, DC, April, 1975. Discusses the evaluation of women criminals in terms of who they are rather than on their criminal behavior.

E.0044 Baro, Agnes (1994). *A case study of the sexual abuse and exploitation of women incarcerated in the state of Hawaii: 1980-1993.* Paper presented at the ACJS Annual Meeting, 1994, Chicago, IL. Discusses the abuse and exploitation of women prisoners both in Louisiana and Hawaii.

E.0045 Barros, Colleen, et al. (1971, May). *Movement and characteristics of Women's Detention Center admissions, 1969: Research report #39.* Washington, DC: Department of Corrections. Information on daily intake and release at the center and inmate characteristics.

E.0046 Barry, Ellen (1991, Spring). Jail litigation concerning women prisoners. *The Prison Journal, 71*(1), 44. Discussion of women in jail.

E.0047 Barry, Ellen (1989, Spring). Pregnant prisoners. *Harvard Women's Law Journal, 12*, 189-205. Discusses the treatment of incarcerated pregnant women.

E.0048 Barry, Ellen (1987, Winter). Imprisoned mothers face extra hardships. *National Prison Project Journal, 14*, 20-25. Discusses the separation of incarcerated mothers from their children.

E.0049 Barry, Ellen (1985, November/December). Quality of prenatal care for incarcerated women challenged. *Youth Law News, 6*(6). Reviews prenatal care for incarcerated women.

E.0050 Bartolo, Ann (1992, Spring). A journey to understanding and changes. *Federal Prisons Journal: Special issue: Focus on the female offender,* 3(1), 15. Discusses programming in women's prisons.

E.0051 Baruch, Marcia (1992a). The 5-South Unit at MCC, New York. In ACA *Female offenders: Meeting the needs of a neglected population* (pp. 101-104). Laurel, MD: American Correctional Association. Describes an awaiting trial unit for women in New York City.

E.0052 Baruch, Marcia (1992b, Spring). The 5-South Unit at MCC New York. *Federal Prisons Journal Special Issue: Focus on the female offender, 3*(1), 4-6. Describes a typical day at the awaiting trial unit at MCC, New York and discusses why it is a difficult place to work.

E.0053 Baugh, C. (1985). *Women in jail and prison: A training manual for volunteers and advocates.* New York, NY: National Council of Churches. Manual for volunteers to women's prisons.

E.0054 Baunach, Phyllis (1992). Critical problems of women in prison. In I. Moyer (Ed.), *The changing roles of women in the criminal justice system* (pp. 99-110). Prospect Heights, IL: Waveland Press. Discusses problems of incarcerated women including conditions of confinement, loss of love and family, lack of meaningful training programs and options for the future.

E.0055 Baunach, Phyllis (1985). *Mothers in prison.* New Brunswick, NJ: Transaction Books. Descriptive analysis of two programs for inmate mothers. Explores inmate mothers' perceptions of the effects of separation on themselves, their children, and the mother-child relationship.

E.0056 Baunach, Phyllis (1982). You can't be a mother in prison, can you? Impacts of the mother-child separation. In N. Price and B. Sokoloff (Eds.), *The Criminal Justice System and Women* (pp. 70-85). New York, NY: Clark Boardman Company. Discusses the separation of incarcerated women from their children.

E.0057 Baunach, Phyllis (1977). *A pilot study of the self-perceptions and institutional behaviors of inmate mothers as a function of their level of separation and contact with their children during incarceration.* Washington, DC: National Institute of Law Enforcement and Criminal Justice. Study of the effects of separation on incarcerated women and their children.

E.0058 Baunach, Phyllis, & Morton, T. (1973, Fall). Women in prison: An awakening minority. *Crime and Corrections: Journal of California Probation Parole and Correctional Association, 1*(2), 4-12. Discussion of women in prison.

E.0059 Beavers-Luteran, Brenda (1983, June). Mother/child retreats. *Corrections Today, 45*, 93+. Discusses programs in women's prisons to unite incarcerated women with their children.

E.0060 Beckerman, Adela (1994, January). Mothers in prison: Meeting the prerequisite conditions for permanency planning. *Social Work, 39*(1), 9-14. Study of mothers incarcerated in New York state prisons who have children in foster care.

E.0061 Beckerman, Adela (1991, Fall). Women in prison: The conflict between confinement and parental rights. *Social Justice, 18*(3), 171-183. Discusses the rights of incarcerated women.

E.0062 Beckerman, Adela (1990). *The implementation of permanency planning legislation with incarcerated mothers: An exploratory study of mother-child contact and mother-caseworker contact.* Dissertation, Rockefeller College of Public Affairs and Policy. Examines specific aspects of the Implementation of the Adoption Assistance and Child Welfare Act of 1980 (P.L. 96-272) pertaining to incarcerated mothers.

E.0063 Beckerman, Adela (1989). Incarcerated mothers and their children in foster care: The dilemma of visitation. *Children and Youth Services Review, 11*(2), 175-183. Discusses the difficulty of maintaining contact between natural mothers and their children when the mother is incarcerated.

E.0064 Behrendt, C., et al. (1994, May). Voluntary testing for HIV in a prison population with a high prevalence of HIV. *American Journal of Epidemiology, 139*(9), 918-925. Tested 2,842 entrants into the Maryland prison system. 7.9% of the men and 15.3% of the women tested positive.

E.0065 Bergen, Donna (1982, October). A mold that fits Nebraska's mothers in prison. *Corrections Today, 44*(5), 12, 42. Program for incarcerated mothers and their children in Nebraska.

E.0066 Bergmann, Ilene (1979, September). The federal female offender. *Prison Law Monitor, 2*, 92-94. Discusses the female offender in federal prisons.

E.0067 Berk, Richard, et al. (1983). Prisons as self-regulating systems: A comparison of historical patterns in California for male and female offenders. *Law and Society Review, 17*(4), 547-586. Looks at efforts to regulate the flow of individuals through the California prison system.

E.0068 Bhattachan, Krishna (1984). *Nepali women in prison: A study of female prisoners in Kathmandu.* Kathmandu: Research Centre for Nepal & Asian Studies. Study of female prisoners in Nepal.

E.0069 Bickell, Nina, et al. (1991, October). Human papillomavirus gonorrhea, syphilis, and cervical dysplasia in jailed women. *American Journal of Public Health, 81*(10), 1318-1320. Looks at health problems of women in jail.

E.0070 Bigda-Peyton, F. (1988, April). Managing conflicts in a women's prison: Individual styles and institutional pressures. *Journal of Offender Counseling, 8*(2), 44-56. Interview data on how female inmates and correctional officers approach conflict.

E.0071 Birecree, Elizabeth, et al. (1994, Fall). Diagnostic efforts regarding women in Oregon's prison system: A preliminary report. *International Journal of Offender Therapy and Comparative Criminology, 38*(3), 217-230. Collected data from 91 women in the Oregon prison system using a combination of psychometric testing and clinical interviews.

E.0072 Bishop, N., et al. (1987). *Drug free program at the Hinsberg prison for women.* Norrkoping, Sweden: National Prison and Probation Administration. Describes a program at the Hinsberg Prison for women in Sweden and presents findings of a follow-up study.

E.0073 Bloom, Barbara, et al. (1994). *Women in California prisons: Hidden victims of the war on drugs.* San Francisco, CA: Center on Juvenile Justice. Examines the increased incarceration of women in California prisons and mandatory sentencing guidelines.

E.0074 Bloom, Barbara, & Steinhart, D. (1993). *Why punish the children?: A reappraisal of the children of incarcerated mothers in America.* San Francisco, CA: National Council on Crime and Delinquency. Looks at what happens to the children of incarcerated women.

E.0075 Bloom, Barbara (1992). Incarcerated mothers and their children: Maintaining family ties. In ACA *Female offenders: Meeting needs of a neglected population* (pp. 60-68). Laurel, MD: American Correctional Association. In 1986 nine out of ten incarcerated women had children under the age of eighteen, and six out of ten had more than one child.

E.0076 Bloom, Barbara (1989). Mothers in prison: A neglected population. *Centerforce Journal, 18*, 7. Looks at incarcerated mothers and what happens to their children.

E.0077 Bonitz, G. (1971). Sociopsychiatric views on delinquency in elderly women. In G. Verlay (Ed.), *Medicolegal borderline questions, Vol. II.* Analyzes the structure of delinquency in elderly women. Indicates property offenses are the most common.

E.0078 Boor, Myron, & Bair, Jeffrey (1992, June). Comment on Witherspoon, Long, and Nickell's study of speaking anxiety, self-esteem, crime, and educational achievement of female offenders. *Psychological Reports, 70*(3, Pt. 1), 961-962. Argues that Witherspoon et al. did not demonstrate that female inmates' anxiety about speaking was related to dropping out of school.

E.0079 Bottomley, K., & Fielding, N. (1986, August). Women in the penal system. *The Howard Journal of Criminal Justice, 25*(3). Discusses the treatment of women in prisons.

E.0080 Boudin, Kathy (1993, Summer). Participatory literacy education behind bars: AIDS opens the door. *Harvard Educational Review, 63*(2), 207-233. Personal account of an inmates' experience as a literacy instructor at Bedford Hills Correctional Facility for women.

E..0081 Boudouris, J. (1983). *Prisons and kids.* Des Moines, IA: Iowa Department of Social Services Division of Adult Corrections. Survey of programs for incarcerated mothers and their children in 55 correctional institutions in all 50 states.

E.0082 Bowman, J. T., et al. (1974, December). Pre-release training of female public offenders. *Psychological Reports, 35*(3), 1193-1194. Assessment of prerelease training of 16 incarcerated women and eight controls.

E.0083 Bowker, Lee (1978). *Women, crime, and the criminal justice system.* Lexington, MA: Lexington Books. Part I looks at early theories of women and crime and Part II looks at the treatment of women in the criminal justice system.

E.0084 Breece, Connie (1979). Women in prison. In *Breaking the silence: Seven courses in women's studies* (pp. 125-143). Cambridge, MA: Goddard College, Graduate Program in Social Change. A six-session course on Women in Prison presented in 1978 to two high schools in Boston.

E.0085 Brennan, R., & Stalkus, S. (1988, Summer). Beginning of a new day. *American Jails, 2*(2), 50-52. Information on New York City Department of Corrections jail facility for women, the Rose M. Singer Center (RMSC), and methods of female inmate management.

E.0086 Brett, Crista (1992, Spring). The cycle from victim to victimizer. *Federal Prisons Journal, special issue: Focus on the female offender, 59-62.* Discusses programs on domestic violence in women's prisons.

E.0087 Brewer, Kathleen, et al. (1974, August). *Prison nursery study: A summary report of findings to date.* New York, NY: Junior League of the City of New York. Looks at programs in women's prisons where newborns remain with their mothers.

E.0088 Brick, H., et al. (1965). A comparison of the effects of amitriptyline and protriptyline on anxiety and depressive states in female prisoners. *International Journal of Neuropsychiatry, 1*(4), 325-336. Looks at the use of anti-depressants in women's prisons.

E.0089 Brislin, Virginia (1984, October). The effect of immediate versus delayed separation from infants on several dimensions of inmate-mothers perception and enactment of the maternal role. *Dissertation Abstracts International, 45*(4), 1317. Data explores differences in maternal role enactment and perception between two groups of inmate-mothers.

E.0090 Brodie, Donna (1982, Spring). Babies behind bars: Should incarcerated mothers be allowed to keep their newborns with them in prison? *University of Richmond Law Review, 16*(3), 677-692. Discusses prison nursery programs, pros and cons.

E.0091 Brodsky, Annette (1975). *The female offender.* Beverly Hills, CA: Sage Publications. Collection of ariticles on the female offenders divided into empirical research and future planning.

E.0092 Brodsky, Annette (1975). Planning for the female offender. In A. Brodsky (Ed.), *The female offender* (pp. 100-108). Newbury Park, CA: Sage Publications. Discusses areas of concern in future planning for female offenders.

E.0093 Bronner, Augusta (1944, March-April). The woman offender of today: Medical and psychiatric services for women offenders. *Prison World, 6*(2), 9, 28. Discusses the importance of regular medical checkups for incarcerated women.

E.0094 Brooks, Jennifer, & Bahn, Kimberly (1994, Winter). "It's a family affair": The incarceration of the American family: Confronting legal and social issues. *University of San Francisco Law Review, 28*, 271-308. Discusses what happens to the children when parents are incarcerated.

E.0095 Brown, Jennie (1978, January). A field study of two subsystems in a women's prison: Implications of differences in values and goals. *Dissertation Abstracts International, 38*(7-A), 3891-3892. Analyzes two processes of socialization in the New Jersey Correctional Institute for Women, unisex fictive families and other fictive kinship relationships.

E.0096 Brown, Marjorie (1990). *Women in jail: Problems, programs, and resources.* Washington, DC: U.S. Department of Health, Education, and Welfare. Report on women in jail in the U.S.

E.0097 Browne, Dorothy (1989, June). Incarcerated mothers and parenting. *Journal of Family Violence, 4*(2), 211-221. Describes a 24-week primary prevention program for incarcerated women aimed at enhancing parental childrearing capablilities and knowledge.

E.0098 Brownstone, D., & Swaminath, R. (1989, April). Violent behavior and psychiatric diagnosis in female offenders: *Canadian Journal of Psychiatry, 34*(3), 190-194. Retrospective study of 91 female offenders (15-58 yrs. old) admitted to a psychiatric hospital between 1981 and 1985.

E.0099 Buckles, D., & Fazia, M. (1973). Child care for mothers in prison. In B. Ross & C. Cheremain (Eds.), *Social work practice and social justice.* New York, NY: National Association of Social Workers. Discusses foster care for children of incarcerated women.

E.0100 Bularik, Mary (1984). The Dedham temporary asylum for discharged female prisoners, 1864-1909. *Historical Journal of Massachusetts, 12*(1), 28-35. Reviews the history of a halfway house in Dedham, MA. Looks at reformers and inmates and their bonds of sisterhood.

E.0101 Bularik, Mary (1982). Sex, crime, and justice: Women in the criminal justice system of Massachusetts, 1900-1950. *Dissertation Abstracts International, 43*(4), 1262-A. Examines the experiences of women as administrators and inmates in Massachusetts, 1900-1995.

E.0102 Burden, O. (1983, April 4). Changing times bring better-than-equal opportunity for growing female inmate ranks. *Law Enforcement News, 9*(7), 13. Discusses programs for female inmates.

E.0103 Bureau of Prisons (1977). *Female offenders in the Federal Prison System.* Lompoc, CA: Federal Prison Industries. Brief history of the federal prison system and overview of the female prison population. Looks at living conditions of female inmates.

E.0104 Burke, Carol (1992). *Vision narratives of women in prison.* Knoxville, TN: University of Tennessee Press. Reports on an innovative program for incarcerated women.

E.0105 Burke, P., & Adams, L. (1991). *Classification of women offenders in state correctional facilities: A handbook for practitioners.* Washington, DC: National Institute of Corrections. Handbook for corrections administrators and those making decisions affecting female offenders.

E.0106 Burkhart, Kathryn (1973). *Women in Prison.* Garden City, NY: Doubleday. Discusses dehumanizing aspects of prisons for women such as forced physical exams and body searches.

E.0107 Burns, V. (1934). *Female convicts.* New York, NY: Macaulay. Early writings on incarcerated women.

E.0108 Butler, Anne (1989, February). Still in chains: Black women in Western prisons, 1865-1910. *Western Historical Quarterly, 20*(1), 19-35. Historical view of the incarceration of black women.

E.0109 California Department of Corrections (1992). *Description of population characteristics for the "forever free" drug treatment program at the California Institution for Women, Frontera, California.* Sacramento, CA: California Department of Corrections. Analysis of demographic characteristics of the 131 female inmates who volunteered for drug treatment.

E.0110 California State Commission on the Status of Women (n.d.). *Women in transition: Volunteer counselors for women in a county jail.* Sacramento, CA: California State Commission on the Status of Women. Describes an action project to test the effectiveness of community volunteers in providing services to incarcerated women.

E.0111 Calisti, K. M. (1986, March). Post-GED writing curriculum for incarcerated women. *Journal of Correctional Education, 37*(1), 8-13. Proposed writing curriculum for female inmates.

E.0112 Callahan, Christine (1986, June). *Women in prison: Does the justice system do them justice?* Anchorage, AK: Alaska Women's Commission. Historical perspective of the female offender in Alaska and a profile of female offender programs and services.

E.0113 Camp, John (1974). *Holloway Prison: The place and the people.* North Pomfret, VT: David & Charles. Description of Holloway Prison, a prison for women in London.

E.0114 Campbell, Charles (1980). *Serving time together: Men and women in prison.* Fort Worth, TX: Texas Christian University Press.

E.0115 Canadian Journal of Corrections (1969, January). Brief on the woman offender. *Canadian Journal of Corrections, 11*(1), 26-60. Overview of women prisoners in Canada.

E.0116 Canadian National Advisory Committee on the Female Offender (1977). *Female offender: Selected statistics.* Ottawa, Ontario: Canadian National Advisory on the Female Offender. Statistical tables, charts, and related narratives regarding female offenders grouped according to Canadian police and correctional institution statistics.

E.0117 Canestrini, Kathy (1986). *Characteristics of female inmates held under custody: 1975-1985.* Albany, NY: New York Department of Correctional Services. Reports on female commitments including, profiles, recidivism, women who commit murder, and inmate mothers.

E.0118 Cardoos, R. I. (1973, Spring). The status of the female offender in the New England region. *The New England Correctional Digest,* 33-46. Discussion of incarcerated women.

E.0119 Carlen, Pat (1985, June). Law, psychiatry and women's imprisonment: A sociological view. *British Journal of Psychiatry, 46,* 618-621. Looks at the treatment of women prisoners.

E.0120 Carlen, Pat (1983). *Women's imprisonment: A study in social control.* London: Routledge. Research on women's prisons in Scotland. Quotes from women inmates

E.0121 Carlen, Pat (1982). Papa's discipline: An analysis of disciplinary modes in the Scottish women's prison. *The Sociological Review, 30*(1), 97-124. Analytic case study of sociobiographies of 20 female inmates. Data collected in interviews with prisoners, judges, and prison officials.

E.0122 Carlson, Norman (1981). Statement of Norman A. Carlson. In *Female Offender* (pp. 3-44). Rockville, MD: National Institute of Justice. Report on 1,325 women serving sentences in Federal Institutions in 1979-1980.

E.0123 Carmouche, Joyce, & Jones, Josetta (1989, Fall). Her children, their future: Learning to parent in federal prison. *Federal Prisons Journal, 1*(2), 23, 26-27. Describes pilot parenting program, Parents and Children Together (PACT) at the Federal Correctional Institution in Lexington, KY.

E.0124 Carp, Scarlett, & Schade, Linda (1992a). Tailoring facility programming to suit female offenders needs. In ACA *Female offenders: Meeting needs of a neglected population* (pp. 37-42). Laurel, MD: American Correctional Association. Discusses programming for female offenders that focuses on their roles as parents, histories of abuse, educational levels, and work skills.

E.0125 Carp, Scarlett, & Schade, Linda (1992b, August). Tailoring facility programming to suit female offenders needs. *Corrections Today, 54*(6), 152-159. Recommends programs that teach self-sufficiency, improved interpersonal relationships, and responsible behavior.

E.0126 Casale, Silvia (1989). *Women inside: The experience of remand prisoners in Holloway.* London, England: Civil Liberties Trust. Looks at woman recidivists in Hollaway prison.

E.0127 Casey, Karen (1994a, March). The effect of visitation on the disciplinary adjustment of incarcerated females. *Dissertation Abstracts International, 54*(9), 3601. Explores the nature of prison visiting and examines factors that are related to visitation.

E.0128 Casey, Karen (1994b, March). *The disciplinary adjustment of maximum security female inmates.* Paper presented at the 1994 ACJS Annual Meeting, Chicago, Illinois. Examines the disciplinary behavior of 222 women from a large maximum security prison.

E.0129 Cassel, R. N., & Clayton, Julia (1961, April). A preliminary analysis of certain social self-concepts of women in a correctional institution. *Sociology and Social Research, 45*(3), 316-319. Looks at the effects of incarceration on self-concept.

E.0130 Cassel, R. N., & Van Vorst, R. B. (1961, January/February). Psychological needs of women in a correctional institution. *American Journal of Corrections, 23*, 22-24. Presents psychological profiles of incarcerated women.

E.0131 Catan, L. (1989). The development of young children in prison mother and baby units. *Research Bulletin, 26*, 9-12. Studied 74 babies between April, 1986 and August, 1987.

E.0132 Cavior, Helene, et al. (1974, December). Physical attractiveness of female offenders: Effects on institutional performance. *Criminal Justice and Behavior, 4*(1), 321-331. Measured physical attractiveness for consequences both in judicial and non-judicial settings.

E.0133 Chandler, Edna (1973). *Women in prison.* Indianapolis, IN: Bobbs Merrill Co. Results of interviews and questionnaires at one women's prison.

E.0134 Chapman, Jane, et al. (1981). Criminal justice programs for women offenders. In *Female Offender, 1979-1980* (pp. 528-566). Washington, DC: U.S. Department of Justice. Summarizes findings of a 15-month study of needs, policies, and practices in correctional programming.

E.0135 Chapman, Jane (1979). The treatment of convicted female offenders in the criminal justice system. In C. Griffiths & M. Nance (Eds.), *The female offender* (pp. 195-200). Burnaby, BC: Simon Fraser University. Looks at the treatment of women in prison.

E.0136 Chase, Dorothy (1977, June). Empathy and trustworthiness in female prisoners. *Dissertation Abstracts International, 37*(12), 6318. Study of empathy and trust in women's prisons.

E.0137 Chesney-Lind, Meda (1992, August). Women's prisons: Putting the brakes on the building binge. *Corrections Today, 54*(6), 30-34. Suggests the solution to criminality in women may be in studying why women commit crimes rather than in building more prisons.

E.0138 Chesney-Lind, Meda (1987). *Prisoners in paradise: Women's prison problems in Hawaii.* Honolulu, HI: University of Hawaii at Manoa. Looks at the increases in women's incarceration from 1975-1985. Considers factors that contributed to the increase.

E.0139 Chesney-Lind, Meda, & Rodriguez, Noelle (1983, September). Women under lock and key: A view from the inside. *The Prison Journal, 63*(2), 47-65. Profile of women incarcerated at the Oahu Community Correctional Center in 1982. Data collected through in-depth interviews.

E.0140 Chonco, Nobuhle (1991). The mentally ill female inmate: Do labels matter behind bars? *Dissertation Abstracts International, 52*(5), 1903-1904. Discusses four categories of female inmates identified by the mental health staff at Huron Valley Women's Facility.

E.0141 Church, Angela (1992a). Turning up the lights: Hospices in women's prisons. In ACA *Female offenders: Meeting the needs of a neglected population* (pp. 85-88). Laurel, MD: American Correctional Association. Describes the Hospice Program at the Federal Correctional Institution for Women in Lexington, KY.

E.0142 Church, Angela (1992b, Spring). Turning up the lights: Hospices in women's prisons. *Federal Prisons Journal: Special issue on the female offender, 6*(2), 8-11. Discusses the need for Hospice programs in women's prisons and gives examples of the activities volunteers promote.

E.0143 Chwast, J. (1971). Special problems in treating female offenders: Sociopsychological aspects. *International Journal of Offender Therapy, 15,* 24-27. Looks at adaptation and adjustment problems to incarceration as well as previous mental health problems.

E.0144 Clark, J., & Boudin, Kathy (1990, Summer). Community of women organize themselves to cope with the AIDS crisis: A case study from Bedford Hills Correctional Facility. *Social Justice, 17*(2), 293-351. Looks at the prison environment and coping with AIDS at Bedford Hills.

E.0145 Clark, M., & Grier, P. E. (1987). *Female sexual offenders in a prison setting.* St. Louis, MO: Behavioral Science Institute. Discusses women incarcerated for sex offenses.

E.0146 Clark, Ramona (1979). *Inmate mothers: Their perceptions of their mothering functions.* Dissertation, Oklahoma State University. Investigated inmate mothers perceptions of their functions in relation to their children using a Family Relations Scale.

E.0147 Clayton, E. T. (1951, October). Babies in prison. *Negro Digest,* 24-28. Early look at the children of women in prison.

E.0148 Clement, Mary Jo (1993). Parenting in prison: National survey of programs for incarcerated women. *Journal of Offender Rehabilitation, 19*(1-2), 89-100. Responses from 43 state and federal corrections departments, June, 1989. Profiles of prisons, female inmates, and programs.

E.0149 Climent, Carlos, et al. (1977, January). Epidemiological studies of female prisoners: IV. Homosexual behavior. *Journal of Nervous and Mental Disease, 164*(1), 25-29. Data collected from 95 female inmates at a Massachusetts prison on the existence of homosexual behavior.

E.0150 Climent, Carlos, et al. (1973, September). I. Epidemiological studies of women prisoners: Medical and psychiatric variables related to violent behavior. *American Journal of Psychiatry, 130*(9), 985-990. Investigated medical and psychiatric correlates of violent behavior. Data collected from 95 female inmate volunteers.

E.0151 Cloninger, C. R., & Guze, S. B. (1973a, June). Psychiatric illnesses in the families of female criminals: A study of 288 first-degree relatives. *British Journal of Psychiatry, 122*(571), 697-703. Interviews and records of relatives of convicted women criminals.

E.0152 Cochrane, R. (1971). The structure of value systems in male and female prisoners. *British Journal of Criminology, 11,* 73-79. Looks at how value systems are formed in women's prisons.

E.0153 Coid, J. (1993). Self-mutilation in female remanded prisoners II: A cluster analytic approach towards identification of a behavioral syndrome. *Criminal Behavior and Mental Health, 3*, 1-14. Study of self-mutilation in women recidivists.

E.0154 Colley, Ella, & Camp, Althea (1992, April). Creating programs for women inmates. *Corrections Today, 54*(2), 208-209. A guide of programs for women prisoners.

E.0155 Community Research Center (1984). *Locking up the female offender: An assessment of women in Kentucky prisons and jails.* Champaign, IL: University of Illinois. Report on the status of women in Kentucky jails and prisons betweeen December 1980 and May, 1981.

E.0156 Comstock, Harriet (1927, March). The woman offender in Illinois. *Welfare Magazine, 18,* 311-313. Early report of women prisoners in Illinois.

E.0157 Connolly, Janet (1983, Autumn-Winter). Women in county jails: An invisible gender in an ill-defined institution. *Prison Journal*, *63*(2), 99-115. Looks at facilities, population size, sentences, types of offenses, programming, and staff in Pennsylvania jails.

E.0158 CONTACT Inc. (1982). Women offenders. *Corrections Compendium* (Lincoln, NE), *7*(1), 6-11. Results of a survey of correctional institutions for women throughout the U.S. Data on population, crimes, alcohol/drug use, and educational opportunities for incarcerated women.

E.0159 Cookson, H. M. (1977, October). A survey of self-injury in a closed prison for women. *British Journal of Criminology, 17*(4), 332-347. Compared psychological, criminal, and social characteristics of self-mutilating incarcerated women with the general prison population.

E.0160 Cooper, Sheelagh (1987). The evolution of the federal women's prison. In E. Adelberg & C. Currie (Eds.), *Too few to count: Canadian women in conflict with the law* (pp. 127-144). Vancouver, BC: Press Gang Publishers. Historical overview of the development of women's prisons in Canada.

E.0161 Cordero, L., et al. (1992, September). Perinatal outcome for women in prison. *Journal Perinatol, 12*(3), 205-209. Pregnancy outcome for 233 women in prison with multiple perinatal high-risk factors.

E.0162 Cordero, L., et al. (1991). Duration of incarceration and perinatal outcome. *Obstetrics and Gynecology, 78*(4), 641-645. Perinatal outcome of 53 women with short-term incarceration (less than 90 days) and 53 women with long-term incarceration (more than 120 days).

E.0163 Corrections Digest (1994, February 23). Carswell AFB to become medical center for all federal women inmates. *Corrections Digest, 25*(4), 9-10. Discusses the use of base facilities for incarcerated women.

E.0164 Corrections Digest (1991, March). AIDS infection rate higher among female prisoners. *Corrections Digest, 22*(6), 5-6. Looks at AIDS in incarcerated women.

E.0165 Corrections Digest (1989, November 15). Prison pregnancy studies. *Corrections Digest, 20*(33), 3-4. Discusses prison pregnancies and outcomes.

E.0166 Corrections Digest (1982, December 20). Number of women inmates rises, but there's a space shortage. *Corrections Digest, 13*(26), 1-3. Discusses the need for more prisons for women.

E.0167 Corrections Digest (1977, April 13). New York women inmates sue state over posting of male officers. *Corrections Digest,* 10. Discusses a lawsuit by female inmates in New York state.

E.0168 Corrections Digest (1975, March 5). Women lead California jail riot: Violence blamed on overcrowding. *Corrections Digest, 6*(5), 2. Discusses conditions of jails where women are held.

E.0169 Corrections Digest (1975, July 20). Congress on problems of women prisoners, sponsored by Lewis University Special Services Division. *Corrections Digest, 6*(17), 7-8. Discussions on problems and special needs of incarcerated women.

E.0170 Corrections Today (1990, December). Women in prison: Unequal justice. *Corrections Today, 52*(7), 160. Discusses discriminatory practices in prisons for women.

E.0171 Cottle, Thomas (1976, April). Angela: A child-woman. *Social Problems, 23*(4), 516-523. Case study of a 12-year-old girl whose mother was in prison.

E.0172 Cox, Janine (1982, November). Self-perceived health and aging of older females in prison: An exploratory age group case study. *Dissertation Abstracts International, 43*(5), 1433. Investigated demographics, health status, and perceptions of aging of women in prison.

E.0173 Craig, Mary (1981, July). The development of a Freire-based literacy/conscientization program for low-literate women in prison. *Dissertation Abstracts International, 42*(1), 68. Discusses a literacy/conscientization program designed for prisoners in the Huron Valley Women's Facility.

E.0174 Crawford, V. G., et al. (1990). *Five-year plan for female inmates.* Springfield, IL: Illinois Department of Corrections. Proposed plan for female inmates in Illinois discusses administration, housing and, educational and vocational planning.

E.0175 Criminal Justice Newsletter (1975, November 24). Education at women's prisons assessed. *Criminal Justice Newsletter, 6*(23), 2-3. Assessed educational programs at women's prisons.

E.0176 Criswell, T. C. (1989, August). Step in the right direction. *Corrections Today, 51*(5), 200-202, 208. Examines the Lifesteps Program at the Mabel Bassett Correctional Center for women in Oklahoma City, Oklahoma.

E.0177 Crites, Laura (1976). *The female offender.* Toronto: DC Heath. Essays on the female offender divided into 3 parts, female offenders, law and the courts, and women prisoners.

E.0178 Crowell, Suzanne (1974). The Federal Reformatory for women - what does it accomplish? *Civil Rights Digest, 7*(1), 26-33. Maintains that female inmates engage in stereotypical women's work, receive vocational training in low-paying jobs, and have limited educational opportunities.

E.0179 Crowley, Joan, & Adrian, Lynn (1992). Women misdemeanants in the Allegheny County Jail 1892-1923. *Journal of Criminal Justice, 20*(4), 311-330. Traces patterns of incarceration of women using records from the 1892-1923 Daybooks of the Allegheny County Jail in Pittsburgh.

E.0180 Culbertson, R. G., & Fortune, E. P. (1986, Spring). Incarcerated women: Self-concept and argot roles. *Journal of Offender Counseling, Services and Rehabilitation, 10*(3), 25-49. Analyzes female inmates' self-concepts and role adaptations during incarceration.

E.0181 Cunningham, Gloria (1963, December). Supervision of the female offender. *Federal Probation, 27*(4), 12-16. Discusses special problems posed by male officers supervising female inmates.

E.0182 Curran, Len (1987). AIDS in prison. In B. J. McGurk et al. (Eds.), *Applying psychology to imprisonment: Theory and practice* (pp. 341-360). London, England: HM Stationery Office Books. Discusses women in prison with AIDS.

E.0183 Curriden, Mark (1993, September). Prison scandal in Georgia: Guards traded favors for sex. *The National Law Journal, 16*(3), 8. Discusses sexual misconduct of prison guards in a women's prison in Georgia that resulted in the firing of 14 guards.

E.0184 Daehlin, Diane, & Hynes, Jane (1974). Discussion group in a women's prison. *Child Welfare, 53*(7), 464-470. Looks at how a discussion group helps mothers in prison in Minnesota awaiting release, readjust to their families and to life outside.

E.0185 Dale, M. J. (1990). The female inmate: An introduction to legal rights and issues. *American Jails, 4*(4), 56-58. Discusses the legal rights of incarcerated women.

E.0186 Dalley, Bronwyn (1993, Winter). Prisons without men: The development of a separate women's prison in New Zealand. *New Zealand Journal of History, 27*(1), 37-60. Discusses the first women's prison opened in 1913 in New Zealand based on the American penal model.

E.0187 Dalley, Bronwyn (1993, Winter). Following the rules? Women's responses to incarceration. New Zealand, 1880-1920. *Journal of Social History, 27*(2), 309-325. Examines compliance and cooperation of women prisoners with the penal regime in New Zealand.

E.0188 Daly, Kathleen, et al. (1988, Fall). Litigation driven research: A case study of lawyer/social scientist collaboration. *Women's Rights Law Reporter, 10*(4), 221-241. Discusses a class action suit filed in 1983 on behalf of the inmates at the women's prison at Niantic, CT.

E.0189 Daniel, Anasseril, et al. (1988). Lifetime and six-month prevalence of psychiatric disorders among sentenced female offenders. *Bulletin of the American Academy of Psychiatry and the Law, 16*(4), 333-342. Study of female offenders admitted to a correctional system over a 7-month period. Data collected from 100 women prisoners.

E.0190 Daniel, Anasseril, et al. (1981, September). Differences between mid-life female offenders and those younger than 40. *American Journal of Psychiatry, 138*(9), 1225-1228. Data collected from two groups of female offenders, one in their 20's and one in their 40's.

E.0191 Datesman, Susan, & Cales, G. L. (1983, Autumn/Winter). I'm still the same mommy: Maintaining the mother/child relationship in prison. *The Prison Journal, 63*(2), 142-154. Study advocating visitation policies encouraging frequent contact between mothers and their children.

E.0192 Dauton-Fear, M. W. (1975). *Women as participants in the criminal justice system.* Woden, Australia: Australian Institute of Criminology. Addresses women as personnel, victims, and offenders in the criminal justice system.

E.0193 Davis, R. A. (1984, Spring/Summer). Women in prison. *Prison Journal, 64*(1). Update on the status of incarcerated women in the U.S.

E.0194 Davis-Berman, J., & Brown, D. (1990, October). AIDS knowledge and risky behavior by incarcerated females: IV and non-IV drug users. *Sociology and Social Research, 75*(1), 8-16. R Examines differences between IV and Non-IV drug users and discusses AIDS awareness.

E.0195 Deck, Mary (1988, May). Incarcerated mothers and their infants: Separation or legislation? *Boston College Law Review, 29*, 689-713. Discusses state legislation regarding the rights of incarcerated mothers.

E.0196 DeConstanzo, Elaine, & Valente, Janet (1984, Spring/Summer.). Designing a corrections continuum for female offenders: One state's experience. *The Prison Journal, 64*(1), 120-128. Looks at long-range planning for female offenders.

E.0197 DeCorse, Helen (1944, March/April). The woman offender of today: The institutional employment program. *Prison World, 6*(2), 11. Discusses the institutional inmate employment program as the foundation of the female inmate's prison life.

E.0198 Dell, Susanne, et al. (1971). Remands of women offenders for medical reports. *Medicine, Science and the Law, 11*(3), 117-127. Data from 95 female remand prisoners diagnosed as psychotic at Holloway prison. Few had committed serious offenses.

E.0199 Dennett, R., & York, J. S. (1966). Group therapy in one women's correctional institution. *American Journal of Corrections, 28*(1), 21-25. Discusses the use of group therapy in a women's prison.

E.0200 Desmond, A. M. (1991, March). The relationship between loneliness and social interaction in women prisoners. *Journal of Psychosocial Nursing and Mental Health Services, 29*(3), 4-10. Study of loneliness experienced by women prisoners.

E.0201 Dimick, Kenneth (1979). *Ladies in waiting: Behind prison walls.* Muncie, IN: Accelerated Development Inc. Looks at the incarceration of women in the U.S.

E.0202 Dobash, Russell, et al. (1986). *The imprisonment of women.* Totowa, NJ: Basil Blackwell. Women's prisons in Great Britain from 18th to the 20th century.

E.0203 Dolan, Bridget, & Mitchell, Elaine (1994). Personality disorder and psychological disturbance of female prisoners: A comparison with women referred for NHS treatment of personality disorder. *Criminal Behavior and Mental Health, 4*(2), 130-143. Assessed prevalence of personality disorder and psychological distrubance in 50 female inmates housed at HM Holloway.

E.0204 Dorn, N., et al. (1992). *Women, HIV, drugs: Criminal justice issues.* London: Institute for the Study of Drug Dependence. Articles discussing the issue of treatment of women offenders in England who are drug users and/or HIV positive.

E.0205 Downey, G. P., et al. (1994, May 28). Management of female prisoners with abnormal cervical cytology. *British Medical Journal, 308*(6941), 1412-1413. Study indicates female prisoners are at higher risk for developing cervical neoplasia and cervical cancer than the general population.

E.0206 Dressel, Paula, & Barnhill, Sandra (1994, October). Reframing gerontological thought and practice: The case of grandmothers with daughters in prison. *Gerontologist, 34*(5), 685 691. Indicates that grandmothers with daughters in prison are among the neediest older persons.

E.0207 Driscoll, Dorothy (1985, August). Mother's day once a month. *Corrections Today, 47*(5), 18, 20. Discusses a visiting program for the children of incarcerated women.

E.0208 DuBose, D. (1975). *Problems of children whose mothers are imprisoned.* New York, NY: Institute of Women's Wrongs. Looks at problems experienced by children of incarcerated women.

E.0209 Duncan, Donna (1992, February). Survey examines programs for women offenders. *Corrections Today, 54*(1) 114. Examined women offenders involvement in correctional programs. Most were involved in sewing, data processing, reupholstering, microfilming, and telemarketing.

E.0210 Durham, Marian, et al. (1981). *Women, families and prison.* Raleigh, NC: Governors Council on Children and Youth. Looks at services to imprisoned women under the age of 21 and effects of incarceration on inmate mothers and their children.

E.0211 Earnest, Marion (1971, Fall). Criminal self-conceptions of female offenders in a penal community. *Wisconsin Sociologist, 8*(3-4), 98-105. Study of female offender volunteers.

E.0212 Easteal, Patricia (1993). Overseas-born female inmates in Australia: A prison within a prison. *Journal of Criminal Justice, 21*(2), 173-184. Profiles fifty-six women in Australian prisons.

E.0213 Edwards, N. (1988, Spring/Summer). AIDS among incarcerated females. *National Journal of the Black Nurses Association, 2*(2), 36-46. Discusses the problems of incarcerated women with AIDS.

E.0214 Edwards, Susan (1994, May). The social control of women in prison. *Criminal Justice: Magazine of the Howard League, 12*(2), 9-10. Looks at social control in women's prisons.

E.0215 Egley, C. C., et al. (1992, February). Outcome of pregnancy during imprisonment. *Journal of Reproductive Medicine, 37*(2), 131-134. Comparative study of 69 incarcerated pregnant women over a one-year period. Controls were matched for age, parity, and race.

E.0216 Ellis, D. P., & Austin, Penelope (1971, September). Menstruation and aggressive behavior in a correctional center for women. *Journal of Criminal Law, Criminology, & Police Science, 62*(3), 385-395. Discusses aggressiveness during the menstrual cycle in incarcerated women.

E.0217 Elton, P. J. (1988, January). Mothers and babies in prison. *British Journal of Hospital Medicine, 39*(1), 9. Editorial.

E.0218 Epperson, Douglas, et al. (1982, September). Women incarcerated in 1960 and 1980: Implications of demographic education and personality characteristics from earlier research. *Criminal Justice and Behavior, 9*(3), 352-363. Profiles the population of female inmates in Iowa.

E.0219 Evans, Maureen (1989). *A survey of institutional programs available to federally sentenced women.* Ottawa, Ontario: Ministry of the Solicitor General of Canada. Looks at prison programs for women in Canada.

E.0220 Evenson, M. (1964). Research with female drug addicts at the prison for women. *Canadian Journal of Corrections, 6,* 21-27. Looks at research with women drug addicts incarcerated in Canada.

E.0221 Eyman, Joy (1971). *Prisons for women: A practical guide to administration.* Springfield, IL: Thomas. Guide for administration and personnel in women's prisons.

E.0222 Eyman, Joy (1966). The myth of the father-image in women's prison. *American Journal of Corrections, 28*(2), 10-11. Study of the Tennessee Prison for Women, Nashville: TN.

E.0223 Eysenck, Sybil, & Eysenck, Hans (1973, December). The personality of female prisoners. *British Journal of Psychiatry, 123*(577), 693-698. Results of a personality questionnaire given to 264 female prisoners.

E.0224 Fabian, Sharon (1979, Fall). Towards the best interests of women prisoners: Is the system working? *New England Journal of Prison Law, 6*, 1-60. Overview of what is happening to incarcerated women during and after incarceration.

E.0225 Fagin, Alan, & Reid, Arlene (1991, January-February). Moms in jail. *Children Today, 20*(1), 12-13. Discusses a program in Nassau County, New York Correctional Facility for women designed to help incarcerated mothers understand behaviors that lead to child abuse.

E.0226 Faily, Anwar, et al. (1980). A study of the maintenance of discipline with regard to rule infractions at the Louisiana Correctional Institute for women. *Corrective and Social Psychiatry and Journal of Behavior Technology Methods and Therapy, 26*(4), 151-155. Discusses variables related to rule infractions of 171 female inmates incarcerated for 6 months or longer.

E.0227 Faily, Anwar, & Roundtree, G. A. (1979). A study of aggression and rule violations in a female prison population. *Journal of Offender Counseling, Services & Rehabilitation, 4*(10), 81-87. Looks at behavioral profiles of incarcerated women.

E.0228 Fair, Susan, & Meisler, R. (1986, Spring). Detroit women in prison. *Michigan Quarterly Review, 25*, 387-401. Looks at women incarcerated in Detroit, Michigan.

E.0229 Faith, Karlene (1987). Media myths and masculinisation: Image of women in prison. In E. Adelberg & C. Currie (Eds.), *Too few to count: Canadian women in conflict with the law* (pp. 181-219). London: Press Gang Publishers. Looks at how media images set norms for general ideas about incarcerated women.

E.0230 Faith, Karlene (1982). Love between women in prison. In M. Cruikshank (Eds.), *Lesbian studies: Present and future* (pp. 187-193). Old Westbury, CT: The Feminist Press. Looks at love relationships among incarcerated women.

E.0231 Families in Society (1994, March). An anger-management workshop for women inmates. *Families in Society, 75*(6), 172-175. Results of an anger-management workshop for incarcerated women.

E.0232 Family Law Reporter (1986, April 22). Mother has no constitutional rights to breast-feed infant in prison. *The Family Law Reporter: Court Opinions, 12*(24), 1296-1297. Reveiws of rights of incarcerated mothers.

E.0233 Farrell, Ann (1994). The experience of young children and their incarcerated mothers. A call for humanly-responsive policy. *International Journal of Early Childhood, 26*(2), 6-12. Describes the IMCIPE Project (Incarcerated Mothers and Children: Impact of Prison Environments).

E.0234 Farris, Lawrence (1975). An ex-offender evaluates correctional programming for women. In A. Brodsky (Eds.), *The female offender* (pp. 96-99). Beverly Hills, CA: Sage. Discusses the need for programming that prepares women to return to work.

E.0235 Federal Register (1986, December 30). Control, custody, care, treatment, and instruction of inmates: Interim rule. *Federal Register, 51*(249), 471-479. Rulings on birth control, pregnancy, child placement, and abortion.

E.0236 Feinman, Clarice (1983, November 2). Historical overview of the treatment of incarcerated women: Myths and realities of rehabilitation. *Prison Journal, 63*(2), 12-26. Discusses failures in prison reform and rehabilitation programs for incarcerated women.

E.0237 Feinman, Clarice (1976). *Imprisoned women: A history of the treatment of women incarcerated in New York City, 1932-1975.* Dissertation, New York University. Historical study of incarcerated women in New York City.

E.0238 Fernald, Mabel, et al. (1920). *A study of women delinquents in New York state.* New York, NY: Century. Early study contrasts native and foreign born women in prison.

E.0239 Field, Xenia (1963). *Under lock and key: A study of women in prison.* London: M. Parrish. Overview of women in prison in the 60's.

E.0240 Filo, Barbara (1982). *Reclaiming those poor unfortunates: The movement to establish the first federal prison for women.* Dissertation, Boston University Graduate School. Discusses the establishment of the first federal prison for women at Alderson, WV, and some early reformers.

E.0241 Fink, Carolyn (1991). School life-histories of incarcerated women with learning problems: A retrospective study. *Dissertation Abstracts International, 52*(9), 3244. Study on what education means to women prisoners with disabilities.

E.0242 Fisher, K. L. (1977). *The determination of some personality characteristics of women who escaped from prison.* Dissertation, University of Washington. Profile of women escapees.

E.0243 Fishman, S. H. (1982, Fall). The impact of incarceration on children of offenders. *Journal of Children in Contemporary Society, 15*(1), 89-99. Estimates that in 1979 over 900,000 children were affected by parental incarceration.

E.0244 Fitzgerald, Anne (1992, July 31). The secret torture. *New Statesman and Society, 5*(213), 21-22. Deals with the custodial rape of women prisoners.

E.0245 Fjarstedt, S. (1994). Women prisoners in Sweden. *Prison Service Journal, 96,* 15-22. Surveyed female prisoners on attitudes towards women's prisons and their needs.

E.0246 Flanagan, LaMont (1995, June). Meeting the special needs of females in custody: Maryland's unique approach. *Federal Probation, 59*(2), 49-53. Describes programs designed and implemented in Maryland to prepare female offenders for reintegration into the community.

E.0247 Fleming, Grant (1993, June). Neuropsychological characteristics associated with psychopathy in female prisoners. *Dissertation Abstracts International, 53*(12), 6547. Results of psychological tests administered to 64 female inmates sentenced to the Wyoming Women's Center.

E.0248 Fletcher, Beverly, et al. (1993a). *Women prisoners: A forgotten population.* Westport, CT: Praeger. Preliminary results of a multi-disciplinary longitudinal study of women incarcerated in Oklahoma. Explores causes of recidivism.

E.0249 Fletcher, Beverly, et al. (1993b). The woman prisoner. In B. Fletcher et al. (Eds.), *Women prisoners: A forgotten population* (pp. 15-26). Wesport, CT: Praeger. Profiles women prisoners in Oklahoma.

E.0250 Fletcher, Beverly, et al. (1992). *Project for recidivism research and female inmate training.* Paper presented at the 1992 ACJS Annual Meeting, Pittsburgh, PA. Discusses a research project to determine causes of recidivism in women incarcerated in Oklahoma.

E.0251 Fletcher, Beverly, et al. (1991). *Profile: The female inmate.* Paper presented at the Fourth National Workshop on Women Offenders, Washington, DC. Discusses incarcerated women in Oklahoma.

E.0252 Flint, M. (1964). Narcotics addiction in women offenders. *Canadian Journal of Corrections, 6,* 246-265. Looks at drug addiction in female inmates.

E.0253 Flint, M. (1960, July). An experiment in the rehabilitation of women offenders. *Canadian Journal of Corrections* (Ottawa), *2,* 240-254. Discusses programming in women's prisons.

E.0254 Floch, M. (1946, October). Group therapy in a women's prison. *Federal Probation, 10,* 34-36. Early look at group therapy with incarcerated women.

E.0255 Flynn, Elizabeth Gurley (1963). *The Alderson story.* New York, NY: International Publishers. History of the First Federal Institution for women at Alderson, West Virginia.

E.0256 Fogel, Catherine (1993, October/December). Hard time: The stressful nature of incarceration for women. Special Issue: Socially vulnerable populations. *Issues in Mental Health Nursing, 14*(4), 367-377. Data collected from 55 women (ages 17-59) during their first weeek of incarceration and after 6 months in prison.

E.0257 Fogel, Catherine, & Martin, S. L. (1992, February). The mental health of incarcerated women. *Western Journal of Nursing Research, 14*(1), 30-40. Discussion of mental health of women in prison.

E.0258 Fogel, Catherine (1991, Summer). Health problems and needs of incarcerated women. *Journal of Prison and Jail Health, 10*(1), 43-57. Results of structured interviews with 135 women during their first week of incarceration and with 55 of these after 6 months in prison.

E.0259 Fogel, Catherine (1988, December). Health status of incarcerated women. *Dissertation Abstracts International, 49*(6), 1582-A. Study conducted in a state prison in the South looks at incarcerated women's health status and predictive factors that may influence health.

E.0260 Fogel, Catherine, et al. (1986, November/December). Expecting in prison: Preparing for birth under conditions of stress. *Journal of Obstetrical Gynecology and Neonatal Nursing, 15*(6), 454-458. Looks at programs for pregnant incarcerated women.

E.0261 Fondren, D. L. (1976). *A comparison of institutionalized female offenders with non-offender females according to vocational self-concept, acquiescent response style, and vocational anxiety.* Dissertation, University of Southern Mississippi. Data collected from 40 female offenders.

E.0262 Footes, L. E. (1974, June). Effect of achievement motivation training on women prisoners. *Criminal Justice and Behavior, 1*(2), 131-138. Looks at motivation training in women prisoners.

E.0263 Fordham Urban Law Journal (1992, Winter). Has Connecticut thrown out the baby with the bath water? Termination of parental rights and in re Valerie D. [595 A.2d 922 (Conn.)]. *Fordham Urban Law Journal, 19,* 535-561. Discusses parental rights of incarcerated women.

E.0264 Forsythe, Bill (1993, August). Women prisoners and women penal officials, 1840-1921. *British Journal of Criminology, 33*(4), 525-540. Examines aspects of prison discipline relating to women, 1840-1921. Discusses Dobash (1986) and Zedner (1991).

E.0265 Fortune, Eddyth, & Ballach, Margaret (1985). Project MET: A community based educational program for women offenders. In I. Moyer (Ed), *The changing role of women in the criminal justice system* (pp. 113-129). Prospect Heights, IL: Waveland Press. Discusses a 16 week project for job training in skills normally associated with male dominated occupations.

E.0266 Foster, Euphesenia (1977). *Female offenders in the Federal Prison System.* Washington, DC: U.S. Department of Justice. Describes what happens to women in the Federal Prison System. Discusses counseling, education, training and recreation available to them.

E.0267 Foster, Euphesenia (1973). *Female offenders in the Federal Correctional System.* Washington, DC: U.S. Bureau of Prisons. Booklet with brief history of Federal Women's prisons and information on women prisoners.

E.0268 Foster, Thomas (1975, February). Make-believe families: A response of women and girls to the deprivations of imprisonment. *Journal of Criminology and Penology, 3*(1), 71-78. Compared data from 6 different institutions to explore pseudo-kinship relationships among female inmates.

E.0269 Fox, Denamae (1972). *The influence of perception training on communication between polarized groups of officers and inmates at the Colorado Women's Correctional Institution.* Dissertation, University of Colorado. Data collected from both female inmates and officers revealed the potential of perception training for changing initial concepts.

E.0270 Fox, James (1984, March). Women's prison policy, prisoner activism, and the impact of the contemporary feminist movement: A case study. *The Prison Journal, 64*(1), 15-36. Discusses the effects of the women's movement on current prison policy.

E.0271 Fox, James (1982). Women in prison: A case study in the social reality of stress. In R. Johnson & H. Toch (Eds.), *Pains of imprisonment* (Chapter 12). Newbury Park, CA: Sage Publications. Presents a case study of New York's Bedford Hills facility in the 1970's.

E.0272 Fox, James (1976). Self-imposed stigmata: A study of tattooing among female inmates. *Dissertation Abstracts International, 37*(5-A), 3201. Looks at the significance of tattooing for female imates.

E.0273 Franey, Ross (1989, November 10). The lower depths. *New Statesman & Society, 2,* 15-16. Case of Carole Richardson, an English woman who was falsely imprisoned.

E.0274 Freedman, Estelle (1984). Sentiment and discipline: Women's prison experiences in nineteenth century America. *Prologue, 16*(4), 249-259. Discusses the first women's prisons, The Indiana Women's Prison (1873) and The Massachusetts Reformatory for Women.

E.0275 Freedman, Estelle (1981). *Their sister's keepers: Women's prison reform in America, 1830-1930.* Ann Arbor, MI: The University of Michigan Press. Discusses 19th-century reformers who proclaimed a sisterhood with imprisoned women.

E.0276 Freedman, Estelle (1974). Their sisters keepers: An historical perspective on female correctional institutions in the United States, 1870-1900. *Feminist Studies, 2,* 77-95. Looks at the first correctional insitutions for women in the U.S.

E.0277 Freeman, R. (1994, March). *Correctional officer attitudes toward inmates and discretionary rule enforcement: A study of professional orientation.* Paper presented at the 1994 ACJS Annual Meeting, Chicago, IL. Data from inmate discipline reports completed by officers at the Maryland Correctional Institution for Women.

E.0278 Fritsch, Travis, & Burkhead, John (1982, January). Behavioral reactions of children to parental absence due to imprisonment. *Family Relations, 30*(1), 83-88. Explored problematic behavior in children who have a parent incarcerated.

E.0279 Fuller, Lisa (1993, December). Visitors to women's prisons in California: An exploratory study. *Federal Probation, 57*(4), 41-47. Profiles visitors to female inmates at 3 institutions in California. Data collected by interview.

E.0280 Fuller, W. C. (1977). *Life scripts of female offenders at the Kentucky Correctional Institution for women.* Dissertation, Louisville Presbyterian Theological Seminary. Profiles of women incarcerated in Lexington, Kentucky.

E.0281 Furlong, Carol (1991). *A study of female offenders in Canada with particular reference to educational programs.* Ottawa, Ontario: National Library of Canada. Looks at educational programs for incarcerated women in Canada.

E.0282 Gabel, Katherine, et al. (1982). *The legal issues of female inmates.* Washington, DC: National Institute of Corrections. Data collected in interviews with 109 female inmates in 4 women's prisons concerning their legal needs, the resources available, and constraints on use of resources.

E.0283 Gallup, M. F. (1944, March/April). The woman offender of today: How can we educate the female? *Prison World, 6*(2), 12, 29. Discusses the difficulties of program planning with transient populations. Emphasizes that program planning must be a "re-education" process.

E.0284 Garma, Joan (1985, July). Investigation of grief with the female inmates at the end of incarceration and implications for pastoral care. *Dissertation Abstracts International, 46*(1), 301. Explains grief reaction model using Kubler-Ross stages of death and dying. Seven case studies of female inmates.

E.0285 Gattone, E., et al. (1976). *Women in the Vermont correctional system.* Montpelier, VT: Vermont Department of Corrections. Assessment of program needs of female inmates. Data collected from the staff at the Vermont Department of Corrections in 1974 and 1976.

E.0286 Gauch, Sarah (1989, Summer). When mothers go to prison. *Human Rights, 16*(2), 32-35. Addresses what happens to family life when mothers are incarcerated. Looks at one model program.

E.0287 Gaudin, J. M. (1984). Social work roles and tasks with incarcerated mothers. *Social Casework, 65*(5), 279-286. A model for social work practice for the maintenance of relationships between imprisoned mothers and their children.

E.0288 Gauper, I. H. (1962, November-December). Missouri State Penitentiary for women. *American Journal of Corrections, 24*(6), 26-30. Reviews prison philosophy on educational programs.

E.0289 Geballe, S., & Stone, M. (1988, Spring). New focus on medical care issues in women's prison cases. *Journal of the National Prison Project, 15*, 1-7. Discusses health care for women inmates, medical-care issues in litigation and types of relief rendered..

E.0290 Gelfand, Elissa (1983). *Imagination in confinement: Women's writings from French prisons.* Ithaca, NY: Cornell University Press. Examines the writings of five French women imprisoned in the 18th, 19th, and 20th centuries. A sociohistorical and literary analysis.

E.0291 Geller, G. A., et al. (1993, October). HIV infection in the women's jail, Orange County, California, 1985 through 1991. *American Journal of Public Health, 83*(10), 1454-1456. Assesses incidence of HIV infection among women tested at the Orange County, CA, Women's Jail from 1985-1991.

E.0292 Genders, Elaine, & Player, Elaine (1995). Women lifers: Assessing the experience. In T. J. Flanagan (Ed.), *Long-term imprisonment: Policy, science and correctional practice* (pp. 117-127). Thousand Oaks, CA: Sage Publications. Focuses on the initial period of assessment for women lifers in the Main Center, role of the staff, and how women experience the initial stages.

E.0293 Genders, Elaine, & Player, Elaine (1990, Spring-Summer). Women lifers: Assessing the experience. *Prison Journal, 80*(1), 45-57. Assessment of the Main Center for Women at H-Wing, Durham, Great Britain, where work and educational opportunities are limited.

E.0294 Genders, Elaine, & Player, Elaine (1987). Women in prison: The treatment, the control, and the experience. In P. Carlen & A. Worrall (Eds.), *Gender, crime and justice* (pp. 161-175). Philadelphia: Open University Press. Looks at treatment of women prisoners.

E.0295 Genders, Elaine, & Player, Elaine (1986, October). Women's imprisonment: The effects of youth custody. *British Journal of Criminology, 26*(4), 357-371. Explores changes in women's prisons in Great Britain. Interviews with 254 women prisoners and 134 prison staff.

E.0296 Genty, P. M. (1988). Protecting the parental rights of incarcerated mothers whose children are in foster care: Proposed changes to New York's termination of parental rights law. *Fordham Urban Law Journal, 17*(1), 1-26. Discusses 1983 legislation in New York to protect parental rights of incarcerated women whose children are in foster care.

E.0297 Geoffrey, A., & Wiorkowski, John (1977, Fall). Female prisoners and legal services. *Quarterly Journal of Corrections, 1*(4), 28-33. Looks at women prisoners use of legal services.

E.0298 Georgia Department of Offender Rehabilitation (1982). *Female offenders in the eighties: A continuum of services.* Atlanta, GA: Georgia Department of Offender Rehabilitation. Looks at programs for incarcerated women in Georgia.

E.0299 Ghosh, Shubhra (1986). *Female criminals in India.* New Delhi: India. Examines behavioral patterns of 69 inmates of Nari Bandi Niketan, a women's unit in Lucknow, India.

E.0300 Giallombardo, Rose (1966a). *Society of women: A study of a women's prison.* New York, NY: John Wiley. Empircal research on women's prisons.

E.0301 Giallombardo, Rose (1966b, Winter). Social roles in a prison for women. *Social Problems, 13*(3), 268-288. Explores social roles of female inmates, such as snitches and inmate cops.

E.0302 Gibbs, Carole (1971, April). The effect of the imprisonment of women upon their children. *British Journal of Criminology, 11*(2), 113-130. Looks at children of incarcerated women.

E.0303 Gibson, Helen (1976). Women's prisons: Laboratories for penal reform. In L. Crites (Ed.), *The female offender* (pp. 93-119). Toronto: DC Heath. Brief history of women's correctional institutions and reforms pioneered by women.

E.0304 Gibson, Helen (1973). Women's prisons: Laboratories for penal reform. *Wisconsin Law Review, 1*, 210-233. Looks at contemporary adaptations in prisons for women and perceptions of women's needs.

E.0305 Gibson, Suzanne (1978). *Developing program models and prototype training materials to meet occupational training needs of adult women offenders from a correctional institution.* Washington, DC: Office of Education. Eighteen month project to evaluate educational training materials in female corrections education in Virginia.

E.0306 Gildert, Colleen (1994, Spring). A survey of federal female offenders. *Masters Abstracts International, 32*(1), 131. Results of interviews with 30 women prisoners to determine their needs and how they perceived these needs were addressed during their incarceration.

E.0307 Ginsberg, Charlotte (1980). Who are the women in prison? *Corrections Today, 42*, 56-59. Profile of women incarcerated in the 1980's.

E.0308 Gladwin, Bridget (1993, August). My story: Taconic warden finds volunteers have much to offer women inmates. *Corrections Today, 55*(5), 88+. Warden discusses the use of volunteers in a women's prison.

E.0309 Glick, Ruth (1977). *National study of women's correctional programs.* Washington, DC: U.S. Department of Justice. Empirical research on women's prisons.

E.0310 Goetting, Ann, & Howsen, R. M. (1983, Autumn-Winter). Women in prison: A profile. *Prison Journal, 63*(2), 27-46. Results of a 1979 self-report survey of 11,397 inmates in state prisons.

E.0311 Gold, Sally (1972). Women, the criminal code and the correctional system. In S. Gold (Ed.), *Women and social services* (pp. 512-515) New York, NY: Discus Books. Study of women in prison and the culture of women's prisons.

E.0312 Golden Gate University Law Review (1986, Fall). Women and children first: An examination of the unique needs of women in prison. *Golden Gate University Law Review, 16*(6), 455-474. Looks at the children of incarcerated women and programs available to them.

E.0313 Goldsborough, P. A. (1988a). *North Carolina women in corrections: Women in crisis.* Winston-Salem, NC: Women of Convictions. Data on North Carolina.

E.0314 Goldsborough, P. A. (1988b). *Irreverence for life: A story of some federal prisoner mothers and their babies.* Winston-Salem, NC: Women of Convictions. First-person account of policies, practices, and problems of pregnant women and their infants. Data from 1985-1986.

E.0315 Goodman, Nancy, & Price, Jean (1967). *Studies of female offenders.* London: Research Unit Report. Analysis of women offenders in the Metropolitan Police District in 1957, a day's population of women in prison on January 1, 1965, and girls sentenced to Borstal in 1963.

E.0316 Gordon, Mary (1922). *Penal discipline.* London: Routledge. Incarcerated women included.

E.0317 Grace, S. (1990). Needs of women prisoners. *Research Bulletin, 29*, 42-46. Review of literature on concerns and needs of female prisoners in Great Britain.

E.0318 Greening, B. (1978). Prison for moms and kids. *Youth Authority Quarterly, 31*, 25-30. Discusses prison programs for incarcerated women with children.

E.0319 Greenfield, Lawrence, & Minor-Harper, Stephanie (1991). *Women in prison.* Washington, DC: U.S. Department of Justice, Bureau of Justice Statistics. Bureau of Justice Statistics.

E.0320 Greenspan, Judy (1994, Summer). Struggle for compassion: The fight for quality care for women with AIDS at Central California Women's Facility. *Yale Journal of Law and Feminism, 6,* 383-395. Discussion of quality of life for women in prison with AIDS.

E.0321 Gregory, Jeanne (1995, August). Persistence and irony in the incarceration of women in the Texas penitentiary, 1907-1910. *Masters Abstracts International, 33*(4), 1133. Study of the convict lease system and the sexual misconduct of guards with female prisoners.

E.0322 Griffith, J. (1984, Fall/Winter). Evidence of unidimensionality of locus of control in women prisoners: Implications for prisoner rehabilitation. *Journal of Offender Counseling, Services and Rehabilitation, 9,* (1-2), 57-70. Investigates the LOC construct in a prison sample.

E.0323 Griffiths, A. (1896). *Female prisoners.* London: Windsor. Early study of women in prison.

E.0324 Griggs, Mildred, & Oppert, Judy (1974). Teachers behind bars. *Adult Leadership, 23*(4), 112-114. Results of a project conducted in a women's prison by a university.

E.0325 Grodd, Barbara, & Norton, Linda (1982). Mothers in prison: Ties to the outside world. *Practice Digest, 5*(1), 30-33. Discusses the Incarcerated Mothers Program (IMP) at the women's unit of Westchester County Jail, Valhalla, New York.

E.0326 Grossman, Michelle (1992, July-October). Two perspectives on aboriginal female suicides in custody. *Canadian Journal of Criminology, 34*(3-4), 403-415. Deprivation and importation theories of suicide are reviewed using data on incarcerated aboriginal women in Canada.

E.0327 Gubar, Susan, & Hedin, Anne (1981, December). A jury of our peers: Teaching and learning in the Indiana women's prison. *College English, 43*(8), 779-789. Explores difficulties of teaching and learning women's literature in a women's prison.

E.0328 Gwinn, Bobbie (1992, Spring). Linking inmate families together: The L.I.F.T. program at FPC Alderson. *Federal Prisons Journal: Focus on the Female Offender,3*(1) 37-40. Reports on Linking Inmate Families Together (LIFT) a program for incarcerated mothers.

E.0329 Hadley, A. (1985, August 28). Women behind bars. *Nursing Times, 81*(35), 24-26. Looks at health care for incarcerated women.

E.0330 Hadley, J. G. (1981). *Georgia women prison inmates and their families.* Atlanta, GA: Georgia Department of Offender Rehabilitation Office. Statistical information about women incarcerated in Georgia.

E.0331 Hairston, Creasie (1991a, March). Family ties during imprisonment: Important to whom and for what? *Journal of Sociology and Social Welfare, 18*(1), 87-104. Research on social functions of prisoner family ties.

E.0332 Hairston, Creasie (1991b, Summer). Mothers in jail: Parent-child separation and jail visitation. *Affilia: Journal of Women and Social Work, 6*(2), 9-27. Fifty-six incarcerated mothers' views on separation from children and children visiting them in prison.

E.0333 Hairston, Creasie, & Hess, Peg (1989, April). Family ties: Maintaining child-parent bonds is important. *Corrections Today, 51,* 102-106. Results of a 1988 survey of state policies governing parent-child relations in correctional settings.

E.0334 Hairston, Creasie, & Lockett, Patricia (1987, March-April). Parents in prison: New directions for social services. *Social Work, 32*(2), 162-164. Describes a program known as "Parenting in prison" which offers family support services for prisoners.

E.0335 Hale, Donna (1988). Impact of mothers' incarceration on the family system: Research and recommendations. In F. Hagan & M. Sussman (Eds.), *Deviance and the family* (pp. 143-154). New York, NY: Halworth Press. Reviews systems theory and studies of the family as a system. Examines impact of maternal incarceration.

E.0336 Hale, Donna (1987). The impact of mothers' incarceration on the family systems: Research and recommendations. *Marriage and Family Review, 12*(1-2), 143-154. Review of the literature on the systems approach to family research. Reports on affects of separating offender and family.

E.0337 Haley, Kathleen (1980). Mothers behind bars: A look at the parental rights of incarcerated women. In S. Datesman & F. Scarpitti (Eds.), *Women, crime, and justice* (pp. 34+). New York, NY: Oxford University Press. Looks at the legal rights of incarcerated mothers.

E.0338 Haley, Kathleen (1977, Fall). Mothers behind bars: A look at parental rights of incarcerated women. *New England Journal on Prison Law, 4*(1), 141-155. Considers the legal rights of incarcerated mothers.

E.0339 Halfon, A., et al. (1971). The Baxtrom women: A four year follow-up of behavior patterns. *Psychiatric Quarterly, 45*(4), 518-527. Examined patterns of 47 women transferred to civil mental hospitals from a hospital for the criminally insane.

E.0340 Halsam, P. (1964). The female prisoner. *Canadian Journal of Corrections, 6*(4), 463-466. Overview of women in prison in Canada (1960's).

E.0341 Halsey, Peggy (1983, May). Meeting the needs of incarcerated women. *Engage/Social Action, 11*(5), 35-40. Discusses programming for incarcerated women.

E.0342 Haltom-Fox, C., & Lobel, K. (1992). *HIV, AIDS and reproductive health: A peer trainer's guide.* Little Rock, AK: Women's Project. A 4-hour course given to 368 incarcerated women covering facts about HIV transmission and risk-reduction behaviors, symptoms, and testing.

E.0343 Hammer, Max, & Ross, Michael (1977). Psychological needs of imprisoned adult females with high and low conscience development. *Corrective and Social Psychiatry and Journal of Behavior Technology Methods and Therapy, 23*(3), 73-78. Study of 110 imprisoned female adults to distinguish psychopathic groups by the absence or presence of guilt.

E.0344 Hammer, Max (1965). Homosexuality in a women's reformatory. *Corrective Psychiatry and Journal of Social Therapy, 11,* 168-169. Looks at homosexuality among incarcerated women.

E.0345 Hampton, Blanche (1993). *Prisons and women.* Kensington, NSW, Australia: New South Wales University Press. Looks at prisons for women in Australia.

E.0346 Hands, J., et al. (1974). Mensturation and behavior in a special hospital. *Medicine, Science, and the Law, 14*(1), 32-35. Looks at institutionalized women criminals.

E.0347 Hankins, Catherine, et al. (1994, October). HIV infection among women in prison: An assessment of risk factors using a nonnominal methodology. *American Journal of Public Health, 84*(10), 1637-1640. Results of a study conducted in Canada revealing that incarcerated women under the age of 25 are more likely to be infected with HIV than similarly aged incarcerated men.

E.0348 Hannum, T. E., et al. (1978, September). Self-concept changes associated with incarceration in female prisoners. *Criminal Justice and Behavior, 5*(3), 271-279. Results of admissions test battery administered to 57 female prisoners at the Iowa Women's Reformatory.

E.0349 Hannum, T. E., et al. (1973). Differences in female prisoner characteristics: 1960-1970. *Corrective and Social Psychiatry and Journal of Applied Behavior Therapy, 19*(3), 39-41. Study of patterns of women's offenses over the years 1960-1970.

E.0350 Hannum, T. E., & Warman, R. E. (1964, July). The MMPI characteristics of incarcerated females. *Journal of Research in Crime and Delinquency, 1*(2), 119-126. Studied the admission scores of 139 female inmates at the Iowa Women's Reformatory.

E.0351 Hannum, T. E., & Warman, R. E. (1963). The use of inmate "counselors" in the orientation of new inmates. *Corrective Psychiatry and Journal of Social Therapy, 9*(2), 95-99. Discusses a program at the Women's Reformatory, Rockwell City, Indiana.

E.0352 Hanson, Laurie (1983). Women prisoners: Freedom from sexual harassment: A constitutional analysis. *Golden Gate University Law Review, 13*(667). Looks at sexual harassment of female inmates in women's prisons.

E.0353 Hardesty, Constance, et al. (1993). Self-esteem and the woman prisoner. In B. Fletcher, et al. (Eds.), *Women prisoners: A forgotten population* (pp. 27-44). Westport, CT: Praeger. Explores the relationship between self-esteem and the experiences of women prisoners. Considers existing research on the issue of self-esteem as a predictor of recidivism.

E.0354 Hargrove, Ann, & Faucett, Jan (1978). *Women offenders in non-traditional work.* Washington, DC: Wider Opportunities for Women. Describes a project in which women prisoners were trained and placed in non-traditional jobs in the Washington, DC, area.

E.0355 Harland, Anne (1987). *An evaluation of reconviction rates for female corrective trainees.* Wellington, New Zealand: New Zealand Department of Justice. Examines reoffending among females sentenced to "corrective training" a three-month custodial sentence introduced in 1981.

E.0356 Harm, Nancy (1992, Spring). Social policy on women prisoners: A historical analysis. *Affilia: Journal of Women and Social Work, 7*(1), 90-108. Traces history of social policy toward female offenders as a basis for understanding the current status of women in the correctional system.

E.0357 Harm, Nancy (1990, April). *Women incarcerated in Illinois state prisons, 1843-1915: An exploratory study in social policy.* Dissertation, University of Illinois at Chicago, 1990. History of the Illinois state women's prison and characteristics of women prisoners from 1843-1915.

E.0358 Harper, Ida (1952, October). The role of the "fringer" in a state prison for women. *Social Forces, 31*, 53-60. Looks at social roles in women's prisons.

E.0359 Harris, Jean (1992, August). Troubling the stars. *American School Board Journal, 179*(8), 37-38. Harris talks about the parenting course she taught to inmate mothers.

E.0360 Harris, Jean, & Alexander, Shana (1991). *Marking time: Letters from Jean Harris to Shana Alexander.* New York, NY: Charles Scribner's Sons. Correspondence between Jean Harris and Shana Alexander, during Harris' incarceration at the Bedford Hills Correctional Facility.

E.0361 Harris, Jean (1988). *They always call us ladies: Stories from prison.* New York, NY: Charles Scribner's Sons. Personal memoir including a history of Bedford Hills Correctional Facility and a portrait of Katherine Davis, the first woman to advocate prison reform, in 1901.

E.0362 Harris, Mary Belle (1936). *I knew them in prison.* New York, NY: Viking Press. Early study of women's prisons by Mary Belle Harris a reformer and activist.

E.0363 Harris, Sara (1967). *Hellhole: The shocking story of the inmates and life in the New York City House of Detention for women.* New York, NY: E. P. Dutton, Inc. Daily life of women incarcerated in New York City (1960's).

E.0364 Hartnagle, Timothy, & Gillan, Mary (1980, January). Female prisoners and the inmate code. *Pacific Sociological Review, 23*(1), 85-104. Discusses the social structure of a women's prison.

E.0365 Hatty, Suzanne (1984, June). *Women in the prison system: Proceedings, June 12-14, 1984.* Brisbane: Australian Institute of Criminology. Discusses characteristics of female offenders, and how the Australian prison system regards incarcerated women.

E.0366 Hayes, Lindsay, et al. (1989). *The female offender in Delaware: Population analysis and assessment.* Alexandria, VA: National Center on Institutions and Alternatives. Statistics on female offenders in Delaware, 1980's.

E.0367 Hayes, Lindsay, et al. (1988). *Technical assistance report presenting a population analysis of the Women's Correctional Institution in Claymont, Delaware as of October, 1988.* Assesses programs available for female offenders in the state.

E.0368 Hazard, Helen (1942, February). The reformatory for women, Dwight, Illinois. *Illinois Welfare Bulletin, 33*, 5-6. Early look at women's prison in Illinois.

E.0369 Heffernan, Esther (1993). Alderson: The early years. In ACA *Female offenders: Meeting needs of a neglected population* (pp. 17-25). Laurel, MD: American Correctional Association. History of the founding of the first federal institution for women at Alderson.

E.0370 Heffernan, Esther (1972). *Making it in prison: The square, the cool, and the life.* New York, NY: John Wiley. Study of women's prisons using data from the Women's Reformatory at Occoquan, VA.

E.0371 Heidensohn, Frances (1981). Women and the penal system. In A. Morris and L. Gelsthorpe (Eds.), *Women and crime* (pp. 125-139). Cambridge, England: University of Cambridge Institute of Criminology. Looks at the treatment of women in prison.

E.0372 Heidensohn, Frances (1975). The imprisonment of females. In S. McConville (Ed.), *The use of imprisonment* (pp. 43-56). London. Looks at treatment of incarcerated women.

E.0373 Heidensohn, Frances (1969). Prison for women. *Howard Journal of Criminology and Crime Prevention, 12*, 281-288. Discusses women in prison.

E.0374 Hendrix, Omar (1972, July 15). *A study in neglect: A report on women prisoners.* New York, NY: Women's Prison Association. Results of a demographic study of the New York City Correctional Institute for Women and a national survey of female inmates.

E.0375 Heney, Jan (1990). *Report on self-injurious behavior in the Kingston Prison for women.* Ottawa: Ministry of the Solicitor General. Discusses self-mutilation of women prisoners.

E.0376 Henriques, Zelma (1982). *Imprisoned mothers and their children: A descriptive and analytical study.* Lanham, MD: University Press of America. Discusses major concerns of 30 incarcerated mothers relating to their children.

E.0377 Henry, Joan (1952). *Women in prison.* Garden City, NY: Doubleday. A look at incarcerated women through observation and interviews.

E.0378 Herjanic, M., et al. (1977, May). Forensic psychiatry: Female offenders. *American Journal of Psychiatry, 134*(5), 556-558. Looks at the psychiatric treatment of incarcerated women.

E.0379 Herman, A. M. (1970). If she were a carpenter: Non-traditional apprenticeships for women in prison. *Corrections Today, 41*, 24-25+. Looks at non-traditional training programs for incarcerated women.

E.0380 Herman, Helen, et al. (1991, February). Hidden severe psychiatric morbidity in sentenced prisoners: An Australian study. *American Journal of Psychiatry, 148*(2), 236-240. Evaluated types and prevalence of severe mental disorders among sentenced prisoners in Australia.

E.0381 Herndon, Michelle (1992). *A descriptive study of programs for pregnant inmates in state correctional institutions.* Masters Thesis, Central Missouri State University. Identifies number of pregnant inmates in state correctional institutions and accessibility of programs.

E.0382 Hickey, J. A. (1992, Spring). Gibson v. Matthews [926 F.2d 532 (1991)] the Sixth Circuit and the stillbirth of the reproductive rights of incarcerated women. *The University of Toledo Law Review, 23*, 599-617. Case study of reproductive rights of incarcerated women.

E.0383 Hinck, K. E. (1989, Summer). Second class prisoners: New Hampshire's placement policy for female offenders. *New England Journal on Criminal and Civil Confinement, 15*(2), 225-24. Study of New Hampshire's female offenders. Includes historical overview and discussion of New Hampshire's policy of sending women prisoners out of state.

E.0384 Hindson, N. A. (1988). Treatment of mentally disordered women within the prison system in England and Wales. In A. Morris & C. Wilkinson (Eds.), *Women and the penal system* (pp. 94-117). Cambridge, England: University of Cambridge Institute of Criminology. Looks at psychiatric treatment of incarcerated women.

E.0385 Hironimus, Helen (1944, March/April). The woman offender of today: Problems of administration. *Prison World, 6*(2), 7, 25. Early discussion of the problems of operating a women's prison on a limited budget.

E.0386 Hodge, J. (1988, October). Group work with women in a maximum security unit. *Prison Service Journal, 72*, 6-8. Looks at group therapy in a prison for women.

E.0387 Hoffman, K. S. (1983). Women offenders and social work practice. In A. Roberts (Ed.), *Social work in juvenile and criminal justice settings* (pp. 247-329). Springfield, IL: Charles C. Thomas. Describes treatment of female offenders and how social workers can work with them.

E.0388 Hoffman, Susan (1977). *What happens when a mother goes to prison? An overview of relevant legal and psychological considerations.* Paper presented at the Annual Meeting of the American Psychology-Law Society, Snowmass, Colorado, June 26-28, 1977. Presents state dispositions towards children of incarcerated women.

E.0389 Hokanson, S. (1986). *Women offender in Minnesota profile, needs and future directions.* St. Paul, MN: Minnesota Department of Corrections. Report on female offenders in Minnesota. Includes inventory of services available and overview of the development and training needs of correctional staff involved with female inmates.

E.0390 Holdman, Sharlette (1980, July 9). *Babies born in prison and other women prisoners' issues.* Memorandum from the Florida Clearinghouse on Criminal Justice. Tallahassee, Florida. Florida's disposition on babies born in prison.

E.0391 Holland, Terrill, et al. (1979, October). Preferences of prison inmates for male versus female institutional personnel. *Journal of Applied Psychology, 64*(5), 564-568. Investigated preferences of California prison inmates including 77 female felons, and 89 female addicts.

E.0392 Holmes, Michelle, et al. (1993, April). Chlamydial cervical infection in jailed women. *American Journal of Public Health, 83*(4), 551-555. Discusses prevalence of and risk factors for chlamydial infection in women in a New York City jail as well as policies for testing.

E.0393 Holt, Karen (1982). Nine months to life: The law and the pregnant inmate. *Journal of Family Law, 20*(3), 523-543. Discusses legal rights of pregnant prisoners.

E.0394 Holt, K., & Mattes, S. (1987). *Transinstitutionalization in the human service sector: An examination of female population movement between mental health and correctional institutions.* Boston, MA: Massachusetts Department of Corrections. Time series analysis of mental health histories of adult women incarcerated in Massachusetts.

E.0395 Home Office Prison Department (1972). *Education in establishments for women and girls.* Maidstone, England: Home Office Prison Department, H.M. Prison. Looks at prison programming for women incarcerated in England.

E.0396 Hopper, Columbus, & McCance, Kathleen (1983). *The forgotten sufferers: Children of inmates.* Paper presented at the Annual Meeting of the Southwestern Social Science Association, Houston, Texas, March 14-17, 1983. Discusses how children are influenced by their parents' incarceration.

E.0397 Hovey, M. (1971, January). The forgotten offenders. *Manpower, 13*(1), 38-41. Addresses employment problems of women offenders.

E.0398 Howard, Gwendolyn (1976). *The perceptions of incarcerated black mothers and their concerns for their children: A exploratory study with implications for schools.* Dissertation, Atlanta University. Looks at concerns of incarcerated black mothers for their children.

E.0399 Howard, E. M., & Howard, Joyce (1974). Women in institutions: Treatment in prisons and mental hospitals. In V. Franks & V. Burtle (Eds.), *Women in therapy: New psychotherapies for a changing society* (pp.357-382). New York, NY: Brunner/Mazel. Looks at psychiatric treatment of incarcerated women.

E.0400 Howe, Adrian (1990). Prologue to a history of women's imprisonment: In search of a feminist perspective. *Social Justice, 17*(2), 5-22. History of women's imprisonment from a feminist perspective.

E.0401 Huft, Anita, et al. (1992a, Spring). Care of the pregnant offender. In ACA *Female offenders: Meeting needs of a neglected population* (pp. 54-59). Laurel, MD: American Correctional Association. Discusses various aspects of care for the pregnant female offender including clinical dilemma, social networking, team delivery of services, and mothering in prison.

E.0402 Huft, Anita (1992b, April). Psychosocial adaptation to pregnancy in prison. *Journal of Psychosocial Nursing and Mental Health Services, 30*(4), 19-22. Looks at childbearing for incarcerated women and the displacement of the maternal role functions after birth.

E.0403 Humphrey, Elaine (1992, April). *Female offenders committed to state prison.* Albany, NY: New York Department of Correctional Services. Department of Corrections Statistics on women in prison in New York.

E.0404 Hungerford, Gregory (1993). *The children of inmate mothers: An exploratory study of children, caretakers, and inmate mothers in Ohio.* Dissertation, Ohio State University. Examined the children of inmate mothers in Ohio. Data collected from 150 inmate mothers.

E.0405 Hunt, G., et al. (1989, June). Wretched, hatless and miserably clad: Women and the inebriate reformatories from 1900-1913. *British Journal of Sociology, 40*(2), 244-270. Details of the Farmfield Reformatory for Women open from 1900-1915 as a result of the Inebriate Act of 1898.

E.0406 Hunter, Susan (1985, February). The relationship between women offenders and their children. *Dissertation Abstracts International, 45*(8), 2660. Explores the relationship between female offenders and their children before, during, and after incarceration.

E.0407 Hunter, Susan (1984a). *Rehabilitation between women offenders and their children.* Washington, DC: National Institute of Justice. Discusses programs for incarcerated women with children.

E.0408 Hunter, Susan (1984b, March). Issues and challenges facing women's prisons in the 1980's. *The Prison Journal, 64*(1), 129-135. Discusses problems with women's prisons and looks at what the future holds for incarcerated women.

E.0409 Hurley, William, & Dunne, Michael (1991, December). Psychosocial distress and psychiatric morbidity in women prisoners. *Australian and New Zealand Journal of Psychiatry, 25*(4), 461-470. Results of screening 91 female inmates for psychological distress and psychiatric morbidity.

E.0410 Hutchings, J., et al. (1974). Into Europe: A study of four women's prisons. *Social Work Today, 4*(25), 793-796. Describes 1972 visits of seven probation officers from London to women's prisons in West Germany, Sweden, Denmark, and Holland.

E.0411 Iacovetti, R. G. (1975). *Corrections and the female offender.* Paper presented at the Southern Conference on Corrections, February 27, 1975. Discusses inadequate and inappropriate facilities, treatment, and programs for women in the correctional environment.

E.0412 Iglehart, Alfreda, & Stein, Martha (1985, March). The female offender: A forgotten client. *Social Casework, 66*(3), 152-159. Discusses how Social Workers can use program planning to empower female offenders to manage their lives productively.

E.0413 Iglehart, Alfred (1981). Personal and social characteristics of female offenders. In J. Figueria-McDonough et al. (Eds.), *Females in prison in Michigan, 1968-1978: A study of committment patterns.* Ann Arbor, MI: University of Michigan. Profiles women incarcerated over a ten-year period.

E.0414 Illinois Department of Corrections (1990). *Women and children residential program feasibility study.* Springfield, IL: Illinois Department of Corrections. Results of a feasability study of child and female parent residential programming in Illinois.

E.0415 Immarigeon, Russ, & Chesney-Lind, Meda (1993). Women's prisons: Overcrowded and overused. In R. Muraskin & T. Alleman (Eds.), *It's a crime: Women and justice* (pp. 242-259). Englewood Cliffs, NJ: Prentice Hall. Discusses some problems with women's prisons in the 1990's.

E.0416 Immarigeon, Russ (1989). Four states study policies affecting women offenders. *Journal of the National Prison Project, 19*, 4-6. Results of studies on policies for incarcerated women in four states.

E.0417 Immarigeon, Russ (1987, Summer). Few diversion programs are offered female offenders. *National Prison Project Journal, 12*, 9-11. Discusses scarcity of programs for diverting women offenders from prison. Describes 3 programs that existed at the time of this writing.

E.0418 Immarigeon, Russ, & Chesney-Lind, Meda (1991). *Women's prisons: Overcrowded and overused.* Washington, DC: National Council on Crime and Delinquency. Presents evidence that the current level of women's imprisonment is disproportionate to the need for confinement.

E.0419 Inman, Debra (1977, January). Differentiation of intrapunitive from extrapunitive female inmates. *Journal of Clinical Psychology, 33*(1), 95-98. Results of a battery of psychological tests.

E.0420 Jefferson, Laurie, & Smith, Betsy (1985, Fall). A health program for black incarcerated women. *Sage: A Scholarly Journal on Black Women, 2*(2), 60-64. Describes a Black women's health program at the Massachusetts Correctional Institution for women in Framingham, MA.

E.0421 Jensen, Gary, & Jones, Dorothy (1976, March). Perspective on inmate culture: A study of women in prison. *Social Forces, 54*(3), 590-603. Data collected from 172 female felons and misdemeanants incarcerated in a prison for women.

E.0422 Johnson, Elizabeth (1991a). Pregnancy in prison. *Dissertation Abstracts International, 52*(6), 2993. Data from 17 women incarcerated at a Federal Prison for Women. All had confirmed pregnancies. Assessed women's descriptions of their pregnancies.

E.0423 Johnson, Elizabeth (1991b). Women's prisons in Japan: A comparative analysis. *International Journal of Comparative and Applied Criminal Justice, 15*(2), 1-14. Addresses gender issues and criminality, trends for women inmates and the uniqueness of the Japanese correctional system.

E.0424 Johnson, Elizabeth (1969). *Childbirth to women under sentence: Characteristics and outcome.* Dissertation, Southern Illinois University, Carbondale. Study on childbirth in prison.

E.0425 Johnston, Judy (1988, Spring). Female prisoners in New South Wales, 1788. In D. Biles (Ed.), *Current Australian trends in corrections* (pp. 126-130). Annandale, Australia: Federation Press. Discusses women prisoners, unit living and participatory management.

E.0426 Johnston, W. C. (1968). A descriptive study of 100 convicted female narcotic residents. *Corrective Psychiatry and Journal of Social Therapy, 14*, 230-236. Study of drug addiction in women prisoners.

E.0427 Jones, Richard (1993). Coping with separation: Adaptive responses of women prisoners. *Women and Criminal Justice, 5*(1), 71-99. Analysis of adaptation of female inmates and how women's relationships outside of prison affect their responses to prison.

E.0428 Jones, Richard (1987). Mitchellville: A study of adaptation responses of women in prison. *Dissertation Abstracts International, 47*(11), 4196-A. Study of incarcerated women focusing on adaptation.

E.0429 Jordan, Judith (1979). *Female offenders in New Jersey: Compilation of information on program needs and priorities.* Trenton, NJ: New Jersey Advisory Committee on the Status of Women. Report on the programming needs of women incarcerated in New Jersey (1970's).

E.0430 Jordan, T. E. (1990). For their countrys' good: The convict women of the ship Harmony: 1829. *International Journal of Comparative and Applied Criminal Justice, 14*(1), 83-95. Discusses the ship "Harmony" which transported 96 female convicts from Great Britain to Australia in 1829.

E.0431 Jose-Kampfner, Cristina (1995). Health care on the inside. In D. Adams (Ed.), *Health issues of women of color: A cultural diversity perspective* (pp. 164-183). Thousand Oaks, CA: Sage. Looks at the lack of health care for incarcerated women and some of the problems they face.

E.0432 Jose-Kampfner, Cristina (1992, Winter). Reflections from the inside: Women's health in prison. *Health Bulletin, 22*(4), 15. Discusses the health care needs of incarcerated women.

E.0433 Jose-Kampfner, Cristina (1991a). Coming to terms with existential death: An analysis of women's adaptation to life in prison. *Social Justice, 17*(2), 10-23. Looks at the life of incarcerated women and how they adapt to long-term imprisonment.

E.0434 Jose-Kampfner, Cristina (1991b, August). Michigan program makes children's visits meaningful. *Corrections Today, 53*(5), 132-134. Data collected from the Huron Valley Correctional Facility in Ypsilanti, Michigan. Report on the children's visitation program.

E.0435 Jose, Maria Cristina (1985). Women doing life sentences: A phenomenological study. *Dissertation Abstracts International, 46*(7), 1877. First person accounts of seven women serving long sentences in three different prisons. Concerns about children are prominent.

E.0436 Journal of the American Medical Association (1992, July 1). HIV prevention in the US correctional system, 1991. *Journal of the American Medical Association, 23*(2), 268. Study indicates that 15% of all women entering U.S. prisons may test positive for AIDS.

E.0437 Journal of the American Medical Association (1992, July 1). Varicella outbreak in a women's prison: Kentucky. *Journal of the American Medical Association, 23*(2), 193+. Discusses disease control in women's prisons.

E.0438 Journal of Family Law (1981-1982). Nine months to life: The law and the pregnant inmate. *Journal of Family Law, 20,* 523-543. Looks at legal rights and sanctions for pregnant inmates.

E.0439 Journal of Juvenile Law (1991). Incarceration and termination of parental rights. *Journal of Juvenile Law, 12,* 70-78. Looks at state statutes on parental rights of incarcerated women.

E.0440 Justice of the Peace (1974). Unsupported mothers and first prison sentences. *Justice of the Peace, 138*(18), 250-251. Discusses what happens to the children of incarcerated women.

E.0441 Juvenile Justice Digest (1993, July 21). Female inmates testify to problems of raising children in prison. *Juvenile Justice Digest, 21*(4), 6-8. Results of interviews with female inmates regarding their children.

E.0442 Juvenile Justice Digest (1975, October). Pre-schoolers attend classes in Washington women's prison. *Juvenile Justice Digest, 3*(20), 5. Discusses a program for children of incarcerated women in Washington, DC.

E.0443 Kalny, Cheryl (1989). Daughters of Eve: Female offenders and the criminal justice system. *Dissertation Abstracts International, 50*(12), 4074-4075. Focuses on women in the Minnesota criminal justice system from early Minnesota statehood to the onset of the Great Depression.

E.0444 Kaminer, Anita (1992, August). Life events stress, social support, and maternal-fetal attachment in incarcerated pregnant women and non-incarcerated pregnant women. *Dissertation Abstracts International, 53*(2), 769. Data collected from 70 incarcerated pregnant female inmates.

E.0445 Kaplan, Mildred (1988). A peer support group for women in prison for the death of a child. *Journal of Offender Counseling, Services, and Rehabilitation, 13*(1), 5-13. Describes a peer support group for mothers imprisoned for murdering a child.

E.0446 Karsai, H., et al. (1988, October 15). Cervical intraepithelial neoplasia in female prisoners in British Columbia. *Canadian Medical Association Journal, 139*(8), 733-736. Discussion of health issues of incarcerated women.

E.0447 Kassebaum, Gene, & Chandler, Susan (1994). Polydrug use and self control among men and women in prisons. *Journal of Drug Education, 24*(4), 333-350. Tested an instrument to determine the extent and variety of alcohol and drug use in prison populations.

E.0448 Kassebaum, Gene, et al. (1962, Fall). Job related differences in staff attitudes toward treatment in a women's prison. *Pacific Sociological Review, 5*(2), 83-88. 1961 data from staff on etiology of crime, penalties for offenders, and management of female inmates.

E.0449 Kates, Elizabeth (1955, October). Sexual problems in women's institutions. *Journal of Social Therapy, 1*, 187-191. Looks at relationships in women's prisons.

E.0450 Kates, Erika (1984, May). *Litigation as a means of achieving social change: A case study of women in prison.* Dissertation, Brandeis, 1984. Discusses why female inmates seldom resort to litigation to improve their situations.

E.0451 Katrin, Susan (1974, March). Effects on women inmates of facilitation training provided correctional officers. *Criminal Justice and Behavior, 1*, 5-12. Discusses the effects of a 40-hr. 13-week facilitation training program for 14 female 25-56 year-old correctional officers.

E.0452 Katrin, Susan (1973, February). The effects on women inmates of facilitation training provided correctional officers. *Journal of Abnormal Psychology, 81*(1), 87-95. Discusses the treatment of female inmates and efforts to change.

E.0453 Kauffman, Kelsey (1990, Spring). The prison as a just community. *New Directions for Child Development, 47*, 77-80. Discusses the democratic approach to moral education as it is applied to a prison setting at the Connecticut State Prison for Women.

E.0454 Kay, Barbara (1961). *Differential self perceptions of female offenders.* Master's Thesis, Ohio State University. Study of 324 female offenders in a state reformatory on socialization, alienation, and institutional impact.

E.0455 Kearns, Anthony, & O'Connor, Art (1988, June). The mentally handicapped criminal offender: A 10-year study of two hospitals. *British Journal of Psychiatry, 152*, 848-851. Case notes of 92 patients referred on hospital order to 2 mental hospitals. Study includes female offenders.

E.0456 Kelley, J. (1967). *When the gates shut: HM prison for women, Holloway.* London: Longmans, Green & Co. Ltd. Data collected from the open prison for women, Askham Grange, and the closed prison for women, Holloway, on architecture, schedules, population, and staff.

E.0457 Kelley, J. (1955). Askham Grange: Open prison for women. *Howard Journal of Criminal Justice, 9*(2), 124-130. Overview of the open prison for women in England.

E.0458 Kemper, Kathi, & Rivera, Frederick (1993, August). Parents in jail. *Pediatrics, 92*(2), 261-264. Describes characteristics and criminal histories of incarcerated parents and attempts to determine the number of children with incarcerated parents in the United States.

E.0459 Kendall, Kathleen (1993). *Literature review on therapeutic services for women in prison.* Ottawa: Ministry of the Solicitor General, Corrections Branch. Report on services for women prisoners in Canada.

E.0460 Ketterling, Marvin (1964). *Rehabilitation of women in the Milwaukee County Jail: An exploratory experiment.* Dissertation: Greeley, CO; Colorado State College. Looks at an experimental program for women in the Milwaukee jail (1964).

E.0461 King, P. (1964). The woman inmate's contacts with the outside world. *American Journal of Corrections, 26*(3), 18-21. Information about Julia Tutwiler Prison in Wetumpka, Alabama.

E.0462 Kinsella, Nina (1944, March/April). The woman offender of today: These are our jails. *Prison World, 6*(2), 6, 24. According to the Census Bureau in April, 1940, there were 9,209 women fourteen years of age and over held in local jails and workhouses.

E.0463 Kirkaldy, A.D. (1978). *Incarcerated women in British Columbia Provincial Institutions.* Victoria, BC: British Columbia Department of the Attorney General. Discusses statistical information on women in correctional institutions in British Columbia.

E.0464 Kiser, G. (1991, September). Female inmates and their families. *Federal Probation, 55*(3), 56-63. Explores relationships of female inmates and their families. Discusses inmates preoccupation with family relationships and children.

E.0465 Kline, Sue (1992a). A profile of female offenders in state and federal prisons. In ACA *Female offenders: Meeting the needs of a forgotten population* (pp.1-6). Laurel, MD: American Correctional Association. Reports on the 5,103 women housed in thirteen Federal Bureau of Prisons facilities as of June, 1992.

E.0466 Kline, Sue (1992b). A profile of female offenders in the Federal Bureau of Prisons. *Federal Prisons Journal, 3*(1), 33-36. Reports a 254% increase in a 10-year period.

E.0467 Knight, Barbara (1992). Women in prison as litigants: Prospects for post-prison futures. *Women and Criminal Justice, 4*(1), 91-116. Examines court decisions regarding rights of women in prison, with special reference to right to prenatal care, rehabilitation, and visitation.

E.0468 Koban, Linda (1983). Parents in prison: A comparative analysis of the effects of incarceration on the families of men and women. *Research in Law, Deviance, and Social Control, 5,* 171-183. Assesses gender differences in perceptions about separation from and prospective reunions with children. Data collected from 70 female and 62 male inmates in Kentucky prisons.

E.0469 Kolman, Anita Sue (1983, Autumn/Winter). Support and control patterns of inmate mothers: A pilot study. *The Prison Journal, 63*(2), 155-166. Examines mother-child interactions in three types of correctional settings.

E.0470 Koppel, Sheree (1987). *Assessing vocational needs in a female correctional institution.* Paper presented at the Annual Meeting of the American Educational Research Association, Washington, DC, April 20-24, 1987. Results of a study to determine female inmates' occupational aspirations and educational needs.

E.0471 Kratcoski, P., & Scheuerman, K. (1974, Spring). Incarcerated male and female offenders perceptions of their experiences in the criminal justice system. *Journal of Criminal Justice, 2*(1), 73-78. Compared institutionalized females and males convicted of a criminal offenses.

E.0472 Krause, F. H., et al. (1972, Winter). An itinerate psychological services program in a women's prison. *Correctional Psychologist, 5*(3), 171-177. Looks at psychological services for incarcerated women.

E.0473 Kreft, Katherine, & Brittain, Thomas (1983). A prisoner assessment survey: Screenings of a municipal prison population. *International Journal of Law & Psychiatry, 6*(1), 113-124. Study included 122 female prisoners screened to determine service needs.

E.0474 Kremer, Gary (1990, April). Strangers to domestic virtues: Nineteenth-century women in the Missouri prison. *Missouri Historical Review, 84*(3), 293-310. Examines the position of women convicts in Missouri after 1830.

E.0475 Kromm, Jane, et al. (1982, Summer). Occupational therapy in the assessment of a woman accused of murder. *Psychiatric Quarterly, 54*(2), 85-96. Case of a 17-yr.-old female. Author illustrates ways in which occupational therapy offers advantages for evaluation.

E.0476 Kropova, Olga (1990, July). Life behind bars: The Soviet perspective. *Corrections Today, 52*(4), 133-234, 136-137. Views a minimum security women's reformatory for first offenders in southern Russia. Most women were serving time for theft, drug trafficking, or murder.

E.0477 Kruttschnitt, Candace (1981). Prison codes, inmate solidarity, and women: A reexamination. In Warren (Ed.), *Comparing female and male offenders.* Newbury Park, CA: Sage Publications.

E.0478 Kruttschnitt, Candace, & Krmpotich, S. (1990, January). Aggressive behavior among female inmates: An exploratory study. *Justice Quarterly, 7*(2), 371-389. Study of violence in a women's correctional facility.

E.0479 Kurshan, Nancy (1992). Women and imprisonment in the U.S.: History and current reality. In W. Churchill & J. Vander Wall (Eds.), *Cages of steel: The Politics of imprisonment in the US* (pp. 331-357). Washington, DC: Maisonneuve Press. Discusses the imprisonment of women against the backdrop of patriarchal relationships.

E.0480 LaChance-McCullough, Malcolm, et al. (1994). HIV infections among New York state female inmates: Preliminary results of a voluntary counseling and testing program. *Prison Journal, 74*(2), 198-219. Explores HIV infection among female inmates. Data collected from records of 216 voluntary participants.

E.0481 Ladu, Lena, & Garrison, K. C. (1931, December). Study of emotional instability and intelligence of women in the penal institutions of North Carolina. *Social Forces, 10,* 209-216. Early study of mental health of incarcerated women.

E.0482 Lamb, H. R., et al. (1983). Mentally ill women in a county jail. *Archives of General Psychiatry, 40*(4), 363-368. Looks at mental illness in a population of women in jail.

E.0483 Larson, James, & Nelson, Joey (1984). Women, friendship, and adaptation to prison. *Journal of Criminal Justice, 12*(6), 601-615. Application of Thomas & Peterson's (1977) prisonization model expanded to include friendship. Data collected from 121 incarcerated women.

E.0484 Launay, Giles, & Slade, Peter (1981). The measurement of hallucinatory predisposition in male and female prisoners. *Personality and Individual Differences, 2*(3), 221-234. Describes the development of the Hallucinatory Predisposition Scale and its uses.

E.0485 Lavin, John (1977). Changing lives. *Change, 9*(12), 49-50. Discusses a program in Michigan for female inmates training as nurse-attendants and teachers' aides in special education.

E.0486 Lawson, T. L., & Fawkes, L. S. (1992, Spring). HIV, AIDS, and the female offender. *Federal Prisons Journal: Focus on the Female Offender 3*(1), 27-32. Discusses AIDS and related issues in correctional facilities for women.

E.0487 Lechich, M. L. (1984, October-November). Health education in a women's prison. *Health Education, 15*(6), 34-36. Discusses health education for incarcerated women.

E.0488 Le Flore, Larry, & Holston, Mary Ann (1989). Perceived importance of parenting behaviors as reported by inmate mothers: An exploratory study. *Journal of Offender Counseling, Services and Rehabilitation, 14*(1), 5-22. Compared inmate mothers' attitudes about parenting behaviors with those of non-inmate mothers.

E.0489 Legal Services for Prisoners with Children Publications (1991, Fall). *Pregnant women in California prisons and jails: A guide for prisoners and legal advocates.* San Francisco, CA: Legal Services for Prisoners with Children. A booklet addressing legal and practical concerns of incarcerated women in the perinatal period.

E.0490 Leger, R. G. (1987, December). Lesbianism among women prisoners: Participants and nonparticipants. *Criminal Justice and Behavior, 14*(4), 448-467. Identifies factors related to lesbianism in women's prisons using the importation-deprivation debate.

E.0491 Lehtinen, M. W. (1977, Fall). Women's corrections: Problems and future prospects. *Quarterly Journal of Corrections, 1*(4), 34-39. Considers factors contributing to the lack of attention to women's corrections and problems caused by this lack of attention.

E.0492 Lekkerkerker, E. C. (1931). *Reformatories for women in the US.* Gronigen: J.B. Wolters. Early empirical research on women's prisons.

E.0493 Lennon, Anne (1993, Spring). Infants in prison: A study of the health status of babies incarcerated with their mothers at a maximum security correctional facility. *Masters Abstracts International, 31*(1), 300. Describes health status of infants incarcerated with their mothers at a New York State maximum security correctional facility. Sample includes 116 infants.

E.0494 Levy, B. (1978). Art therapy in a women's correctional facility. *Art Psychotherapy, 5*(3), 157-166. Describes an art therapy program at a correctional institute for women in Kentucky. Looks at 9 sessions with one group of 10 female inmates (20-32 yrs. old) in detail.

E.0495 Lewis, Diane, & Bresler, Laura (1981). *Is there a way out? A community study of women in the San Francisco jail.* Boston, MA: Unitarian Universalist Service Committee. Investigates service programs available to female offenders in jail and in the community.

E.0496 Lewis, E. B. (1974). The Georgia female inmate - who is she? *Georgia Journal of Correction, 3*(2), 74-79. Profile of women incarcerated in Georgia.

E.0497 Liebling, Alison (1994, February1). Suicide amongst women prisoners. *Howard Journal of Criminal Justice, 33*(1), 1- 9. Discusses women's vulnerability in prison. 1972-1992 data from English and Welsh prisons shows the rate of suicide among female prisoners is underestimated.

E.0498 Lindquist, Charles (1980, Summer). Prison discipline and the female offender. *Journal of Offender Counseling, Services and Rehabilitation, 4*(4), 305-318. Compared backgrounds and sanctions received for one female and one male incarcerated population.

E.0499 Lindquist, Charles (1978). *Disciplinary offense patterns of male and female inmates.* Tallahassee, FL: Florida State University Center for Professional Development. Looked at disciplinary offenses and offenses for which prisoners were incarcerated.

E.0500 Literacy Volunteers of New York City (1992). *Bars coming near: An anthology by men and women new writers in prison.* New York, NY: Literacy Volunteers of New York City. Writings of incarcerated males and females.

E.0501 Lockwood, K. (1980). Mothers as criminals. *Women's Law Review, 9*, 78-86. Looks at the crimes women commit and the consequences of incarcerating mothers.

E.0502 Logan, Gloria (1992, August). In Topeka: Family ties take top priority in women's visiting program. *Corrections Today, 54*(6), 160-162. Information about the Women's Activites and Learning Center for female offenders and their families.

E.0503 Lombardi, N. J. (1979). The absence of suicide in New York City's Women's House of Detention. *Dissertation Abstracts International, 40*(11), 5411. Study of suicide amongst incarcerated women.

E.0504 Lorant, L. (1983). *Women in jail: A description of the awaiting trial unit at the Massachusetts Correctional Institution at Framingham.* Boston, MA: Massachusetts DOC. Analyzes population movement of women at the Awaiting Trial Unit (ATU) at MCI Framingham.

E.0505 Lorimer, Anne, & Heads, M. (1962, December). The significance of morale in a female penal institution. *Federal Probation, 26*, 38-44. Discusses morale among incarcerated women.

E.0506 Lory, Marie Loretta (1985, July). Women and the criminal justice system: A study of women offenders involvement with the criminal justice system. *Dissertation Abstracts International, 46*(1), 347. Explores the relationship among societal attitudes, social structures, and women offenders.

E.0507 Lowe, P., & Stewart, C. (1983). Women in prison. In S. Spence & B. Shepherd (Eds.), *Developments in social skills training.* New York, NY: Academic Press. Discusses programs in social skills for incarcerated women.

E.0508 Lundstrom, Francesca (1988, December). The affective responses of women prisoners to two discrepant penal systems. *Criminal Justice and Behavior, 15*(4), 411-432. Contrasts a retributive justice system (Irish) with a rehabilitative system (Swedish).

E.0509 MacKenzie, Doris, et al. (1995). Long-term incarceration of female offenders: Prison adjustment and coping. In T. J. Flanagan (Ed.), *Long-term imprisonment: Policy, science, and correctional practice* (pp. 128-137). Thousand Oaks, CA: Sage Publications. Discusses long term offenders in Louisiana.

E.0510 MacKenzie, Doris, et al. (1989, June). Long-term incarceration of female offenders: Prison adjustment and coping. *Criminal Justice and Behavior, 16*(2), 223-238. Data from 141 female offenders, serving short and long-term sentences in Louisiana.

E.0511 MacLeod, L. (1986). *Sentenced to separation: An exploration of the needs and problems of mothers who are offenders and their children.* Ontario, Canada: Canadian Solicitor General. Discusses policies and practices of criminal justice personnel and service agencies with female offenders that inhibit the development of mother-child relationships.

E.0512 MacMillan, Jane, & Baldwin, Steve (1993, July). A pilot study of an alcohol educatior course for young women offenders: What's good for the goose? *Alcohol and Alcoholism, 28*(4), 499-504. Tested the relevance of a course in alcohol education in treating women offenders.

E.0513 Madden, Allison, et al. (1994, Spring). A criminological and psychiatric survey of women serving a prison sentence. *British Journal of Criminology, 34*(2), 172-191. Uses case notes and interviews of women serving prison sentences in England and Wales.

E.0514 Magura, Stephen, et al. (1993, October). HIV risk among women injecting drug users who are in jail. *Addiction, 88*(10), 1351-1360. Examined women's patterns of HIV risk behaviors related to drugs and sex and identified behavioral and attitudinal correlates of HIV serostatus.

E.0515 Mahan, Edna (1944, March/April). The woman offender today: Reflections on institutional discipline. *The Prison World, 6*(2), 14, 30. Discusses the use discipline to educate incarcerated women. Focuses on training programs in women's institutions.

E.0516 Mahan, Sue (1984, September). Imposition of despair: An ethnography of women in prison. *Justice Quarterly, 1*(3), 357-383. An ethnographic study of observations and interviews at two minimum-security prisons for women in New Mexico in light of Hall's culture theory.

E.0517 Mahan, Sue (1982). *Unfit mothers.* Palo Alto, CA: R. & E. Research Associates. Discusses the legal status of incarcerated mothers.

E.0518 Mahan, Sue (1980, November). The women's honor unity: Case study of a women's prison. *Dissertation Abstracts International, 41*(5), 2305. Study of eleven female inmates at the Women's Honor Unit of the New Mexico State Department of Corrections in Albuquerque.

E.0519 Mandaraka-Sheppard, Alexandra (1986). *The dynamics of aggression in women's prisons in England.* Brookfield, VT: Gower. Data gathered from a self-report misbehavior questionnaire to a stratified sample of 334 female inmates of 6 British prisons.

E.0520 Mandel, N. G., & Vinnes, H. B. (1968). *Effects of short-term group psychotherapy on the intra institutional behavior of female felons.* St. Paul, MN: Minnesota Department of Corrections. Discusses the use of group therapy in a women's prison.

E.0521 Mane, K. V. (1972, June). Volunteering behavior and personality characteristics of women prisoners. *Dissertation Abstracts International, 32*(12-B). 7293-7294. Looks at volunteering amongst women prisoners. Who volunteers and why.

E.0522 Marcus, David, & Bibace, Roger (1993, September). A developmental analysis of female prisoners' conceptions of AIDS. *Criminal Justice and Behavior, 20*(3), 240-253. Reviews female prisoners ideas about causes and transmission of AIDS in two womens prisons in Texas.

E.0523 Martin, J. W., & Much, D. H. (1988, April). Sexually transmitted diseases in a prison for women. *Pathology and Medicine, 91*(4), 40-42. Discusses the health of women prisoners and sexually transmitted diseases.

E.0524 Martin, Ronald, et al. (1979). The evaluation of diagnostic concordance in follow-up studies: II. A blind perspective follow-up of female criminals. *Journal of Psychiatric Research, 15*(2), 107-125. Reports on diagnostic concordance in a blind six year follow-up of 66 female felons.

E.0525 Masci, David (1993, July 3). Harris an advocate for prison moms. *Congressional Quarterly, 51*, 1747. Report on advocacy by Jean Harris for mothers in prison.

E.0526 Massachusetts Department of Corrections (1988). *Female offenders advisory group report.* Boston, MA: Massachusetts Department of Corrections. Examined the needs of female inmates at MCI Framingham and recommended improvements. Data collected from interviews.

E.0527 Mawby, R. I. (1982, January). Women in prison: A British study. *Crime and Delinquency, 28*(1), 24-39. Data collected from responses of 27 female inmates of Askham Grange, a British open prison. Similarities between female inmates in U.S. and Great Britain are noted.

E.0528 Maxey, J. W. (1986, April). Designing a women's prison. *Corrections Today, 48*(2), 140-142. Discusses future designing of women's prisons.

E.0529 McBurney, Kathleen (1989). *Women in prison: A survey of nutrition-related health problems as perceived by female inmates and ex-offenders.* Dissertation, University of California at Berkeley. Describes health problems among incarcerated women and women in community-based reentry programs. Data collected at Pleasanton, California, and Alderson, West Virginia.

E.0530 McCall, Carol, et al. (1985). *Pregnancy in prison: A needs assessment of perinatal outcome in three California penal institutions.* Oakland, CA: Prison MATCH. Looks at programs in California for pregnant inmates.

E.0531 McCall, Carol (1972, April). An investigation of language deficiency in a female prison population. *Dissertation Abstracts International, 32*(10-B), 6101. Study of language abilities of a women's prison population.

E.0532 McCalley-Whitters, Mona (1989). *Subtypes of sociopaths in male and female inmates.* Dissertation, University of Iowa, Iowa City, Iowa. Investigated whether two distinct subtypes of Antisocial Personality Disorder inmates existed in a sample of female and male felons.

E.0533 McCarthy, Belinda (1980, Spring). Inmate mothers: The problems of separation and reintegration. *Journal of Offender Counseling, Services, and Rehabilitation, 4*(3), 199-212. Looks at inmate mothers problems of separation. Discusses the effects of home visit programs.

E.0534 McClain, Mildred (1983, December). Educational achievement in prison schools among black women. *Dissertation Abstracts International, 44*(6), 1934. Discusses relationships and resources which positively impact academic achievement in the prison environment. Focuses on black female offenders at MCI Framingham in Massachusetts.

E.0535 McCraner, Alana (1990, Spring). Women and HIV/AIDS. *Prison Service Journal, 78*, 17-19.

E.0536 McCubbin, Elizabeth (1967). The something different at one women's prison. *Journal of Social Work Process, 16*, 89-106. Interviews with women prisoners pointed to concerns about their crime and punishment, loved ones, and not being able to adjust to prison.

E.0537 McGaha, G. S. (1987, Fall-Winter). Health care issues of incarcerated women. *Journal of Offender Counseling Services and Rehabilitation, 12*,(2), 53-59. Looks at gynecological services, health education, and services related to childbearing and parenting for incarcerated women.

E.0538 McGowan, Brenda, & Blumenthal, Karen (1978). *Why punish the children? A study of children of women prisoners.* Hackensack, NJ: National Council on Crime and Delinquency. Discusses effects of mother's imprisonment on children.

E.0539 McGowan , B., & Blumenthal, K. (1976). Children of women prisoners: A forgotten minority. In Laura Crites (Ed.), *The female offender* (pp. 121-135). Lexington, MA: Lexington Books. Discusses what happens to the children of incarcerated women.

E.0540 McGurk, B. J., et al. (1987). The vocational interests of female prisoners. In B. J. McGurk et al. (Eds.), *Applying psychology to imprisonment: Theory and practice* (pp. 393-410). London, England: HM Stationery Office Books. Research on vocational interests of female prisoners.

E.0541 McGurrin, Mary Catherine (1993, Winter). Pregnant inmates' right to health care. *New England Journal on Criminal and Civil Confinement, 20,* 163-194. Discusses health care programs and the lack of programs for pregnant incarcerated women.

E.0542 McHugh, Gerald (1980). Protection of the rights of pregnant women in prisons and detention facilities. *New England Journal on Prison Law, 6*(2), 231-263. Discusses the legal rights of the pregnant female offender to medical care and abuses such as coercion by prison officials to abort.

E.0543 McKinney, J. D. (1994, March). *Impact of social learning experiences on adult female inmates.* Paper presented at the 1994 ACJS Annual Meeting, Chicago, IL. Discusses the impact of social learning experiences on the behavior of female inmates.

E.0544 McRandle, C. D., & Goldstein, R. (1986, December). Hearing loss in two prison populations. *Journal of Correctional Education, 37*(4), 147-155. Conclusions of screening of inmates by pure-tone audiometry and by acoustic commitance procedures. Twenty female inmates included.

E.0545 Meadow, Mary Jo (1982, April). Value issues in counseling women: Pt. 2. *Counseling and Values, 26*(3), 154-179. Describes the mother-daughter relationship of women offenders and the use of counseling techniques.

E.0546 Mebane, Bette (1977, May). Differential life history factors among incarcerated female offenders. *Dissertation Abstracts International, 37*(11-B), 5836-5837. Study on life histories of female inmates.

E.0547 Metzler, Donna (1994, August). Neglected by the system: Children of incarcerated mothers. *Illinois Bar Journal, 82,* 428-432. Looks at the children of incarcerated women.

E.0548 Meyer, Doreen (1992, Winter). A prison of their own: The contradictions behind Canada's prison for women. *Masters Abstracts International, 31*(4), 1597. Examines women and crime in Canada and the debate around closing Canada's only Prison for Women, P4W.

E.0549 Michigan Women's Commission (1993, July). *Unheard voices: A report on women in Michigan county jails.* Lansing, MI: Michigan Women's Commission. Discusses women incarcerated in Michigan for non-violent offenses and economically motivated crimes and reports by female inmates of being sexually harassed or assaulted by male correctional officers.

E.0550 Miller, Marsha (1990). *Perceptions of available and needed programs by female offenders in Delaware*: Wilmington, DE: Delaware Council on Crime and Justice.

E.0551 Miller, W. G., & Hannum, T. E. (1963). Characteristics of homosexually involved incarcerated females. *Journal of Consulting Psychology, 27*(3), 277. Looks at homosexuality and its characteristics in incarcerated women.

E.0552 Miller-Ashton, Jane (1993). Canada's new federal system for female offenders. In ACA *Female offenders: Meeting needs of a neglected population* (pp. 105-111). Laurel, MD: American Correctional Association. Report on federally sentenced women in Canada.

E.0553 Miller-Ashton, Jane (1992, Spring). Canada's female offenders: New options in the federal system. *Federal Prisons Journal Special Issue: Focus on the Female Offender*, 63-83. Study of women incarcerated in Canada.

E.0554 Mills, R., & Barrett, H. (1990, September-October). Meeting the special challenge of providing health care to women inmates in the 90's. *American Jails, 4*, 55-57. Looks at health care for incarcerated women, existing programs and needs.

E.0555 Milstei, F. (1971). Special problems in treating female offenders: Clarifying the patients sense of identity. *International Journal of Offender Therapy, 15*, 16-20. Discusses treatment problems with women prisoners.

E.0556 Milton, Catherine (1976). *Female offenders: Problems and programs.* Washington, DC: American Bar Association. Looks at programs for female offenders.

E.0557 Minnesota Department of Corrections (1979). *Institutional placement of the woman offender, 1979 legislative report.* St. Paul, MN: Minnesota Department of Corrections. Comprehensive study of correctional facilities for female offenders in Minnesota.

E.0558 Misch, C., et al. (1982). *National survey concerning female inmates in provincial and territorial institutions.* Ottawa: Canadian Association of Elizabeth Fry Societies. Results of a survey of Canadian institutions housing female inmates.

E.0559 Mitchell, Arlene (1975). *Informal inmate social structures in prisons for women: A comparative study.* San Francisco, CA: R. & E. Associates. Looks at relationships among inmates in women's prisons.

E.0560 Mitchell, M. P. (1982). *A study of children of women prisoners.* Dissertation, Emory University. Looks at the effects of maternal incarceration on children.

E.0561 Moffat, Kelly (1991). Creating choices or repeating history: Canadian female offenders and correctional reform. *Social Justice, 18*(3), 184-203. Looks at the treatment of women prisoners in Canada.

E.0562 Mogal, D. P. (1969). A research project in teaching in a women's prison. *Community Mental Health Journal* (Qunicy, MA), *5*(3), 247-255. Discusses a project at the House of Detention for Women in New York City. Explored teaching commercial subjects to female inmates.

E.0563 Montague, Mary Ella (1963). Women prisoners respond to contemporary dance. *Journal of Health, Physical Education, Recreation, 34*(3), 25-26, 74. Discusses the use of dance with women prisoners.

E.0564 Moore, J. Z., et al. (1988, Fall/Winter). Health locus of control of female inmates from the Virginia Correctional Center for Women measured by the multidimensional Health Locus of Control Scale. *Journal of Prison and Jail Health, 7*(2), 98-108. Data from 161 female inmates of the Virginia Correctional Center for women.

E.0565 Morales, Richard (1981, May). History of the California Institution for Women, 1927-1960. *Dissertation Abstracts International, 41*(11), 4814. Considers women reformers who helped change attitudes on sex roles. Also presents institutional history.

E.0566 Morgan, A. M. (1964). Women in preventive detention. *Prison Service Journal (Wakefield, England), 4*(13), 11-25. Discusses women in Holloway prison.

E.0567 Morris, Allison, & Wilkinson, Christine (1988, March). *Women and the penal system: Papers presented to the 19th Cropwood Round-Table Conference.* Cambridge, UK: Institute of Criminology. Anthology of papers dealing with various topics on female inmate populations, women in Holloway prison, and penal policy and practices for women.

E.0568 Morris, Ruth (1987). Women in prison. *Canadian Dimension, 20*(8), 10-12. Examines lives of women prisoners in Canada through a review of the experiences of Bettina Harris.

E.0569 Moses, Marilyn (1995, October). Keeping incarcerated mothers and their daughters together: Girl Scouts beyond Bars. *National Institute of Justice Journal.* Discusses the scouting program for mothers and daughters at the Maryland Correctional Institution for Women.

E.0570 Moses, Marilyn (1993, August). Girls Scouts behind bars: New program at women's prison benefits mothers and children. *Corrections Today, 55*(5), 132-135. Looks at a scout program in a women's prison for incarcerated mothers and their daughters.

E.0571 Morton, Joann (1992). The older offender. In ACA *Female offenders: Meeting the needs of a neglected population* (pp. 80-84). Laurel, MD: American Correctional Association. Describes physical and mental problems of older incarcerated women.

E.0572 Morton, Joann (1992, Spring). The older female offender: Suggestions for correctional policymakers. *Federal Prisons Journal Special Issue: Focus on the Female Offender, 3*(1), 11-14. Looks at aging in the female inmate population.

E.0573 Moss, Etta (1986, Summer/Fall). Women in prison: A case of pervasive neglect. *Women and Therapy: A Feminist Quarterly, 5*(2-3), 177-185. Discusses the lack of programs for the physical and mental health of incarcerated women.

E.0574 Moyer, Imogene (1984). Deceptions and realities of life in women's prisons. *Prison Journal, 54,* 45-56. Looks at the realities of women's incarceration.

E.0575 Moyer, Imogene (1980). Leadership in a women's prison. *Journal of Criminal Justice, 8,* 233-241. A study of social interaction in a southeastern correctional institution for women.

E.0576 Moyer, Imogene (1978). Differential social structures and homosexuality among women in prison. *Virginia Social Science Journal, 13,* 13-19. Looks at relationships and social structures in women's prisons.

E.0577 Moyses, C. D. (1982). *The effects of three treatment approaches on locus of control of incarcerated females.* Dissertation, Auburn University. Looks at treatment programs for incarcerated women.

E.0578 Muller, Rachel (1991). Social constructs of AIDS and prostitution: A descriptive study among women in jail. *Masters Abstracts International, 29*(2), 266. Explores understanding of prostitution and AIDS with twenty-three incarcerated women.

E.0579 Munger, Elizabeth (1941, July). Passing reflections: Problems encountered in dealing with the female prisoner. *Prison World, 3,* 13-16. Looks at early treatment programs for female inmates.

E.0580 Musk, H. A. (1982). Programs for incarcerated women and their children: Psychodynamic considerations and implications. *Dissertation Abstracts International, 42*(8), 3460. Looks at programs for incarcerated women and their children.

E.0581 Myles-Nixon, Charlotte (1994, April). An assessment of the potential effectiveness of an educational program for incarcerated females in maximum security prisons who have low adaptability levels and who are intellectually challenged. *Dissertation Abstracts International, 54*(10), 3901. Study conducted in 1993.

E.0582 National Review of Criminal Science (1959, November). Women convicts in Egypt, UAR.: A statistical analytical study. *National Review of Criminal Science* (Cairo), *2*, 305-437. Discusses women prisoners in Egypt (1951).

E.0583 Nesbitt, C. A. (1988). Creativity in programming for female offenders: In E. Watts (Ed.), *One hundred and seventeenth Annual Congress of Correction of the American Correctional Association Proceedings* (pp. 39-76). Laurel, MD: American Correctional Association. Discusses innovative programs for female inmates in telemarketing and mass mailings.

E.0584 Neto, V. V., & Bainer, L. M. (1983). Mother and wife locked up: A day with the family. *Prison Journal, 63*(2), 125-141. Examined visiting practices in women's institutions including extended daytime and overnight visits with families. Data collected in 1980.

E.0585 Neto, V. V. (1981). Expanding horizons: Work and training for female offenders. *Corrections Today, 43*, 66-72. Looks at training programs for incarcerated female offenders.

E.0586 New York State Department of Corrections (1990). *Review of Department of Correctional Services research on female commitments.* Albany, NY: New York State Department of Corrections. Reports on characteristics of female inmates in New York State.

E.0587 New Zealand Ministerial Committee of Inquiry into the Prison System (1989). Women in prisons. In *Prison review-Te ara hou: The new way* (pp. 151-171). Wellington, New Zealand: New Zealand Ministerial Committee of Inquiry into the Prisons System. Discusses issues concerning women in prison including the rights of children in regards to incarcerated parents.

E.0588 Nicholls, Delia (1987, Summer). Mothers in prison. *Barrister, 14*, 14-18. Discusses the rights of incarcerated mothers.

E.0589 Nickell, Eugenie, et al. (1989, December). Decreasing speech anxiety of female prisoners. *Psychological Reports, 65*(3, Pt. 2), 1351-1357. Looks at treatment porgrams for decreasing speech anxiety in female inmates.

E.0590 Norris, Linda (1974, February). Comparison of two groups in a southern state women's prison: Homosexual Behavior vs. non-homosexual behavior. *Psychological Reports, 34*(1), 75-78. Estimates the incidence of homosexual behavior in one southern state women's prison.

E.0591 North Carolina Central Law Journal. (1981, Spring). Women, prison, and the eighth amendment. *North Carolina Central Law Journal, 12*, 434-460. Looks at the legal rights of incarcerated women.

E.0592 North, Jeanne, & Annis, William (1994, March). New Hampsire's state-sentenced female offender. *Journal of Correctional Education, 45*(1), 38-47. Analysis of records of 168 female offenders in New Hampshire prisons.

E.0593 Norton, Lee, et al. (1987). *Improving vocational programs for female inmates: A comprehensive approach to quality programs.* Columbus, Ohio: Ohio State University. Guidelines for corrections administrators in improving quality and quantity of programs.

E.0594 Novak, Kathy, & Harris, Ruth (1978). *Orientation to health aide careers mini-course & sanitarian aide course for female prisoners.* Blacksburg, VA: Virginia Polytechnic Institute. Curriculum guide for teachers of women offenders. Contains outlines on six topics.

E.0595 Nova Scotia Department of the Attorney General (1977). *The female offender, Nova Scotia and New Brunswick.* Halifax, Nova Scotia: Department of the Attorney General. Statistical profile of women inmates in Novia Scotia.

E.0596 O'Connor, Art, & O'Neill, Helen (1991, September). Female prison transfers to the Central Mental Hospital: A special hospital. *Irish Journal of Psychological Medicine, 8*(2), 122-123. Data on 99 female prison transfers to the Central Mental Hospital in Ireland 1983-1988.

E.0597 O' Dwyer, J., et al. (1987). Women's imprisonment in England, Wales, and Scotland: Recurring issues. In P. Carlen & A. Worrall (Eds.), *Gender, crime, and justice* (pp. 176-190). London: Milton Keynes, Open University Press. Focuses on harassment in women's prisons.

E.0598 O'Dwyer, J., & Carlen, Pat (1985). Surviving Holloway and other women's prisons. In P. Carlen (Ed.), *Criminal women.* Cambridge, England: Polity. Presents life at Holloway Prison.

E.0599 O'Leary, Margaret, & Weinhouse, D. (1992, August). A class act: Colorado facility helps women overcome barriers to education. *Corrections Today, 54,* 194+. Looks at an educational program in a Colorado facility for women.

E.0600 O'Malley, E. P., & Bluestone, H. (1965). Trials and tribultations in conducting a drug study in a women's prison. *Psychosomatics, 6*(2), 95-99. Discusses difficulties of studying addiction with a population of women prisoners.

E.0601 One America Inc. (1980). A *descriptive study of vocational education programs in nine state correctional institutions for women.* Washington, DC: One America, Inc. Assessment of vocational needs and aspirations of 390 incarcerated women.

E.0602 O'Reilly, C., et al. (1968). Sentenced women in a county jail. *American Journal of Corrections, 30*(2), 23-25. Discusses treatment of women in county jails.

E.0603 Orlick, T. D. (1978). *Sport and the inmates dilemma: Time to kill or time to live.* Paper presented at the Annual Conference of the North American Society for the Psychology of Sport and Physical Activity, Tallahassee, Florida, May 21-24, 1978. Results of interviews with female and male inmates to determine role of sports in their prison lives.

E.0604 Ousterhout, Ann (1994). *Women in prison: Can they establish goals?* Paper presented at the Academy of Criminal Justice Sciences Annual Meeting, March 8-12, 1994, Chicago, IL. Describes a program at the Oregon prison for women for goal setting through group identity, common activites and group counseling.

E.0605 Owen, Barbara, & Bloom, Barbara (1994, March). *Women prisoners: Their lives prior to incarceration.* Paper presented at the 1994 ACJS Annual Meeting, Chicago, IL. Information on life experiences of women before incarceration. Data collected from 297 women inmates.

E.0606 Owens, Laura (1983, April). That's no granny: That's the warden. *Corrections Today, 45,* 90-91. Looks at the female warden of one women's prison.

E.0607 Oxley, Deborah (1993, December). Convict maids. *Dissertation Abstracts International, 54*(6), 2268. Describes convict women transported from Britain to New South Wales.

E.0608 Padel, Una, & Stevenson, P. (1988). *Insiders: Women's experience of prison.* London: Virago. Description of life in a women's prison.

E.0609 Padilla, Felix, & Santiago, Lourdes (1993). *Outside the wall: A Puerto Rican woman's struggle.* New Brunswick, NJ: Rutgers University Press. One woman discusses the experience of incarceration.

E.0610 Page, Richard, & Sanders, J. J. (1979). Some characteristics of imprisoned female drug abusers and implications for rehabilitation. *Rehabilitation Counseling Bulletin, 23*(1), 59-62. Investigated the need for counseling services among imprisoned female drug users.

E.0611 Page, Richard, & Kubiak, L. (1978, August). Marathon groups: Facilitating the personal growth of imprisoned black female heroin abusers. *Small Group Behavior, 9*(3), 409-416. Data collected from 22 black female heroin addicts incarcerated in Florida.

E.0612 Palmer, Richard (1972). The prisoner mother and her child. *Capital University Law Review, 1*, 127-144. Looks at legal status of incarcerated mothers and the determination of parental rights.

E.0613 Panagopoulos, Jennifer (1980, December). A study of a Greek prison for women offenders. *Dissertation Abstracts International, 41*(6), 2795. Compares attitudes of female inmates to attitudes of prison custodial staff at Korydullo, the only prison for women offenders in Greece.

E.0614 Panton, James, & Kiefer, Stephan (1980). Development of an MMPI index to predict acting-out hostility among female inmates within an institutionalized population. *Research and Communications in Psychology, Psychiatry and Behavior, 5*(3), 323-333. Data collected from MMPI profile of 25 acting-out hostile and 40 non-acting-out female prison inmates.

E.0615 Patterson, Richard (1992). *An examination of the demographic and personality characteristics of Wyoming female penitentiary inmates.* Dissertation, University of Wyoming. Study of women incarcerated in Wyoming.

E.0616 Paul, Gail (1992, Spring). Women's spirituality in prison. *Federal Prisons Journal Special Issue: Focus on the Female Offender,* 3(1), 40-43. Discusses spirituality in its broad sense, i.e., not just a relationship with a God, but also with others and with oneself.

E.0617 Pearson, A. (1971, May). Education in the new Holloway prison for women. *Adult Education* (Great Britain), *44*(1), 33-36. Looks at educational programs for women prisoners in England.

E.0618 Pearson, Jennifer (1994, April). *The gentle hand of Mexico's family based corrections: 1965-1968.* Dissertation, University of California, Berkeley. Field study of a prison for women in Mexico City where the female inmates family is incorporated into the correctional process.

E.0619 Pearson, Jennifer (1993, Fall) Centro Femenil: A women's prison in Mexico. *Social Justice, 20*(3-4), 85-128. Discusses a facility for women where penal treatment is based on cultural and social values that seek to strengthen the familial, communal, and cultural traditions

E.0620 Pelka-Slugocka, M., & Slugocka, L. (1980, December). The impact of imprisonment on the family life of women convicts. *International Journal of Offender Therapy and Comparative Criminology, 24*(3), 249-259. Data collected from 320 female inmates in a Polish prison who completed professional training 1963-1966. Similar follow-up-research 1974-1976.

E.0621 Pendergrass, Virginia (1975). Innovative programs for women in jails and prisons. In A. Brodsky (Ed.), *The female offender* (pp. 67-76). Newbury Park, CA: Sage Publications. Looks at programs for women incarcerated in jails and prisons.

E.0622 Pendergrass, Virginia (1974, December). Innovative programs for women in jail and prisons: Trick or treatment? *Criminal Justice and Behavior, 1*(40), 350-368. Reports on programs instituted in 1972 at the Dade County, Florida, Detention Center for Women.

E.0623 Perry, Mary Elizabeth (1990). With brave vigilance and a hundred eyes: The making of women's prisons in counter-reformation Spain. *Women and Criminal Justice, 2*(1), 3-17. Historical overview of women's prisons in Spain.

E.0624 Perry, Wingfield (1973, Fall). The forgotten victim: An exclusive report on the families of prisoners. *Mental Health, 57*(4), 10-14. Discusses impact of incarceration on families of both female and male prisoners. Perspectives of prisoners family members and correctional officers.

E.0625 Petersen, A. M. (1922-1923). The administrative problems of a women's reformatory. *Journal of the American Institute of Criminal Law and Criminology, 13*, 438-445. Early essay on adminstration of a women's reformatory.

E.0626 Peterson, Michael, & Johnstone, Bryan (1995, January-February). The Atwood Hall health promotion program, Federal Medical Center, Lexington, KY: Effects on drug-involved federal offenders. *Journal of Substance Abuse Treatment, 12*(1), 43-48. Discusses a residential drug treatment program and 43 female offenders who volunteered to participate.

E.0627 Peterson, Thomas, et al. (1985, September). A comparison of two social interest measures with female convicts. *Individual Psychology Journal of Adlerian Theory, Research and Practice, 41*(3), 349-353. Data collected from 36 female inmates (19-55 yrs. old) and 36 female university employees (19-64 yrs. old).

E.0628 Pfouts, J., & Meyer, Q. (1961, March/April). Examination of a sample of inmates in a southern women's prison. *American Journal of Corrections, 23*, 7-12. Profile of female inmates.

E.0629 Phillip, E. (1988, August). Pregnancy in women prisoners. *British Journal of Hospital Medicine, 40*(2), 150+. Discusses programs for pregnant inmates.

E.0630 Phillip, E. (1987, January). Gynecology in prison. *British Journal of Clinical Practice, 41*(1), 549-552. Looks at the health care of pregnant inmates.

E.0631 Picton, W., & Picton, H. (1931). The women's prison in Berlin. *Howard Journal of Criminal Justice, 3*, 77-79. Early study of a women's prison in Germany.

E.0632 Pierce, F. J. (1963). Social group work in a women's prison. *Federal Probation, 27*(4), 37-43. Looks at group work in a prison for women.

E.0633 Pollack, Shoshana (1994, Fall). Opening the window on a very dark day: A program evaluation of the peer support team at the Kingston Prison for women. *Masters Abstracts International, 32*(3), 859. Interviews with twelve female inmates trained as peer counselors.

E.0634 Pollock-Byrne, Joycelyn (1990). *Women, prison, and crime.* Pacific Grove, CA: Brooks Cole Publishing Co. Comprehensive look at women imprisoned in the United States. Discusses treatment of women inmates, correctional staff, and legal issues confronting women inmates.

E.0635 Pollock-Byrne, Joycelyn (1984, March). Women will be women: Correctional officers perceptions of the emotionality of women inmates. *The Prison Journal, 64*(1), 84-91. Looks at correctional officers perceptions of women prisoners and their emotions.

E.0636 Potter, Cathy (1985). *Neglected population: Women prisoners at Bayview.* New York, NY: Correctional Association of New York. Assesses treament of women the New York state correctional system during 1983-1984.

E.0637 Potter, Ellen (1977, Fall). The problems of women in penal and correctional institutions. *Quarterly Journal of Corrections, 1*(4), 9-14. Originally published in 1934, this article describes problems of imprisoned women in the 1920s and early 1930s.

E.0638 Potter, Ellen (1931, April). How shall we plan for children of unmarried mothers in correctional institutions? *Hospital Social Services, 23*, 403-412. Early essay on incarcerated women.

E.0639 Potter, Joan (1979, September). Women in prison. *Prison Law Monitor, 2*(73), 96-97. Looks at women in prison.

E.0640 Potter, Joan (1978, December). In prison, women are different: The number of female prisoners has increased. *Corrections Today, 4*, 14-24. Looks at crowding in women's prisons.

E.0641 Powell, Robert, et al. (1991). Female offenders and their guards: A program to promote moral and ego development of both groups. *Journal of Moral Education, 20*(2), 191-203. Focuses on a program with an experimental group of female prisoners and their guards.

E.0642 Power, K. G., et al. (1992, January). Intravenous drug-use and HIV transmission amongst inmates in Scottish prisons. *British Journal of Addictions, 87*(1), 35-45. Data collected from a sample which included 79 female inmates.

E.0643 Pritchard, Constance (1980, March). *Teaching women prisoners to write.* Paper presented at the Annual Meeting of the Conference on College Composition and Communication, Washington, DC, March 13-15, 1980. Report on the University of South Carolina's college composition program at the Women's Correctional Center, a minimum security state prison, in Columbia.

E.0644 Pritchard, Constance (1978). *Getting acclimated: Language in a women's prison.* Paper presented at the Annual Symposium on Language and culture in South Carolina, March 10, 1978. Refers primarily to lexicon used at the Women's Correctional Center in Columbia, SC.

E.0645 Public Health Reports (1992, May/June). New "health link" substance abuse program targets women and teens before and after jail. *Public Health Reports, 107*, 363. Looks at substance abuse programs for incarcerated women.

E.0646 Quay, Herbert, & Love, Craig (1989, July). *Behavioral classification for female offenders: Research report.* Washington, DC: National Institute of Corrections. Measured behavior of newly admitted inmates and inmates past behavior.

E.0647 Quinn, Kelli (1984, Fall/Winter). The killing ground: Police powers and psychiatry: Special Issue: Woman and mental health. *Women and Therapy, 3*(3-4), 71-77. Authors experience of victimization as an institutionalized psychiatric female inmate.

E.0648 Quinlan, Michael (1992, Spring). The female offender: A prologue. *Federal Prisons Journal Special Issue: Focus on the female offender, 3*(10), 2. Discusses the treatment of women historically in the criminal justice system and the need for "gender-specific" treatment.

E.0649 Radosh, Polly (1988). Inmate mothers: Legislative solutions to a difficult problem. *Journal of Crime and Justice, 11*(1), 61-76. Catalogs legislatively established programs in the United States for in-house care of children by inmate mothers.

E.0650 Rafter-Hahn, Nicole (1990). *Partial justice: Women, prisons, and social control.* New Brunswick, NJ: Transaction Publishers. Essays on the treatment of incarcerated women.

E.0651 Rafter-Hahn, Nicole (1987, Spring). Even in prison, women are second-class citizens. *Human Rights, 14,* 28-31. Discusses discriminatory practices in women's prisons.

E.0652 Rafter-Hahn, Nicole (1985). *Partial justice: Women in state prisons, 1800-1935.* Boston, MA: Northeastern University Press. Historical overview of the incarceration of women, 1800-1935.

E.0653 Rafter-Hahn, Nicole (1983a). Chastising the unchaste: Social control functions of the women's reformatory system. In A. Scull & S. Cohen (Eds.), *Social control and the state: Comparative and historical essays* (pp. 288-311). New York, NY: St. Martin's Press. Discusses prison operation from 1894-1931. Focuses on the punishment of women for failing to conform to societal norms.

E.0654 Rafter-Hahn, Nicole (1983b). Prisons for women, 1790-1980. In M. Tonry & N. Morris (Eds.), *Crime and justice: An annual review of research* (pp. 129-181). Chicago, IL: University of Chicago Press. Contends that differential care of female prisoners has remained a constant.

E.0655 Rafter-Hahn, Nicole (1982). Hard times: Custodial prisons for women and the example of the New York State Prison for women at Auburn, 1893-1933. In N. Rafter-Hahn & E. Stanko (Eds.), *Judge, lawyer, victim, thief.* Boston, MA: Northeastern University Press. Looks at prisons for women historically.

E.0656 Rahman, Anisur, & Husain, Afreen (1984). Personality and female criminals in Bangladesh. *Personality and Individual Differences, 5*(4), 473-474. Results of translated version of the Eysnic Personality Questionnaire standardized in Bangladesh.

E.0657 Ramsey, Mary Lou (1980, Fall). GENESIS: A therapeutic community model for incarcerated female drug offenders. *Contemporary Drug Problems, 9*(3), 273-281. Discusses the first federally funded therapeutic community for incarcerated females.

E.0658 Rann, Julie (1993, July-August). Women in jail: Michigan conducts study. *American Jails,* 25-26. Study of women in Michigan jails.

E.0659 Rastogi, P. (1954, September). Female prisoners in Uttar Pradesh. *Journal of Correctional Work* (Lucknow, India), *1,* 39-45. Looks at women incarcerated in India.

E.0660 Raulerson, Clare (1981, February 4). *Current status and history of mothers and babies in Florida's prisons as of 2/4/81.* Tallahassee, FL: Florida Clearinghouse on Criminal Justice. Memorandum. Report on programs in Florida for women prisoners and their babies.

E.0661 Reaves, Lynne (1983, August). Babies in jail: Suit asks rights for moms. *American Bar Association Journal, 69,* 10-14. Discusses legal rights of incarcerated mothers.

E.0662 Reddish, S. (1994, March). Prison and the perfect woman: Are outsiders inside? *Prison Service Journal, 92,* 64-67. Examines the treatment of female offenders by the criminal justice system in the UK.

E.0663 Reid, S. (1985, Spring). "Reproduction" of women's dependence as a factor in "treating" the female offender. *Canadian Criminology Forum, 7*(2), 129-143. Discusses the socialization of women in Canada and how the women's prisons perpetuate dependency.

E.0664 Reid, Sue (1976). Female prison community. In S. Reid (Ed.), *Crime and criminology* (pp. 606-607). Hinsdale, IL: The Dryden Press. Looks at women's prisons.

E.0665 Reilly, Shannon (1992, Winter/Summer). Incarcerated mothers and the foster care system in Massachusetts. *New England Journal of Criminal and Civil Confinement, 18,* 147-181. Looks at legal rights of incarcerated mothers.

E.0666 Reisner, Susan (1978, Summer). Balancing inmates rights to privacy with equal employment of prison guards. *Women's Rights Law Reporter, 4*(4), 243-251. Reviews the constitutional basis for a prison inmate's right to be free from observation by guards of the opposite sex.

E.0667 Resnik, Judith, & Shaw Nancy (1980). Prisoners of their sex: Health problems of incarcerated women. *Prison Law Monitor, 3*(3), 57, 68-83. Reviews literature confirming inadequate health care for female offenders in jails and prisons across the U.S. First of a 4-part work.

E.0668 Richie, Beth (1991). *The empowerment program: A curriculum for health education groups for women at Rikers Island.* New York, NY: Hunter College, School of Health Sciences. Describes how women inmates take an active part in reducing their risk of HIV infection.

E.0669 Richards-Ekeh, Kaylene (1981, September). Voluntary association membership of female inmates: A case study. *Dissertation Abstracts International, 42*(3), 1327. Examined voluntary associations among female inmates at the Women's Reformatory, York, Nebraska.

E.0670 Richmond, R. (1970). The homosexual in prison. *Canadian Journal of Corrections, 12*(9), 533-555. Asserts that overt homosexuality is more prevalent in women's prisons than in men's.

E.0671 Rippin, J. D. (1918). Municipal detention for women. *National Conference of Social Work, 1918,* 132-139. Contains statistics and information on what social workers were doing to help incarcerated women in the early 1900's.

E.0672 Rizzo, Elaine (1995, August). The creation of the New Hampshire state prison for women: Some unintended consequences of legal reform (female offenders). *Dissertation Abstracts International, 56*(2), 711. Describes the establishment of New Hampshire's first women's prison in 1989 as the result of a lawsuit filed by inmates.

E.0673 Robbins, A. J., et al. (1986, January). Missouri classification system applied to female offenders: Reliability and validity issues. *Journal of Behavior Technology Methods and Therapy, 32*(1), 21-30. Reports first phase of a project to evaluate the classification system for female offenders used by the Missouri Department of Corrections since 1983.

E.0674 Rocheleau, A. M. (1987). *Joining incarcerated mothers with their children: Evaluation of the Lancaster visiting cottage program.* Boston, MA: Massachusetts Department of Corrections. Evaluates first year operation of a program extending incarcerated mothers' visits with children.

E.0675 Rodgers, Karen (1993, Spring). The political discourse on women prisoners and the issue of co-corrections in Canada. *Masters Abstracts International, 31*(1), 168. Explores the political discourse on women in prison and the issue of co-corrections in Canada.

E.0676 Rodgers McCarthy, Belinda (1980). Inmate mothers: The problems of separation and reintegration. *Journal of Offender Counseling, Services & Rehabilitation, 4*(3), 199-210. Discusses problems faced by inmate mothers as a result of their separation from their children.

E.0677 Rogers, Helen (1922). *A digest of laws establishing reformatories for women in the United States.* New York, NY: Bureau of Social Hygiene. Early laws governing reformatories for women.

E.0678 Rogers, S., & Carey, C. (1979). *Child-care needs of female offenders.* Toronto: Ministry of Correctional Services. Report on child care need of incarcerated women in Canada.

E.0679 Rootes, L. E. (1974, June) The effect of achievement motivation training on women prisoners. *Criminal Justice and Behavior, 1*(2), 131-138. Hypothesized increased motivation to achieve and compete would improve the probability of rehabilitation for female inmates.

E.0680 Rosenkrantz, Louise, & Joshua, Virdia (1982). Children of incarcerated parents: A hidden popualtion. *Children Today, 11*(1), 2-6. Describes Prison MATCH/Pleasanton Children's Center inside the fence of the Federal Correctional Institution for Women in Pleasanton, California.

E.0681 Ross, J., & Heffernan, Esther (1977). Women in a coed joint. *Quarterly Journal of Corrections, 10*, 24-28. Discussion of women in a co-ed prison.

E.0682 Ross, Robert, & Fabiano, Elizabeth (1986). *Female offenders: Correctional afterthoughts.* Jefferson, NC: McFarland & Company Inc. Addresses need to teach female offenders basic life skills such as budgeting, banking, obtaining housing, and household management.

E.0683 Ross, Susan (1992, December). A rhetorical analysis of the writings of women prisoners; A thematic examination. *Dissertation Abstracts International, 53*(6), 1726A. Analysis of writing of women lifers in Pennsylvania. Focuses on writing as a tool of empowerment.

E.0684 Ross, T. (1991). Imprisonment and tuberculosis in HIV-infected women. *Journal of the Association of Nurses in AIDS Care, 2*(3), 9-15. Examined medical records of HIV-positive women prisoners for TB, and compared them with HIV-positive women who were not prisoners.

E.0685 Rothman, David, & Rothman, Sheila (1987). *Women in prison: 1834-1928.* New York, NY: Garland. Pamphlets on Progressive Reform's response to female criminals in the 19th-20th centuries.

E.0686 Rotner, S. (1963). Design for a women's prison: An architect's view. *Howard Journal of Criminal Justice, 11*(2), 134-144. Proposes a plan for a prison to house 200 women who have committed non-aggressive crimes for three months or more.

E.0687 Roundtree, George, et al. (1980). Determinants of female aggression: A study of a prison population. *International Journal of Offender Therapy and Comparative Criminology, 24*(3), 260-269. Study on aggression in incarcerated women.

E.0688 Roundtree, George, & Faily, Anwar (1980). The impact of educational programs on acts of aggression and rule violations in a female prison population. *Corrective and Social Psychiatry and Journal of Behavior Technology, Methods and Therapy, 26*(3), 144-145. Hypothesized that frequency of aggressive acts and of rule violations would be affected by education.

E.0689 Roy, Marjorie (1979). *Women in jail:. Problems, programs, and resources.* Washington, DC: Office of Education. Manual designed to help those responsible for developing educational and vocational programs for women in jail. Models and descriptions of existing programs.

E.0690 Ruback, R., & Carr, T. (1984, January/February). Crowding in a woman's prison: Attitudinal and behavioral effects. *Journal of Applied Social Psychology, 14*(1), 57-68. Results of two studies assessing the impact of crowding on female inmates.

E.0691 Rucker, Lila (1994, March). Coercive versus cooperative environments: The collateral effects in prisons. *Prison Journal, 73*(20), 74-75. Study compares a coercive penal setting with a co-operative workshop setting for a group of women imprisoned in a maximum security prison.

E.0692 Rucker, Lila (1992, August). Creating nonviolent niches within a medium security prison for women. *Dissertation Abstracts International, A: The Humanities and Social Sciences, 53*(2), 628-A. Looks at ways in which women in prison avoid violence.

E.0693 Ryan, T. A., & Grassano, J. B. (1992). Pregnant offenders: Profile and special problems. In ACA *Female offenders: Meeting needs of a neglected population* (pp. 49-53). Laurel, MD: American Correctional Association. Reviews literature on pregnant female offenders, and presents a profile of the pregnant offender.

E.0694 Ryan, T. A., & Grassano, James (1992, August). Taking a progressive approach to treating pregnant offenders. *Corrections Today, 54*, 184-186. Discusses the treatment and care of pregnant inmates.

E.0695 Ryan, T. A., & Grassano, J. B. (1988). *Survey of pregnant adult offenders.* Columbia, SC: University of South Carolina Press. Results of a study of pregnancy in female inmates in SC.

E.0696 Ryan, T. A. (1984). *Adult female offenders and institutional programs: A state of the art analysis.* Washington, DC: U.S. Department of Justice. Analyzed the population of adult female offenders in the U.S. as well as programs and services available to them.

E.0697 Ryan, T. (1979). *Generalized model for planning and evaluating programs for female offenders.* Columbia, SC: University of South Carolina. Planning model for administrators and mid-management personnel for correctional programs for women offenders.

E.0698 Sack, William, & Seidler, J. (1978). Should children visit their parents in prison? *Law and Human Behavior, 2*(3), 261-266. Discusses the effects of visiting a parent in prison.

E.0699 Sack, William, et al. (1976, October). The children of imprisoned parents: A Psychosocial exploration. *American Journal of Orthopsychiatry, 46*(4), 618-628. Data collected from state correctional institutions in Salem, OR. Study included eleven imprisoned mothers and children.

E.0700 Sacks, Barbara (1978, Spring). The case for coeducational institutions. *Offender Rehabilitation, 2*(3), 255-259. A study of women prisoners examines several things including negative self-images and low self-esteem, lack of work-orientation, and lack of education and literacy.

E.0701 Salm, Don (1992). *Women offenders in the correctional system: Memo #1.* Madison, WI: Wisconsin State Legislative Council. Describes programs and services available to incarcerated women in Wisconsin.

E.0702 Sametz, Lynn (1980, July). Children of incarcerated women. *Social Work, 25*(4), 298-303. Discusses female offender's responsibilities and familial ties. Proposes prison reforms that foster relationships between incarcerated women and their children.

E.0703 Sanborn, B. (1925-1926). An analysis of the population of the reformatory for women at Framingham, Massachusetts. *Journal of the American Institute of Criminal Law and Criminology, 16*, 127-150.

E.0704 Saubin, Beatrice (1994). *The ordeal: My ten years in a Malaysian prison.* New York, NY: Arcade. Personal account of prison experience.

E.0705 Sanyal, Shubhra (1975, July). An empirical study of certain personality characteristics and attitudes of 25 female convicts of Nari Bandi Niketan. *Social Defence, 11*(41), 30, 31-43. Data collected from 25 women imprisoned for at least 3 years, most of them for murder.

E.0706 Sarri, Rosemary (1987). The female offender and the criminal justice system. In D. S. Burden & N. Gottlieb (Eds.), *The woman client: Providing human services in a changing world* (pp. 177-194). New York, NY: Tavistock & Routledge. Summarizes information on the female offender and their treatment in the criminal justice system.

E.0707 Scanlon, Matthew (1993, November). Women in prison. *Psychology Today, 26*(6) 44-47. Interviews with four female inmates at Bedford Hills Correctional Facility.

E.0708 Scheffler, Judith (1986). *Wall tappings: An anthology of writings by women prisoners.* Boston, MA: Northeastern University Press. Writings by incarcerated women.

E.0709 Scheffler, Judith (1984, Fall). Prison writings of early Quaker women: We were stronger afterward than before. *Quaker History, 73*(2), 25-37. Describes the writings of 17th-century British Quaker women imprisoned for religious beliefs. Letters and memoirs of five women.

E.0710 Schweber, Claudine (1984, March). Beauty marks and blemishes: The coed prison as a microcosm of integrated society. *The Prison Journal, 64*(1), 3-14. Examines effects of co-correctional prisons. Literature review and interviews conducted with prison administrators in 1976.

E.0711 Schweber, Claudine (1982). The government's unique experiment in salvaging women criminals: Cooperation and conflict in the administration of a women's prison: The case of the Federal Industrial Institution for women at Alderson. In N. Rafter-Hahn & E. Stanko (Eds.), *Judge, lawyer, victim, thief* (pp. 277-303). Boston, MA: Northeastern University Press. Discusses the administration of women's prisons in the 1920's. Focuses on Dr. Mary Belle Harris.

E.0712 Scott, Edward (1977). Therapy with female offenders. *International Journal of Offender Therapy and Comparative Criminology, 21*(3), 208-220. Offers a typology of the female offender based on ten years of therapy work with female inmates.

E.0713 Scott, Norman, et al. (1982, August). Assessment of depression among incarcerated females. *Journal of Personal Assessment, 46*(4), 372-379. Results of the use of the Abridged Beck Depression Inventory as a depression screening device for 65 incarcerated female felons.

E.0714 Scott, Norman, et al. (1980, January). The applicability of the Bell-Panton MMPI escape index to female felons. *Journal of Clinical Psychology, 36*(1), 360-363. Tested the MMPI Bell-Panton Escape Index with 168 minimum security incarcerated female felons.

E.0715 Scott, Norman, et al. (1977, September). MMPI and demographic correlates and predictors of female prison escape. *Criminal Justice and Behavior, 4*(3), 285-300. Data from female felons incarcerated in the Iowa Women's Reformatory between 1960 and 1974.

E.0716 Scott, Norman (1976, October). Correspondence on the MMPI and Mini-Mult among female reformatory inmates. *Journal of Clinical Psychology, 32*(4), 792-794. Comparison of the MMPI and mini-Mult for a sample of 168 incarcerated female felons.

E.0717 Scott, Sandra (1979). *Information needs and reading interests of adult prisoners.* Santa Fe, NM: New Mexico State Library. Analyzed prisoner questionnaires from New Mexico prisons to assess reading interest of adult prisoners. Study included incarcerated women.

E.0718 Scraton, P., et al. (1991). Life in the prison submarine: Long-term imprisonment for women. In Scraton et al. (Eds.), *Prisons under protest* (pp. 147-150). Philadelphia: Open University Press. Looks at the effects of long-term incarceration on women.

E.0719 Segal, Ruth (1982). *The prison nursery: Bedford Hills Correctional Facility.* Master's Thesis, Bank Street College of Education, New York, NY. Examines the nursery of the Bedford Hills Correctional Facility for Women. Reviews history from its beginnings to its current status.

E.0720 Serna, Idella (1992). *Locked down: A lesbian in prison.* New York, NY: New Victoria Publishing. Story of Mary Dortch.

E.0721 Shakur, Assata (1981, November-December). Women in prison: How we are. *Black Scholar, 12*(6), 50-57. Reprint of a 1978 article that describes the alienation and escapism that prevailed among Black women inmates of Riker's Island prison in New York City.

E.0722 Shaw, Margaret (1992, Autumn). Issues of power and control: Women in prison and their defenders. *British Journal of Criminology, 32*(4), 438-452. A study of female offenders in Canada completed for the Canadian Task Force on Federally Sentenced Women set up in 1989.

E.0723 Shaw, Margaret (1990, November). *Survey of federally sentenced women: Report.* Ottawa: Solicitor General Canada. Report on federally sentenced women in Canada.

E.0724 Shaw, Nancy, et al. (1985, Spring). Eating more and enjoying it less: U.S. prison diets for women. *Women and Health, 10*(1), 39-57. Study of weight and diets of female prisoners.

E.0725 Shaw, Nancy (1982). Female patients and the medical profession in jails and prisons: A case of quintuple jeopardy. In N. Rafter-Hahn & E. Stanko (Eds.), *Judge, lawyer, victim, thief: Women, gender roles, and criminal Justice* (pp. 261-273). Boston, MA: Northeastern University Press. Discusses the situation of women who are incarcerated as medical patients and their rights.

E.0726 Shaw, Nancy (1981a, Spring/Summer). Female prisoners view their health. *Journal of Prison Health, 1*(1), 30-43. Looks at health concerns of female prisoners.

E.0727 Shaw, Nancy, et al. (1981b, Spring-Summer). Sexism and medical care in a jail setting. *Women and Health, 6*(1-2), 5-24. Compared clinic visits by female and male prisoners in NYC.

E.0728 Shelton, B., & Gill, D. (1989, July/August) Childbearing in prison: A behavioral analysis. *Journal of Obstetrical Gynecology and Neonatal Nursing, 18*(4), 301-308. Looks at prenatal care for incarcerated women.

E.0729 Shekar, S. (1981, January). Special problems of women in correctional institutions. *Indian Journal of Social Work, 41*(4), 347-356. Focuses on correctional institutions for women in Maharashtra state, India.

E.0730 Shepard, D., & Zemans, E. (1950). *Prison babies.* Chicago, IL: John Howard Association. Early discussion of prison pregnancies.

E.0731 Shortum, J. R., et al. (1970, July). The relationship of self-concept and parent image to rule violations in women's prison. *Journal of Clinical Psychology, 26*, 284-287. Discusses rule violations in women's prisons.

E.0732 Shover, Neal, & Einstadter, W. (1988). Women's prisons. In N. Shover & W. Einstadter (Eds.), *Analyzing American corrections* (pp. 93-105). Belmont, CA: Wadsworth Publishing. Overview of women's prisons in America.

E.0733 Showers, Jacy (1993, September). Assessing and remedying parenting knowledge among women inmates. *Journal of Offender Rehabilitation, 20*(1-2), 35-46. Assessed the level of knowledge among female inmates about child development and child behavior management.

E.0734 Siegal, Harvey, et al. (1993, January-February). Conducting HIV outreach and research among incarcerated drug abusers. *Journal of Substance Abuse Treatment, 10*(1), 71-79. Report of an outreach/early intervention research project conducted in Ohio and targeted at women inmates.

E.0735 Sikka, K. D. (1986, July). Women in Indian prisons: Major issues. *Indian Journal of Social Work, 47*(2), 201-206. Looks at denial of programs to incarcerated women.

E.0736 Silbaugh, David (1992, June). The cognitive style questionnaire: A cross-validation study, utilizing the MMPI and the Hare Psychopathy checklist with a population of incarcerated females. *Dissertation Abstracts International, 53*(12), 6574. Study to establish parameters of validity for the Cognitive Style Questionnaire applied to a population of incarcerated females.

E.0737 Simmons, I. (1975). Interaction and leadership among female prisoners. *Dissertation Abstracts International, 36*(10), 6990. Investigates structure of a state correctional institute for women. Looks at relationships and types of inmate interaction found in a women's prison.

E.0738 Simon, Rita (1994). Women in prison. In C. Culliver (Ed.), *Female criminality: The state of the art.* New York, NY: Garland. Research on women in prison today.

E.0739 Sims, Anne (1992, Spring). Women's prisons: Their social and cultural environment. *Federal Prisons Journal: Focus on the Female Offender, 3*(1), 44-48. Describes differences in institutional cultures of women confined within the Federal Bureau of Prisons.

E.0740 Sims, Patsy (1976). Women in Southern jails. In L. Crites (Ed.), *The female offender* (pp. 137-146). Lexington, KY: DC Heath. Discusses conditions in 20 Southern jails the author visited and interviewed more than 50 women.

E.0741 Singer, Linda (1973, Winter). Women and the correctional process. *The American Criminal Law Review, 11*(2), 300-308. Discusses the legal rights of incarcerated women. Focuses on equality in programs.

E.0742 Singer, Mark, et al. (1995, January). The psychosocial issues of women serving time in jail. *Social Work, 40*(1), 103-113. Results of interviews with 201 female inmates at a municipal jail.

E.0743 Sledge, Andrea (1987). *Mother infant literacy knowledge.* Paper presented at the Annual Meeting of the American Educational Research Association, Washington, DC, April 20-24, 1987. Describes the Mother-Infant Literacy Knowledge (MILK) program at the Bedford Hills Correctional Facility, New York's maximum security prison for women.

E.0744 Smith, Anne (1962). *Women in prison: A study in penal methods.* London, England: Stevens and Sons. Describes women's prisons in Great Britain from 1500-1961.

E.0745 Smith, Babette (1992). *A cargo of women: Susannah Watson and the convicts of the Princess Royal.* Melbourne, Australia: Sun. Discusses women convicts in Australia.

E.0746 Smith, Betsy, et al. (1985). *Expectant mothers in Massachusetts criminal justice system.* Boston, MA: Women's Health and Learning Center. Discusses needs of the 50+ pregnant women who were incarcerated at the MCI Framingham at the time of the study.

E.0747 Smith, Beverly (1990, December). The female prisoner in Ireland, 1855-1878. *Federal Probation, 54*(4), 69-81. Discusses female criminality and prison treatment in 19th century Ireland.

E.0748 Smith, Brenda (1990, August 17). *Women in prison and HIV infection: Perspectives and recommendations.* Washington, DC: National Women's Law Center. Overview of HIV and incarcerated women.

E.0749 Smith, Larry, et al. (1994, March). An anger-management workshop for women inmates. *Families in Society, 75*(3), 172-175. Discusses 3-week workshop at the Utah State Prison in which 11 female inmates participated.

E.0750 Smith, Lynda, et al. (1988, February). Validity of the Megargee-Bohn MMPI typology with women incarcerated in a state prison. *Psychological Reports, 62*, 107-113. Discusses results of validity testing.

E.0751 Smith, Perry, et al. (1991, May). HIV infection among women entering the New York State correctional system. *American Journal of Public Health, 81*, 35-40. Results of a 1988 study conducted on 480 New York female prison inmates, at the time of their admission.

E.0752 Smith, R. (1984). Women in prison. *British Medical Journal, 288*, 630-633. Looks at mental and physical health of incarcerated women.

E.0753 Smykla, John (1980). *Coed prison.* New York, NY: Human Science Press. Thirteen essays on administrative, interpersonal, and research issues related to sexually integrated prisons.

E.0754 Smykla, John (1979). *Co-Corrections: A case study of a coed federal prison.* Washington, DC: University Press of America. Case study of a coed prison.

E.0755 Snell, Tracy (1992). *Women in jail, 1989.* Washington, DC: U.S. Department of Justice. Report on women in U.S. jails in 1989.

E.0756 Snell, Tracy (1994, March). *Women in prison: Survey of state prison inmates, 1991.* Washington, DC: Bureau of Justice Statistics special report. Report of women in prison as of 1989-1990

E.0757 Snow, E. (1931, January 17). Hard lot of women prisoners in Hon Sanso. *China World, 55*, 255+. Discussion of women incarcerated in China.

E.0758 Sobel, Suzanne (1982, Winter). Difficulties experienced by women in prison. *Psychology of Women Quarterly, 7*(2), 107-118. Identifies problems of incarcerated women such as a lack of occupational, educational, and social programs, and inadequate health services.

E.0759 Social Welfare (1993, December 1). New hope for women prisoners. *Social Welfare, 40*(10), 25. Looks at programming for women in prison.

E.0760 Sohoni, Neera (1989). *Women behind bars.* New Delhi: Vikas. Women in prison in India.

E.0761 Sohoni, Neera (1974, July). Women prisoners. *Indian Journal of Social Work, 35*(2), 137-148 Looks at the characteristics of the 62,000 women imprisoned in India between 1961-1965.

E.0762 Solursh, Lionel, et al. (1993). Is there sex after the prison door slams shut? *Medicine and Law, 12*(3-5), 439-443. Observations on sex in prison between inmates, between male guards and female prisoners, and HIV infection.

E.0763 Somander, Lis (1993). *Women prisoners.* Norrkoping, Sweden: Swedish Prison and Probation Administration. Explores the Swedish prison system and its female inmates. Data collected by questionnaire from 119 female inmates in Sweden in 1992.

E.0764 Sorenson, Virginia (1981, May/June). Educational and vocational needs of women in prison. *Corrections Today, 43*(3). Looks at educational and vocational needs of incarcerated women.

E.0765 Southern California Law Review (1991, March). Women in prison with AIDS: An assault on the Constitution? *Southern California Law Review, 64*, 741-796. Discussion of the AIDS issues with women in prison.

E.0766 Sowards, Patricia (1986, October). A correlational and predictive study of depression in women prisoners following abortion. *Dissertation Abstracts International, 47*(4), 1746. Data collected from 109 female inmates and college students who had previously had abortions.

E.0767 Spaulding, Edith (1923). *An experimental study of psychopathic delinquent women.* New York, NY: Rand McNally. Early description of cases treated at the Psychopathic Hospital connected with the Laboratory of Social Hygiene, Bedford Hills, NY.

E.0768 Spaulding, Edith (1914). The results of mental and physical examinations of 400 women offenders with particular reference to their treatment during commitment. *Journal of the American Institute of Criminal Law and Criminology, 5*, 704-717. Early report on health of women prisoners.

E.0769 Spitz, J. (1976). *Overview of Manpower programs for incarcerated women:* Rockville, MD: National Criminal Justice Research. Survey of educational and vocational programs for women incarcerated in state institutions. Model program at MCI Framingham.

E.0770 Stafford, Norma (1975). *Dear somebody: The prison poetry of Norma Stafford.* San Francisco, CA: Unitarian-Universality Service Committee. Prison writings of an incarcerated woman.

E.0771 Stanton, Ann (1980). *When mothers go to jail.* Lexington, MA: DC Heath. Investigates children separated from incarcerated mothers. Compares them to children of women convicted of similar crimes who were granted probation without jail time.

E.0772 Stanton, Ann (1977). *Female offenders and their children: The effects of maternal incarceration on children.* Dissertation, Stanford University. Data collected from 75 mothers and children (ages 4-18) from four California counties.

E.0773 Stefanowicz, J., & Hannum, T. (1971, January). Ethical risk-taking and sociopathy in incarcerated females. *Correctional Psychologist, 4*(4), 138-152. Data from 38 incarcerated women.

E.0774 Stein, L., & Mistiaen, V. (1988, February). Pregnant in prison. *Progressive, 36*(2), 18-21. A state sponsored study found inadequate medical care, harsh treatment, lack of exercise, unsanitary cell conditions, and physical abuse of women prisoners in California.

E.0775 Sternbach, J. D. (1974). *Philadelphia services for women offenders: Final evaluation report.* Harrisburg, PA: Pennsylvania Governor's Justice Commission. Assessment of community treatment, resources, and Manpower development for women offenders.

E.0776 St. John's Law Review (1993, Fall/Winter). Women in the criminal justice system. *St. John's Law Review, 66,* 933-1045. Looks at treatment of women offenders in the criminal justice system.

E.0777 Stoffer, S. S., et al. (1969). Behavior in ex-addict female prisoners participating in research. *Comprehensive Psychiatry, 10.* 224-232. Looks at research on female prisoners.

E.0778 Stohr, Mary (1994). *Sexual harrassment in women's jails.* Paper presented at the ACJS Annual Meeting, 1994, Chicago, IL. Uses staff survey data to explore instances of sexual harrassment in five exclusively women's jails. Considers who reports it and what action is taken.

E.0779 Strange, Carolyn (1985a). Criminal and fallen of their sex: The establishment of Canada's first women's prison, 1874-1901. *Canadian Journal of Women and the Law, 1*(1), 79-92. Historical overview of what led to the establisment of Canada's first women's prison.

E.0780 Strange, Carolyn (1985b, December). Unlocking the doors on women's prison history. *Resources for Feminist Research, 14*(4), 13-15. Looks at the history of women's prisons.

E.0781 Strick, S. E. (1989, Fall). Demographic study of 100 admissions to a female forensic center: Incidence of multiple charges and multiple diagnosis. *Journal of Psychiatry and Law, 17*(3), 435-448. Study of a statewide sample of 100 initial admissions to a female forensic center in Pennsylvania over a 3-year period.

E.0782 Strickland, Katherine (1976). *Correctional institutions for women in the United States.* Lexington, MA: Lexington Books. Looks at women's prisons in the US.

E.0783 Stricklin, Ann, & Penk, Mildred (1980, August). Levels of imagery and personality dimensions in a female prison population. *Journal of Personality Assessment, 44*(4), 390-395. Assessment of female prisoners characteristics.

E.0784 Stumbo, Norma, & Little, S. (1991, August). Campground offers relaxed setting for children's visitation program. *Corrections Today, 53*(5), 136-144. Program at Dwight Correctional Center in Illinois allows inmates and their children to be together overnight.

E.0785 Sturges, T. (1965). Experiment in Holloway: A new approach to prison visiting. *Prison Service Journal* (Wakefield, Eng.), *4*(14), 22-29. Report of students' visit to Holloway women's prison.

E.0786 Suarez, J. M., et al. (1972). The establishment of a therapeutic community within a women's correctional facility. *Journal of Forensic Science, 17*(4), 561-567. Looks at a therapeutic program in a woman's prison.

E.0787 Sullivan, E. A. (1917). Syphilis and its treatment in a reformatory for women. *American Prison Association Proceedings, 1917,* 214-218. Early report on syphilis in women's prisons.

E.0788 Sultan, Faye, & Long, Gary (1988, Spring/Summer). Treatment of the sexually/physically abused female inmate: Evaluation of an intensive short-intervention program. *Journal of Offender Counseling Services & Rehabilitation, 12*(2), 131-143. Treatment model for physically and/or sexually abused female inmates. Data collected from 15 incarcerated women.

E.0789 Sultan, Faye, et al. (1986, Fall). The application of psychodidactic support groups to facilitate female offenders' adjustment to prison. *Psychotherapy, 23*(3), 469-471. Looks at the use of group work in a women's prison.

E.0790 Sultan, Faye, et al. (1984, Fall/Winter). The female offenders adjustment to prison life: Comparison of psychodidactic and traditional supportive approaches to treatment. *Journal of Offender Counseling Services, and Rehabilitation, 9*(1-2), 49-56. Assesses the most effective strategy for facilitating womens' adjustment to prison.

E.0791 Sutker, Patricia, & Moan, C. (1973, November). A psychosocial description of penitentiary inmates. *Archives of General Psychiatry, 29*(5), 663-667. Fifty-one female inmates from Louisiana prison farms are included.

E.0792 Tavano, Suzanne (1981, June). Incarceration in an urban jail. *Dissertation Abstracts International, 41*(12), 4693. Looks at the experience of pre-sentence incarceration, in effect, imprisonment before one is proven to be a criminal. Study of fourteen included six adult females.

E.0793 Taylor, A. J. (1970). Tattooing among male and female offenders of different ages and in different types of institutions. *Genetic Psychology Monographs, 81*(1), 81-119. Discusses the significance of tattooing among female inmates.

E.0794 Terr, Lenore (1972). Children of Chowcilla: Study of psychic trauma. *Psychoanalytic Study of the Child, 34*, 547-623. Study of the effects of parental incarceration on children.

E.0795 Thomas, D. J. (1987). *Effects of autogenic training, biofeedback and guided imagery on anxiety and locus of control in a female prison population.* Dissertation, California Institute of Integral Studies, San Francisco, CA. Looks at programming for women offenders.

E.0796 Thomas, Robert (1994). *Self-esteem improvement for incarcerated women at Northern California Women's Facility, Stockton, California.* Dissertation, Golden Gate Baptist Theological Seminary. Explores the idea that low self-esteem impacts incarcerated women.

E.0797 Thomas, Ruth (1981, June). De-institutionalization: Managing independent living: An adult education program for incarcerated women. *Journal of Correctional Education, 32*(4), 11-14. Looks at programs preparing women prisoners to leave prison.

E.0798 Thomas, Suzie, & Stein, Nancy (1990, Summer). Criminality, imprisonment & women's rights in the 1990's. *Social Justice, 17*(5), 135. A case study from Bedford Hills Correctional Facility for Women, of women inmates who organized themselves to cope with the AIDS crisis.

E.0799 Thompson, G. R. (1968). Institutional programs for female offenders. *Canadian Journal of Corrections, 10*(2), 438-444. Looks at programming for female inmates (1960's).

E.0800 Treece, Catherine (1977, October). Narcotic use in relation to selected ego functions among incarcerated women. *Dissertation Abstracts International, 38*(4-B), 1909-1910. Study of the effects of drug use in women.

E.0801 Triano, S. (1991). *Before I used to be scared.* New Castle, Delaware: Women's Correctional Institution. Comic book using characters living in a women's prison to talk about safe sex. Material contains sexually explicit language and/or pictorials.

E.0802 Tucker-Allen, S., et al. (1994, March/April). Health care of women in prison: An overview. *ABNF Journal, 5*(2), 52-56. Reviews written matter on health care for women in prison.

E.0803 Turner, T. H., & Tofler, D. S. (1986, March 8). Indicators of psychiatric disorder among women admitted to prison. *British Medical Journal, 292*(6521), 651-653. Data from 708 women admitted to Holloway Prison.

E.0804 U.S. Congress (1982, May 6). *District of Columbia female offenders in the federal prison system, oversight hearing.* Washington, DC: 97th Congress, 2d session. Discusses incarceration of District of Columbia female offenders in federal prisons that are located far from the DC area.

E.0805 U.S. Department of Labor (1982). *Female offender workshop guide.* Washington, DC: U.S. Department of Labor. Guide for workshops on female offenders. Lists resources.

E.0806 U.S. Library of Congress (1977). *A selected list of songs dealing with women in prison.* Washington, DC: U.S. Library of Congress Archive of Folk Songs.

E.0807 U.S. National Institute of Law Enforcement and Criminal Justice (1977). *National study of women's correctional programs.* Examines programs and services for women in state prisons, county jails, and community-based correctional programs, 1970's .

E.0808 U.S. Senate Committee on the Judiciary (1993, June 29). *Women in prison: Programs and alternatives.* Washington, DC: U.S. Senate. Focuses on S. 1158, a bill authorizing grants to states to implement family unity projects for women prisoners.

E.0809 U.S. Women's Bureau (1980). *The women offender apprenticeship program: From inmate to skilled craft worker: Pamphlet #21.* Washington, DC: U.S. Women's Bureau. Information on the Women Offenders Apprenticeship Program. Focuses on vocational training for women inmates.

E.0810 U.S. Women' s Bureau (1977). *Employment needs of women offenders: A program design.* Washington, DC: U.S. Women's Bureau. Explores employment related problems of women offenders and proposes solutions based on data collected in Baltimore, Boston, and Miami.

E.0811 Vacho, Marla, et al. (1994). Women in prison. *Forum on Corrections Research, 6*(10), 3-48. Features 12 papers on women's imprisonment in Canada. Topics include policy changes in the areas of placement, programming and visitation.

E.0812 Van Balen, Sister Susan (1992). The unique pastoral needs of incarcerated women. In ACA *Female offenders: Meeting the needs of a neglected population* (pp. 69-79). Laurel, MD: American Correctional Association. Describes pastoral needs of incarcerated women and explores the differences between needs of men and women.

E.0813 Van Wormer, Katherine (1987, Winter). Female prison families: How are they dysfunctional? *International Journal of Comparative and Applied Criminal Justice, 11*(2), 263-271. Questions the typical structure in women's prisons of disjointed family units.

E.0814 Van Wormer, Katherine (1981, Summer). Social functions of prison families: The female solution. *The Journal of Psychiatry and Law, 9,* 181-191. Describes the Julia Tutwiler prison in Alabama and the female inmates incarcerated there.

E.0815 Van Wormer, Katherine, & Bates, Frederick (1979, September). A study of leadership roles in an Alabama prison for women. *Human Relations, 32*(9), 793-801. Leaders in women's prisons tend to be women with serious types of offenses.

E.0816 Van Wormer, Katherine (1978). *Sex role behavior in a woman's prison: An ethological analysis.* San Francisco, CA: R. & E. Research Associates. Investigated sex-role behavior, or traits of masculinity and femininity in a prison classroom with 33 female inmates.

E.0817 Vasallo Barrueta, Norma, & Smith Alayon, Irene (1993, Fall). The influence of labor activity in the rehabilitation of women prisoners. *National Women's Studies Association Journal, 5*(3), 343-348. Looks at programming for female inmates.

E.0818 Velimesis, Margery (1981, February). Sex roles and mental health of women in prison. *Professional Psychology, 12*(1), 128-135. Focuses on concerns regarding women's mental health in prison such as suicide, depression, and the use of psychotropic drugs.

E.0819 Velimesis, Margery (1975, March). The female offender. *Crime and Delinquency Literature, 7,* 94-112. Review of research between 1970-1975. Includes topics such as parole, recidivism, programs, and the courts' treatment of women.

E.0820 Velimesis, Margery (1972, April 20). *Women in county jails and prisons.* Philadelphia, PA: Pennsylvania Program for Women and Girl Offenders. Report on women in county jails.

E.0821 Viadro, C., & Earp, J. (1991). AIDS education and incarcerated women: A neglected opportunity. *Women and Health, 17*(2), 105-117. Results of focus group interviews with 40 short-term inmates who expressed concern about HIV in prison and institutional policies.

E.0822 Vukson, T. (1988). Inmate abortion funding in California: A constitutional analysis. *California Western Law Review, 24*(1), 107-126. Discusses constitutionality of California's DOC policy of funding inmate abortions performed in the first trimester but not beyond.

E.0823 Wagner, Cynthia, et al. (1983, July). Communicative disorders in a group of adult female offenders. *Journal of Communication Disorder, 16*(4), 260-277. Results of screening of 50 female offenders (18-44 yrs) for articulation, hearing, and receptive language fluency (stuttering).

E.0824 Waite, Robert (1985). Necessary to isolate the female prisoners: Women convicts and the women's ward at the old Idaho penitentiary. *Idaho Yesterdays, 29*(3), 2-15. Discusses the occasional sentencing and incarceration of women in the late 1800's and early 1900's in Idaho.

E.0825 Waldron, J. A., & Angelino, H. R. (1977). Shock probation: A natural experiment on the effect of a short period of incarceration. *Prison Journal, 57*(1), 45-52. Studied 136 women prisoners.

E.0826 Walford, Bonny (1987). *Lifers: The stories of eleven women serving life sentences for murder.* Montreal: Eden. Stories of eleven women imprisoned for murder at the Prison for Women (P4W) in Kingston, Ontario under the Parties Act.

E.0827 Ward, David, & Kassebaum, Gene (1965). *Women's prisons: Sex and social structure.* Chicago, IL: Aldine. Study of the social structure of women's prisons.

E.0828 Ward, David, & Kassebaum, Gene (1964). Homosexuality: A mode of adaptation in a prison for women. *Social Problems, 12*(2), 159-177. Looks at homosexuality among female inmates.

E.0829 Ward, Joyce (1973, Aug. 16). Women inside. *New Society, 25*(567), 388-390. Data from observations of a minimum-security prison for women.

E.0830 Waring, Nancy, & Smith, Betsy (1991). The AIDS epidemic: Impact on women prisoners in Massachusetts: An assessment with recommendations. *Women and Criminal Justice, 2*(2), 117-143. Profile of incarcerated women with HIV infection in MCI Framingham.

E.0831 Warman, R. E., & Hannum, T. E. (1965). MMPI pattern changes in female prisoners. *Journal of Research in Crime and Delinquency, 2,* 72-76. Looks at MMPI patterns with female inmates.

E.0832 Washington, Pat, & Diamond, R. J. (1985). Prevalence of mental illness among women incarcerated in five California county jails. *Research in Community & Mental Health, 5,* 33-41. Results of interviews with 115 female inmates.

E.0833 Watson, Catherine (1981, October). Women prisoners and modern methods of prison control: A comparative study of two Canadian women's prisons. *Dissertation Abstracts International, 42*(4), 1806-A. Comparative study of two contemporary women's prisons in Canada.

E.0834 Watterson, Kathryn (1995). *Women in prison: Inside the concrete womb.* Boston, MA: Northeastern University Press. Study of women in prison.

E.0835 Weber, C. R. (1981). *A study of the effects of structured short-term therapy employing G.A.S. on self-concept and internal-external locus of control with an incarcerated female substance abuse population.* Dissertation, St. John's University. Study of short-term therapy with incarcerated women.

E.0836 Weintraub, J. F. (1987, November). Mothers and children in prison. *Corrections Compendium, 11*(17), 5-13. Study by the United National Alliance of Non-governmental Organizations looked at countries that permit children to remain in prison with their mothers.

E.0837 Weisheit, Ralph (1985). Trends in programs for female offenders: The use of private agencies as service providers. *International Journal of Offender Therapy and Comparative Criminology, 29*(1), 35-42. Looks at privatization in women's prisons.

E.0838 Weitzel, Susan, & Blount, William (1982, Summer). Incarcerated female felons and substance abuse. *Journal of Drug Issues, 12*(3), 259-273. Data collected from 176 incarcerated women. Categories were created on the basis of intensity and duration of self-reported drug intake.

E.0839 Welshe, A. M. (1907). Prison discipline for women. *National Prison Association Proceedings, 1907,* pp. 252-256. Early essay on disciplining women in prison.

E.0840 West, Angela (1994, March). *AIDS education in U.S. prisons: The need for gender-specific and culturally sensitive programs.* Paper presented at the 1994 ACJS Annual Meeting, Chicago, IL. Addresses the need for gender/culturally-specific prison programming for AIDS.

E.0841 West's Education Law Reporter (1995, June 1). Women prisoners of the District of Columbia Department of Corrections v. District of Columbia (877 F.Supp. 634). *West's Education Law Reporter, 98*, 681-737. Discusses lawsuit filed by women prisoners of the District.

E.0842 Whalen, J. W. (1990). *Mothers attributions of control and children's attachments in a prison sample.* Dissertation, California School of Professional Psychology, University of California at Berkeley. Looks at effects of maternal incarceration on children and mothers.

E.0843 Wheeler, C. L. (1978). Preparation of male and female offenders for the occupation of home-making. *Federal Probation, 42*(3), 17-22. Looks at a home-economics course for prisoners.

E.0844 Wheeler, Martha (1975). The current status of women in prison. In A. Brodsky (Ed.) *The female offender.* Newbury Park, CA: Sage Publications. Looks at treatment and issues of incarcerated women.

E.0845 Whetsell, Charles (1991, October). The relationship of beliefs about AIDS to knowledge about AIDS in three groups of female inmates: General population, IV drug-using, and HIV-super(+). *Dissertation Abstracts International, 52*(4-B), 2284-2285. AIDS instructions with female inmates.

E.0846 Whittaker, Richard (1990, December). Manning a women's prison: One officer's viewpoint. *Corrections Today, 52*(7), 158-159. A correctional officer's comments on working in a women's prison.

E.0847 Whitson, Karin (1978). *A comparison of the adult performance levels of women offenders in the Texas Department of Corrections and Free-world women in Texas.* Paper presented at the Annual Adult Education Research Conference. Compared competencies of 131 women offenders incarcerated in Texas to competencies of 868 free-world women in Texas.

E.0848 Widom, Cathy (1978, March). Empirical classification of female offenders. *Criminal Justice and Behavior, 5*(1), 35-52. Taxonomy of female offenders is developed on the basis of personality profiles of 66 women at MCI Framingham.

E.0849 Wilfley, Denise, et al. (1986, April). Angry women offenders: Case study of a group. *International Journal of Offender Therapy and Comparative Criminology, 30*(1), 41-51. Reports on a group approach to assist women in acknowledging, accepting, and constructively releasing anger.

E.0850 Wilkens, John, & Coid, Jeremy (1991). Self-mutilation in female remanded prisoners: I. An indicator of severe psychopathology. *Criminal Behavior and Mental Health, 1*(3), 247-267. Tested hypothesis that a history of self-mutilation in women prisoners is an indication of severe and extensive psychiatric morbidity. Seventy-four female inmates and 62 controls were interviewed.

E.0851 Williams, John (1983). Irish female convicts and Tasmania. *Labour History* (Australia), *44*, 1-17. Describes the transportation of Irish female prisoners to Tasmania between 1803 and 1853.

E.0852 Williams, J. E. (1975). Female offenders. In J. E. Williams (Ed.), *Changing prisons* (pp. 182-185). London: Peter Owen, Ltd. Looks at women prisoners place in the prison system.

E.0853 Williams, Larry (1978). *An analysis of recreational programs in state women's correctional institutions of the United States with suggested guidelines for recreation services.* Dissertation, University of Maryland, 1978. Investigated women's prisons in 33 states to ascertain the status of prison recreational services for women.

E.0854 Williams, V., & Fish, M. (1974). *Convicts, codes and contraband: The prison life of men and women.* Cambridge, MA: Ballinger. Essays on prisons and prison life for men and women.

E.0855 Wilson, J. (1993, January). Childbearing within the prison system. *Nursing Standard, 7*(18), 25-28. Describes health care for incarcerated women who are pregnant.

E.0856 Wilson, J., & Leasure, R. (1991, February). Cruel and unusual punishment: The health care of women in prison. *Nursing Practice, 16*(2), 32-34, 36-39. Explores need for innovative methods of delivering health care to women in prison. Discusses most frequent medical problems.

E.0857 Wisconsin Program for Women and Girl Offenders. (1975). *The woman offender in Wisconsin jails: A survey.* Milwaukee, WI: Wisconsin Program for Women and Girl Offenders, Benedict Center for Criminal Justice. Report on women in Wisconsin jails.

E.0858 Women's Health and Learning Center (1986). *Expectant mothers residence program design.* Boston, MA: Women's Health and Learning Center. Prison program in Massachusetts for expectant mothers assists in caring for families while women are in transition.

E.0859 Women's Prison Association of New York. (1858). *Annual report of the Woman's Prison Association of New York: The Isaac T. Hopper Home.* New York, NY: Women's Prison Association.

E.0860 Woods, Caroline (1869). *Woman in prison.* New York, NY: Gillian. A prison matron's personal experiences.

E.0861 Woods, P. J. (1972, Spring). Study of anger in the Federal Reformatory for women. *Catalog of Selected Documents in Psychology, 2*, 73-74. Looks at therapy with women in prison.

E.0862 Woodside, M. (1974). Women offenders and psychiatric reports: Notes from a Scottish hospital. *Social Work Today, 5*(11), 341-342. Looks at therapy with female inmates.

E.0863 Wooldredge, John & Masters, Kimberly (1993, April). Confronting problems faced by pregnant inmates in state prisons. *Crime and Delinquency, 39*(2), 195-203. Study of types of policies in U.S. prisons to care for pregnant inmates.

E.0864 Yale Law Journal (1985, April). Women's prisons: An equal protection evaluation. *Yale Law Journal, 94*, 1182-1206. Looks at discrimination in women's prisons.

E.0865 Yang, S. S. (1990). The unique treatment needs of female substance abusers in correctional institutions: The obligation of the criminal justice system to provide parity of services. *Massachussetts Medicine and Law, 9*(4), 1018-1027. Discusses the lack of drug and alcohol abuse treatment programs for female offenders.

E.0866 Zalba, Serapio R. (1964). *Women prisoners and their families.* Los Angeles, CA: Delmar. Looks at the families of incarcerated women.

E.0867 Zambran, Norma (1992, Spring). My experience with the L.I.F.T. program. *Federal Prisons Journal Special Issue: Focus on the Female Offender,* 3(1), 40. Account of a Bolivian woman incarcerated at FPC Alderson who participates in the L.I.F.T (Linking Inmate Families Together) program.

E.0868 Zebrowski, E. (1991, November). Physics poetry in a women's prison. *The Physics Teacher* (Stony Brook, NY), *29*(8),536-537.

E.0869 Zehner Moore. J. E., et al. (1988, Fall/Winter). Health locus of control of female inmates from the Virginia Correctional Center for Women measured by the Multidimensional Health Locus of Control Scale. *Journal of Prison and Jail Health, 7*(2), 98-108. Study of 161 female inmates from the Virginia Correctional Center for Women.

E.0870 Zupan, Linda (1994, March). *Reel women behind bars: Hollywood's depiction of women in prison.* Paper presented at the 1994 ACJS Annual Meeting, Chicago, IL. Analysis of plots, characters, content, and messages in Hollywood films about women in prison.

E.0871 Zupan, Linda (1992, July). Men guarding women: An analysis of the employment of male correction officers in prisons for women. *Journal of Criminal Justice, 20*(4), 297-309. Assesses the extent to which male officers are employed in prisons for women.

6

PROBATION AND PAROLE

Halfway Houses; Recidivism

F.0001 Acorn, Linda (1992, June). Elizabeth Fry Center: California program helps offenders make smooth transition. *Corrections Today, 54*(4), 102. Discusses the Elizabeth Fry Center in San Francisco which serves as a transition for incarcerated women into the community.

F.0002 Acorn, Linda (1990, June). Coming home: Parolee offers glimpse into life as a former fugitive and inmate. *Corrections Today, 52,* 118+. Personal account of a parolee.

F.0003 Adler, C., & Bazemore, G. (1980). Issues in the application of parole guidelines to females. In C. Griffiths & M. Nance (Eds.), *The female offender.* Burnaby, B.C.: Simon Fraser University, Criminology Research Center. Looks at problems with parole guidelines for females.

F.0004 Albitson, Catherine (1994). The social meaning of the Norplant condition: Constitutional considerations of race, class, and gender. *Berkeley Women's Law Journal, 9,* 9-57. Looks at the use of Norplant as a condition for parole.

F.0005 Banks, Martha, & Ackerman, R. J. (1983). *Women prisoners: Reintegration into family and community.* Paper presented at the 92nd Annual Convention of the American Psychological Association, Toronto, Ontario, August 24-28, 1984. Examines the effectiveness of group psychotherapy in assisting women prisoners to make the transition to the community.

F.0006 Bartrum, T. E. (1991-1992). Birth control as a condition of probation: A new weapon in the war against child abuse. *Kentucky Law Journal, 80,* 1037-1053. Looks at the use of Norplant for a condition of probation for female inmates.

F.0007 Bedford, A. (1974, April). Women and parole. *British Journal of Criminology, 14*(2), 106-117. Studied 287 women considered for parole between April, 1968 and June, 1971. Looked at several areas including offenses, age, length of sentence, and previous convictions.

F.0008 Benson, Margaret (n.d.). *Women on probation in Metropolitan Toronto.* Toronto: Elizabeth Fry Society. Looks at women on probation in Canada.

F.0009 Berecochea, J. E., & Spencer, Carol (1972). *Recidivism among women parolees: A long term survey.* Sacramento, CA: Research Division, Department of Corrections. Study of 626 California women parolees over an eight-year period

F.0010 Berk, Richard, et al. (1983). Prisons as self-regulating systems: A comparison of historical patterns in California for male and female offenders. *Law and Society Review, 17*(4), 547-586. Discusses the use of parole in California to regulate prison crowding.

F.0011 Birg, Laura (1981). Support systems of female felons. *Dissertation Abstracts International, 42*(2), 865. Explored the quantity and quality of support systems of 22 women who entered a Work-Release Program administered by the Salvation Army in Chicago.

F.0012 Black, Hartzel, et al. (1993). *"Life after prison": Successful community reintegration programs reduce recidivism in Illinois.* Chicago, IL: Southeastern Illinois College Correctional Eudcation Division. Discusses a program in Chicago designed to encompass 12 areas of an ex-offenders life.

F.0013 Bohlander, E. W. (1973). *Shock probation: The use and effectiveness of an early release program as a sentencing alternative.* Dissertation, Ohio State University. Study of the effectiveness of shock probation. Subjects included 7 females who went through shock probation.

F.0014 Bowman, J. T., et al. (1974, December). Pre-release training of female public offenders. *Psychological Reports, 35*(3), 1193-1194. Looks at pre-release programming for female inmates.

F.0015 Bularik, Mary (1984). The Dedham temporary asylum for discharged female prisoners, 1864-1909. *Historical Journal of Massachusetts, 12*(1), 28-35. Historical look at a halfway house for female offenders in transition.

F.0016 Burke, Melissa (1992, Fall). The constitutionality of the use of the Norplant contraceptive device as a condition of probation. *Hastings Constitutional Law Quarterly, 20,* 207-246. Looks at the use of Norplant as a condition for probation for women prisoners.

F.0017 Campbell, Emily (1992-1993). Birth control as a condition of probation for those convicted of child abuse. *Gonzaga Law Review, 28,* 67-102. Looks at the use of Norplant as a condition for parole of female inmates.

F.0018 Channing, L. Bete Co. (1991). *What you should know about AIDS while on parole.* South Deerfield, MA: Channing L. Bete Company, Inc. Covers general information about AIDS, focusing of HIV transmission and prevention. Written for female and male inmates.

F.0019 Cloninger, C., et al. (1973, August). Psychiatric disorders and criminal recidivism: A follow-up study of female criminals. *Archives of General Psychiatry, 29*(2), 266-269. Study of 66 convicted female felons on parole. Analyzes rates of criminal recidivism.

F.0020 Dando, J. B. (1976). *Women's Project Newgate.* Minneapolis, MN: U.S. Department of Justice Law Enforcement Assistance. Progress report on two halfway houses for female ex-offenders in Minneapolis, MN from April 1, 1976 to May 26, 1976.

F.0021 Davies, Patricia (1993, July). Community action! Goal: Job skills for women offenders. *Chatelaine, 66*(7), 24. Discusses a job and life-skill training program in Toronto. Women on probation or parole learn life-skills, job-search techniques and employment skills.

F.0022 Devault, B. M. (1965). Woman parolees: Parole performance of women referred to a mental health service unit. *Crime and Delinquency, 11*(3), 272-282. Discusses mental health services for female parolees.

F.0023 Ding, L. K., & Chan, L. Y. (1970). A study of ex-prisoner female narcotic addicts in Hong Kong. *Bulletin on Narcotics, 22,* 7-11. Looks at post-prison experience of female narcotic addicts.

F.0024 District of Columbia (1974). *From program to citizen: Programs for the woman offender.* Washington, DC: District of Columbia Commission the Status of Women. Looks at programs that prepare women prisoners to return to the community.

F.0025 Dowell, David, et al. (1985). Evaluation of a halfway house for women. *Journal of Criminal Justice, 13*(3), 2217-226. Evaluated a halfway house for female offenders in Long Beach, California.

F.0026 Eaton, Mary (1993). *Women after prison.* Buckingham: Open University Press. Discusses the after prison experiences of thirty-four women. Explores the structural preconditions for change and the blocks which ex-offenders encounter.

F.0027 Erez, Edna (1992, March). Dangerous men, evil women: Gender and parole decision making. *Justice Quarterly,* 105-106. Looks at discriminatory practices in parole decisions.

F.0028 Erez, Edna (1989). Gender, rehabilitation, and probation decisions. *Criminology, 27*(2), 307-327. Examines structure of probation decision-making.

F.0029 Ericson, D. (1978). *New hope for women ex-offenders: Project Esperanza, San Jose, California.* Washington, DC: U.S. Department of Labor Manpower Administration. A manual describing a residential program in San Jose, California that helps female ex-offenders readjust to society.

F.0030 Fenton, N. (1955, November-December). Placing women inmates in other state facilities before parole. *American Journal of Corrections, 17,* 29-30. Looks at what happens to women after parole.

F.0031 Fessler, Susan (1991, September). Mothers in the correctional system: Separation from children and reunification after incarceration. *Dissertation Abstracts International, 52*(3), 1084-A. Includes a parole study investigating actual reunification as evidenced in parole records.

F.0032 Fletcher, Beverly, et al. (1992). *The project for recidivism research and female inmate training.* A conference paper presented at the ACJS Annual Conference, Pittsburgh, Pennsylvania. Discusses a longitudinal study in Oklahoma to determine why women recidivate.

F.0033 Frei, Irene (1993). *Relationship between experience in a specialized therapeutic program and behavior of women prisoners after release from jail.* Dissertation. Study of post-prison experiences of women prisoners.

F.0034 Ginzberg, Janet (1992, Fall). Compulsory contraception as a condition of probation: The use and abuse of Norplant. *Brooklyn Law Review, 58,* 979-1019. Looks at the use of Norplant as a condition for probation.

F.0035 Hallett, Kaitlin (1992). *Stopping the revolving door: Profile, problems, and prospects of female recidivists in Minnesota.* Paper, Macalester College Department of Political Science. Paper on recidivism of women offenders.

F.0036 Himmel, S. (1966). Jobs for the girls? *Probation* (London), *12*(3), 96-101. Discusses whether male probation officers should work with female offenders.

F.0037 HM Inspectorate of Probation (1991). *Report on women offenders and probation service provision: Report of thematic inspection.* Great Britain: HM Inspectorate of Probation. Looks at probation of women prisoners in England.

F.0038 Hoffman, Peter (1982, March). Females, recidivism, and salient factor score: A research note. *Criminal Justice and Behavior, 9*(1), 121-125. Examines the recidivism rates of federal prisoners, including 193 females.

F.0039 Horton, A. M., & Whitesell, L. J. (1979). Prediction of recidivism by sex and number of siblings. *Psychological Reports, 45*(1), 98. Looks at ways of predicting recidivism.

F.0040 Hunt, Dana, et al. (1989). AIDS in probation and parole. Washington, DC: U.S. Department of Justice. Report discussing men and women leaving prison with AIDS.

F.0041 International Journal of Comparative and Applied Criminal Justice (1979, Fall). Measures tending to combat recidivism among women offenders. *International Journal of Comparative and Applied Criminal Justice, 3*(2), 209-219. Survey research designed to determine the international status of women offenders and measures taken to combat their recidivism.

F.0042 Johnson, David, et al. (1974). Correctional education and recidivism in a woman's correctional center. *Adult Education, 24*(2), 121-129. Study did not support the hypothesis that successful participation in academic educational programs by women inmates reduces recidivism.

F.0043 Johnson, S. M. (1980). Beyond incarceration: A women's alternative. In C. T. Griffiths & M. Nance (Eds.), *The female offender.* Burnaby, B. C.: Simon Fraser University Criminology Research Center. Discusses a community-based program for female offenders in Seattle, Washington.

F.0044 Jurik, Nancy (1983, November). The economics of female recidivism: A study of TARP women ex-offenders. *Criminology: An Interdisciplinary Journal, 21*(4), 603-622. Examined the effect of economic incentives on the rearrest rates of 125 women ex-felons.

F.0045 Jurik, Nancy (1980). *Women ex-offenders: Their work and rearrest patterns.* Dissertation, University of California. Study of rearrest rates of women offenders.

F.0046 Kemshall, H., & Wright, L. H. (1994). Feminist probation practice: Making supervision meaningful. *Probation Journal, 41*(2), 73-80. Argues supervision needs to take into account the differences in female offenses and in women's lives if it is to be a positive resource for women.

F.0047 Kikstra, C. (1967). *Parole outcome of female felony offenders from the Detroit House of Correction.* Lansing, MI: Michigan Department of Corrections. Study compares parole violators with nonviolators. Data from the files of the Michigan Department of Corrections.

F.0048 Landolfi, J. (1976). *Charlotte House Pre-Release Center for Women: A profile of participants and a recidivism follow up.* Boston, MA: Massachusetts Department of Correction. Study to determine individuals who complete the program and those who do not.

F.0049 LeClaire, D. P. (1978). Home furlough program effects on rates of recidivism. *Criminal Justice and Behavior, 5*(3), 249-259. Study looked at inmate mother's attitudes about parenting and compared those to the attitudes of mothers who were not incarcerated.

F.0050 Leiberg, L., & Parker, W. (1975, January-February). Mutual agreement programs with vouchers: An alternative for institutionalized female offenders. *American Journal of Corrections, 2,* 3-50. Discusses an experimental program for women in Wisconsin and Arizona that used a contract between female inmate, administration, and parole board.

F.0051 Lewis, Diane (1982, January). Female ex-offenders and community programs: Barriers to service. *Crime and Delinquency, 28*(1), 40-51. Results of a 7-month study of services to women released from a local jail in a Western U.S. city.

F.0052 Lipton, Jack, & Campbell, Colin (1989, Spring). The constitutionality of court-imposed birth control as a condition of probation. *New York Law School Journal of Human Rights, 6,* 271-298. Looks at Norplant as a condition for parole.

F.0053 Long, Gary, et al. (1984, Fall-Winter). The psychological profile of the female first offender and the recidivist: A comparison. *Journal of Offender Counseling, Services and Rehabilitation, 9*(1-2), 119-124. Compares female first offenders with women who had served previous terms in prison.

F.0054 Mabil, Jerome, et al. (1985, Spring). Prerelease stress in prison inmates. *Journal of Offender Counseling, Services, & Rehabilitation, 9*(3), 43-56. Examines prerelease stress in male and female inmates at a minimum security federal correctional institution.

F.0055 Maddux, Hilary (1975, June). At a New Jersey prison: Furloughs for women. *Corrections Magazine, 1*(6), 57-58. Looks at a furlough program for women inmates in New Jersey.

F.0056 Mair, George, & Brockings, Nicola (1988, May). Female offenders and the probation service. *Howard Journal of Criminal Justice, 27*(2), 117-126. Considers the position of female offenders in relation to the work of the probation service in Great Britain. Investigates disparities.

F.0057 Manpower Information Service (1974, September 11). Case study: Women offenders in bank jobs. *Manpower Information Service,* 573-575. A program at Chase Manhattan Bank in NYC for women ex-offenders. Includes training in banking skills and placement.

F.0058 Martin, Ronald , et al. (1978, February). Female criminality and the prediction of recidivism: A prospective six-year follow-up. *Archives of General Psychiatry, 35*(2), 207-214. Investigated 64 convicted female felons for six years after their release from prison.

F.0059 Mazzotta, C. (1981). *Pilot programs for women offenders: A job-readiness training manual.* Washington, DC: U.S. Department of Justice. A manual presenting a job-readiness pilot program that served as a pre-employment training model for female ex-offenders.

F.0060 McArthur, Virginia (1974). *From convict to citizen: Programs for the woman offender.* Washington, DC: Manpower Administration. Booklet to inform community groups about problems of women ex-offenders and to present descriptions of programs to assist them.

F.0061 McCarthy, Belinda (1979). *Easy time: Females on temporary release.* Lexington, MA: Lexington Books. Looks at a temporary-release program for female inmates.

F.0062 Metz, B. H. (1967). Alienation among female probationers. *Journal of the California Probation, Parole and Corrections Association, 4,* 37-45. Looks at mental health of female probationers.

F.0063 Molof, M. J. (1970, January). *Statistical prediction of recidivism among female parolees in the California Youth Authority: Research Report #57.* Sacramento, CA: California Department of Youth Authority, Research Division. Used a large sample of women released on parole in 1963 and 1964 to predict recidivism within 15 months of release.

F.0064 Mosley, William, & Gerould, Margaret (1975, Spring). Sex and parole: A comparison of male and female parolees. *Journal of Criminal Justice, 3*(1), 47-58. Compared 1,573 female parolees and 1,619 male parolees on three factors for two years.

F.0065 Moyer, Imogene, & Rogers, J. W. (1970). The relationship between type of offense and successful post-institutional adjustment of female offenders. *Criminology, 7*, 68-76. Looks at adjustment after prison for female offenders.

F.0066 Mubaraki, Monica (1992, Fall). The constitutionality of court imposed contraception as a condition of probation. *Criminal Justice Journal, 14,* 385-405. Looks at Norplant as a condition for probation.

F.0067 Mugge, Robert (1954). *Recently released women prisoners: A report prepared for the Adult and juvenile delinquency Committee of the North Carolina Conference for Social Service.* Raleigh, NC: State Board of Public Welfare. North Carolina report on post-prison adjustment of women offenders.

F.0068 Nelson, G. (1970). *Female offender: After release where? Proceedings of the One Hundreth Annual Congress of Correction.* Laurel, MD: American Correctional Association. Discusses the role of half-way houses in the reorientation of female releasees.

F.0069 Nelson, Hilde, & Nelson, James (1995, January). Feminism, social policy, and long-acting contraception. *Hastings Center Report, 25*(1), S30-S32. A feminist perspective on the use of Norplant as a condition for probation.

F.0070 N. K. V. (1960, February). The principles of rehabilitation applied to recidivism in women. *Indian Sociologist, 2*(2), 38-41. Recommended approaching the whole individual by including the family and the community as well as programs of prevention .

F.0071 Norland, Stephen, & Mann, Priscilla. (1984, March). Being troublesome: Women on probation. *Criminal Justice and Behavior, 11*(1), 115-135. Examined women's violations against probation and compared them with those filed against males.

F.0072 Parsloe, P. (1972). Cross-sex supervision in probation and after-care service. *British Journal of Criminology, 12*(3), 269-279. Discusses the implications of the 1971 Criminal Justice Act which made it possible for male probation officers to supervise females on probation.

F.0073 Pauze, V. K. (1982). *Parole prediction in Iowa.* Des Moines, IA: Iowa Women's Reformatory. Report of parole predictions of women prisoners in Iowa.

F.0074 Pearson, Virginia (1973). A study of relationships between the Porteus Maze Test and recidivism rates of female correctional institution inmates. *Dissertation Abstracts International, 33*(6), 2791-A. Investigated correlations between the Qualitative score of the Porteus Maze Test and age and rates of recidivism of female correctional institution inmates.

F.0075 Petraglia, G. G. (1965). *Female parole violators: An analysis of the situational aspects of their failure.* Dissertation, Fordham University. Study of reasons women violate parole.

F.0076 Pigeon, Helen (1944, March-April). The woman offender today: Probation and parole. *Prison Journal, 6*(2), 15, 27. Early look at women on probation and parole.

F.0077 Price, A. M. (1988, April). Managing women: A probation officers perspective. *Prison Service Journal, 70,* 27-29. Discusses the management of probation for female offenders.

F.0078 Pung, L. J. (1978, April). The effects of a stressful transition experience on dreams: An analysis of dreams of women undergoing release from prison. *Dissertation Abstracts International, 38*(10), 5040-5041-A. Study of the effects of stress in women preparing to leave prison.

F.0079 Raisin, B. C. (1952). *Factors associated with parole adjustment in an area of New Jersey.* Dissertation, New York University. Study to determine and describe the differences between a group of adult female sex offenders who violated parole in New Jersey and a comparable group who adjusted under supervision.

F.0080 Ramos, M. O. (1982). *Prisonization as an inhibitor of Puerto Rican female inmates' effective resocialization.* Dissertation, University of Missouri, Columbia. Looks at the effects of incarceration on a woman's ability to readjust to society after prison.

F.0081 Rasche, C. E. (1972). *Problems, expectations and the post-release adjustment of the female felon.* Dissertation, University of Washington. Looks at the adjustment of women after prison.

F.0082 Rogers, Joseph (1985). Probation, parole, power, and women offenders: From patriarchal parameters to participatory empowerment. In I. Moyer (Ed.), *The changing roles of women in the criminal justice system* (pp. 131-142). Prospect Heights, IL: Waveland, Press. Looks at probation and parole, and the empowerment of women prisoners.

F.0083 Russell-McMillin, S. (1993). *Attitudes of female offender toward transitional housing.* MHR Research Paper. Portland, OR: George Fox College. Discusses how women prisoners feel about transitional housing.

F.0084 Schoonmaker, Meyressa, & Brooks, Jennifer (1975, April). Women in probation and parole, 1974. *Crime and Delinquency, 21*(2), 109-115. Discusses the employment of women as probation and parole officers.

F.0085 Schulke, Beverly (1993). Women and criminal recidivism: A study of social constraints. *Dissertation Abstracts International, 54*(4), 1551. Examined female recidivism to explore rates of recidivism in men and women.

F.0086 Schweber, Claudine (1984a). *The politics of parole reform: The case of women in the District of Columbia.* Paper presented at the ACJS Annual Meeting, Chicago, IL. Looks at the way women parolees are treated in the District of Columbia.

F.0087 Schweber, Claudine, & Feinman, Clarice (1984). Criminal justice politics and women: The aftermath of legally mandated change on women prisoners. *Women and Politics, 4*(3), 1-10. Looks at sex-based discrimination in the granting of paroles in DC and New Jersey.

F.0088 Selmore, A. P. (1981). *Evaluation of the Orleans Parish criminal sheriff's pre-release/work release program for women.* New Orleans, LA: Mayors Criminal Justice Coordinating Council. Evaluates the Women's Prerelease/work release program set up in Orleans Parish, LA, to provide rehabilitative services for nonviolent female offenders awaiting release from prison.

F.0089 Shaver, Lynda (1993). The relationship between language culture and recidivism among women offenders. In B. Fletcher et al. (Eds.), *Women prisoners: A forgotten population* (pp. 119-134). Westport CT: Praeger. Explores dilemmas from the perspectives of inmates and staff that may contribute to recidivism.

F.0090 Shore, Elsie, & McCoy, M. L. (1987, September-October). Recidivism among female DUI offenders in a Midwestern American City. *Journal of Criminal Justice, 15*(5), 369-374. Compared women who were arrested in Wichita, Kansas, more than once during a 5-year period for Driving Under the Influence to those who were arrested only once.

F.0091 Simmons, I. L., & Rogers, J. W. (1970). The relationship between type of offense and successful post-institutional adjustment of female offenders. *Criminology: An Interdisciplinary Journal, 7,* 68-76. Study of 246 women released by the Kansas Correctional System from 1961-1965. Success was defined as the completion of parole or conditional release periods without violations.

F.0092 Simon, Rita (1979). Parole system: How women fare. In F. Adler & R. Simon (Eds.), *Criminology of deviant women.* Boston, MA: Houghton Mifflin Co. Compares statistics on parole outcomes for women and men throughout the nation for 1968-1970.

F.0093 Spencer, Carol, & Berocochea, J. (1972, July). Recidivism among women parolees: A long-term survey. In F. Adler & R. Simon (Eds.) *The criminology of deviant women* (pp. 372-379). Boston, MA: Houghton-Mifflin. Study of 626 California women parolees over an eight-year period to determine effects of agency decisions on parole outcome.

F.0094 Spencer, Carol, & Berecochea, J. (1971, January). *Vocational training at the California Institution for Women: An evaluation, Research Report #41.* California Department of Corrections. Studied the extent to which paroled women find employment in the field in which they received training.

F.0095 Steinitz, L. Y. (1982). Garnes decree in reality: Determining parole eligibility for District of Columbia women. In M. Morash (Ed.), *Implementing criminal justice policies.* Newbury Park, CA: Sage Publications. Looks at parole decisions regarding women in DC.

F.0096 Stevenson, Janet (1994). Stopping fetal abuse with no-pregnancy and drug treatment probation conditions. *Santa Clara Law Review, 34,* 295-372. Looks at no-pregnancy policies as conditions for probation.

F.0097 Sullivan, Katharine (1973). *Girls on parole.* Westport, CT : Greenwood Press. Study of parole policies and outcomes for girls and women.

F.0098 Taitt, A. L. (1974). Counseling and recidivism: A study of women participants in the Teachers College, Columbia University, Rikers Island Correctional Institution for Women project. *Dissertation Abstracts International, 35*(6), 3438-A. Looks at the use of counseling for women on probation and/or parole.

F.0099 Taskar, K. T. (1960, February). Recidivism among women. *Indian Sociologist, 2*(2), 14-18. Discusses the lack of rehabilitative techniques and things that contribute to recidivism in women.

F.0100 Taylor, James (1992, July). Court-ordered contraception: Norplant as a probation condition in child abuse. *Florida Law Review, 44,* 379-416. Looks at the use of Norplant as a condition for probation.

F.0101 Thomas, Ruth, et al. (1980). *De-institutionalization: Managing independent living: An adult education program for incarcerated women in transition.* St. Paul, MN: Minnesota Higher Education Coordinating Board. A manual providing materials for implementation of a Managing Independent Living Program for adult female offenders in a state residential facility.

F.0102 Van Horne, B. A. (1979). *A study of selected variables, including the MMPI, as predictors of adult female recidivism.* Dissertation, University of Wisconsin. Looks at the MMPI as a predictor for recidivism in women.

F.0103 Vankatwyk, P. L. (1978). *The re-entry process of women parolees: A case study in a socialization counseling model in pastoral care.* Dissertation, School of Theology at Claremont. Looks at pastoral counseling with women on parole.

F.0104 Venter, J. D. (1962, May). The pattern of crimes committed by white female recidivists. *Journal of Social Research, 12*(2), 137-149. Looks at recidivism in white female offenders.

F.0105 Waldron, J. A., & Angelino, H. R. (1977). Shock probation: A natural experiment on the effect of a short period of incarceration. *Prison Journal, 57*(1), 45-52. 136 female inmates studied.

F.0106 Walker, Kristyn (1993, March). Judicial control of reproductive freedom: The use of Norplant as a condition of probation. *Iowa Law Review, 78,* 779-812. Looks at the use of Norplant as a condition for probation and/or parole.

F.0107 Walsh, A. (1984, August). Gender-based differences: A study of probation officers attitudes about, and recommendations for, felony sexual assault cases. *Criminology, 22*(3), 371-387. Looks at differences in male and female attitudes among probation officers.

F.0108 Washborn, Lucy (1950, August). Special problems in dealing with women on parole. *Public Welfare in Indiana, 60,* 12-14. Discusses problems of women on parole.

F.0109 Webb, A. P., & Riley, P. V. (1970). Effectiveness of casework with young female probationers. *Social Casework, 51*(9), 566-572. Looks at social work with female probationers.

F.0110 Western State University Law Review (1991, Fall). Birth control as a probation condition for child abusers: Creative alternative or unconstitutional condition? *Western State University Law Review, 19,* 289-307. Looks at the use of Norplant as a condition for probation.

F.0111 Wexler, Harry, et al. (1991). *Evaluation of an AIDS prevention program for "at risk" parolees.* Paper presented at the 99th Annual Convention of the American Psychological Association, San Francisco, CA. August 16-20. Discusses an AIDS prevention and education program for prison parolees with histories of intravenous drug use.

F.0112 Wilkinson, C. (1988). The post-release experience of female prisoners. In A. Morris & C. Wilkinson (Eds.), *Women and the penal system.* Cambridge, England: Institute of Criminology, Cropwood Series #19. Looks at experiences of female inmates on probation and parole.

F.0113 Wilson, Mrs. F. R. (1944, March-April). The woman offender today: Her readjustment to society. *Prison World, 6*(2), 18, 31. Early look at women prisoners on probation and parole.

F.0114 Worall, Anne (1989). Working with female offenders: Beyond alternatives to custody. *British Journal of Social Work, 19*(2), 77-93. Reports on research into the attitudes of probation officers about female offenders.

F.0115 Wylie, Elizabeth (1993, Spring). Birth control for child abusers: Statutory concerns and privacy issues in court-enforced contraception. *The Review of Litigation, 12,* 489-512. Looks at the use of Norplant as a condition for probation and/or parole.

F.0116 Zimbal, Camilla (1983, September). Hiring women ex-offenders: What can we do. *Federal Probation, 46*(3), 42-45. Discusses the dual employment problems of the female ex-offender and proposes a program to increase their employability and to decrease recidivism rates.

7

POLITICAL PRISONERS

Personal Accounts; Official Reports

G.0001 Andersen, Marguerite (1985, December). Women silenced. *Resources for Feminist Research, 14,* 56-57. Discusses women as political prisoners.

G.0002 Antonius, Soraya (1980, Spring). Prisoners for Palestine: A list of women political prisoners. *Journal of Palestine Studies, 9,* 29-80. Presents a list of women political prisoners.

G.0003 Amnesty International (1988, August). *Summary report: USA, the high security unit, Lexington Federal Prison, Lexington, Kentucky.* London: Amnesty International . Report on the women who were held as political prisoners at the Federal Prison in Kentucky.

G.0004 Backiel, Linda (1991, November). Incarceration of a movement lawyer: A letter from Linda Backiel. *Humanity and Society, 15*(4), 429-430. Author discusses her life as an activist for Puerto Rican independence and her life in a women's prison where she was incarcerated in 1990.

G.0005 Baumel, Judith (1995). Social Interaction among Jewish women in crisis during the holocaust: a case study. *Gender & History, 7*(1), 64-84. Discusses the *Zehnnerschaft (Group of ten)* formed at the Plaxzow labor camp in Poland in 1943.

G.0006 Bloom, Lynn (1987). "Til death do us part": Men's and women's interpretations of wartime internment. *Womens Studies International Forum, 10*(1), 75-83. A study of the experiences of 500 male and female prisoners of war under the Japanese at Camp Holmes in the Phillipines.

G.0007 Bowen, Helene (1988). Women and treason in pre-war Japan: The prison poetry of Kanno Suga and Kaneko Fumiko. *Lilith, 5,* 9-25. Discusses the motivations, political attitudes, and characters, of two Japanese women anarchists. Poetry written from 1901-1926.

G.0008 Bryan, Helen (1954). *Inside.* London: Peter Davies. Personal account of Helen Bryan, an American woman sentenced for refusing to assist the House Un-American Activities Committee.

G.0009 Cade, Julia (1988, Fall). Court denounces practices at Lexington control Unit. *National Prison Journal, 17.* Discusses the unit in Kentucky that was closed.

G.0010 Celmina, Helene (1985). *Women in Soviet prisons.* New York, NY: Paragon House Publishers. Autobiographical account of life in a Soviet Labor Camp. Presents a portrait of female inmates, crimes they committed, and the workings of the Soviet Judicial System for women.

G.0011 Churchill, Ward, & Wall, J. J. (1990). *Cages of steel: The politics of imprisonment in the United States.* Washington, DC: Maisonneuve Press. Contends that there are political prisoners and prisoners of war in US prisons today.

G.0012 Clayton, Cherry (1991). *Post-colonial, post-apartheid, post-feminist: Family and state in prison narratives by South African women.* Denmark: Aarhus. Looks at South African women political prisoners.

G.0013 Cruz-Bernal, Mairym (1995, July). A note on Maria Elena Cruz Varela. *American Poetry Review, 24*(4), 26. Life and works of the Cuban poet Maria Elena Cruz Varela.

G.0014 Dai, Qing (1992, September). My imprisonment. *Index on Censorship, 21*(8), 20-27. A Chinese journalist imprisoned for supporting and participating in political turmoil.

G.0015 Deming, Barbara (1966). *Prisons that could not hold: Prison Notes, 1964 - Seneca, 1984.* New York, NY: Grossman. Authors memoirs during incarceration for political activism.

G.0016 Diaz, N. (1992). *I was never alone: A prison diary from El Salvador.* Talman. Personal prison memoir.

G.0017 El Saadawi, Nawal (1994). *Memoirs from the women's prison.* Berkeley, CA: University of California Press. Prison memoirs.

G.0018 Flynn, Elizabeth (1963). *The Alderson story: My life as a political prisoner.* New York, NY: International Publisher. Personal prison memoir.

G.0019 Freeman, Alexa, & Adjoa, Aiyetoro (1988). Report on the high security unit for women, Federal Correctional Institution, Lexington, Kentucky. *Social Justice, 15*(1). Looks at the security unit at the Federal Women's prison which has since been closed.

G.0020 Gelissen, Rena, & Macadam, Heather (1995). *Rena's promise: A story of sisters in Auschwitz.* Boston: Beacon Press. Memoir of a Polish woman's three years imprisoned at Auschwitz.

G.0021 Gnazela, Sindiswa (1985, December). The female target: Behind bars in South Africa. *Resources for Feminist Research, 14,* 23-25. Considers women political prisoners in South Africa.

G.0022 Halsey, Peggy (1991, July). Women political prisoners, a new stage: High security unit at Marianna, Florida. *Christianity and Crisis, 51,* 305-306. Discusses the transfer of the women political prisoners from the High Security Unit in Lexington, KY, to Mariana, Florida.

G.0023 Halsey, Peggy (1988, March). Undue process: Political prisoners Alejandrina Torres, Susan Rosenberg and Silvia Baraldini. *Christianity and Crisis, 48,* 81-84. Discusses the women political prisoners, now being held in Mariana, Florida.

G.0024 Harlow, Barbara (1992). *Barred women: Women, writing, and political detention.* University Press of New England: Wesleyan University. Looks at women's writings during incarceration.

G.0025 Harlow, Barbara (1986, Fall). From the women's prison: Third world women's narrative of prison. *Feminist Studies, 12,* 501-524. Memoirs of political prisoners.

G.0026 Inglis, Jean (1981). What made me like this? The prison memories of Fumiko Kaneko. *Ampo: Japan-Asia Quarterly Review, 13*(2), 34-39. Fumiko Kaneko was convicted of conspiring to assassinate the Emperor of Japan and hanged herself in prison while awaiting execution.

G.0027 Kaneko, Fumiko (1991). *The prison memoirs of a Japanese woman.* Armonk, NY: M. E. Sharpe. Fumiko Kaneko was convicted of conspiring to assassinate the Emperor of Japan and hanged herself in prison while awaiting execution.

G.0028 Korn, R. (1988). Effects of confinement in the high security unit at Lexington. *Social Justice, 15(1).* Looks at the women political prisoners held in Kentucky and transferred to Florida.

G.0029 Kropova, Olga (1990, July). Life behind bars: The Soviet perspective. *Corrections Today, 52*(4), 132-134. Prison memoirs of political incarceration in Russia.

G.0030 Loughran, Christina (1986, Summer). Armagh and feminist strategy: Campaigns around Republican women prisoners in Armagh jail. *Feminist Review, 23,* 59-79. Discusses the struggles of Republican women prisoners in Armagh jail in Northern Ireland.

G.0031 Manning, Michele (1992). Angels of mercy: The army nurse corps on Bataan and Corregidor. *Parameters, 22*(1), 86-100. Discusses the capture of U.S. nurses stationed on the Philippines during the Japanese invasion of 1941.

G.0032 Mellon Research University Press (1991). *Criminal experiments on human beings in Auschwitz and war research laboratories: Twenty women prisoners' accounts.* (1991). Chicago, IL: Mellon Research University Press. Memoirs of twenty women prisoners from Auschwitz.

G.0033 Norman, Elizabeth & Eifried, Sharon (1995). How did they all survive? An analysis of American nurses' experiences in Japanese prisoner-of-wora camps. *Nursing History Review, 3,* 105-127. Discusses the internment of U.S. military nurses at Santo Tomas Internment Camp.

G.0034 O'Hare, Kate (1923). *In prison, by Kate Richards O'Hare sometimes federal prisoner # 21669.* New York, NY: Knopf. Personal experiences of Kate O'Hare during a fourteen-month confinement in the Missouri State Penitentiary.

G.0035 O'Hare, Kate (1919). *Prison letters: Appeal to reason.* Girard, KS: People's Pocket Series #66. Discusses conditions under which women were confined in the Missouri State Penitentiary.

G.0036 O'Melveny, Mary (1992). Portrait of a U.S. political prison: The Lexington High Security Unit for Women. In W. Churchill & J. Vander Wall (Eds.), *Cages of steel: The politics of imprisonment in the US* (pp. 112-122). Washington, DC: Maisonneuve Press. Looks at the unit which has since been closed that held women as political prisoners in Kentucky.

G.0037 Passerini, Luisa (1992). Lacerations in the memory: Women in the Italian underground organizations. *International Social Movement Research, 4,* 161-212. Report on a continuing seminar with former women prisoners of the Carceri Nueve prison in Turin.

G.0038 Pogrebin, Letty (1989, November). Cruel and unusual punishment. *Ms., 18,* 36-37. Anne Pollard was sentenced to five years in prison for removing from her apartment documents that incriminated her husband, Jonathan, who was later convicted of spying for Israel.

G.0039 Porter, C. (1976). Five women: The first to be terrorists. *New Society, 35*(698), 382-384. Discusses Sofya Perovskaya, Vera Figner, Tatiana Lebedeva, Anna Yakimova, and Olga Lyubatovich, five women who committed themselves to fight against the patriarchal Russian autocracy.

G.0040 Ratushinska, Irina (1991). *In the beginning.* New York, NY: Knopf. Discusses her life as a prisoner in Russia.

G.0041 Ratushinska, Irina (1989). *Grey is the color of hope.* New York, NY: Vintage. Discusses her life as a prisoner in Russia.

G.0042 Rinser, L. (1987). *A woman's prison journal: Germany, 1944.* New York, NY: Schocken Books. Prison memoir.

G.0043 Rodriguez, Ana, & Garvin, Glenn (1994). Diary of a survivor: Nineteen years in a Cuban woman's prison. Personal memoir.

G.0044 Rosenberg, Susan (1992). Reflections on being buried alive. In W. Churchill & J. Vander Wall (Eds.), *Cages of steel: The politics of imprisonment in the US* (pp. 128-130). Washington, DC: Maisonneuve Press. Looks at political prisoners in the U.S.

G.0045 Russell, Diane (1989). Life in a police state: A black South African woman speaks out. *Womens Studies International Forum, 12*(2), 157-166. Discusses Jean Pease, a black school teacher and anti-apartheid activist, who was detained during the 1985 state of emergency.

G.0046 Shackelford, Jole (1993, Summer). A reappraisal of Anna Rhodius: Religious enthusiasm and social unrest in seventeenth-century Christiania, Norway. *Scandinavian Studies, 65*, 349-389. Anna Frederksdatter was a German women convicted of libel.

G.0047 Stevens, Doris (1920). *Jailed for freedom.* New York, NY: Boni. Prison espisodes of a militant suffragette.

G.0048 Stout, Kate, & Dello-Buono, Richard (1987, November). Political prisoners in the U.S.: A call to action for humanists. *Humanity and Society, 11*(4), 533-539. Discusses women as political prisoners in the U.S. and how the aim of the prison administration is to reform them.

G.0049 Strokata, Nina (1986, March-April). Women prisoners of conscience in the Soviet Union. *Ukranian Review, 34*(3), 76-82. Disccusses women political prisoners in the USSR condemned for religious or human rights activities.

G.0050 Susler, Jan (1989, Fall). The women's high security unit in Lexington, Kentucky. *The Yale Journal of Law and Liberation, 1*(1). A look at the place where women political prisoners were held, which has since been closed.

G.0051 Tibbetts, Alexandra (1994). Mama's fighting for freedom in Kenya. *Africa Today, 41*(4), 27-48. Discusses the history of women's activism in Kenya against colonial authorities over the past 70 years.

G.0052 United Methodist Church (1987). *Report of visit by General Board of Global Ministries team to the high security unit for women, Federal Correctional Institution, Lexington, KY.* New York, NY: General Board of Global Ministries. Report on the unit where women political prisoners were held, which is now closed.

G.0053 Zwerman, G. (1988). Special incapacitation: The emergence of a new correctional facility for women political prisoners. *Social Justice, 15*(1), 31-47. Discusses the high-security unit which was located at the Federal penitentiary in Lexington, KY.

8

BIBLIOGRAPHIES

H.0001 Abel, Ernest (1987). *Homicide: A bibliography.* New York, NY: Greenwood Press.

H.0002 Abramson, Catherine (1977). *Spouse abuse: An annotated bibliography.* Washington, DC: Center for Women's Policy Studies.

H.0003 Aday, R. H. (1988). *Crime and the elderly: An annotated bibliography.* New York, NY: Greenwood Press.

H.0004 Bennett, James, & McIver, Barbara (1992). Political trials and prisoners in the United States: A classified and annotated bibliography. *Free Speech Yearbook, 30,* 173-194.

H.0005 Bowker, Lee (1978). *Prisons and prisoners: A bibliographic guide.* San Francisco: R & E Research Associates.

H.0006 Brantley, James, & Kravitz, Marjorie (1979). *Alternatives to institutionalization: A definitive bibliography.* Washington, DC: U.S. Department of Justice, Law Enforcement and Criminal Justice.

H.0007 Brewer, Julie (1988). Bibliography of resources on American law and literature on prostitution. *Wisconsin Women's Law Journal, 4,* 63-93.

H.0008 Brooks, J. F. (1975, September). *Women offenders and the criminal justice system: A bibliography.* East Lansing, MI: Michigan State University School of Criminal Justice.

H.0009 Bullough, Vern, et al. (1992). *Prostitution: A guide to sources, 1960-1990.* New York, NY: Garland.

H.0010 Bullough, Vern, et al. (1977). *A bibliography of prostitution.* New York, NY : Garland. Nearly 6,500 books and articles in English and Western languages.

H.0011 Christenson, S. J., & Swanson, A. Q. (1974). Women and drug use: An annotated bibliography. *Journal of Psychedelic Drugs, 6*(4), 371-413.

H.0012 Connecticut State Library (1918, April 5). *List of references on reformatory work for women.* Hartford, CT: Connecticut State Library, Legislative Reference Department.

H.0013 Cook, Rebecca (1992, Winter). Women's international human rights: A bibliography. *New York University Journal of International Law and Politics, 24,* 857-888.

H.0014 Davis, Nanette (1993). *Prostitution: An international handbook on trends, problems, and policies.* Wesport, CT: Greenwood Press.

H.0015 DeCoste, F., et al. (1991). *Feminist legal literature: A selective annotated bibliography.* New York, NY: Garland Publishers.

H.0016 Desrosiers, Danielle (1992). *Women and the criminal law: A selective bibliography of Canadian material.* Ottowa, Canada: Library of the Supreme Court of Canada.

H.0017 De Young, Mary (1985). *Incest: A bibliography.* Jefferson, NC: McFarland.

H.0018 Doerkson, Lorna (1985). Women and crime: A bibliography. *Resources for Feminist Research, 14*(4), 60-61. Lists more than 50 books and articles concerning women and crime.

H.0019 Doleschal, E. (1970). The female offender: A guide to published materials. *Crime and Delinquency Literature, 2,* 639-645. A review essay followed by an annotated bibliography, topically arranged, of female criminals in North America, Britain, and Western Europe.

H.0020 Elizabeth Fry Society (1972). *Bibliography: Female offenders.* Toronto: Elizabeth Fry Society.

H.0021 Engelbarts, R. (1972). *Books in stir: A bibliographic essay about prison libraries and about books written by prisoners and prison employees.* Metuchen, NJ: Scarecrow Press.

H.0022 Flynn, Robert (1992). *The Borden murders: An annotated bibliography.* London: King Philip Publishing.

H.0023 Franklin, Bruce (1982). *American prisoners and ex-prisoners, their writings: An annotated bibliography of published works, 1798-1981.* Westport, CT: L. Hill.

H.0024 Gelsthorpe, Loraine (1986). *Gender issues in juvenile justice: An annotated bibliography.* Lancaster, England: Lancaster Information Services.

H.0025 Glaser, Daniel (1978). *Handbook of criminology: An annotated bibliography.* Chicago, IL: Rand McNally.

H.0026 Gleason, J. (1974). *Ex-offender: A bibliography of programs and aids.* Washington, DC: National Clearinghouse for Criminal Justice Planning and Architecture.

H.0027 Goyer-Michaud, Francyne (1974). The adult female offender: A selected bibliography. In A. Brodsky (Ed.), *The female offender* (pp. 48-64). Beverly Hills, CA: Sage.

H.0028 Goyer-Michaud, Francyne (1974). The adult female offender: A selected bibliography. *Criminal Justice and Behavior, 1*(4), 340-356. Over 200 articles in French and English that have appeared in professional legal, medical, criminological, psychiatric, and social work journals published between 1959-1974 inclusive.

H.0029 Grauerholz, Elizabeth, & Koralewski, Mary (1991). *Sexual coercion: A sourcebook on its nature, causes, and prevention.* Lexington, MA: Lexington Books.

H.0030 Hallett, Michael, & Palumbo, Dennis (1993). *U.S. criminal justice interest groups: Institutional profiles.* Westport, CT: Greenwood Press. Directory of 100 groups in the U.S. that work to affect public policies on criminal justice issues.

H.0031 Hartz, Fred, et al. (1987). *Prison librarianship: A selective, annotated, classified bibliography, 1945-1985.* Jefferson, NC: McFarland.

H.0032 Hawley, Donna (1985). Prostitution in Canada: A bibliography. *Resources for Feminist Research, 14*(4), 61-63. Lists over 65 books and articles relating to prostitution in Canada.

H.0033 Horton, Davis, & Kravitz, Marjorie (1979). *The female offender: A selected bibliography.* Germantown, MD: Aspen Systems Corp. Focuses on literature from 1965 through 1978, classics are included. Three themes include criminological theory of female crime, legal mechanics of justice administration and, the management of female offenders.

H.0034 Hubbard, Robert, et al. (1980). *Rural crime and criminal justice: A selected bibliography.* Germantown, MD: Aspens Systems Corporation. 140 items on crime and the administration of criminal justice in rural America between 1921-1979, primarily in the 1970's.

H.0035 Huls, Mary Ellen (1993). *U.S. Government documents on women, 1800-1990: A comprehensive bibliography, Social Issues.* Westport, CT: Greenwood Press.

H.0036 Hunt, Ezra (1931). *A selected bibliography on the female offender.* NewYork, NY: Women's Prison Association.

H.0037 International Reference Organization in Forensic Medicine and Sciences (1972). *Bibliography of references on the battered child and infanticide.* Wichita, KS: International Reference Organization in Forensic Medicine and Sciences.

H.0038 Jerath, Bal, & Jerath, Rajinder (1993). *Homicide: A bibliography.* Boca Raton, FL: CRC Press, Inc. Contains both contemporary and historical references from journals and other publications.

H.0039 Johnson, Carolyn (1980). *The literature of higher education in criminology and criminal justice: An annotated bibliography.* Washington, DC: National Institute of Corrections. 500 items on programs, services, and other issues pertaining to higher education in criminology and criminal justice. Covers the 1950's-1970's.

H.0040 Johnson, Carolyn, & Kravitz, Marjorie (1978). *Prison industries: A selected bibliography.* Washington, DC: National Institute of Law Enforcement and Criminal Justice.

H.0041 Jones, K. M. (1971). *Bibliography on personal violence: An index for understanding and prevention, 1950-1971.* Galveston, TX: Moody Foundation.

H.0042 Journal of Criminal Law, Criminology, and Police Science (1968, March). Bibliography: 1945-1967. *Journal of Criminal Law, Criminology, and Police Science, 59*(1), 41-56. Over 300 unannotated items from two decades on the rehabilitation of criminals through various "group" methods. Focus is on group counseling, group therapy, and group psychological methods used in correctional institutions.

H.0043 Kent, David, & Flynn, Robert (1992). *The Lizzie Borden sourcebook.* London: Branden. Resources for information on the case of Lizzie Borden.

H.0044 Klien, Dorie (1970). The etiology of female crime: A review of the literature. *Issues in Criminology, 8,* 3-30. A selection of twenty-seven influential or representative works dating from the turn of the century to the early seventies.

H.0045 Klein, Sandra (1990). Your right to privacy and the AIDS virus: A selective bibliography. *Legal Reference Services Quarterly, 13,* 105-116.

H.0046 Koneski-White, Bonnie (1991-1992). AIDS and HIV: The legal dimensions: A selective bibliography. *Journal of Law and Health, 6,* 131-172.

H.0047 Laska, Vera (1990, Winter). The heritage of the Holocaust: A bibliographic essay on sources. *New England Journal of History, 47*(3), 52-59. Reviews 12 available bibliographies of Holocaust literature.

H.0048 Livesey, Sharon, et al. (1975). *Survey of legal literature on women offenders.* Pittsburgh, PA: Entropy Limited. Reviews 26 references on female offenders. Includes material on rape and prostitution, criminal law, and the legal status of women.

H.0049 Lystad, Mary (1974). *Violence at home: An annotated bibliography.* Rockville, MD: National Institute of Health, Division of Mental Health Programs.

H.0050 McDade, T. M. (1961). *The Annals of murder: A bibliography of books and pamphlets on American murders from Colonial Times to 1900.* Norman, OK: University of Oklahoma Press.

H.0051 Mersky, R. M., et al. (1978). *Authors guide to journals in law, criminal justice, and criminology.* New York, NY: Haworth Press.

H.0052 Nash, J. R. (1981). *Look for the woman.* New York, NY: M. Evans. A narrative encyclopedia of female poisoners, kidnappers, thieves, extortionists, terrorists, swindlers and spies from Elizabethan times to the present.

H.0053 Nash, Stanley (1994). *Prostitution in Great Britain 1485-1901: An annotated bibliography.* Metuchen, NJ: Scarecrow Press. 390 entries.

H.0054 National Criminal Justice Reference Service (1989). *Topical bibliography: Adult female offender.* Rockville, MD: National Criminal Justice Reference Service.

H.0055 National Institute of Justice (1991). *Topical bibliography: Prison violence.* Rockville, MD: National Institute of Justice.

H.0056 National Institute of Justice (1989-1990). *Topical bibliography: Trends in alternatives to incarceration.* Rockville, MD: National Institute of Justice.

H.0057 National Prison Project (1985). *Bibliography of material on women in prison.* Washington, DC: National Prison Project.

H.0058 National Victims Resource Center (1992). *Topical Bibliography: The criminal justice response to child abuse.* Rockville, MD: National Victims Resource Center.

H.0059 Newton, Michael (1988). *Mass murder: An annotated bibliography.* New York, NY: Garland Publishers.

H.0060 Olm, Jane, et al. (1971, June). *Criminal justice and related topics: A selected bibliography.* Austin, TX: Tarleton Law Library, University of Texas.

H.0061 Pointer, Donald, & Kravitz, Marjorie (1980). *Correctional staff and development and training: A selected bibliography.* Washington, DC: Department of Justice, National Institute of Justice. Abstracts of 232 documents on training for personnel in adult corrections.

H.0062 Powell, Scott (1987, April). Sentencing juvenile offenders: Societal and legal aspects: A selective bibliography. *Record of the Association of the Bar of the City of New York, 42,* 393-401.

H.0063 Radinowicz, Leon, & Hood, Roger (1976). *Criminology and the administration of criminal justice: A bibliography.* Wesport, CT: Greenwood Press.

H.0064 Reinertsen, Gail (1986, Fall-Winter). Bibliography on public access to legal materials. *Legal Reference Services Quarterly, 6*(3-4), 181-193. Categorized in three sections, public access to legal information and materials in law libraries, in non-law libraries, and non-prison libraries.

H.0065 Rosenzweig, Mariana, & Brodsky, Annette (1976, March). *Psychology of the female offender: A research bibliography.* Tuscaloosa, AL: University of Alabama, Center for Correctional Psychology, Report #32. Annotated selections on theory, research, and treatment of adult and juvenile offenders. Material from correctional, sociological, and psychological literature published between 1950 and 1975.

H.0066 Santamour, Miles, & West, Bernadette (1978). *Retardation, corrections, and retarded offenders: A bibliography of relevant reserach, programs, and literature with annotations.* Washington, DC: Department of Health, Education and Welfare, President's Committee on Mental Retardation.

H.0067 Sarri, R., et al. (1975, August). *The female offender: An annotated bibliography.* Ann Arbor, MI: University of Michigan, School of Social Work. Annotations and critiques about issues related to female offenders. In addition to adult female corrections it covers juveniles, legal issues, mental institutions, abortion, rape, and prostitution.

H.0068 Scheffler, Judith (1984, March). An annotated bibliography of writing by women prisoners. *The Prison Journal, 64*(1), 68-83.

H.0069 Seagrave, Kerry (1992). *Women serial and mass murderers: A worldwide reference, 1580 through 1900.* Jefferson, NC: McFarland & Co.

H.0070 Smandych, Russell, et al. (1987). *Canadian criminal justice history: An annotated bibliography.* Toronto: University of Toronto Press.

H.0071 Sturgeon, Susan, & Rans, Laurel (1975). *The woman offender: A bibliographic sourcebook.* Pittsburgh, PA: Entropy Ltd. Annotations of 257 books, journals articles, and other documents, plus 400 source listings.

H.0072 Sturgeon, Susan (1973). *Women in prison: An annotated bibliography.* Honolulu, HI: Graduate School of Library Science., University of Hawaii. Fifty three annotations of journals, magazines, and newspaper articles and books on female offenders published since 1965. Most material is taken from alternative press publications and written from a feminist perspective.

H.0073 Tompkins, Dorothy (1964). *Probation since World War II: A bibliography.* Berkeley, CA: Institute of Government Studies, University of California, Berkeley.

H.0074 Tompkins, Dorothy (1963). *The Offender: A bibliography.* This bibliography supplements the Culver Bibliography of crime and criminal justice 1932-1937 and covers twenty-five years after. Women Offenders as well as several types of offenders are included.

H.0075 U.S. Library of Congress (1916, October 28). *List of references on women criminals.* Washington, DC: U.S. Library of Congress, Division of Bibliography. #136.

H.0076 Waki, F. A. (1987). *Law and women: Select bibliography.* Saskatchewan, CN: University of Saskatchewan.

H.0077 Walsh, Dermot, & Poole, Adrian (1983). *A dictionary of criminology.* London: Routledge & Kegan Paul.

H.0078 Washington State Library (1970). *Women offenders: A bibliography.* Olympia, WA: Washington State Library. Citations are divided into four sections: Books, journals, research projects, and special publications which originated primarily in state agencies. Covers the period from 1940-1970. Over 180 citations listed.

H.0079 Watts, Tim (1989). *Justifiable homicide or manslaughter: The battered woman defense in murder trials, a bibliography.* Monticello, IL: Vance Bibliographies.

H.0080 Weinke, Lavonne (1974, July). *Female offenders: A bibliography.* Washington, DC: Law Enforcement Assistance Administration. 345 books, journal articles, reports, and theses on female delinquents and offenders published between 1893 and 1973.

H.0081 Williams, Jane (1990). Sentencing guidelines: A selective bibliography of state materials. *Legal Reference Service Quarterly, 10*(1-2), 7-27.

H.0082 Willis, Michael, et al. (1978). *Resources for educators of adults: Annotated bibliography for the education of public offenders by descriptive subject headings.* Syracuse, NY: Clearinghouse of Resources for Educators of Adults.

H.0083 Wilson, N. K. (1976). *Bibliography: Female offender.* Carbondale, IL: Southern Illinois University, Center for the Study of Crime, Delinquency, and Corrections.

H.0084 Wise, Sue (1988). Doing feminist social work: An annotated bibliography and introductory essay. *Studies in Sexual Politics, 21,* 1-71.

SUBJECT INDEX

Letters refer to chapters and numbers refer to citations.

AUTHOR INDEX

About the Compilers

KATHLEEN O'SHEA is currently working on her doctorate in Social Work at the Catholic University of America in Washington, D.C. Ms. O'Shea has over twenty-five years of experience teaching adults and children of all ages and people with special needs, including the blind and those with mental challenges. She has extensive counseling experience and served as a Catholic nun for twenty-two years. Among her publications is a chapter on women on death row in *Women Prisoners: A Forgotten Population*, edited by Beverly Fletcher (Praeger, 1993).

BEVERLY R. FLETCHER is Principal Associate conducting justice research for the Institute for Law and Justice, and has served as Adjunct Professor at both the University of Maryland and the American University in Washington, D.C. She is a member and consultant for the NTL Institute for Applied Behavioral Sciences and is conducting research on juvenile violence in Washington, D.C. She is the editor of *Women Prisoners: A Forgotten Population* (Praeger, 1993) and the author of *Organization Transformation Theorists and Practitioners: Profiles and Themes* (Praeger, 1990).

www.ingramcontent.com/pod-product-compliance
Ingram Content Group UK Ltd.
Pitfield, Milton Keynes, MK11 3LW, UK
UKHW020249290926
15470UKWH00002B/834